Hiob Ludolf

A new History of Ethiopia

Being a full and accurate description of the Kingdom of Abessinia

Hiob Ludolf

A new History of Ethiopia
Being a full and accurate description of the Kingdom of Abessinia

ISBN/EAN: 9783742812681

Manufactured in Europe, USA, Canada, Australia, Japa

Cover: Foto ©Thomas Meinert / pixelio.de

Manufactured and distributed by brebook publishing software
(www.brebook.com)

Hiob Ludolf

A new History of Ethiopia

A NEW

HISTORY

OF

ETHIOPIA.

BEING

A Full and Accurate DESCRIPTION

OF

The Kingdom of Abessinia.

Vulgarly, though Erroneously, called

The EMPIRE of *PRESTER JOHN*.

IN FOUR BOOKS.

Wherein are Contained,

I. An Account of the Nature, Quality, and Condition of the Country, and Inhabitants; their Mountains, Metals, and Minerals; their Rivers, (particularly, of the Source of the *Nile* and *Niger*;) their Birds, Beasts, Amphibious Animals, (as the River-Horse and Crocodile,) Serpents, &c.

II. Their Political Government; the Genealogy and Succession of their Kings; a Description of their Court, and Camp; their Power, and Military Discipline; their Courts of Justice, &c.

III. Their Ecclesiastical Affairs; their Conversion to the Christian Religion, and the Propagation thereof, their Sacred Writings, their Sacraments, Rites, Ceremonies, and Church-Discipline; the Decreale of the *Romish* Religion, their Contentions with the *Jesuits*, their Separation from the *Greek Church*, &c.

IV. Their Private Oeconomy, their Books and Learning, their common Names, their Diet, Marriages, and Polygamies, their Mechanick Arts and Trades; their Burials; their Merchandise and Commerce, &c.

Illustrated with Copper Plates.

By the Learned JOB LUDOLPHUS, *Counsellor to His Imperial Majesty and the Dukes of* Saxony, *and Treasurer to His Highness the Elector* Palatine.

The Second Edition.

TO WHICH IS ADDED,

A New and Exact Map of the Country: As also, a Preface, shewing the Usefulness of this History; with the Life of *Gregorius Abba*; and the Author's Opinion of some other Writers concerning *Ethiopia*. Translated out of his Learned Manuscript Commentary on this History.

Made *English* by J. P. Gent.

LONDON,

Printed for *Samuel Smith* Bookseller, at the *Princes Arms* in St. *Paul's* Church-yard, 1684.

THE

PREFACE

OF THE

BOOKSELLER

TO THE

READER.

THevenotius, when he published some things, in the Fourth Part of his *Curious Voyages*, taken out of *Tellezius*, begins with these Words: *Never any Author had greater Reason to publish his History than* Tellezius; *for all that we had before him, concerning* Ethiopia, *was Fabulous*, &c. We may affirm the same of our Author, with much more reason. For *Tellezius* did onely write in the *Portuguese* Language, for the sake of his own Countrymen; besides, he too much favours the Jesuits, whose Actions he every where defends; and, on the other side, is all along severe upon the *Habessins*: although as to things of Fact, he gives a true Account, and therefore is both approved of, and commended by our Author. But our Author writ in *Latin*, that his History of Things unknown, or at least which had been conveyed to us under many Mistakes, might be truly communicated to all Learned Men. Whereas it would be very considerable to have a more certain Account of the Kingdom of the *Habessins*, as well of their Ecclesiastical State, as Civil; especially, when so many things worthy of being remarked, concerning some Wonders of Nature, as the *Nile*, stupendious Rocks, and the most lofty tops of Mountains, the true Situa-

tion

tion of this Country, and its Chorographical Map, the ancient Family of the Kings, Ecclesiastical Antiquities, and the like, are here to be met with, which stretch themselves through all Learning, and its several Parts. For example; Should any one design to write an Universal History, either Sacred or Profane, to give an Account of the Geography, the Manners, the Languages, the Literature of Nations, or any thing of the like Nature, they cannot be without this Excellent Work. Let onely the Table of the Chapters of this Book be looked upon, from these we may easily discern the Multitude and Variety of Things here treated of. Which is the Cause which prevailed with me to procure its Translation into *English*, so that the Curious and Inquisitive Wits of our Nation (to whom probably the *Latin* Tongue is not so familiar) may understand all these things, and make use of them, or at least satisfie their Curiosity.

It will be also very useful to those who travel into *India*, and to the *Red Sea*, in order to their Converse with the *Habessines* (should they accidentally happen on any of them) both to understand their Language, as also to make Observation of those things which are necessary for the Continuation of this History, and for the more perfect Knowledge of the present State of *Habessinia*, and for the giving us a true Relation of what they find there.

It is not significant that I should speak any thing of our Honourable and Learned Author, he being already so well known to most of our Nation, as well on the account of his eminent Learning, as from his prudent Management of the Publick Affairs of State, and therefore he cannot want my Recommendation. Neither can there be the least reason why any should doubt of his Fidelity, when through his whole Work he doth so ingenuously mention his Authors; so that in the very Concern of Religion, in which generally Men are partial, he would not have his Reader credit him so much as his Authors every where cited and referred to: So that indeed those who profess a different Religion from his, cannot reasonably suspect him, as the Reader may easily discern through his whole Book. But our Translator may need some Apology, for not exactly expressing, in some few places, the Sense of our Author, and falling short of that Elegancy and Brevity which he uses. For all know, who have been concerned in

the

the Verſion of Books, that no Tranſlation can reach the Propriety of Expreſſion in the Original. Neither can thoſe pertinent Sentences, and witty Sayings of one Language, retain their Agreeableneſs in another, as will eaſily appear to the Reader. I might here mention equivocal Words, which can ſcarce ever be turned by Words of another Language which are exactly of the ſame Force and Signification. For exemple: When our Author writes, *Immanes Gallanis ſignum occiſi hominis maſculi afferre, atque projicere, & cumulare coram exercitu, quaſi barbara iſta fortitudo ſine teſtibus eſſe non poſſet.* Alſo, *A moribus Solomonis alienum non fuiſſe, ut poſt tot ænigmata, etiam Reginæ Sabæ ceſtum ſolverit*: and many others of the like nature. Wherefore we both beg, and hope for Pardon from our Author, and all others.

But probably, ſome Mens Curioſity may prompt them to inquire, How, and by what means, thoſe things of which the remaining part of this Preface chiefly conſiſts, and which gives ſo much Light to the enſuing Hiſtory, ſo happily fell into my Hand? Of this, *Reader*, take this brief Account.

The Honourable Author, Mr. *Jobus Ludolfus*, coming lately into *England*, did confer with ſome Learned Men of our Nation, concerning his Commentary on his *Ethiopick* Hiſtory, and happing on this Tranſlation of his Work, wiſhed that he had had the View of it before its publiſhing, that ſo he might have been able to have given ſome neceſſary Advice about it, and, where need requires, more fully explained his Senſe: For example; *L.* 2. *c.* 18. the Word *Servus* is tranſlated *Servant*, when indeed in that place it ought to be turned *Slave*: with ſome other ſlight Miſtakes, which will eaſily appear, and may as eaſily be corrected, by thoſe who pleaſe to compare this Verſion with the *Latin* Original. But being requeſted by me, That he would vouchſafe to communicate ſomething towards a Second Edition in *Engliſh*, this Honourable Perſon, with great Courteſie, gave me leave to tranſlate what here follows, out of his moſt Learned Commentary.

After his Diſcourſe of *Balthazar Tellezius*, he gives us this following Relation of *Gregorius* the *Habeſſin*, from whom he received the Notice of many particular Things mentioned in his Hiſtory, of which we have no Account from any other Author: To whom alſo he was obliged, for his more accurate Knowledge in the *Ethiopick* Tongue.

The History of Gregorius Abba the Habessin. Collected out of Mr. Job Ludolph's Commentary.

GRegorius was esteemed a Person of great Credit, and on whose Authority any one may securely rely, not onely by me, but by the Prince himself, *Ernestus* Duke of *Saxony*, and his Counsellors. And therefore we think it worth our pains to treat a little more largely of him, that not onely his Manners and Understanding may be known, but also the Reader may be acquainted how he came into *Germany* to me, and what he did at *Gota*. Being requested by me, before he came into *Germany*, to give briefly an Account of his Country, Family, and Life; in a Letter writ to me the Sixteenth of *October*, 1650. he thus answers. *My Beloved Friend, Let not my Family seem to you to be of a low Condition; for it is of the* Amharican *House, the Linage of Nobles, who are Governours of the* Ethiopian *People, Princes, Generals, and Counsellors of the King of Kings of* Ethiopia; *who promote to Dignities, and depose from them; they Command and Rule in the Place of the King. I also my self have been conversant with the King, Princes, and Nobles, &c.* Being descended from an Honourable Family in a Town of *Amhara*, called * *Macarwelact*, about the beginning of this Century, † in his Childhood he applied himself to the Study of Good Letters, and made so considerable a Progress in them, that amongst his own Countrymen he was accounted Eminent, and extraordinary Learned, for which Reason he was styled *Abba*. So that *Alphonsus Mendez*, the *Portuguese* Patriarch, considering his great Wit, made him the Governour of those Noble Youths whom he brought up in his own House, as in a Seminary. For this *Gregorius* was at that time a Disciple of the Fathers of the Society, which were also in great Reputation with the King, and many of the Nobility. He was so much an Admirer of their Doctrine and excellent Learning, that afterwards when they grew into less esteem, and were banished, he followed them into *India*. But not finding there what he expected, because of his speaking something freely of the Fathers Actions, he designed to come into *Portugal*. Going aboard, he was commanded by the Master of the Ship to go back, just as they were setting Sail, in vain asking the reason, he was put into the Boat, and carried to Shore without the Necessaries for his Voyage he had put on board, which he, crying out *Minha roupa, minha roupa*, did to no purpose desire. So being deprived of all Hope, he fitted

* *Alvarez makes mention of this Town*, cap. 63, 64.

† *He was of a middle stature, a blackish colour; he had curled hair, as other* Ethiopians *have, but a more ingenuous Countenance.*

ted himself to return into his own Country, and went aboard a small *Indian* Vessel, which landing him on the *Arabian* Shore, he underwent many grievous Trials from his own Countrymen; for the *Habessins* being taken Captive in their Youth, and sold to the petty Princes of *Arabia*, and abandoning the Christian Religion, for the excellency of their Wit, are made Governours of the Sea-Ports and Cities; (as we have shewed in our History,) These afterwards do sollicite others, by the pretence of Rewards, and their own Example, to embrace the Religion of the *Saracens*. Afterwards being arrived at *Suaquem*, he found three Capuchin Friars (after the Banishment of those Jesuits sent from *Rome*) travelling into *Habessinia*. They did very much rejoyce, that they had hapned on a Man by whom they might send their Letters, unwarily indited, to the King of *Ethiopia*, concerning their Coming and Mission. They importune *Gregorius* that he would undertake the Message; but he being too cautious, would not hazard the Reward that the Authors of them met with, *viz.* the loss of their Heads. And therefore the Letters were conveyed by the *Arabians*, as is declared in our History; and he coming alone to the Court, was soon reconciled to the King: For he returned satisfactory Answers to all the Questions which were cunningly proposed to him by the King, concerning the Condition of the *Portuguese* in *India*, in relation to their Wars, Commerce, and Shipping, what the Jesuits did with their Patriarch, and what they did design? But not long after, it was laid to his charge by his Rivals, chiefly the Monks, that he had followed the Jesuits as a Traytor, out of the Kingdom; and being a Disciple of those *Loyalites*, he was loaden with Chains. But by the Kings contrivance (who could not defend him against so many Enemies) being privately set at liberty, he made his Escape, as if the Chains had been broke, and once more left the Kingdom. He came by Land into *Egypt*, from thence into *Italy*, and at last to *Rome*. *Tellezius* writes thus concerning him: Abba Gregorius, *the* Habessin, *was very conversant in the House of the Patriarch; he was well versed in* Ethiopick *Books, who returned out of* India *with a design to help his Native Country, which he was forced a second time to forsake, by reason of those grievous Persecutions he there met with from the Monks.* But being entertained at *Rome* in the College of the *Habessins*, he, with three others, L.6.c.37.

were

were maintained at the Pope's Charge: Amongst whom, *Antonius de Andrade*, whose Father was a *Portuguese*, and his Mother an *Habessinian*, was wont to say *Mass*, which he did always hear standing, according to the Custom of his own Country, as he did also in other Places. For the ancient Popes did prudently allow the Liberty of their own Rites to Forreign Christians, that by this means they might draw the more to *Rome*; and they also gave an House, with the Chappel of St. *Stephen* in the *Vatican*, behind St. *Peter's* Church, where the *Habessins* have lived above an hundred Years, and before ever they were accounted Hereticks or Schismaticks, as they now are, did celebrate *Mass* after their own way, in the *Ethiopick* Tongue, as *Joh. Potken*, in his Preface to the *Ethiopick Psalter*, put out at *Rome*, *Anno* 1513. testifies. They have also printed their *Liturgies*, *Anno* 1548. which are now extant together with the *New Testament*, and in the *Bibliotheca Patrum*, are found translated into *Latin*; which nevertheless the Jesuits did disapprove of in *Ethiopia*.

Three Months after him, *viz.* *Anno* 1649. I also came to *Rome*, to enquire after some ancient *Swedish* Records and Manuscripts, which were supposed to have been carried thither by *Johannes Magnus* Archbishop of *Upsal*, and Primate of *Swethland*, who left his Country on the account of the Alteration of Religion. For *Ericus* the Son of *George*, otherwise called *Tegel*, a *Swede*, writes, in his History of *Gustavus* I. King of *Swethland*, thus: *Dr.* Johannes Magnus, *Elect Archbishop of* Upsal, (*when he intended to leave* Swethland) *did put up whatever he had which was valuable, together with the most ancient and choicest Acts, Epistles, Annals, Genealogies, and other Records, which had been preserved in the Cathedral of* Upsal, *and other Places, and carried them to* Rome *with him. Out of which Acts and ancient Monuments, he afterwards writ a Chronologie in* Latin, *of all the Kings of* Swethland, *who have Governed that Nation from the Flood to the Reign of* Gustavus; *as also, concerning the Government of our Ancestors the* Goths, *and their Transactions with other Nations.* But *Christina* Queen of *Swethland* commanding that eminent Person *Sheringus Rosenhane*, her Embassadour to the *French* King, that he should send some fit Person to *Rome* to enquire about the said Records, he committed the Management of this Affair to me, that privately, under the pretence of studying Antiquity, I should search for them, and having once found

them,

them, should use all means to recover them. And that I might the better succeed in this Affair, besides very many others, he also obtained the King's Letters, by which I was recommended to the Marquess *de Fontenay Mareuil*, the *French* Embassador. But those Manuscripts were either never conveyed to *Rome*, or in the Reign of *Sigismund* were carried into *Poland*. Going therefore all over the City to no purpose, I enquired for the *Habessine*, whom I had heard lived at *Rome*, whom at last I found in their College before-mentioned. I addressed to them, and acquainted them how desirous I was to learn the *Ethiopick* Language: They surround me, and wonder, and at length demand the Reasons; to which, being heard, they return this Answer: *That that could not be done out of* Ethiopia, *for it was a thing of great Labour, and much Time: That there was indeed one* Gregorius *there, a very Learned Man,* (whom they shewed me) *but that he neither understood* Latin, *nor* Italian. I desired they would onely resolve some Doubts, and satisfie my Difficulties, for that I had already acquired the Rudiments of that Language. *Gregorius* understanding from his Companions what I desired, immediately runs in, and fetches a great Parchment Book, curiously writ, and bids me read, (it was the Book of the Councils, which I describe in my History.) *Lib. 3.* At which they could not abstain from Laughter, especially *Gregorius*, who said, *He reads like Father Athanasius*, meaning *Kircher*, who had learned to pronounce it, as I had done, not from the Instructions of any Master by word of Mouth, but from the printed * *Alphabets* of *Potkenus* and *Marianus Victorius*; out of which none can learn to read well; for in them both the Consonants and Vowels are expressed very unfitly by *Latin* Letters, without any Direction. But when I went about to interpret, they turned their Laughter into Admiration, scarce believing that that Language, which seemed so difficult (as they said) to the Fathers of the Society, who abode so long in *Ethiopia*, could be learned without a Master. For afterwards *Gregorius* writ thus to me: *The Fathers* (meaning the Jesuits) *who came from* Italy *and* Portugal, *were many Years in our Country, and we find none amongst them able to perform what you do, in writing and interpreting Epistles in our Language, notwithstanding they were learned in Books, and Divines.*

* *Syllabarum.*

So getting acquaintance with them, I daily visited *Gregorius*: But at the beginning we did not converse in Discourse;

for he understood no *European* Language besides the *Portuguese*, and that not very perfectly, which then I had not learned. He was then beginning to learn the *Italian*: So that we did a long time confer by an Interpreter, *Antonius d'Andrade*, and at last began to discourse imperfectly our selves. Afterwards we conversed in the *Ethiopick*, which neither of us had ever before spoke; for amongst the *Habessines* the *Amharick* Dialect is used in speaking through the whole Kingdoms, the *Ethiopick* onely in Writing. Concerning speaking the *Ethiopick*, I had not so much as dreamed. So that we were forced, that we might understand each other, to use a Tongue to which neither of us had been accustomed. *Gregorius* was very knowing in the Affairs of his own Country; for he had followed the Court very long, first in a Private Capacity, and then as a Domestick of the Patriarch. He was well acquainted with the Royal Family, the Nobility, and the several Affairs which had been acted in this Age. Besides this, he was Eloquent, and Witty, and behaved himself courteously and affably to all, and did not conceal from me any thing I asked him, and communicated to me as many Books as he had there. In requital, I gave him an Account of the Affairs of *Europe*, he desired to know. After my departure, he expressed his earnest Desire of seeing me again by frequent Letters, and accepted of the Condition I had offered him of coming into *Germany* at my Charges. I had invited him to *Erford*, into my Country, where my Mother did then live; but I had not writ the Name of *Erfurt* plain enough in *Ethiopick* Characters, so that he read it *Erfart*, which in the *German* Language is pronounced *Ehrfahrt*, that his Friends whom he consulted, told him they knew no such Place; and it might be, that I, being casually asked, had so answered. So that one Letter or Point, not rightly placed or read, occasioned the Mistake. For the same Reason *Aulexus*, an inconsiderate *Habessinian* young Man, following *Gregorius*, without any Recommendation, enquired for the City of *Erfurt* in *Germany*, and losing his Labour, at last returned into *Italy*, (as I have shewn in my History.) An Accident not unlike this hapned to the most eminent Bishop *Walton*, who desired to have my Assistance in the *Ethiopick*, when he put forth the *Polyglot Bible*; but he directing some of his Letters to *Hervordia* in *Westphalia*, whereas he should have directed them *Erfordiam*, or *Erfurtum*, was the

cause

cauſe they never came to my Hand; from whence it was, that I could not give my Aſſiſtance to ſo great a Work, as I willingly would have done, nor prevent not a few Miſtakes in the *Ethiopick* Verſion, and the *Latin* Interpretation of it.

But to return to *Gregorius*, who was now on his Journey, when the moſt Serene Prince, *Ernestus* Duke of *Saxony*, to whom I had given an Account of the whole Matter, commanded that I ſhould bring him to *Gota*, to his Court, for that he was very deſirous to underſtand the Truth of the Affairs of the *Habeſſins*, whom he had heard to have been ancient *Chriſtians*, and that he would bear all the Expence of his Journey. I was not unwilling, by this means, to be freed from the Burden of his Expences, and ſo I wrote to *Gregorius*, who was already come into *Germany*. He being wholly ignorant which way he went, or which way he ſhould return, or by whom he was ſent for, anſwered, *That he was at my diſpoſal, that I might do what ſeemed to me juſt and right.* I went therefore as far as *Nurnberg* to meet him; there, as ſoon as I ſaw him, he fell into an Eſtaſie of Joy, moſt affectionately embracing me, that he almoſt drew Tears from me, reflecting, that I, but a private Perſon, and a young Man, not yet ſetled in the World, nor as yet knowing the Charitable Intention of the Prince of *Gota*, had prevailed with that good Man, being more than Fifty Years old, and alſo lame in his Feet, to come from Foreign Countries, into the Heart of *Germany*.

Duke *Ernestus* commanded him firſt to be carried to his Caſtles of *Heldburg* in *Franconia*, and after to that of *Tenneberg* in *Thuringia*, that his Qualities being found out, he might the better know how to entertain and treat him. When therefore nothing that was diſagreeable was related of his Perſon, Manners, and Inclinations, being clothed in the *German* Faſhion, he was brought to the Caſtle of *Gota*, called *Friedenſtein*, and there placed in a convenient Apartment with me. Afterwards, on an appointed day, being called to the Prince, the Chancellor, and the reſt of his Counſellors, both Secular and Eccleſiaſtical, being preſent, after he had made his Obeiſance, he ſaid, *That he gave Thanks to the Immortal God, that had granted him the good Fortune both to behold and ſpeak to a Chriſtian Prince, beyond his hope and expectation, in the remote Countries of the North, whoſe Piety and Prudence, ſince his coming into theſe Parts, he had heard highly ſpoken of; neither could he hope leſs from his Clemency, mercy and Benevolence, who had entertained him, who was a Stranger, and unknown, so charitably, and had admitted him to kiss his Hand.* To which the Prince replied, *That it was not less acceptable to him, to see a Christian, from such remote Parts, in his Court: That the Divine Providence was to be adored with the greatest Praises, that had preserved the* Ethiopick *Church in* Africa *through so many Ages, amongst so many barbarous People, amongst so many Persecutions of the Mahumetans; and commanded him not at all to doubt of his Benevolence.* Which when I was about to interpret in *Italian*, that the By-standers might understand what I said, he cried out in the *Amharick* Dialect, *Metzhafetu, Metzhafetu; In* Ethiopick, *in* Ethiopick. All admiring what he meant, he told them, *Whereas he had to do with a Prince, he ought to understand most accurately what he spake, that he might know what to answer him; and therefore he did desire, that I would discourse with him in the* Ethiopick *Tongue.* Which I did as well as I could. Then he replied, *That it was true, that the Christian Religion had been miraculously preserved in his Country so many Ages, and did wonderfully extol the Antiquity of it.* The Prince answered, *That the principal Reason of his Invitation of him was, that he should declare the State of Religion and Civil Affairs in his Native Country, for that many and great things were every where in* Europe *reported of his Country; concerning which he did desire to be better satisfied from his Mouth, and that nothing of our Affairs should be concealed from him.* So he was kindly dismissed, and soon after Counsellors were assigned, who were to discourse him. These, at the Princes command, collected out of certain ancient Books (because at that time they had not any others at hand) whatsoever had been reported of the Affairs of the *Habessins* by our Writers. The greatest part of those things which were ancient, were taken out of that strange Confession of Faith of *Tzaga-Zaabus*, (which we hereafter mention, l. 3. c. 1.) which sometimes caused *Gregorius* to laugh, sometimes to be angry, as we shall shew. To those things therefore that were proposed, he answered, and also sometimes discoursed more copiously of them, that the State of Religion, and the Civil Government, might sufficiently be understood from him. But we then wanted the later Writings of the Fathers of the Society of *Jesus*, and their Annual Relations published in *Portuguese*, and therefore never or seldom seen in *Germany*; which if we had had, we could have examined things more nar-

rowly,

rowly, and discoursed with him more particularly. So that being asked onely of what was Antique, Whether they were true or false? he did often consistently affirm and deny them, according to the diversity of Times.

He was knowing in the Holy Scriptures, and in the Three first General Councils, (which are onely received in *Ethiopia*) and in the Symbolical Books of the *Habessines*: Yet he had imbibed some things from the Doctrine of the Fathers of the Society, which caused him to relate the Opinions of the *Ethiopians* which are different from ours, sometimes ambiguously, and sometimes more agreeably, as afterwards I easily discovered from the Relations of *Tellezius*, and other Fathers. The Prince himself did often times confer with him; he often sent for *Gregorius* to him, and frequently came alone to him. When he heard his ready and solid Answers, how he pertinently cited the *Psalter* and the *New Testament*, (for he had no other *Ethiopick* Books with him) and presently found and shewed the cited Places, he had a value for the Man, and bestowed considerable Favours on him; of which he being sensible, with a Modesty mixt with Freedom, satisfied the Princes Questions, and demonstrated his Respect by the most dutiful Expressions. When for some time he had not seen the Prince, he told him, *That a Cloud of Sadness had overshadowed his Mind, whereas he had not been enlightned with the Sun of his Clemency*: (for he frequently made use of the like kind of *Ethiopick* Elegancies to him.) Duke *Ernestus* answered, *That the Minds of Christians could not be obscured with Grief, so long as the Sun of Righteousness shined upon them.*

At this time, Prince *Johannes Ernestus*, the Duke's eldest Son, being about Eleven years old, a Child of an excellent Wit, was alive, whose Governour *I* afterwards was. He coveted to be very frequently with *Gregorius*, and to discourse with him; which opportunity his Masters made use of, pretending, that he ought to discourse in *Latin* (which at another time he did with some reluctancy) with such a Stranger. He complied, and that with good success, although he was sufficiently sensible there was need of my Interpretation. Therefore he often visited *Gregorius*, who by receiving him with Compliance, and praising him for giving the right Meaning of some difficult things in the Bible, did wonderfully obtain upon him.

After his departure out of *Italy* to go into his Country, he took his leave of this his Patron, in an *Ethiopick* Epistle: But a little after, hearing that he was dead, he gave a Testimony of his Grief by a written Lamentation, and an *Ethiopick* * Funeral Song. But he did chiefly esteem Prince *Frederick* the second Son, who now governs his Ancestor's Dominions, who, though then but six Years old, had a mixture of Gravity and Courtesie, in his Going, his Speech, and Countenance.

* Epicedium, or Funeral Poem. Some distinguish Epicedium and Epitaphium. The Epicedium is before the Burial of the Body; Epitaphium is after the Burial.

In the mean time *Gregorius* was not uninquisitive into our Affairs, but enquired narrowly into the State of the Dominion, the Reason of the Government, and the Manners of the Court. When therefore he understood, that Duke *Ernestus* enjoyed the Chief Privileges of Kingly Government in his Dominion; that he had the Chief Power in Ecclesiastical Things; that he published Laws and Edicts; that he determined Controversies, without Appeal; that he imposed Taxes, that he raised Armies, that he convoked the States of his Dominion, that he coined Money, with many other Rights which the Princes of *Germany* claim in their Territories, by the Laws of our Empire, or the Concessions of Emperours; he wondring, said, *We should call such a Prince a King.* But when he heard, there were many more, and those richer, Princes in *Germany*, both Ecclesiastical and Secular, Counts and Abbots, as also Free Cities, and all united in one Body, under the Emperour, as their Head; he was ready to imagine, that some *Platonical* Polity was feigned; replying, *How Great an Emperour must he needs be, who rules, and keeps within the Boundaries of their Duty, Men of such a various Condition and Religion? How can they live in Peace amongst themselves?* * For *Aristocracy* and *Democracy* are unknown Forms of Government to them, and he understood nothing of their Foundation and Constitution, before he came into *Europe*: For *Africa* knows no other Government besides *Monarchy*. Indeed many People live at large, without any Government; and some obey their Chieftains for some set time. Their Kingdoms, for the most part, are so constituted, that One is Lord, and the rest are accounted Slaves. But when he heard, and saw, that with us the Subjects enjoyed a reasonable Liberty, that the Prince was intent on the Business of his Government, that he acted nothing by violence, nothing rashly, but managed all things by mature Counsel, the Matter being well weighed;

* N. B.

that

that he daily frequented the Assemblies of his Counsellors; that he was easie to be addressed to, and ready to receive the Petitions of such who presented them, which he did not throw aside, but took care of their dispatch; he declared, *That those People are happy who are thus governed.* But when he considered the Court, and found all things to be there managed orderly, without Pride and Luxury; that the Prince himself did most strictly observe the Hours of Divine Worship, and Prayers, as if they had been Canonical; that he did carefully educate his Children in Piety, and Ingenuous Arts; that the Family was called Morning and Evening to Prayers; that Dinner and Supper were begun and ended at appointed Hours; that Discipline and Good Manners were observed, as if it had been in a * Monastery; that Idleness and Wantonness were absent; he exclaimed his wonted *O wonderful!* and acknowledged, that scarce his *Itegue* (the Chief of their Monks) could live more holily.

* *Monasterium &c. Accordingly, a Place inhabited by Monks, who lived in a more strict Example of Virtue, and under a more severe Discipline; from whence they are called Ascetics.*

Neither did he less admire the Duke's Care in re-beautifying the City, in building a new Castle, and busying himself even about Private Affairs. For the Prince himself was always present, he prepared all things, he left few things to be onely done by his Ministers, so careful was he to provide for Posterity. When he saw Grain gathered in, and even Hay, (as is necessary in *Europe*) to be stored up, *How excellent* (says he) *would such Provision be against Locusts, which indeed destroy every green and leaved thing, from whence proceed, scarcity of Food, from thence Famine, and the Death of Men and Cattel.* What his thoughts were of our Affairs, and what he related of those of his Country, we shall mention in their due place. When he heard so many vain and fabulous Stories to be reported concerning the *Habessins*, by our Writers, he did with indignation say, *That the* Europeans *were sick of a certain Itch of Writing, and did both write and publish whatsoever they heard, whether true or false; That his Countrymen were wholly heretofore ignorant of this their Humour, otherwise they would have answered more cautiously to their questions, so that our Interpreters might have understood them rightly: That when he first saw the famous Library of* Alphonsus *the* Portuguese *Patriarch, and the Books put out with the Royal Privilege, and the Licence and Approbation of Great Men, he looked on Printing as some Sacred Invention, to be reckoned amongst the* Regalia *of Princes, and supposed that nothing was printed, but what was true, and good, and useful to the Publick; but that he was amazed when he found, that many fictitious, vain, and trifling things, and indeed hurtful to the Publick, were daily sent to the Press.*

But in Composing my *Ethiopick Lexicon*, he willingly assisted me, and with a great deal of readiness did explain the more difficult Places of Authors, and Words more rarely used: and this he did with much exactness, if the Words were pure *Ethiopick*; but in Words and Things which were Exotick, or Forreign, he most frequently mistook, and presently ran to the *Saufau*, *i. e.* the great *Dictionary* of his Country. But he was wholly ignorant how to compose a *Dictionary* or *Grammar*, and did not at all understand how to place Words according to their * Primitives, and at the first was much against it, (as *I* have shewed in my History.) But when he observed me to set in order both what *I* read and heard from him, and to refer the Derivatives to their Primitives, he frequently repeated his *O wonderful!* And when he had discoursed concerning the different Signification of any Word, he would add, *Now do you dispose that according to your Art*. *I* did also explain to him the Mysteries (as he called them) of the *Latin Grammar*, and by this means he became more ready in answering my Questions. When *I* had explained to him the Terms of Art, *viz.* The *Declensions*, *Conjugations*, *Cases*, *Tenses*, and the like, with much labour, in the *Ethiopick* Tongue, as soon as he understood the End and Use of them, *It is revealed*, says he, *to God be the Praise*: And, *All things have their Names in* Europe; meaning, Terms of Art. For he was so desirous to learn the *Latin* Tongue, that in my absence from him for two days, this hopeful Scholar proposed to himself for his Task, to learn by Heart, by frequent reading and repeating, the whole *Etymologie*, the *Declensions*, and all the *Conjugations*. Therefore beginning in the Morning, by constantly reciting till late at Night, and endeavouring by himself, none molesting him, he had so disturbed his Head, that at my return *I* found him ill of a *Vertigo*, or Dizziness. A Physician was called, who enquiring diligently into the Cause of this unwonted Distemper, at last we found that it proceeded from too much attention in Studying. But he did after complain, that the Fathers of the Society, when they lived in *Ethiopia*, could not possibly be prevailed with to teach the Children of his Country the *Latin* Tongue. The Reason of this we have

* Radices [illegible]

given

given an Account of in our History. Indeed *Gregorius* had earnestly desired to learn this amongst us, that he might be able to understand *Latin* Authors; and for that very thing, made no mention of his Departure: But it seemed good to the Prince to send him back before Winter, lest he, being a Person accustomed to a warmer Climate, and growing old, might be impaired in his Health, by the unwonted Cold; especially as well because he so earnestly desired to return to his Country, as also that he might shortly relate to the King and Nobles of *Ethiopia* what he had seen and heard amongst us. He departed therefore from *Gota*, with a Resolution and Promise to return into his Country, although the Patriarch *Alphonsus* by Letters had disswaded him. But he staid in *Italy* between hope and fear, as also in *Egypt* and *Palestine*, longer than he intended. At his arrival in *Italy* (the return into his Country being unsafe) Duke *Ernestus* sent to him a Stipend, to support him in his Banishment, which he accepted with a thankful Mind, as he did sufficiently acknowledge by Letters writ in *Ethiopick* to the Prince.

He refused a competent Support, which was offered him, if he would return into *Germany*; so prevalent in him was the Love of his Country: and therefore he did once more make an Attempt to return into it. But it pleased the Almighty, in stead of conducting him to his Earthly Country, to open to him an Heavenly one. For after he had sailed over the *Mediterranean* with a prosperous Gale, going to *Alexandretta* in a small Boat, he, with Twenty four others, not far from the Shore, was cast away. The *French* Consul at *Aleppo* caused his Body to be found and buried.

This is that *Gregorius* whom we every where commend, and on whose Credit we depend about the *Ethiopian* Affairs, which are found in no other Author. If amongst them any thing should chance to be not so perfectly related, let the Mistake be imputed to me, who at the beginning of our Acquaintance, perchance, might not so well understand him. For he was of that sincerity and integrity of Mind, that he would not designedly affirm any thing to me that was false, though he might, through Humane Weakness, commit some Errour.

After this Account of *Gregorius*, whose Credit our Honourable Author hath sufficiently vindicated; it cannot be amiss,

Reader, to acquaint thee with his Judgment of some others, who pretend to write of *Ethiopia* and *Habessinia*. For upon whose Authority can we more reasonably rely, than on his, who has had so many Advantages, with a discerning Sagacity, and profound Judgment, to enquire into the Affairs and Languages of that Nation? And how can we hope for a better Guide in Things of so great Obscurity?

The first Fabulous Author he takes notice of, is *Jacobus Baratti*. This Man, being not at all affrighted at the Infamy of *Urreta*, directly treads his Footsteps; and under the Title of an *Itinerarium*, or, *An Account of his Travels*, has ventured lately to impose on the Learned, by his fictitious *Habessinian* Relations. This *Jacobus Baratti* was an *Italian*, who is therefore more to be blamed, because, since *Godignus* and *Tellezius* their Histories were extant, he endeavours to perplex and obscure the Light of Truth. For he boldly affirms, That *the ancient Possessions of the King of the* Habessins *did equal the largest Empires in the World; that he hath very great Revenues; that* Congo *is a Bordering Kingdom to* Habessinia; *that the* Negus, *or Emperour, is whiter than the rest of that Nation, God himself, by this, having particularly distinguished him from all others; that his Children, as soon as they have received their Names, are conveyed into a certain delicious Place, in the midst of a large Mountain, called* Amark, *where a stately Castle is built, encompassed with the River* Borohr, (where note his Boldness, in feigning Proper Names) *and fortified with a strong Wall: thither, as soon as the Father is dead, the principal Nobility go, and chuse the eldest Son, unless he be uncapable of so great an Honour, to succeed in the Government; that there is there a very large Library, of above Ten thousand Volumes, all Manuscripts; a Seminary for the Education of the Sons of Noblemen; and a Bishop, with several of the Inferiour Clergy, for the Instruction of Youth.* These, and the like Trash, he heard, and transcribed from *Urreta*, and other trifling Authors. But in that, he is guilty of the grossest Falshood, where he writes, *That he was permitted to go into the Library, and that there he saw some Books made of the* Ægyptian Papyrus, *and others of old Parchment, that did bear the Marks of Antiquity; and, that the Library-keeper told him, that the Books worn out by age, were wont to be transcribed; and for that intent, Twenty three Scribes were maintained at the Emperour's Charge.* This indeed seemed to him becoming, and necessary in a great Library; and therefore, by this Example, he

would

would perswade Kings and Princes to the same; as also by that which he relates concerning the King's Children, and the Children of the Principal Nobility, being educated by the Bishop, (whom he affirms (with his Clergy) to have here a Palace.) And these are not all the Mistakes this Man is guilty of; for he affirms, *That the Emperour speaks the* Arabick, Persian, *and* Hebrew *Languages, with many others; that he is skilful in Philosophy and Astronomy; that he first puts on a Crown of Thorns, before he is Crowned with the Imperial Diadem; that the Captain of the Emperour's Guards is stiled* Diriharvah Negus (which is an unknown Word.) He calls also many other Court-Officers by strange and unknown Names. He reports, *That when the King goes abroad, all fall on their Knees; that the King is eminently devout, and his Courtiers imitate his Example*; and, *that one* (a new and almost unparallell'd Instance) *for the meer suspicion of Adultery, was deprived of his Employment; that if there is no Heir male, the eldest Daughter succeeds in the Government; that the Daughters are taught the* Hebrew *and* Arabick *Languages, Philosophy, and the Principles of Christian Religion, and many other things, which are vain and false.*

I have no particular knowledge of this Author; but he seems to me to be a Soldier, and wholly ignorant of all Ingenuous Arts, and not rightly to apprehend Military Affairs, to which he pretends: for he strangely inveighs against Learned Princes, whom he imagines Swords and Guns to become better than Books. By this Discourse of his, he seems to endeavour to inform the *Italian* Princes how their Children are to be educated, as if they did not sufficiently understand, that the Arts of Peace, as well as War, are necessary for a good Prince; and that those Governours of Kings Children are very injurious to the Commonweal, who inure them to nothing but Arms, Fights, and besieging Cities; who propose no Examples to their Imitation, besides *Alexander the Great*, and *Julius Cæsar*, those two Depopulaters of the World. For by this means they cause them to desert Justice, and neglect the Good of the Commonweal, which they are to Govern, and to esteem Military Glory, acquired with the effusion of the Blood of so many Innocents, with the Ruine of so many Towns and Cities, their Chiefest Good. For it generally happens, that Men endeavour to excel in those Arts which they learned in their Youth.

But

But the Folly of *Baratti* has drawn me from my Design. Those things which I have mentioned out of his Book, may be read in the beginning of it. Yet concerning this Author, and his Translators, I will add this one thing, *viz.* That it is a thing much to be wondred at, that this Fabulous Author should be turned into so many various Languages; particularly, into *English*, by *G. D.* who, if he did believe himself, as to those things to which he endeavours to perswade others to assent, in his Dedication to the Worshipful *Thomas Windham* Esq; why did he omit his Name? He uses a very weak Argument, *viz.* That Baratti *durst not have published his Book in* Italy, *had not his Relation been true*: For which he feigns a Reason, *viz.* *That this Gentleman had committed an Act not agreeable to that Judgment that he uses in his Writings, to publish things of a Kingdom so well known to most Parts of* Italy, *by reason of the continual Correspondency that the Princes of it do entertain by their Factors with the Grand* Neguz *or Emperour.* Thus he accumulates one Trifle upon another. He adds, *That had not his Book found an universal Applause, it had not twice been honoured with the Press.* If therefore the Translator thought the Buyers of Books might be deceived by reading the *Second Edition* in the Title Page, it is a wonder that he did not add the *Third Edition* to his Title.

The Authors Opinion of some other Writers.

Our Learned Author seems to have no better Opinion of the Relations of many others concerning *Habessinia*, who have writ their own, or the pretended Travels of other Men, than of *Baratti's* Book. For, says he, most Itineraries are of a suspected Authority, whereas the greatest part of Travellers, without due consideration, commit whatsoever they hear, either from a good or bad Interpreter, to their Table-books, which is afterwards promiscuously divulged. Many of these Itineraries *Nicolaus Roth*, a Bookseller of *Frankfurt*, collected without Judgment and Discretion, and *Anno* 1609. (lest the Press should be idle) printed them.

Lenhardus Rauchwolfe, M. D.

Amongst these, is found the Travels of one *Lenhardus Rauchwolfe*, Doctor of Physick, who, *Lib.* 2. *cap.* 8. writes thus: *That it was told him, that the* Persians, *the twelfth year before their coming into* Palestin, (which was about the Year 1561.) *made a League with* Presbyter John, *and agreed, That if he would send them assistance, the Christian Religion should be brought into* Persia: *Whereupon a certain Patriarch with Priests being sent, they converted above twenty Cities to the Christian Faith.* Philippus

Nicolaus

Nicolaus transcribed this egregious Fable into his Book *De Regno Christi*, as a true Story, expresly affirming, *That the poor Ethiopians did so manage things, that in the short space of twelve years, more than twenty Cities did embrace the Christian Religion; and that Samarcanda was the Metropolis of them*. From which alone the Vanity of this Relator is evident. The same Author, when he had heard, that the King of *Ethiopia Libna, Denghel*, at the time of his Coronation took to himself the Name of *David*, not onely writes in the same place strangely concerning all Kings, but also affirms, That the rest of the Kings of *Ethiopia* did assume to themselves the Name of *David*, to denote their Family.

Next, in his Learned *Commentary*, he gives us an Account of his Thoughts of the Voyage of *Johannes Montevilla* an *English-man*, Doctor, and Knight, in these Words. The Relation of this Mans Voyage scarce deserves a mention; it was writ *Anno* 1310. and is beyond all others most Fabulous. He represents *Presbyter John* (as he ignorantly calls him) to be an *Asiatick* Prince, near *Catayo*; so that indeed this Author seems to have imposed on the Simplicity and Credulity of his own Age. I had not mentioned this Writer, had not a notorious Fiction related by him come into my mind, concerning an Expedition of the *Danes* into *Greece*, and *India*; and of one *John*, Son to a King of *Frisland*, (for the Holiness of his Life stiled *Priest*, or *Presbyter*); which groundless Story was transcribed from him by a later Writer, *who pretends to have read it in the Chronicles of those Countries*. The more than ordinary Folly of this Man doth also appear, in that he entitles *Magnum Tartarorum Chanum*, *Magnum Canem*, *The Great Dog*, *Ibid. Tit. l.* 2. and *l.* 9. in the beginning. Indeed he had for his Leader *Raphael Volaterranus*, in *Geograph. l.* 11. *p.* 130. *Tit. Scythae*, who writes thus, *At this time the King, whom they call* Magalim Canem, *doth govern Cathay, and the rest of* Scythia. The Reason why *Volaterranus* calls him *Magnum Canem*, may probably be in favour of the *Italians*, who cannot pronounce Xan, *Chan*, *Han*, a Prince or King; therefore he has rendred it *Canem*.

Johannes Montevilla.

The next Writer he mentions is *Benjamin Tudelensis* the *Jew*, who was an *Itinerarium* in Rabbinical *Hebrew*. This Author makes mention of *Habessinia*, in these Words: *The Land of* Cus (i. e. Ethiopia) *called* Elhabesh). And a little before, *Phison*, (he means *Gihon*) which descends from the Land of *Cus*,

Benjamin Tudelensis the Jew.

(i. e. *Ethiopia*) over which there rules a King, which they call *Sultan Elhabesh*, which is the true Name of the *Negus*. This Author is indeed very Fabulous, and of small Judgment, as we may easily discern from that Fiction of his concerning a Condensed Sea. Nevertheless, he relates many things truly, which being either not well understood, or unknown, pass for Fables. For example, he writes, *That the* Jews *did inhabit great Mountains, and lived according to their own Law*. This has passed for a Fiction with many; but it was true at that time, as we have shewed in our History.

To discourse of more *Itineraries* signifies not much. Out of those who have given Relations of Voyages into *Palestin*, commonly called the *Holy Land*, and *Egypt*, as also *Arabia*, we generally find something concerning our *Habessines*: But there is need of great Judgment in the Reader, to distinguish the Good from the Bad, and Truth from Falshood. These which follow, deserve the most Esteem and Credit.

Joh. Hugo Linschot. *Joh. Hugo Linschot*, from whom the *Hollanders* learn'd the Way and Manner of Sailing into *India*, cap. 4. mentions the *Habessins*.

Petrus della Valle.

Bernier,

Le Blanc. *Vincentius le Blanc*, who writ *Itinerarium Orientis*, his Travels over the East, and published it in *French*, *Anno* 1616. which has since been translated into *English*, with this Title, *Travels into the East*.

Joh. Cotovicus his *Itinerary*.

Matthæus Armenius. *Matthæus Armenius*, the first Ambassadour of the *Habessines* to *Emanuel* King of *Portugal*. We have the Story of this Person writ at large in *J. P. Maffeius* his History of the *Indian* Affairs, and others who have writ the Life of King *Emanuel*; How he was first received by *Albuquerquius* Viceroy of *India*, and afterwards in *Portugal*; how after some time he was dismissed, and carried back into *Habessinia*; and what he suffered from the *Portuguezes*, for his suspected Embassie.

Tzaga-za-abus. After the mention of this *Matthæus Armenius*, it will not be amiss to give this short remark on *Tzaga-za-abus*, who also spent some time in *Portugal*. This Man has been represented by some to be a Bishop; but it is a great mistake, whereas he was onely an ignorant Monk. The eminent *Joh. Ulricus Wilkins*, D. D. and my singular Friend, in his Disputation of

the

the *Ethiopick* Church, acquaints us, That almost all who have made any mention of this Church, and her belief, *have taken* whatever they have said *from the Confession of Faith of the* Tzaga-za-abus, *which he writ in the Court of* Portugal. And we may reasonably suppose, that a Person in his Circumstances would wrest the Articles of his Faith, as much as possible, to an Agreement with the *Roman* Doctrine, that by this means he might acquire the Favour of the Court, and the good Opinion of the Nation.

Franciscus Alvarez,

Johannes Bermudes.

As to the Annual Relations of the *Jesuits*, we must know, that it is the Custom of the Fathers of that Society, every year, to send an Account of their Managements out of *India*, and other remote Countries of the East and West, from which many things worthy our notice, concerning the State of those Nations, come to our knowledge. But these being for the most part writ in the *Portuguese* Tongue, and seldom or never turned into any other Language, have come late to the knowledge of other Learned Men in *Europe*. And it is for this very Reason that our Countrymen have been so long unacquainted with the History of the *Habessines*. *The Annual Relations of the Jesuits.*

Anno 1606. *Antonius Fernandez* writ an Epistle into *Europe*, from the Town *Gorgorra*, in *Dembea*, which *P. Nicolaus Godignus* made use of in confuting *Urreta*. *F. Ludovicus de Azevedo* writ another about a year before this, *viz.* the Eleventh of *July*, 1605. which is extant in Print, amongst other Relations, *cap.* 13. published at *Lisbon*, *Anno* 1609. Many more things of this nature may be found amongst the books reckoned up by *Antonius de Lepes*. *Antonius Fernandez.*

How much Credit, in things of Fact, I give to *Balthazar Tellezius*, I shall here add nothing; whereas the reading my History will sufficiently manifest my Esteem of that Author. *Balthazar Tellezius.*

Good Reader, I did design here to have put an end to this *Preface*, and no longer to have detained thy Curiosity from the following excellent History, had not the Honourable Author communicated to me, in a sheet of Paper, his Thoughts of these two following, and what Credit they deserve in relation to *Habessinia*; which he commanded me to add to this *Preface*.

The first of these is *Johannes Michael Wansleben*, *Anno* 1679.

there

there was translated into *English*, and published, a small Treatise, with this Title, *A brief Account of the Rebellions and Bloodshed, occasioned by the Antichristian Practices of the* Jesuits, *and other Popish Emissaries, in the Empire of* Ethiopia: *Collected out of a Manuscript History, written in* Latin *by* Jo. Michael Wansleben, *a Learned Papist*. There are many yet in *England* who knew this Man, before he deserted the Reformed Religion, according to the *Augustane* Confession; which he did, being conscious to himself of great Impieties. He was indeed very diligent in collecting and writing Historical Relations; but (to give the true Character of the Man) he was one always of little Judgment, less Faith, and no Honesty. He has onely added some very few things to the History of *Peter Heyling* of *Lubeck*, and transcribed the rest out of *Balthazar Tellezius*, in whom, as also in our History, whatever he mentions, is related far more distinctly and clearly. However, we will remark That *Pag*. 4. he affirms, That the *Abyssins* received the corrupt Opinion of *Eutyches*. But this is false; for they condemn the Heresie of *Eutyches*, though they reject the Council of *Chalcedon*: About which, consult the Ensuing History, *lib*. 3. *cap*. 8. *num*. 13, &c. *Pag*. 5. he says, That Pope *Alexander* the Third was informed by one of his Physicians, named *Peter*, then newly returned out of *Ethiopia*, *That in the Year* 1177. *the* Abissin *Emperour expressed himself very well inclined to the Church of* Rome. But how could he certainly know, that those things are meant of the Emperour of the *Habessines*, which in that History are read of a certain King of *India*, called *Presbyter Johannes*? For this consult the following History, *Lib*. 3. *cap*. 9. *num*. 6. So that what he writes afterwards in the same Page, concerning the Church of St. *Stephen* at *Rome* upon this occasion being granted to the *Habessins*, seems groundless. *Pag*. 6. he affirms, That the Ambassadors of the King of *Ethiopia* carried back with them Letters of Union from his Holiness, as the Acts of that Council signifie, which was begun at *Ferrara*, continued at *Florence*, and ended at *Rome*. It is indeed certain, that Ambassadors were sent from the *Habessines*; but that there was any Union made, or accepted by them, to the *Roman* Church, who can affirm? Indeed, no man, though of the meanest Judgment, can imagine, that an Affair of so great concernment should have been managed so slightly, and perfected so idlely. Is it probable that the Ambassadors had

such

ſuch Inſtructions, that without giving any Account to their Maſter, they could conclude a Matter of ſo great moment? Did the Biſhop of *Rome* ſo expoſe and degrade his Papal Dignity, as to diſpatch Letters of Union, without any Ratification or Approbation of the Acts by the King of the *Habeſſins*? Or if he had never ſo firmly believed, that all things done by the Ambaſſadours would have been ratified and confirmed, it is not eaſily credible, that he would have diſmiſſed them, without ſending along with them ſome *Legate* or *Nuncio*, who might ſee the Heretical King abjure his Hereſie, and by vertue of the Reconciliation order all things according to the Preſcriptions of the *Roman* Church. But I will not either weary my ſelf or the Reader, with any thing more of this nature: The thing it ſelf manifeſts ſufficiently, that no ſuch thing as he here writes, ever entred into the Thoughts of the King of *Ethiopia*.

What he writes, *pag.* 7. concerning *John* the Second, King of *Portugal*'s ſending ſome able Perſons, with his Letters Credential, (as to the moſt remarkable Provinces thereabouts) ſo eſpecially to the Emperour of *Ethiopia*, *&c.* is Fabulous. The Circumſtances of that Matter, and the Names of thoſe which were ſent, may be found more truly related in *Tellezius*, and our Hiſtory.

What he affirms, *pag.* 9. of thoſe Ambaſſadors *who left* Ethiopia, Anno 1529. *and arrived at* Liſbon *in* July *the ſame Year*; *of which one*, viz. Francis Alvarez, *came not to* Rome *till the twenty ninth of* January, Anno 1533. *at which time he delivered the* Ethiopian *Letters to the Pope*, *then* Clemens *the Seventh*, *&c.* ſeems ſcarce credible: For certainly the Buſineſs which this Ambaſſadour came to tranſact, cannot be ſuppoſed great and conſiderable, which admitted a delay of Seven Years.

As to what he tells us in the ſame Page, *That* Claudius, *the Son and Succeſſor of* David, *in the ſame Letters wherein he earneſtly requeſted aids from the King of* Portugal, *againſt one* Grain *King of* Adel, *&c. to render his Requeſt more ſucceſsful, craved an underſtanding Perſon, inveſted by the Pope with the Authority of a Patriarch, and ſome other able Divines, to be ſent under his Conduct into* Habeſſinia. And as to what he ſays, *pag.* 10. *That* Claudius *(having the aids he deſired) had changed his Mind in the Matter of Religion.* Both theſe are falſe and groundleſs: For *Claudius* never deſired a Patriarch from the Pope; and when *Johannes*

Bermudes, and after him *Andreas Oviedus*, came without his leave, and therefore were neglected by him, they never objected, That he had desired that some should be sent from the Pope in their Capacity, and had afterwards changed his Mind; which in reason they would have done, had these Stories of *Wansleben* been true. As to this, let the Relations of *Bermudes* and *Oviedus*, as also the History of *Tellezius*, and mine, which agrees with his, be consulted.

Page 17. he acknowledges *Zaga-Christus*, that infamous Impostor, who came into *France* about the Year 1634. to be the Legitimate Son of *Jacob*, of whom we have discoursed in our History, *Lib.* 2. *cap.* 7. and in our Commentary shall have occasion to say more of him. *Ibid.* he tells us, *That the* Galla *were a People inhabiting between the Kingdom of* Bali *and the Sea, generally esteemed the Race of those* Jews *that were innumerably dispersed by* Salmanassar, Nebuchadnezzar, Titus, Adrian, *and* Severus, *&c.* He inconsiderately says, *they were generally esteemed the Race of those* Jews: For there is no Writer that asserts this vain Figment besides *Tellezius*, which we have in our History sufficiently shewn to be so.

Page 23. he relates the History of *Abba Gregorius* most unfaithfully, as any one may easily see in that Relation which is given of him in this *Preface*, taken out of our Commentary, and which we writ from his own Mouth. Neither did he ever profess himself a *Roman Catholick*, (as *Wansleben* intimates) but expresly affirmed, *That he did not believe many things which the* Roman *Church believed*; which Words a *Roman Catholick* would never utter. As to what he adds, *ibid.* That Gregorius *gave an Account of the whole Matter upon Oath, before* Don Pedro Lippa, *then Secretary to the College* de Propaganda Fide: I never heard any such thing, either from himself, or any of his Companions; neither doth it seem very probable: for (if I do not mistake) the Secretary of the College at that time was not *Don Pedro Lippa*, a *Spaniard*, but *Monsignor Ingoli*. *Ibid.* he writes what is contrary to his own and others knowledge, *viz.* *That* Ernestus *Duke of* Saxony *hearing of this* Habessin's *Arrival and Deposition, immediately sent an Express to invite him to his Court, that he might be informed in a more particular manner from his own mouth.* What Credit this Story deserves, may be judged from what has been already said concerning *Gregorius*. But he doth most notoriously falsifie, in affirming, *That his Highness being not fully*

satisfied

satisfied with his Relation, sent Wansleben *into* Egypt, Anno 1663. *to procure the best Information he could, from such as came from* Ethiopia *to* Grand Cairo. Indeed this inconstant and unstable Person was designed for *Ethiopia*, had not he most perfidiously violated his Promises and Engagements. For the satisfaction of any that may doubt of this, those Letters concerning his Return, by which he obliged himself to his Highness, can be produced. I shall not trouble my self to add more. From what has been already said, it sufficiently appears, that I have not injured *Wansleben*, in representing him as a Man of small Judgment, less Faith, and no Honesty. How much Pains I took, and how great Expences I was at about him, is not now convenient to repeat. I thrice pardoned him, notoriously offending, and as often begging Forgiveness; but alas! I washed an *Ethiopian*: I wish he did not appear Black before the Divine Tribunal. We will therefore end this our Censure of him, with that Relation which he gives us of *Peter Heyling* of *Lubec*, an eminent Person, and well known in *Ethiopia*, *pag.* 27. At the same time (after the Expulsion of the *Jesuit* Patriarch, and another was invited from *Alexandria*, who was *Arsenius*, a *Captus* of the Monastery of St. *Macarius*) there was in *Grand-Cairo* one *Peter Heyling*, a *Lutheran*, of *Lubec*, who, for his better security among the *Roman Catholicks*, passed under the Name of *Petrus Nilungus*, an *Hollander*. * This Man (as is credibly reported) with Ten others of the same Perswasion, emulating the Industry of the *Roman* Church, concurred in a joynt Resolution to disperse the Christian Doctrine, according to the Principles of the *Reformed Religion*, over the whole Earth: And that the Distribution of their Labours might be the better regulated, they cast the several Provinces of the World into a proportionable Division among them, each of them obliging himself to undertake that Part which should fall to him by Lot: In pursuance of which Agreement and Design, the forenamed *Peter* was advanced as far as *Cairo*, the Lot having destined *Egypt* and *Ethiopia* to his Charge. A Person (by my Author's own Confession) of eminent Prudence, well skilled in History, experienc'd in Physick, and in many Languages (as *Greek*, *Hebrew*, *Arabick*, *Ethiopick*) inferiour to none.

* *An Enterprize worthy of the Protestant Religion.*

From *Cairo* he travelled seven days Journey to *Siut*, a City in the upper *Egypt*, but was constrained to return thence by the means of *Agat-Angelus*; wherefore to prevent the like Affront and Disappointment a second time, he determined to procure Licence to accompany *Arminius* the *Ethiopick Metropolitan* in his Journey towards his new Province: for which purpose, that he might ingratiate himself with the Chief of the *Copties*, (at least, as my * Author saith) he not onely professed their Religion, but privately suffered himself to be Circumcised, and by these means obtained Commendatory Letters from the *Alexandrian* Patriarch to the Emperour of *Ethiopia*, as well as Permission to joyn with *Arminius* in his Travels, who left *Cairo* in the Year 1637.

* Which tho' it [illegible] Religion [illegible] Heretick, [illegible] his Apostasion.

And yet the Coherence of my Author's Discourse seems to imply, that *Heyling*'s great Parts and Abilities recommended him to *Arminius*; who, that he might the better veil his own want of Learning under the Covert of such a Man's Company and Assistance, had a private Inducement to obtain the Patriarch's Grant for his Protection and Society, without having recourse to any such indirect Means or base Compliances as are above-specified.

Peter Heyling thus arrived in *Abyssinia*, under the *Metropolitan*'s Favour, took up his abode in a Church, not far from Court: And as soon as he was setled in his new Mansion, he began to practice Physick, and profess the Instruction of Youth in the *Greek* and *Hebrew* Tongues, wherein he quickly became so famous, that even the Principal Nobility accounted it a singular Privilege to have their Sons educated under his Tuition; so that he might easily have amassed a very considerable Treasure, had he been disposed to accept or hoard up all the Gratuities that were offered him: But he either generously refused the Presents when tendered, or else (in case they were urgently pressed upon him) liberally distributed the over-plus among the Poor, after he had made himself a very moderate allowance out of it, for Food and Raiment. A sufficient Evidence (as my Author notes) of his great Abstinence or Self-denial.

These remarkable Qualities and Endowments could not long brook the concealment of a Private Life, but brake out into such an advantageous Report of him, as reached the Emperour's Ears, and won him so high an esteem at Court, that (after some trial had been made of his Capacity for Publick Employments) he was by large steps and degrees quickly

raised

raised to the Principal Charge of the Empire; in which great Office and Trust he acquitted himself with such a prudent Address, that his Great Master obliged him (with a courteous violence) to accept of a Revenue and Attendance equal to the Chief of the Nobility, with a most delightful Apartment in a Place (accounted the Paradise of *Ethiopia*) called *Gener Christos*; yea, and designed him, as 'tis commonly and positively affirmed, his own Daughter in Marriage.

Peter Heyling finding himself so deeply interested in the Princes Favour and Affection, began to remind his Imperial Majesty of all those deplorable Troubles wherein his Dominions had been so often involved, (especially in the Days of his Father) and so effectually represented to him, that those dreadful Commotions, and all their pernicious Consequences, were solely occasioned by the *Jesuits*, and *Popish Emissaries*, warning him of the sudden approach of others on the same Errand, together with the firm Resolution of their Party to persist in the like Treasonable Attempts; that at last his Remonstrance prevailed with the *Ethiopian* Monarch and his Council to establish a Penal Law against all * the People of *Europe*, (of what Country or Perswasion soever) forbidding any Person bearing the Native Distinction of a *White Complexion*, to enter his Territories, upon pain of Death.

* *With regard (we conceive) to a certain old Prophecy, which are* [illegible] *Bel. Cattel* [illegible] *Que gente blanca* [illegible] *That a White People,* [illegible] *shall* [illegible] *them of their Country.*

In the mean time the *Roman* Fathers, *Anno* 1638. proceed on their Journey by *Suaquem*, (an Isle of the *Red Sea*) thence to *Ergiquem*, and so on towards the *Abissin* Court, in the Company of certain Merchants who had liberty of Traffick in those Parts. When they came to *Serave*, where *Barnagassi* the Viceroy of *Midrebahr* had his ordinary Residence, he no sooner saw two White Faces among the Travellers, but he suspected them to be such as had by the late Imperial Edict been banished from all the Coasts of *Ethiopia*: Whereupon (being thereunto advised by the Chief *Abissin* Priest upon the Place) he searched their Sumpture, and therein found Chalices, Stones consecrated for Altars, Sacerdotal Ornaments, and Mass-books, with other things prepared for Ecclesiastical Uses. Having thus discovered their Persons and Designs, the Viceroy informs his Master of the Discovery he had made, and detains the Fathers in Chains until he should receive further notice of his Majesties Pleasure; which was no sooner signified, but they were brought to the Emperour's Presence on the Fifth of *August*, 1638. where, upon reading some Letters which they produced from the Patriarch of *Alexandria*, the Emperour was at first inclined to remand them (without any further mark of his displeasure) to *Grand Cairo*, from whence they came: But being advised to the contrary by *Peter Heyling*, and his new Metropolitan *Arminius*, he changed his purpose, and required them (as a Test resolved on in the late Consult) to receive the Holy Communion after the manner prescribed and practised in the *Abissin* Church; with a Promise, That (in case of their Conformity thereunto) they should not onely have Licence to remain in his Dominions, but be capable of Places of Honour and Trust therein: Provided also, that they bless *S. Dioscorus*, and curse Pope *Leo*; for, all the *Abissins* firmly believe, that in his time the *Roman* Church fell into *Heresie*, and (to let my Author speak in his own Language, *ex Sanctis & Capite, qualem tunc fuisse fatentur, tam factam, dicunt, Caudam & Cathedram Diaboli*) from being Holy and the Head, (as they then owned her) she became, they say, the Tail, and the Chair of the Devil.

This Proposal being utterly rejected by the Friers, his Imperial Majesty (at the urgent Motion of his Mother, the Clergy, and the Commons, whose joynt Vogue accused him of Dissimulation, in case he put not these *Franks* to death according to his own Decree) past Sentence against them; which was speedily executed, they being hanged with those very Ropes which themselves had made use of for their Girdles, and in that posture were intombed by the vast number of Stones which the Multitude of *Abissin* Zealots threw at them; the Heap still remaining a Monument as well of the *Roman* Fathers Resolution, as of *Ethiopian* Severity.

Peter Heyling in process of time (being grown very Rich and Powerful) began to make publick expression of his dislike of divers *Abissin* Customs, decrying especially their Adoration of Saints, and of the Virgin *Mary* her self, as repugnant to True Religion and the Holy Scriptures; having on the same account privately forbidden his Scholars to use their ordinary Forms of Prayer directed to her. This begat him much Ill-will and great Opposition among the Nobles; for all the *Abissins* have a very great Reverence for the Holy Virgin. To express their disgust therefore, they first withdrew their Sons from his Tuition; and after that, made use of their best Ar-

guments

guments and Interest with the Emperour, not onely to remove him from Court, but out of his Dominions also: who hereupon having gently admonished him (at least to be silent, and connive at their Customs, if he could not conform to them) without effect, orders him to quit his Territories for a time, as the best Expedient to avoid the dangerous Efforts of Popular Fury.

Thus this Great Man voluntarily relinquished *Ethiopia*, together with the high Place and Interest he held there, after he had been (as it were) naturalized by Twelve Years Residence in that Country; being accompanied by his usual Retinue, and all the Wealth he had gotten, which was sent along with him as a Mark of the just Esteem and Favour the Emperour ever had for him. But having advanced on his way, thus attended, as far as the Isle *Suaquen*, he fell into the hands of a *Turkish Pasha*, who (to satisfie his Avarice) deprived him at once of his Life and Riches.

Concerning the Learning and Integrity of this Man, and how kindly he was entertained, and highly esteemed by the King, *Gregorius* gave me the same Account, onely adding this, That his Countrymen living at *Rome* through Envy would not endure that he should mention him to any of these Northern Parts, lest others should be encouraged by his Example to come into the Kingdom; for they neither knew what Countryman he was, nor from whence he came. But it happened as I was one Evening walking with *Gregorius*, he asked me, *Whether* Alleman *and* German *were one and the same?* Which, when I replied they were, he wondred. The next Day he again enquired the Reason of these two Names, of which I gave him the Account; and taking notice of his Admiration a second time, I asked him the reason of it; who (having first obliged me to secresie) told me what I have related in my History of *Peter Heyling*. Concerning this Man's Death, there are doubtful and uncertain Reports: As to the rest which *Wansleben* relates of him, I shall not engage to determine the Truth of, but leave it undecided.

This is what I was permitted, by the Honourable and Learned Author, to collect out of his *Commentary*; which kindly accept, till the whole be published.

Good Reader, Before I end this *Preface*, I must acquaint thee with how much security thou maist depend on the Truth of

this

this following History, and what Credit it must deserve from all Men, considering what certain Methods our Honourable and most Judicious Author has used to prevent Errour, both in himself, and Readers. The Names of all those Authors which he has cited, are found prefixed to his Book. He assures thee, he has writ nothing whose Author he is not able to name; and if any should doubt of any Place, or suspect him in Ecclesiastical Affairs, as professing a different Religion from them, he desires them to consult his Authors, and weigh his Reasons, lest without Reason, out of meer Prejudice, they may suspect his Writings. He would have those of the *Roman* Communion treat him with the same Justice that he doth *Tellezius*, even concerning the Religion of the *Habessins*, notwithstanding his being obliged both by his Religion and Order, being a *Jesuit*, to obey the Bishop of *Rome*. For our most Judicious Author excellently distinguishes between his Propagating the Doctrines of the Church of which he professes himself, and defending them, and falsifying Things of Fact, or reporting other Mens Opinions unfaithfully; which two last are highly blameable. I shall add one Argument more to evince the Credit of this History, which is this. Some very few days since, I have been certainly informed, that this *Ethiopick* History has so much obtained in *France*, and gained so considerable an Esteem amongst the Ingenuous, Inquisitive, and Learned of that Nation, that though our excellent Author be different from the *Gallican* Church in the Matter of Religion, yet so much are they convinced of his generous Fidelity, that they have epitomized or contracted his History, and dedicated it to himself: Which none can believe would have been done, had not it been believed to have excelled all Writings of the same Kind and Subject.

THE

J. LUDOLPHUS
TO THE
Courteous Reader.

AT length I present you with my *Ethiopic* Historie, long-promis'd, long expected by my friends. Nor will this delay be wonder'd at by those that consider how I am ty'd to public duty and employment, utterly dissonant from these sort of Studies. Beside which, there were many other Reasons. For I had collected indeed the Body of the matter from the Writings and Discourses of *Gregory* the *Habessinian*, but the Circumstances of time and place, and the names of persons were yet wanting. So that there was Timber and Bricks for the Building, but only Lime and Cement was wanting. Moreover after so many Fables had been Printed upon this subject, I thought it would not be so prudently done to utter more novelty upon the credit of one single person; lest a new truth might be look'd upon as a new Tale. At length having got into my hands *Balthazar Tellez*, from whom as well to supply what I wanted, as also to confirm what might seem to be doubtfull, yet then likewise I wanted Leisure. Which when the most Serene *Saxe-Gotan* Dukes had indulg'd me, I Transferred my family to *Frankfort* upon the *Main*, to the end that I might have the benefit of several famous Libraries in that Noble City, and the opportunity of a Learned Conversation, and by that means accomplish my intended work, which by Gods Assistance I did in six weeks.

After this, when all was ready for the Press, there still wanted what was necessary to forward the Publishing of this work. A proper *Amanuensis* to transcribe the whole matter, and to attend upon the Correction of the Impression; which my occasions would not permit me to do; and then in the next place such Forraign Characters as this work requir'd, which impediments were also at last remov'd. For there was a certain Young Gentleman recommended to me, eminent for his Learning and integritie, by name *John Henry Majus*, a Student in Theology, and the Oriental Tongues. Who being well skill'd in the Hebrew Language, and the Dialect of the Rabbins, by my help easily made himself Master of the *Ethiopic*, and so fitted himself for the imployment I design'd him. He therefore by my directions made the heads of the Chapters, the Sections, the Index, and Translated the *Ethiopic* into Latin, assisted the work and put it forward, taking upon him the whole Correction of it. For which reason I can recommend his deserts the more justly to all good and learned Men.

The Printing part was undertaken by *Balthasar Christopher Wustius*, as well for that he was well known among Forainers, as because he had a Printing House furnished with all sorts of Letters for Foraign Languages. He also caused the *Ethiopic* and *Amharic* Characters to be engrav'd in Copper by the famous *John Adolphus Schmide*, and afterwards to be cast for farther use. But these could not be brought to perfection, so soon

So

as the Compositers requir'd, and therefore there was a necessitie of mixing some old and less elegant, with the new and neater Characters.

As to the Work it self, I have said enough in the Proem: No man understandeth the wants and defects better than my self. Therfore I resolv'd to deferr the Publishing till newer and fuller relations return'd out of *Ethiopia*; or that I might receive them from the bordering Regions, as being furnished for that purpose with very great and most generous Recommendations, till I had brought my design to a full and elaborate perfection. But many Illustrious men, and my most honour'd friends, interceded with me, telling me, *That never any thing came forth perfect at first in all its parts: And that therefore this History was no longer to be conceal'd from the Christian and Learned World, which is concerned to know these things: For that if any thing should fall out hereafter worthy of remark, it might be put into an Appendix or added to a new Edition.* Which makes me hope for pardon from the more Candid Reader, if his desire or expectation be not satisfied in all particulars. For I relate not altogether things beheld with my own eyes, but what I have either read my self or heard from others, yet congruous to Truth and well cohering between themselves. If I have not reach'd the sence of my Authors, I will amend upon admonition, or else return my thanks and satisfaction to the admonisher. That I should please all men, a thing which never mortal yet attained, none in prudence can exact from me, nor dare I hope to have done it. However I propose to my self to injure no man, but every where to study moderation. So they who take offence, ought to be offended with my Authors not with me. There are some perhaps who believe I might have spoken more in matter of Religion, others that I have said too much, certainly I had rather I could have omitted all, so ungratefull to me are the Altercations of Christians among themselves in matters of Religion, chiefly where the Decisions tend to Force and Arms. For they who think mutual Love and Charity is only due to men of their own sect, certainly wander much from the scope of Christian perfection, according to the precepts of Christ and his Apostles.

I have not aim'd at my own advantage, nor my own increase of Reputation, hard to be acquir'd, now the world is so fertile in soaring Genius's, I have only endeavoured to be in some measure profitable to the Commonwealth of Christianity and Learning, out of a peculiar kindness to that, for ought we know, most ancient Nation of the *Habessines*: I confess I have frequently bewail'd their misfortune for this, that the enmities ran so high between them and the Portuguesses, that for their sakes all the other Europeans are suspected to that Nation, and not permitted to have any commerce among them. But it has afforded me much more matter of grief, that there should be such and so great Animosity among the Western Christians, that as things stand, there is no Counsell or help to be afforded for the ease and restitution of the Eastern Church, or for the suppression of those Barbarous *Idolaters*.

[illegible]

The

The Heads of the several Chapters in the following *HISTORY*.

Book I.

Of the Nature of the Country and Inhabitants.

Chap.

Book II.

Of their Political Government.

Chap.

Book III.

Errours

Book IV.

Of their private Affairs.

Of

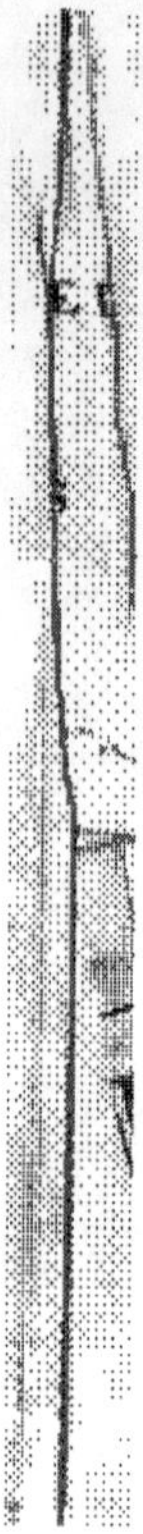

THE HISTORY OF ETHIOPIA:

OR THE KINGDOM *of the* ABESSINES.

I Am now about to write the History of the *Abessines*, concerning whom, there have been many large, but few true Relations. For these People having translated themselves from the Maritime Regions of the *Arabian Gulf*, into the more upland Parts of *Africa*, by reason their Commerce with Foreigners has been very inconsiderable, have been known to very few of the *Europeans*. Besides that the Name of *Ethiopians*, which they assume to themselves, is common to so many Nations, that it has render'd their History very ambiguous; for that many things generally spoken of the *Ethiopians*, were more particularly attributed to the *Abessines*. Neither were they wanting to their own honour, while they appropriated to themselves whatever was said either in Scripture or elsewhere to their advantage.

Others there are, who to wast their idle hours, and designing some fabulous Inventions, or to represent the Platform of some Imaginary Common-Wealth, have chosen *Ethiopia* for the Subject of their Discourse. Believing they could not more pleasantly Romance, or more safely license themselves to fasten Improbabilities upon any other Countrey. Among the rest, *Ludovicus Ureta*, a Monk of *Valentia*, and a most notorious Trifler, has deservedly merited the Lash of *Nicholas Godignus*. In the same Form is *Jacobo Baratti*, an *Italian* of a newer date, but nothing better than the other, either a Transcriber, or casual picker up of feigned Relations, who in his *Itinerario* affirms many things concerning the *Abessines*, not as they really were, but rather as he fancied they were, or desired they should be. I omit to mention others, who in the Relation of their Travels, put down Reports and Hear-says for certain, and experienced Truths, and attribute the manners and dispositions of one or two private Persons to the whole Nation. Which makes me the more careful to leave something more undoubted to Posterity.

The first knowledge of the *Abessine* Emperor was discovered to us by the *Portugals* in the beginning of the preceding Age, but erroneous and very confused, in reference to the misunderstood Denomination of the Word *Prester John*: such as they had learn'd it from the two Ignorant *Habessine* Ambassadors, *Matthew* an *Armenian* Merchant, and *Tzagazabus*, President of the inconsiderable Territory of *Bugna*. *Franciscus Alvarezius*, and *John Bermudes* affords a clearer Light; as having spent some time in *Ethiopia*. However you must take care to prefer what they saw, before what they deliver by report.

Lastly, we have found many things of uncontradicted Truth, which have been Published in the Relations and Epistles of the *Jesuits*. For they by their singular Care and Vigilancy over that Kingdom, have engaged it to themselves and the See of *Rome*, there is hardly any thing that concerns the *Abessine* Nation, that remains concealed and hidden from them. Having therefore gotten into my hands, the *Ethiopian* History of *Balthazar Tellezius*, Provincial of *Portugal*, written in the *Portugal* Language in a pleasant and florid Stile, and finding it to be collected out of the Acts and Instructions of the Fathers of the Society, with a Commentary of *Emanuel Almeyda*, written in *Ethiopia*, and a certain Manuscript History of *Alphonsus Mendeza*, the *Latin Ethiopian* Patriarch, and attested by *Jerome Lupus*, a sworn Witness, I made no question of accomplishing the Work I had taken in hand, more especially observing that all things

exactly

exactly agreed with what *Gregory* the *Abessine*, a Native of *Mecana Selace*, a City in the Kingdom of *Amhara*, had at large related to me. Onely that *Tellezius* takes occasion every where to plead for the *Roman* Religion, and his own Society, to extol the Acts and Proceedings of the Fathers; while on the other side he is very sharp upon the *Abessines*, and very severely censures their Ceremonies, yet with that Candor and Sincerity, that he frequently Commends the good Conditions and Ingenuity of the People.

As for my Self, no difference in Religion, shall make me less Studious of Truth, or less Humane or Charitable towards all sorts of Christians whatsoever. Neither shall any thing of Favour or Hatred either towards the Fathers of the Society, or the *Abessines* in particular, carry me so far to Partiality, but that I shall communicate whatever I heard from others, faithfully and religiously. However least I may be thought to conceal from whence I gathered these my Informations, I have not only plac'd the Names of my Friends in the Margin of the Book, or in the Notes underneath, but also recited their own words in a Commentary which I am preparing to annex to my Work; with Instructions either intire or contracted: And the Reasons that constrain me to differ from others in Opinion. Nor do I bind my self to be any further believed; so that if any thing be understood amiss by my Authors, or not rightly placed, I leave it to be amended by Posterity; and those things to be supplyed which I have omitted, either as uncertain, or altogether unknown.

As to the Person of *Gregory*, upon whose Credit I Relate those *Ethiopic* Affairs and Transactions scarce to be found in any other Authors, and whom I shall frequently mention, more shall be said in our Commentary. Nevertheless I shall not conceal thus much from the Reader, That he, after a Friendship contracted with me at *Rome*, out of a desire to understand the Affairs of *Europe*, and to learn the *Latin* Tongue, came into *Germany* to give me a Visit. Soon after, being sent for to *Gota*, by the Most Serene Prince, Duke of *Saxony*, (of whose Piety and Affection to the Common-weal of Christianity, I have not now time to speak sufficiently) he was by so great a Judgment, after several Discourses with him, found to be a Person of great gravity, and high credit. For being somewhat above fifty years of

Age, and then an Exile, for that contrary to the King's Command, he had followed the Fathers of the Society into *India*, and consequently exercised in Misfortune, he had laid aside all *Levity* and *Ostentation*, the Vices of *Fortunate Youth*. So that although in truth, I was sufficiently able, by vertue of his Instructions, and the knowledge which I obtained from him of the *Ethiopic* Language, to have out-done all those that have gone before me, yet I was unwilling to refell the Errors of others upon the Credit of one single Person, till I had more Authorities to support me.

Nor did I therefore undertake this difficult Task, only to consume my leisure hours in confuting the Errors, or mustering up the different Opinions of Authors, without any prospect of *Publick Benefit*. The History it self of this Nation deserves the Labour of an Accurate Pen. For whether you consider the Temper of the Clime, or the Condition of the Soyl, you shall hardly find in any other Part of the World more frequent Miracles of Nature.

The Country is situated between the *Tropic of Cancer*, and the *Equinoctial Line*, and enjoys a wonderful variety of Air: The Champion Levels feel the Heat, the Hilly Parts are no less subject to Cold. For this reason, the Thunders are most dreadful, and frequent Tempests terrifie both Man and Beasts. Their Prodigious Mountains over-look the Clouds themselves. Neither *Olympus* nor *Athos*, here accounted Wonders; nor *Atlas* it self, which the Ancients fancied to be the Support of Heaven, are to be compared with them. Their Rocks of various Shapes and Figures, so amazingly steep as not to be ascended, yet inhabited. Their surrounded Valleys rugged and representing *Abysses* for profundity. Metals they also have; but chiefly Gold, did they know how to find and dig it forth. Their dryest places in Winter are overflowed in Summer: For those Advantages which the Rains afford the Fields in other places, the Rivers supply in *Ethiopia*. Among those Rivers, *Nilus* for vastness and fame, far exceeds all the Rivers of the whole World: Whose Fountains so diligently sought by the Ancients are not only here found, but it also now appears, that the River *Niger* is no more than its left Channel. Nor do all the Rivers of *Habassia*, as in other Places, empty themselves into the Sea, but are some of them suckt up in the Sand; so that it is more difficult to find the Mouths of those,

than

than the Sources of other Streams. Plants they have of admirable Vertue; and Beasts of all sorts, many of which are unknown to us. The largest also both of Foul and four-footed Beasts are here to be found. The celebrated Unicorn, so curiously sought for in all other Corners of the World, was first seen here. Cattel without number, much larger than ours, feed in the vast Woods, affording Pasture sufficient as well for the Wild as Tame. Nor is the variety of the Nations and People less to be admired; so strangely differing in Language, Customs, and Ceremonies, that it may be thought some distinct Part of the World, rather than a particular Kingdom.

However all *Abessinia* Obeys one King, who by reason of certain Princes that are subject to him, calls himself *Negusa nagast zait ityopia*, King of the Kings of *Ethiopia*. He derives his Descent from *Solomon* King of the *Israelites*, by an ambitious, tho dubious Claim; defending the long series of his Family, whether true or false, with the force of Antiquity. However it be, this is certain, That the Monarchy of the *Abessines*, and the Royal Line, are no less Ancient than any among the *Europeans*. And for their Power, they were formerly more Potent than any other of the *African* Kings: But their Wars in the preceding Age with the *Adelenses*, has brought them very low. Afterwards they were so debilitated by the Fury of the *Gallani*, that *Abessinia* is scarce to be found in *Habessinia* it self, if you compare it with what it was in the times of *Alvarezius*.

But that which deserves the greatest admiration is the antiquity of the Christian Religion, which first began under S. *Athanasius*, Patriarch of *Alexandria*, at what time *Frumentius* Preached among them; the Opinions and Ceremonies of which Church they still retain. So that many Primitive Rites in other Places obsolete, are here still in Use. But that deplorable Schism which arose in the Council of *Calcedon*, for which they alledge other Causes than our Writers do, withdrew the *Abessines* all together from the *Catholick* Church, at that time Flourishing; while they followed the Patriarch of the *Jacobites*, and rejected the Patriarch of the *Melchites*. Yet all this while for so many Ages they have suffered no considerable Change in their Divine Worship till the beginning of this last Century, at what time being split into Divisions by the Artifices of the *Jesuits*, they have been cruelly shaken

with

with Civil Discord and Bloody Wars; some Adhering to the *Romish*, other the *Alexandrian* Religion.

Of which and other things it is our Design to treat more fully in this our History; and so to handle the matter, as to discourse in the First Book, Of Natural Things; as the Situation and Names of the several Countries, the Temper of the Climate, the Condition of the Soyl, the several Customs and Languages of the Nations and Inhabitants. In the Second Book, Of the Political Government, the Succession of their Kings, their Laws, their Acts of War, the Revenue of the Kingdom, and the like. In the Third, Of their Ecclesiastical Affairs, the beginning of the Christian Religion, and its Advance in those Countries, their Differences with the *Greek* and *Latin* Church. And Lastly, in the Fourth Book, Of their Domestick Concerns, and Private OEconomy.

O F

An ETHIOPIC ALPHABET

Divided into seven Orders according to the seven sounds of their vowells.

Hoi	ሀ	ha	ሁ	hu	ሂ	hi	ሃ	ha	ሄ	he	ህ	he	ሆ	ho
Lawi	ለ	la	ሉ	lu	ሊ	li	ላ	la	ሌ	le	ል	le	ሎ	lo
Haut	ሐ	ha	ሑ	hu	ሒ	hi	ሓ	ha	ሔ	he	ሕ	he	ሖ	ho
Mai	መ	ma	ሙ	mu	ሚ	mi	ማ	ma	ሜ	me	ም	me	ሞ	mo
Saut	ሠ	ſa	ሡ	ſu	ሢ	ſi	ሣ	ſa	ሤ	ſe	ሥ	ſe	ሦ	ſo
Rees	ረ	ra	ሩ	ru	ሪ	ri	ራ	ra	ሬ	re	ር	re	ሮ	ro
Sat	ሰ	ſa	ሱ	ſu	ሲ	ſi	ሳ	ſa	ሴ	ſe	ስ	ſe	ሶ	ſo
Kaf	ቀ	ka	ቁ	ku	ቂ	ki	ቃ	ka	ቄ	ke	ቅ	ke	ቆ	ko
Bet	በ	ba	ቡ	bu	ቢ	bi	ባ	ba	ቤ	be	ብ	be	ቦ	bo
Tawi	ተ	ta	ቱ	tu	ቲ	ti	ታ	ta	ቴ	te	ት	te	ቶ	to
Harm	ኀ	ha	ኁ	hu	ኂ	hi	ኃ	ha	ኄ	he	ኅ	he	ኆ	ho
Nahas	ነ	na	ኑ	nu	ኒ	ni	ና	na	ኔ	ne	ን	ne	ኖ	no
Alph	አ	a	ኡ	u	ኢ	i	ኣ	a	ኤ	e	እ	e	ኦ	o
Caf	ከ	ca	ኩ	cu	ኪ	ci	ካ	ca	ኬ	ce	ክ	ce	ኮ	co
Wawe	ወ	wa	ዉ	wu	ዊ	wi	ዋ	wa	ዌ	we	ው	we	ዎ	wo
Ain	ዐ	a	ዑ	u	ዒ	i	ዓ	a	ዔ	e	ዕ	e	ዖ	o
Zai	ዘ	za	ዙ	zu	ዚ	zi	ዛ	za	ዜ	ze	ዝ	ze	ዞ	zo
Jaman	የ	ja	ዩ	ju	ዪ	ji	ያ	ja	ዬ	je	ይ	je	ዮ	jo
Dent	ደ	da	ዱ	du	ዲ	di	ዳ	da	ዴ	de	ድ	de	ዶ	do
Geml	ገ	ga	ጉ	gu	ጊ	ghi	ጋ	ga	ጌ	ghe	ግ	ghe	ጎ	go
Tait	ጠ	ta	ጡ	tu	ጢ	ti	ጣ	ta	ጤ	te	ጥ	te	ጦ	to
Pait	ጰ	pa	ጱ	pu	ጲ	pi	ጳ	pa	ጴ	pe	ጵ	pe	ጶ	po
Zadai	ጸ	tza	ጹ	tzu	ጺ	tzi	ጻ	tza	ጼ	tze	ጽ	tze	ጾ	tzo
Zappa	ፀ	tza	ፁ	tzu	ፂ	tzi	ፃ	tza	ፄ	tze	ፅ	tze	ፆ	tzo
Af	ፈ	fa	ፉ	fu	ፊ	fi	ፋ	fa	ፌ	fe	ፍ	fe	ፎ	fo
Psa	ፐ	pa	ፑ	pu	ፒ	pi	ፓ	pa	ፔ	pe	ፕ	pe	ፖ	po
		a Angl.		ou Gall.		i		a lenam.		e clare		e obscur.		o Long

A Specimen

of their diphthongs

ቈ kuä ኰ kuä ቊ kui ቋ kua

ኈ huä ኍ huä ኊ hui ኋ hua

ጐ guä ጒ gui ጓ gua ጔ gue

ኈ guä ኍ guä ኊ gui ኋ gua

A Specimen

of their numbers or numeral figures taken from the Greek

[illegible] 10000

A Specimen of the Amharic Letters

Sh Engl.	ሸ	sha	ሹ	shu	ሺ	shi	ሻ	sha	ሼ	she	ሽ	she	ሾ	Sho
Ty Hung.	ቸ	tye	ቹ	tyu	ቺ	tyi	ቻ	tya	ቼ	tye	ች	tye	ቾ	tyo
ñ Spanish	ኘ	ña	ኙ	ñu	ኚ	ñi	ኛ	ña	ኜ	ñe	ኝ	ñe	ኞ	ño
Ch Germ.	ኸ	kha	ኹ	khu	ኺ	khi	ኻ	kha	ኼ	khe	ኽ	khe	ኾ	kho
J French	ዠ	ja	ዡ	ju	ዢ	ji	ዣ	ja	ዤ	je	ዥ	je	ዦ	jo
D Bohem.	ጀ	dja	ጁ	dju	ጂ	dji	ጃ	dja	ጄ	dje	ጅ	dje	ጆ	djo
Cia Ital.	ጨ	cha	ጩ	chu	ጪ	chi	ጫ	cha	ጬ	che	ጭ	che	ጮ	cho

OF THE

Nature of the Countrey,

AND THE

INHABITANTS.

BOOK I.

CHAP. I.

Of the Various Names of the Abessines, *and Original of the Nation.*

The Original of the Name of the Abessines *is* Arabian: *But they rather chose to be called* Ethiopians; *more particularly,* Agazian, (i. e.) *Free, as the* Germans *call themselves* Franks. *They transported themselves out of* Arabia-Felix *into* Africa, *for they derive their Original from the* Sabeans, *or* Homerites. *Their Language agrees with the* Arabian. *The* Grecians *call them* Axumites, *others* Indians; *hence confusion of Story: Erroneously called* Caldeans. *The Name of* Abassia *or* Ethiopia, *to be retained.*

IT behoves us to begin with the Name of the Nation. They are now generally called, *Habessines*, by others *Abassines*, or *Abessines*, the Name being given them by the *Arabians*, in whose Language, [*Habesh*] (a) signifies a (b) Confusion, or mixture of People; which Appellation, as being somewhat ignominious, they for a long time despised, neither do they yet acknowledge it in their Writings. For they rather choose to call

(a) *For* Habesha, *speaking of a multitude of People, is no more than* Convenio, *or the multitude gathered together, in the Second Conjugation* Habesha, *congregavit, or Congregated together; From whence the words* Habesh *etc. signifie a multitude of men gathered together from several Tribes of People. So that the* Abessines *may not be improperly called by our* Latin *word,* Convenae, *or such as come together.*

(b) *The* Germans *sound it* Habasch *or* Habesch, *the* Italians, Habassino; *the* French, Habasch, *the* Portuguezes, Abex, *pronounced after the same manner with variety of Letters; in regard of the* Arabick, Habesh, *which is the Original of all these words. It is written* Chabassi *for* Chabesh, *in the* Prolegomena *of* Walton's *Polyglot Bible.* Cap. 15. Pag. 98.

their

their Kingdom, *Manghesta Itiopia*, the Kingdom of *Ethiopia*, and themselves *Itiopiawjan*, *Ethiopians*; assuming the Name from the *Greeks*, though too general, and then formerly common as well to all the swarthy Complexion'd People in *Asia*, as to the Blacks of *Ethiopia*. (c). But if you require a special Name from them, then they call their Kingdom *Geez*: also the Countrey of *Agazi*, or the Land of the *Agazians*, or (d), Freemen, either from the Liberty they enjoy, or their transporting themselves from one place to another, for that the radical Word *Geez* admits of both significations. Perchance, (e) because that in ancient times, translating themselves out of *Arabia* and *Africa*, in search of other Habitations, they assumed that Name in sign of Liberty, as of old, the *Germans*, passing the *Rhine*, gave themselves the Name of *Franks*. (f) For they are not Natives of the Land; but came out of that Part of *Arabia* which is called *The Happy*, which adjoyns to the *Red-Sea*: and from whence there is an easie Passage into *Africa*. For the *Abassines* formerly inhabited *Arabia*, and were reckon'd (g) into the number of the *Sabeans* or *Homerites*, as the ancient Geographers testifie, (h) and many other Convincing Arguments sufficiently prove. For their Ancient Language, which we call the *Ethiopick*, is very near a-kin to the *Arabick*. They have also many Customs, as Circumcision, which are common with the *Arabians*. Their Genius, and the shape of their Bodies, and the Lineaments of their Countenances resemble the *Arabians* much more than the *African Ethiopians*. Besides, that *Severus* the Emperor, among the Vanquished People of *Arabia*, caused the Name of the *Abassines* to be (i) Engraven on his Coyn.

(c) *Hence* Ethiopia *was by the Ancients divided into* Oriental *and* Occidental, *into* African *and* Asiatick: *Of which those Places of Scripture that speak of the* Cushites, *are to be understood. Now adays* Ethiopia *is only Attributed to* Africa.

(d) *For which* Gregory *is my Author in a Letter to my self.*

(e) *See my* Ethiopick Lexicon. *Col.* 425.

(f) *Which I believe, as Agreeing with those Authors cited by* Pontanus *concerning the Original of the* Franks.

(g) *For the* Sabaeans *and* Homerites *are the same from the Region of the* Assamites, *the* Red-Sea *lying between, as saith* Prosop. Castrus *upon the Tenth Chapter of the Third Book of Kings, Ver. 1. upon the words, Queen of Sheba.*

(h) Stephanus *in his Book concerning Cities, upon the word* Abasseni, *writes,* Abaseni, *a Nation of* Arabia, *and relates out of the* Arabicks *of* Uranius, *that they bordered upon the* Sabeans.

(i) Scaliger in Comput. Eccles. Ethiop. de Emendat. temp. *Lib.* 7.

The

The *Habessines* themselves also, while they claim the Queen of *Sheba* for their Princess, betray their Original. For the *Arabians* unanimously confess, That she was descended from the Lineage of the *Homerites*. The *Grecian* Writers, ignorant of the proper Name, from the Royal City *Axuma*, called them *Axumites*. (*k*) Others in reference to their Original, have confus'd them with the *Homerites*; others, by reason of their vicinity, with the *Nubeans*. Most of the Ancients called them *Indians*, as they did all those Nations under the *Torrid Zone*, whose particular Names they understood not. Yea the *Red Sea* it self is by some (*l*) of the Ancients called the *Indian Sea*; so that 'tis no wonder that the Nations bordering upon it should be called *Indians*. Neither did the *Portuguezes* know any other Name in the beginning of the former Century. For *Damianus de Goes* calls their King, the great Emperor of the *Indians*. (*m*) Which diversity of Names has begat no small Confusion in our History. For some things are attributed to our *Abessines*, which are appropriated to the true *Indians*. (*n*) And some things written concerning another Nation of *Ethiopia*, are imposed as peculiar to the *Habessines*. At *Rome*, upon the first Printing of certain *Ethiopick* Books, their Language was said to be *Chaldean*, and they themselves erroneously called, sometimes *Chaldeans*, at other times *Indians*. But the Name of *Abessinia* or *Abassia*, now known to all the World, shall be the Name which (*o*) we shall retain, with that of *Ethiopia* sometimes: More especially when we shall discourse concerning their Kings, their Ancient Language, or their Ecclesiastical Affairs; all which admit themselves to be distinguished by the Title of *Ethiopick*; which the *Abessines* themselvs do also allow.

(*k*) *Stephanus makes mention of these in the word* Axumites. Cedrenus, *An.* 15. *of* Justinian, *and* Ptolomie. Scaliger *mentions the Name of* Axumite *upon certain Pieces of Coyn, in the fore-recited place.*

(*l*) *So* Procopius Gazeus, *cited in his Comment upon the forementioned Tenth of* Kings; *and others, as* Scaliger *observes in* Comp. Ecclef. Ethiop. &c.

(*m*) *In his Relation of the Embassie of* Mattheus *to the King of* Portugal.

(*n*) *Which chiefly happens in the History of the Conversion of the* Habessines, *set forth by* Adesius *and* Frumentius; *which the Writers of Ecclesiastical History, have written almost all of them understood, concerning the true or* Asiatic Indians. Theodoret *in* Hist. Ecclesiast. *Lib.* 1. *Cap.* 22.

(*o*) Paulus *in Præfat.* Psal. Ethiopic. Edit. Rom. Ambrose Theseus *Introd. in Ling. Orient. Pag.* 13.

CHAP.

Of the Situation and Bounds of Abessinia.

The Situation above Egypt, *and degrees of Latitude. The Error of* Jovius, *and the vulgar Tables. The true Latitude. The conjectural Latitude. The Bounds toward the* North, *and toward the* East. *Toward the* South. *Toward the* West.

IN *Africa*, above *Egypt*, beyond (*a*) *Nubia*, lies *Habassia* very near between the Eighteenth and Sixteenth Degree of *Northern* Latitude; being (*b*) called by some the *Upper Ethiopia*. It extends not altogether so far as the *Equinoctial Line*, much less can it be said to cross it. Which notwithstanding, almost all Geographers and Historians have hitherto asserted; whether it were that they did not rightly understand the Sayings and Writings of others, or whether deceived by the Credit of *Paulus Jovius*, who writes that the Kingdom of *Sceva*, (*Sewa* or *Scheva*) beholds the *Antartick Pole* elevated in two and twenty degrees; whereas it is in no place to be seen where *Shewa* lies. Which mistake as seems most probable, he too unwarily drew, not from the *Abessines*, utterly ignorant of those things, but from a certain Ancient Geographical Map of *Africa*; the Author of which has so far extended *Habessinia*, that he has joyned it to another Region known only to himself; fearing to seem ignorant of what lay between by leaving a space. As if it were a shame to be ignorant of that which flies the piercing examination of human wit, and can be no otherwise discovered but by experiment.

But the *Jesuits*, more skilful in *Spherical Discipline*, by the Assistance of the *Astrolabe*, were the first who taught us that same true Latitude, from the *North* to the *South*, already mention'd. But they were not able to make it out: Yet so far as could be rendred most probable and certain, by conjecture, and the length of Journeys, the *Portugals* do reckon this Kingdom, where it is broadest, to contain a a Hundred and Forty of their Leagues. But the longest

---

(*a*) Sub Egypto *most write, but erroneously.*
(*b*) *So* B. Telles, Historia general. de Ethiopia alta.

Journey,

Journey directly *Westward*, is to be accounted from the *Red Sea* to the farthest Limits of *Dembea*. For most sure it is, that the Bounds of this Empire do from the *East* and *West*, as it were Conically lessen; besides that the *Gallans* have torn several of its Members from it.

Toward the *North* it has adjoyning to it, the Kingdom of *Fund*, otherwise *Sennar*, by the *Portugals* called *Fungi*; a part of Ancient *Nubia*. Toward the *East* it was formerly bounded by the *Red Sea*. But now the Port of *Arkiko*, with the adjacent Island of *Mazua* being taken, all that Coast obeys the *Turk*, who are Masters of that Sea. A Sea that affords but little convenience for Harbors, full of Shelves and Quick-sands, and besides that, the Islands which belong to it are Untill'd, ill Inhabited, and labouring under such a scarcity of Water in the midst of the Sea, that they neither afford Accommodation nor Security to Strangers, for which reason they are but little visited. The Mouth of the Streight is very narrow, and of so ill a fame for frequent Shipwracks, that the *Arabians* call it *Bab-elmendeb*, the (c) Port of Affliction. To those that enter into it, the Kingdom of *Dancale* appears upon the left hand. The Prince of this Territory is a Friend to the *Abessines*, and Commands the Port of *Baylur*, where the Patriarch sent from *Rome*, first Landed, and travelled thence into *Abessinia*. More within the Streight lies the King of *Adela*, a *Mahumetan*, a Profest Enemy, and in the last Century, the Scourge of the *Habessines*. Next follow in their Order the Kingdoms of *Dewaro*, *Bali*, *Fatagar*, *Wed*, *Bizamo*, *Cambata*, with several other Provinces, either possessed or wasted by the Barbarous Nation of the *Gallans*. From thence the Countries winding about the Eighth Degree toward the *South*, *Alaba* and *Jendero*, by the *Portugals* called *Gingiro*, Kingdoms of the *Gonzites*, terminate *Habessinia*, till you come to *Enarea*, the last Kingdom, seated between the Eighth and Ninth Degree of Latitude, toward the *Northwest*. Lastly the River *Maleg*, and *Nilus* it self, rolling along through several vast Desarts, close up the *Western* Limits. Nor are there any other Nations worthy to be mentioned thereabout, till you come to the *North*,

(c) *In the Vulgar Mapps, and of latter Editions, mistakenly called* Babelmandel. *The Interpreters of the Nubian* Geographie, *pronounce it* Bab-Almandab, *and render it*, The Dreadful Mouth, Pag. 22.

and the Kingdom of *Sennar*, already nam'd, unless the wandring *Ethiopians*, which the Ancients called *Nomades* and *Troglodytes*; and the *Abessines Shankala*.

CHAP. III.

Of the Division of Habessinia, *into diverse Kingdoms and Regions.*

The Regions and Kingdoms of Habessinia *are variously reputated, and numbred up. Numerical faults.* Gregories *enumeration and pronunciation. The Limits of* Ambara, *and the Provinces.* Angota, Bagemra, *with its Prefectures,* Balis, Bizama, Brigna, Cambata, Conta, Damota, Dewaro, Dambeia, *and its Provinces.* Enarea, Fatagara, Gafata, Gaghe, Gaura, Ganz, Gidm, Gojam. Gombe, Gongia, Guraghe. Ifat, Samen, Sea, Sewa, Shat. Tigra *and its Prefectures. Those which are under* Bahrnagashus, Walaka, Wed. Tellez *reckons more. Others he omits. More remarkable Provinces. What the King of* Habessinia *possesses at this day.*

THE Regions of which *Ethiopia* consists, are neither equally, nor with the same observance of number, but variously set down. Most of them enjoy the Name of the Kingdom, *Menghest*, or *Ethiopia*, in General; perhaps because in ancient times they had their proper Princes and peculiar Laws, as we know that formerly *Spain* was divided into several Kingdoms of the same nature. The rest, in the *Amharic* Dialect, are called *Shumet*, Prefectures, which are not however Governed by *Vice-Roys*, but are under peculiar Governours of their own; which being confounded with the Kingdoms so call'd, must needs render the number of the Kingdoms uncertain. *Paulus Jovius* distinguishes the Empire of the *Habessines* into more than forty Kingdoms; others add yet more, which are more easily set down in writing, than demonstrated. *Matthew the Armenian*, first Ambassador to the *Portugals* from the *Abessines*, will needs have (a) sixty. *Tesfa Sion*, who set forth the *New-Testament* in *Ethiopic*, affirms sixty two Kingdoms in Subjection to his Emperor.

Hist. l. 18.

In Epist. Ev. Johan.

(a) Dam. à Goez. de legat. Indorum ad Emanuel. 5. Lus. Reg.

Lus. Unless

Unless perhaps the Numerical Character for sixty, be mistaken for that denoting only twenty; of which sort, there are most frequent faults both in Prophane and (*b*) Sacred Writers. P. *Nicolaus Godignus*, from the Relation of *John Gabriel*, a *Portugueze* Collonel, a Person of great fame, and one that had long resided in *Ethiopia*, asserts, That the *Abessine* Empire, according to its ancient Right, comprehends no less than twenty six Kingdoms, and fourteen Provinces. But he mixes some Neighbouring Kingdoms, which are no way Subject to the King of the *Abessines*, and some he also omits. (*c*) However most certain it is, that we may safely reckon twenty, computing those which the *Gallans* have subdued. *Gregory* named thirty to me, adding perhaps some small ones, which others allow to be no more than Prefectures. These I shall reckon up from his own mouth, and as he wrote them down himself, that the (*d*) Reader may be assured of their true and genuine Pronunciation. The first, and that the best and most fertile, is the Kingdom of *Tigra*; but for Nobleness *Amhara* exceeds it, which we shall put in the first place, the rest following according to the Order of the *Latin* Alphabet.

Amhara is now the most noble Kingdom of all *Ethiopia*, by reason of those inaccessible Fortified Rocks, *Ghesen* and *Ambacel*, where formerly the Kings Sons, excluded from the Kingdom, were secured; and is therefore accounted the Native Country of the late and present Kings, and of all the Nobility. It lies almost in the Center of *Habessinia*, having on the North the Kingdom of *Begemder*; upon the *West*, *Nile*; and beyond that, the Kingdom of *Gojam*. Upon the *South* it views *Walaka*, and *Eastward* beholds *Angota*. The *Provinces* that belong to it are these that follow:

1 *Akamba*	3 *Ambacit*
2 *Ambacel*	4 *Arman-cm*

(*b*) Ludovic. Capell. in Critic. Sacr. *Lib. 2. Cap. 10. brings an Example of* Sam. Bochart. in Hieroz. P. 1. lib. 2. cap. 25. ad Maccab. 1. 6. 36. *computing thirty two Souldiers upon one Elephant.*

(*c*) *Certainly* Godignus's *numeration is most confused: for the most part ill pronounced, as* Leca, *for* Walaka. *And why does he reckon* Aifala, *and* Dumgaloce *among the number of the Kingdoms, when the latter is only the Metropolis and no Kingdom bounded by the River* Hawash *(for so it ought to be written.) and yet confesses that the Prutonese were no way Subject to the Abessine Emperor.*

(*d*) *This was very necessary by reason of the great variation and corruption of Names, so frequent in all Authors.*

5 *Arونica*

5 *Aronca Marjam*
6 *Beda Bed*
7 *Barara*
8 *Batata*
9 *Beda gadal*
10 *Dada*
11 *Dad*
12 *Demah*
13 *Ephrata*
14 *Ewa za*
15 *Fores Bahr*
16 *Ganata Ghiorghis*
17 *Gesbe-bar*
18 *Griunghe*
19 *Ghel*
29 *Ghesbe*
21 *Ghesbem*
22 *Hagara Christos*
20 *Karna Marjam*
24 *Kuarja*
25 *Lai-Kwita*
26 *Macana Celaxe*, where *Gregory* was Born.
27 *Malza*
28 *Slegia*
29 *Tabor*
39 *Tadbaba Marjam.*
31 *Tat-Kuaja*
02 *Walsa*
33 *Waro*
34 *Wagda*
35 *Wanz-egr*
36 *Zar-amba.*

The Second Kingdom is *Angot*, which is also called *Hangot*.

The Third Kingdom is *Begemder*, in the vulgar Mapps *Bagamdri*, a large and fertile Kingdom, watered with many Rivers. *Gregory* compared it with our *Germany*, saying, *Here is much water, as in Begemder*. The River *Bashlo* divides it from *Amhara*. It is distinguished into several Territories.

1 *Andabet*, the Trumpeters Countrey.
2 *Atena*
3 *Dahr*, more particularly like *Germany*, as *Gregory* said.
5 *Este*
3 *Guna*
6 *Kema*
7 *Maket*, bordering upon *Angota*.
8 *Mashalamja*
9 *Nefasmanca*
10 *Smada*
11 *Tzama*
12 *Wainalga*, famous for the slaughter of *Gradme* in the former Century.
13 *Wudo.*

The fourth Kingdom is *Bali*, most *Easterly*, which the *Gallans* first subdued, and thence afflicted the *Abessines* with so many Calamities.

The

The fifth Kingdom is *Bizamo*, divided from *Gojam* by the River *Nile*.

The sixth Kingdom is *Bugna*, in some Mapps called *Abugana*, a mountanous and small Kingdom.

The seventh Kingdom is *Cambata*, the Inhabitants whereof are called *Hadja*, or *Hadiens*. From whence it comes to pass, that *Adea*, or *Hadea* is in the Mapps erroneously called a Kingdom. It is the last Kingdom toward the *South*, lying not far from *Enarea*; for the most part Christians, but mixed with *Pagans* and *Mahumetans*.

The eighth Kingdom is *Cont*; by the *Portugals* called *Conch*.

The ninth Kingdom is *Damot*; a *Southerly* Kindom, seated beyond *Nile*, and the *Gafats*.

The tenth Kingdom is *Dawaro*; the *Eastern* limits of the Empire, adjoyning to the *Southern* part of *Bali*.

The eleventh Kingdom is *Dembea*, or *Dembia*, a Kingdom now famous for the Royal Camp, continually pitched there. The Prefectures belonging to it are,

1 *Arbja*	9 *Saraka*
2 *Dekal-ariva*	10 *Sera-kara*
3 *Dobhana*	11 *Takuesa*
4 *Ebu*	12 *Tengel*
7 *Gaba*	13 *Tshelga* as it were the Gates of *Abassia* toward *Sennar*.
6 *Guruder*	14 *Walwad*.
7 *Kwara*	
8 *Nara*	

The twelfth Kingdom is *Enarea*, inhabited both by(*d*) Christians and Gentiles. This Kingdom was subdued by *Melech Saghed*, who converted the Governour thereof to the Christian Faith. *Gregory* very much applauded the Inhabitants for their Probity and Integrity: he said it was a fertile Soile, and abounding in Gold, adding *That he had heard from the* Portuguezes, *that this Kingdom was five and thirty days journey distant from the* Indian Ocean; *but would not assert it for Truth.*

The thirteenth Kingdom is *Tatagor*; formerly inhabited by Christians, *Eastward* adjoyning to *Bali*.

(*d*) By the Portugals called Narea, by Godignus Narea. lib. 1. cap. 4.

The

The fourteenth Kingdom is *Gufat*, bordering upon *Damota*.

The fifteenth Kingdom is *Gagghe*; pronounce it as the *French* do, *Gajegue*.

The sixteenth *Gan*, by the *Portuguezes* called *Gaule*.

The seventeenth, *Ganz*. Erroneously joyned with *Bali*, and in the feigned Title of the King, contracted into *Balgada*.

The eighteenth *Gedm*, bordering upon *Damota* toward the *East*.

The nineteenth *Gojam*; (e) pronounce it with the *French*, *Gojam*. A Kingdom wonderful for its situation, and famous for the Fountains of *Nile* therein now discovered. For the River *Nile* almost surrounds it in manner of a *Peninsula*. But that it cannot possibly be the Island of *Meroe*, as *Tellezius* believes, we shall prove in our Commentary. *Godignus* affirms, that it contains twenty Provinces, but conceals their Names.

The twentieth Kingdom is *Gombo*.

The one and twentieth, *Gonga*.

The two and twentieth, *Guragbe*.

The three and twentieth, *Ifat*, adjoyning to *Shewa* toward the *East*.

The twenty fourth is *Samen*; by *Tellezius* called *Cemen*, and numbred among the Provinces.

The twenty fifth *Ser*, whose Inhabitants are *Pagans*.

The twenty sixth *Sewa*, in the *Amharic* Dialect *Shewa*, as the *Portugals* call it *Xoa*, or *Xaoa*, a very large and most opulent Kingdom; formerly much frequented by the *Abessine* Kings, and then more famous than *Amhara*. It is distinguished into the *Upper* and the *Lower*, there are in it several Monasteries and some Towns, as may be seen in our Mapp. *Debra Libanos*, the seat of *Jeghe*, chief Overseer of all the Monks, was formerly in this Kingdom.

The twenty seventh is *Shat*, in *Portugueze*, *Xat*.

The twenty eighth is *Tigre* or *Tigra*; one of the principal Kingdoms, and the first as you enter into *Ethiopia*. The Native Country of the former Kings, who kept their Courts at *Axuma*. The most noble part of it lyes toward the *Red Sea*, and is called *Sabr*, the *Sea*, or *Midra-Bahr*, the *Land of the Sea*, or a Maritim Province, comprehending under it three

(e) *Erroneously* Goyame *in the Mapp.* *Worse* Goiame *by* Godignus. *Lib.* 1. *cap.* 4. *pag.* 15.

Toparchies.

Toparchies. The Governour, *Bahr-Nagash* resides in *Debarwa*. (f) The Prefectures belonging to *Tegre* are,

1 *Abargale*
2 *Afum*, or the Prefecture of *Axum*, the ancient Residence of the Kings.
3 *Adet*
4 *Afa-maciolen*
5 *Agamja*
6 *Amba-Sanet* (g)
7 *Bora*
8 *Upper-Bora*
9 *Lower-Bora*
10 *Beta-Abba Garima*
11 *Daba*, near *Angura*, inhabited by Pagans.
12 *Enderta*
13 *Garalta*
14 *Hagamii*
15 *Memberta*
16 *Nader*
17 *Sabart*
18 *Salawa*
19 *Sanafe*
20 *Sire*
21 *Tadërar*
22 *Tamben*
23 *Torat*
24 *Tzam-a*
25 *Tzerar*
26 *Wag*
27 *Wafrat*.

All which are inhabited by several Nations and People: But there are not so many Governours as Prefectures: For that sometimes two or three Prefectures are under one Governour: For *Bora*, *Salawa*, and *Wag*, are all under one Tetrarch.

The Prefectures under *Bahrnagas*, are

1 *Bahla*, whose Inhabitants are all Graziers, and change their habitations, abiding in the Summer in one place; all the Winter-time in another.
2 *Egala*
3 *Hamacen*, It consists of three Towns, which are subject to the King of the *Habessines*, however they choose their own Magistrates, and are Governed by their own Laws, like a Petty Commonwealth; and often give Protection to Exiles and Fugitives.
4 *Marjan*
5 *Marata*
6 *Sarawe*
7 *Zangaren*.

(f) In the Mapp of [illegible], Erroneously Barua; [illegible] Barua.
(g) By [illegible] Ambacome. Pag. 119.

The twenty ninth Kingdom is *Waleka*, in the *Portuguese* Language *Olera*, or *Holera*.

The thirtieth, *Wed*, by the *Portugals* called *Ogge*.

These are the Kingdoms which *Gregory* numbred up to me, and left the Names of them written down in the *Ethiopic* Characters: to the end I might pronounce them genuinely, and express them as adaptly as could be done in conformity to the *Latin* Letters. *Tellezius* reckons more, which nevertheless, he does not distinguish in his Mapps by great Letters, as he does the other Kingdoms; that is to say,

1 *Alamale*	*Guliar*
2 *Aura*	*Manz*
3 *Bahargamo*	*Murrabet*
4 *Briczamora*	*Mota.*
5 *Buxa*, which nevertheless he says, is a Country of *Enarea*. *l.* 1. *c.* 8.	

On the other side some Kingdoms he omits, some of which however he has inserted in his Geographical Mapp, and of some he makes mention in his History, *l.* 1. *c.* 13. 21.

Fatagar	*Ganga*
Gafat	*Sea*
Guraghe	*Shat*
Gumbo	

The most remarkable Provinces which have their peculiar Governours, are,

1 *Emfras*, between *Bagemdra*, and *Dembea*.	4 *Tzagade*
2 *Mazaga*	5 *Wagara*
3 *Mugar*, near to *Sewa*	6 *Walkayt*

The rest you shall meet with in our Geographick Tables. Now of all these Kingdoms and Provinces the King of the *Abessines* enjoys at present,

1 *Ambara*	3 *Cambata*
2 *Bagemdra*	4 *Damota*

5 *Dembea*
6 *Enarea*
7 *Gojam*
8 *Samen*
9 Part of *Sewa*, with some other Kingdoms of lesser note.

And for Provinces, those of

1 *Emfras*
2 *Mazaga*
3 *Tzagade*
4 *Wagara*
5 *Walkayt*

Which Kingdoms and Provinces comprehend the best part indeed; but not the half of the ancient *Habessia*. The rest the *Gallans* have either subdued, or else utterly laid wast, as we shall relate in due place.

CHAP. IV.

Of the Vulgar Chorographic Table or Mapp of Habessinia, *and the Author's new one.*

The New Mapp of the Habessines. *The first one found fault with as Erroneous; Look'd on as ridiculous by* Gregory, *by reason of the ill writing and because of the ill understood Names of* Barnagassus, Tigremahon, Ambacanticus, *which are explained. The ambiguous power of Letters. Advice to concert a certain Geographical Alphabet. The Authors request about his own Mapp.*

BUT to the end that all things may the more clearly appear, we shall produce a new Chorographical Mapp of *Habessinia*, the old one that goes begging about the World for an Author, being altogether uncertain. I was not a little asham'd to hear the learned *Ethiopian*, *Gregory*, upbraiding as he did, the vanity and carelesness of our People, to obtrude such absurdities upon the Commonweal of Learning, and to defile otherwise such (b) beautiful Pieces of Geography, with such fabulous impertinencies. While they made public to the World Mapps of such consequence,

(b) *Atlasses of* Ortelius, Jansonius, *the Atlas's of* Gerard, Mercator, Blaeu, *and others.*

without any sufficient Authority, or any light by what Pen, of what Nation, or in what Language they were first written, as if they designed on purpose to deceive the Reader, that so he might not be in a Capacity to judge of the Truth; which if it were their aim, they did not miss of their intentions, in regard they led several persons, otherwise eminent, and of great judgment, into foul mistakes, who cryed up the Empire of the *Habessines* for the largest in the World, as being little less than all *Europe*, too unwarily trusting to their fictions.

When I first shewed the vulgar Mapps to *Gregory*, sometimes I made him laugh, sometimes I made him angry. For before I called to mind that the *Latin* Letters were to be pronounced after the *Portugal* manner, I asked him concerning the Kingdoms of *Xoa*, *Gojam*, and other Regions, from whence the *Portugezes* had either taken away; or to which they had added the *Latin* Letters, *a*, *d*, *do*, as being their Articles of declension, (i) without any regard to the Letter *h*. But when I expected an Answer, he knew not what I meant, till I pronounced for *Xoa*, *Shoa*; for *Gojam*, *Gojam*, and so onward: But he laughed outright when I question'd him concerning the Kingdoms of *Barnagassus*, *Tigremahon*, (k) and *Ambiancantiva*. For after a short hesitation he understood them to be compound words, in which the Titles of the *Vice-Roys*, were conjoyned with the Names of the Regions over which they were made Governors; and besides that, very much corrupted by the *Portugal* pronunciation and spelling. For *Barnagassus* in the *Amharic* Language extends it self to *Bahr-Nagash*, a compound word of *Bahr* which signifies the Sea, and *Nagash* a Governour, as much as to say a Commander or Admiral at Sea. *Tigremahon* corruptly for *Tigre-makonnen*, that is to say, Judge or President of *Tigre*. *Ambiancantiva*, for *Dembia-cantiba*, that is, Governour or President of *Dembea*. The same inference happens to the most noble City and Court of Royal Residence, *Axuma*, which never appears in the Mapps, by reason that the *Portugals* pronounce *Axum*, *Acassum*; for they cast away the *A*, as an Article of declension, and adding their own termination *o*, made

(i) *As* Abugno, *for* Bugna; Barua, [illegible] *for* Dobarua; Amara *for* Amhara; [illegible], *for* [illegible], *&c.*

(k) *In the vulgar Tables also you shall find* Tigre *and* Tigremahon, *as if they were two distinct Kingdoms. Which error* B. Tellez *frequently reprehends.* L. 1. Ch. 4.

is *Cassumo*. Upon which City we stood pausing a long time, before we could tell what to make of it. I pass by an innumerable company of other mistakes, which rendred the Mapp altogether useless to me. Nor is it to be doubted but the same thing often falls out in other Exotic Tables: So that unless a Man can divine the Language of the Author, or where he was born; it is impossible but he must read the Names of the places most extravagantly. For we find that because the Modern *Europeans* have no Letters of their own; but onely have accommodated the *Latin* Letters to their own sounds, it comes to pass, that one and the same Letter is variously pronounced by various Nations; which frequently appears in Consonants conjoyned. As for Example, **Ch**, among the *Germans*, *Belgians* and *Polonians*, is a rough Aspiration like the *Hebrew* ח, or the *Greek* Χ. Among the *Italians* Ch, is pronounced like a *k*, among the *French* like an *Hebrew* ש. But among the *English*, *Spaniards* and *Portugueses*, who alone genuinely pronounce the word *China*, there is a kind of hissing compos'd between the Letter ʒ, and ſch. which the *Italians* express by a *C* before *e* or *i*, the *Polonians* by **Ch**, the *Hebrews* more lively in their ש, the *Germans* **Sch**, the *English* by *Sh*, the *French* Ch, the *Italians* Sc before *e*, and *i*; and which the *Portugueses* would do by their Letter X, but that they are unwilling to have it a superfluous Letter in their Alphabet.

For which reason it would be very requisite, that the Publishers of Foraign Mapps, should also Publish their Instructions, and tell the World according to what Pronounciation, the Names of Countries and Cities ought to be read: Or, else that in the compiling of some universal Geographical Work, care might be taken to add such an Index as should be the standard of Pronunciation in every Country, to prevent the common mistakes.

We must acknowledge that our Chorographick Table is not without its defects: For though *Gregorie* were sufficiently skill'd in the Names and Situation of places, yet he was ignorant of the Degrees of the Sphere and Elevation of the Pole. Therefore in the first Mapps of *Habessinia* which I made, I follow'd the Longitude and Latitude of the vulgar Tables; but because I found them false in that too, we thought it more prudence not to Publish any at all. I must confess being in company with certain Persons of Learning

and

and Quality, upon a (1) discourse that happen'd concerning *Ethiopia*, after I had made my Apology, I produc'd a Manuscript exemplar of both sorts: But such they were, that should they ever come to light by any misfortune, I dare not be responsible for their Credit. But at length having happen'd upon the Chorographick Table of *Tellezius*, delineated by the Fathers of the Society, with the help of the *Astrolabe*, I made no scruple to retain the *Degrees*, as by them set down, and then to make them common, together with a new Mapp, for universal information. I have added the Midland Regions, tho without any adventure of justification, in regard those Regions by reason of their vast distance, being so seldom visited by Travellers, afford little of certainty.

(1) Thevenot *makes mention of that which I gave to the Elector of* Mentz, *in his Remarks upon the History of* Ethiopia. *I presented one also to* Frederick 3d. *King of* Denmark, *another to* Charles Lewis *the Elector Palatine, and some others I could not refuse the same satisfaction of their curiosity.*

CHAP. V.

Of the Nature of the Soil, Temper of the Air, Tempests, Winds, and such like Meteors.

The Air various. Wonderful effects of heat. The Torrid Zone nevertheless habitable. The high places cold. No Snow. The temper and wholsomness of the Air. Horrid Thunders. A dirty Winter describ'd by Gregory. *Diversity of Tempests in the same situation. The four seasons of the year different from the* Europeans. *The beginning of the Spring the 25th. of* Septemb. *They have only three seasons of the year; the days and nights almost always equal. Their mornings and evenings very short. The most impetuous Wind, call'd a* Snake. *The two sorts of Whirl-winds,* Presbor *and* Typhon, *very raging and pernicious.*

IN so many and such various Regions, the Constitution of the Air is as various. In low and open places which the *Abessines* call *Kolla*, the heat of the Sun is intolerable, such as Seneca describes in these words. *The flowers shoot as if rear'd in the fire, not onely in the middle of the day, but also toward the evening, the Silver ansilters; the footsteps of men are impatient of the scorching sand. The fastening of the standard melts*

No

No external covering of outward Ornament remains. In which respect both coasts of the *Red Sea* have but a bad report, as also the Ilands, especially *Suaquem*, whose heat *Gregorie* many times us'd to call *Infernal*. For said he, it excoriates the *Skin*, melts hard *Indian* wax in a *Cabinet*, and fears your *Spoon*, like a red hot Iron.

But these Persons consider'd not the nature of those People, that inhabit that Country, much less have they weighed with themselves, the strange Patience of those that covet rule and dominion, who can endure the parching beams of the Sun, and willingly too, though unus'd to those immoderate violences of raging heat. However the ancient Philosophers were in a very great error that believ'd the (m) *Torrid Zone* uninhabitable; or that the middle parts of the Earth, where the Sun continually moves, should be parch'd up with flames, and tosted with the raging fire. (n) Assuredly there are some Philosophers who deliver things uncertain and unprov'd for real and assured truths, and discourse in such a manner of the nature of the Air, the Heavens and the Stars, as if their residence had long been there. For that the Air is colder upon the Mountains, all Nations in their own Countries find by experience; but that the Air is cold of it self, and not warmed but by the repercussion of the Suns beams among the exhalations of the Earth, is the opinion of other sage Philosophers: which exhalations in the lower Region near the Earth rise more close and condens'd, in the upper parts, more thin and rarify'd: so that tho the lower parts frie with heat, high places freez, the cool nature of the Air not suffering any alteration through the defect of heat.

Therefore the higher you ascend the Mountains of *Ethiopia* from the coast of the *Red Sea*, the more temperate you shall feel the Air; insomuch that as *Tellezius* witnesses in many Regions of *Ethiopia*, the Summer heats are more mild then in *Portugal*, so many degrees distant toward the North. Nay there are some Mountainous Countries, as in *Samen* where the cold is more dreaded than the heat. Nevertheless there falls none or very little Snow in those parts, only a certain small sort of Hail sometimes covers the ground, which at a

(m) Aristot. Meteorolog. l. 2. c. 5. and his followers.

(n) [illegible] have a Proverb, he that is [illegible] upon his own Intellect, [illegible]

distance

distance looks like Snow. It was a thing not known to *Gregorie*, for as I Travelled with him over the Mountains of *Tirol*, toward the end of *September*, seeing some Snow that had fallen a little before, crying out *Haritz*, *Haritz*, full of admiration, he called it Meal. From such a temper of the Air it follows that the Country must needs be healthy; and consequently the Inhabitants sane and vivacious, insomuch that some of them live to a hundred years of Age. Onely in *Tigra*, toward the beginning of the *Ethiopic* Spring, that is to say, in the Months of *September* and *October*, Feavers are very rife.

However this variety of the Air is the cause of most dreadful Thunders. Which when *Gregory* describ'd, he astonish'd his hearers. For upon the rising of several Tempests altogether, the Skie is of a sudden cover'd over with black and thick as it were Globes of smokie Clouds; by and by the Thunder breaks forth on every side, ratling continually, with Lightning as incessantly flashing, enough to amaze the most resolute and most accustom'd to the noise. Their Rains are very violent, powering from the Clouds not by drops, but as it were in streams. With those the torrents being swell'd, rowle along with that rapid fury, that they carry Trees and Stones and all things before 'em. All their Rivers overflow; and then the high ways being either covered with water, or else all mirie and dirtie, 'tis a most tedious thing to Travel: And this enduring three Months together renders their Winters very unpleasant. *Gregory* describ'd the *Ethiopian* Winter to me in these words.

" The *Ethiopian* Winters are not caus'd onely by the Rain " which falls from the Skie; for the Earth also opens her " mouth, and vomits up water. There is a Fountain in " every man's house, if it stands low. And therefore we " never Build in low places, but in high grounds. So many and " so great Rivers, and Springs of water out of the Earth; " and such violent Rains are no where the like to be seen as " in our Country.

This tempestuous weather is so troublesome and tedious to Forraigners, that in a dispute which happen'd between an *Abessine* and an *Egyptian*, about the excellency of their Countries, when the first vaunted to the latter, the natural fertilitie of *Abessinia*, the temperateness of the Air, their double Harvests, and other benefits of the Country, adding withall

withall, That the *Egyptians* cannot live without the assistance of *Ethiopia*, in regard that *Nilus* fatten'd *Egypt* with the Mud of *Ethiopia*, without which, both Man and Beast would perish for want of Sustenance; the *Egyptian* retorted upon the *Abyssinian*, upbraiding him with the prodigious Showers, the rapid Torrents, the steep and rugged Mountains, and the dreadful Thunders that render'd the Country so unpleasant; upon which the Victory was allow'd on his side.

Nor does the season of the Winter keep the same Months, nor the same Temperature in all places alike, tho the situation may be the same; for it is not only milder in some places, sharper in others, but also in different Months from our Climate. Which was of old observ'd by (p) *Nonnosus*, Ambassador from the Emperour *Justinian* to the King of the *Axumites*, who travelling those Parts himself.

[illegible], &c.

From the City of the *Adulites* as far as *Ave*, the same Summer and Drouth affects the Air as with us. From *Ave* towards *Axuma*, the Winter is very rigorous, &c. *Gregory* told me, That the Coast of the *Red Sea*, and all that two days Journey, from the Shore to the Mountains of *Ethiopia* the Winter keeps its Station in *November*, *December*, and *January*, as in *Europe*, but they differ nothing in the Degrees of Latitude. So that it is not always true what some (q) Geographers have written, That the *Perioeci*, or those that dwell under the same Meridian, have the same Winter and Summer.

Now what the Winter of that Coast is, you may easily guess, from the answer of *Gregory*, who being ask'd upon a very sultry day, whether it were not very hot in *Germany*, made answer,

To day has been something hot: Such is the Winter in *Suaquena*, which is an Island upon that Coast.

Being ask'd concerning the Seasons of the Year, he answer'd,

(p) *In the History of his Embassy, some Collections out of which are to be seen in* Bibliotheca Photii. n. 3. p.m. 2.

(q) *See the Notes upon* Cluverius's *Introduction to Geography*, l. 1. c. 4. *and* Aristot. l. 2. *de Meteorologic. who without experience writes, That the Heat and Cold do not exceed in regard of the Longitude, but in regard of the Latitude.*

The Season *Matzar*, the Season of Flowers or the Spring.
The Season *Tzadai*, the Season of Harvest or *Autumn*.
The Season *Hagai*, or the Summer.
The Season *Crampt*, or Winter.

Thus he reckon'd the four Seasons: But there is not the same reason for them, nor the same benefits by them, as with us; nor could *Gregory* himself reconcile them with ours.

Matzar indeed may deservedly be call'd the Spring, because it succeeds the Winter, and covers the Fields with Grass and Flowers. It begins upon a certain day of the Month; that is, upon the 25th of *September*.

But the *Tzadai* of the *Ethiopians* cannot be call'd properly *Autumn*, as *Gregory* imagin'd; for it is the second part of the year that succeeds the Spring, and exhilarates the Husbandman with ripen'd Fruits, and therefore ought more truly to be call'd *Summer*. But how *Hagai* is to be interpreted, is a question; it is the third part of the year, yet cannot justly be call'd *Autumn*, in regard the *Habessines* are ignorant of any benefit they receive by it. They get no Vintage in, but are parch'd with extremity of Heat, and therefore they oppose this hottest time of the year to the sharpest Cold of Winter.

For which reason we rather ought to conclude, that there are but three Seasons among the *Abyssines*, that is to say, the Spring which begins upon the 25th of *September*. Then the Summer, which may be divided into two parts; the first, and the best, call'd *Tzadai*, which begins upon the 25th of *December*, and the last, and worst part, call'd *Hagai*, which begins upon the 25th of *June*, and ends upon the (r) succeeding Winter, which is the third part of the *Ethiopic* year.

The Days and Nights in that Climate, being in a right Sphere, are, for the most part, always equal. Their Dawnings and Evenings much shorter than ours. *Gregory* wonder'd, that it should be light when he could not see the Sun; and again, after Sun-set, that the Twilight should last so long. For there immediately after Sun-set it grows dark, and all the Stars, in the absence of the Moon, appear.

(r) Gregory *differs from our* [illegible] *who puts Hagai the* 25th.

The Winds, upon the Mountains frequent and pleaſant, render the Air healthful and temperate; but in open and flat Levels, the Air, for want of motion, grows hot and unwholſom, eſpecially in the Iſlands of the *Red Sea*. This a certain Merchant atteſted, who carrying ſeveral rich *Indian* Commodities from the Port of *Suaquem* to the Court, and being ask'd by one of the King's Daughters, *What there was that could not be purchas'd at the Port of* Suaquem, anſwer'd, *The Winds*; that being only wanting in that place, otherwiſe a happy and pleaſant Iſland.

But all Winds are not equally grateful or beneficial in *Ethiopia*; for there are ſome which are moſt impetuouſly violent; among the reſt, the Whirlwind, called *Sendo*, which in the *Amharic* Dialect ſignifies a *Snake*, a Wind ſo furious, that it throws down all before it, Houſes, Oaks, and Stones, and hurries them along in the Air. The *Belgians* call this Wind Hoos, and report it frequent upon the Coaſts of *Aſia*, as they ſometimes experience to the loſs of their Ships. The Whirlwind by the *Greeks*, called *Typhon*, is that of which *Pliny* thus writes: 'A principal Plague to the Mariners, which 'not only throws down the Maſts, but rives the Ship in pie'ces. And again, 'The ſame Wind meeting oppoſition, 'carries all before it, and ſweeps whatever it meets into the 'Air. *Gregory* affirm'd, it might be ſeen, and that it repreſented the form of a Snake, whoſe thicker part, like the Head, bruſhing upon the ground, the Body advanc'd it ſelf in curls and windings to the Sky. Nor do I believe this Wind to differ much from that Wind which the *Greeks* call Πρηστὴρ (*Preſter*), there being the ſame *Equivocal* in both; for that *Preſter* ſignifies a kind of Serpent, and perhaps may be the ſame which the *Venetians* call *Biſſabova*, *Biſcia* ſignifying a Serpent in *Italian*. Such a Whirlwind laſt *Autumn* happe- *Ann* 1679.
ning in *Dalmatia*, ſwept into the Air, Men, Cattel, Carts and Horſes laden with Hay and great Bells, if there be any faith in Report; and after the ruin of many Houſes, Churches, Towers, and Palaces, left behind it the deplorable Teſtimonies of the havock it had made. *P. Organtin* of *Breſcia* wrote from *Goa*, That a Whirlwind toſs'd up ſeveral empty Ships from the Water into the Air, and carried them beyond the Shore: Which if it be true, thoſe prodigious ſhowers of *Plin. l.* 2.
Stones, Iron, and Bricks, are the leſs to be wonder'd at, *c.* 56.
if we may be allow'd to ſay, That the time has been when it rain'd Men, Ships, and great Bells.

Chap. VI.

Of the high Mountains of Habessinia, *and Rocks of strange forms.*

High Mountains. Lamalmon, *most dangerous.* Amhara *and* Samen *the gibbouse part of* Abyssinia; *higher than the* Alps *and* Pyrenaeans. *Steep Rocks of a wonderful shape, not to be ascended without Ropes and Ladders. Spacious at the top. The Rock where the Kings Sons were formerly kept, describ'd. A Rock in* Gojam *hollow'd like a Looking-Glass. Deep Abysses. Plains very rare, one great one in* Dembea. *The benefits of the Mountains, temperate Air, security and pleasantness of the Fountains.*

ALL *Habessinia* is egregiously Mountainous: So soon as you have travell'd two days Journey from the *Red-Sea*, you must presently climb the high Mountains of *Tigra*, amongst which *Lamalmona* lifts up her head more lofty than the rest, which they that travel to the Royal Camp in *Dembea*, are forc'd to clamber over: The Steps of which, if they may be so call'd, are so dangerous, and the Path or Track so narrow, that if Company meet, Men and Horses giving the way, fall headlong into a bottomless Abyss, never to be any more seen. But not only this Region is the Plain that seems as it were planted with Mountains, *Begemdra*, *Gojam*, *Walaka*, *Shewa*, and all the rest, *Dembea* excepted, are but one continued Chain of Mountains. Among the rest, the vast and high Mountains of *Amhara* and *Samen* are as it were the Embossment of *Habessinia*.

Here are many *Ambas*, or Rocks of an (a) incredible height and ruggedness, in so much, that, as *Tellezius* writes, they strike a terror into the Beholders; the *Alps* and *Pyrenaeans*, compar'd with the *Abessine* Mountains, are but low Hills. The Mountains of *Portugal*, tho very high, are but trifles to them.

Amongst those Mountains, and frequently in the Plain it self, and in the middle of the Fields, rise up Rocks every

(a) *A Rock in* India *called* Aornus, *as being above the flight of a Bird,* Curt. 8. 2. *There are also Lakes of this name, but from another cause, for that the poisonous Exhalations that they send up, kill the Birds that fly over them,* Plin. 2. 4. *by the* Latins *call'd* Averni.

way

way steep, yet varying their shape; some looking a far off like Towers, some like Pyramids, some like four-square Towers built by Art, and so even on the sides, as if the Workman's hand had done it so; so that there is no way to get to the top but by the help of Ladders and Ropes, by which means they Crane up their Cattel, and other necessaries: And yet so spacious at the top, that they contain Woods, Fields, Meadows, Fountains, and which is more wonderful, fish-ponds, and all other conveniencies for humane Support. These sort of Rocks the Natives call *Amba*, as *Amba-Dorba*, (x) &c.

This puts us in mind to describe that famous Rock in the Kingdom of *Ambara*, called *Geshen*, of which, and of the Mountain *Amharel*, we have already made mention, which we shall do in the words of *Tellezius*. *In the Confines of* Ambara, *toward* Shewa, *stands* Amba-Geshen: *It is a Mountain almost impregnable, every way steep, prodigiously high, and in the form of a Castle made all of Free-Stone; At the top it is about half a* Portugal *League in breadth, at the bottom near half a days Journey about; At first easie to be ascended, then steep and rugged, in so much, that the* Abyssine *Oxen, that otherwise will clamber like Goats, must be cran'd up and let down with Ropes.*

Formerly those miserable *Ethiopic* Princes were here cag'd up in wild places, in low Cottages, among Shrubs and wild Cedars, starv'd from all things else but Air and Earth; as if they, who were descended from a high Parentage, were to be confin'd in a high and lofty Exile. In *Gojam*, as (y) *Kercher* tells us, from the Relation of *Peter Pays*, there is a certain Rock so curiously hollow'd by Nature, that afar off it resembles a Looking-Glass, and over against it another, on the top of which there is nothing that can be so softly whisper'd, but may be heard a great way off, and the reverberation of the sound is like the encouraging *Ho up* of Mariners.

Between these Mountains are immense Gulphs, and dreadful Profundities; which because the Sight cannot fathom, Fancy takes them for Abysses; whose bottoms *Tellezius* will have to be the Center of the Earth. Nor did *Gregory* de-

(x) *That is the Rock of the Hen, in the Map erroneously call'd* [illegible].
(y) *In Musurgia sua Univers. T. 2. l. 9. c. 6. where instead of* Iohn Pays, *read* Petrus Pays.

scribe

scribe them otherwise, than as places most dreadful and formidable to the Eye.

Levels are very rare; the largest Plain is *that in Dembea*, near the Lake *Tzanicus*, about twenty *Portugal* Leagues in length, and four or five broad.

A Region so Mountainous, and so like to *Switzerland*, may be look'd upon justly by all people as a most rude and unhusbanded Country; but they that consider the benefits which the *Habessines* receive thereby, will from the same reasons be drawn to an admiring Contemplation of Divine Providence: For that stupendious height of their Mountains contemns the scorching heat, which renders their Country the more inhabitable in those high places, where the people breath a more serene Air. In the next place, Heaven has thereby provided for their security, so many inaccessible Mountains, being like so many Castles, which afford them not only Habitation, but a safe defence against their Enemies. For had it not been for these Fortresses of Nature, they had been ruin'd long e're this, by the *Adelenses* and the *Gallans*. Moreover, thorough all those Mountains you shall find most pleasant Springs of Water, which are wanting in the Levels of the torrid Zone: The reason of which, we shall give you in another place.

Chap. VII.

Of Metals and Minerals.

Abassia abounds in Metals and Minerals, especially Gold, which is found in the Sand of the Rivers; and in Damota *and* Enarea *upon the Superficies of the Earth. Silver they have not, and yet not without Lead. They neither know, nor care to know, what belongs to Metals. Salt plentifully digg'd out of the Earth. Gems they want. They more esteem black Lead, with which they colour their Eye-brows.*

THat so many and so vast Mountains afford plenty of Metals and Minerals, the Fathers of the Society attest. And certainly, 'tis a thing easily credible, that that part of the Earth, lying under the fiercest and most maturing heat of the Sun, cannot be without Metals, and more especially Gold, which is found in the shallows of Rivers, ons, polish'd and pure in great quantities, about the bigness of a Tare or Vetch. Whence it is conjectur'd, that the Gold is brought to perfection in the neighbouring Mountains, and carry'd away together with the Sand, by the forces of the Stream. *Pliny* affirms that sort of Gold to be the finest and most perfect. *Damot*, but more especially *Enarea*, enjoy this advantage, it being the chiefest Tribute which they pay. They are destitute of Silver; whether it be that Nature denies them that benefit, or that they know not how to dig it out and refine it: For they have Lead, which is said to be the Mother of Silver.

But they are altogether ignorant of the Minery Trade. For the digging of Wells, boaring of Mountains, supporting of Mines with massy Timber, hewing of Stones, or forcing Rocks with Gunpowder or Fire, to live in the dark, sometimes hours, sometimes days together, and to be half strangled with Smoke and Damps, to (c) search the Veins of the Earth, and examin the Secrets of Rocks, are things altogether unsuitable to the Genius of the *Habessines*. Rather they count it a piece of folly to pine after Minerals, and heap up Riches, to encourage the *Turk* to make War upon them. They think themselves far more safe in Iron, as being that with which Gold may be won: And for Iron, they have no occasion to delve for it, in regard they find it in great plenty upon the Superficies of the Earth, as *P. Antonio Fernandez* testifies.

Moreover, in the Confines of *Tigra* and *Angota*, from a place call'd the *Land of Salt*, there (a) are natural Mountains of Salt, from whence they supply themselves with inexhaustible quantities, cutting it out of the sides of the Mountains in great pieces of a white and solid Substance. In the Mountain it is soft, and sliver'd off with little labour; but in the Air it hardens. From thence it is fetch'd by great numbers of Merchants, who conveigh it away in Caravans, which are call'd *Cafila*, and vended through all the neighbouring Nations and Countries where it is a scarce Commodity. *Alphonsus Mendez* the Patriarch, writes, That there is in another place a Mountain of Red Salt, very useful in Physic. So propitiously has Heaven compensated their want of Money

(c) *Thus Pliny discourses concerning Minerals.*

(a) *Concerning such kind of Salt, see Pliny, l. 31. c. 7.*

with

with plenty of Salt; which by virtue whereof, as with ready Coyn, in other places they purchase other necessaries. Thus they abound in Salt, which the Life of Man cannot want; but they are destitute of other things that less conduce to the happiness of Human Being. Nor do they desire those things, of whose dazling Beauties and glittering Colours they are ignorant; I mean Gems and Jewels, rarely yet seen in *Ethiopia*, whatever that same Trifler, *Valentinian* Romances. The Royal Diadem it self glitters only with counterfeit Jewels, thinking it not worth their while to send their Salt or Gold to foreign and barbarous Nations to purchase true ones; and admiring at our imprudence, for expending our Money so idly. They much more esteem those Minerals, that conduce to the health and preservation of the Body; chiefly among the rest *Stibium*, or Black Lead, which they in their Language call (*b*) *Cuhel*, or *Cohol*, and believe it to be a great preserver of the Sight; nor do they less esteem it for Ornament, and to beautifie their Faces with it; For being powder'd, they mix it with Soot moisten'd, and with a small Pencil which they call *Mars*, besmear their Eye-brows, according to the frequent and ancient custom of the Orientals.

(*b*) *A word well known in all the Eastern Languages, from the Hebrew word* [illegible] *which signifies Stibium: from* [illegible] *to besmear it with Paint; and whence the* Greek *word* Collyrium, *as it were* Cohollyrium, *some derive it. The Arabic word Alcohol still remains in the* Spanish *Language, wherein there is a Proverb,* Elpolvo de las ovejas, Elcohol es para el Lobo; *The Dust which the Sheep raise is a* Collyrium *to quicken the Wolf's Sight.*

CHAP. VIII.

Of the Rivers of Habessinia, *more especially of* Nile, *its Fountains and Course; as also of the Lake* Tzana.

Many Rivers there more precious than Metals. The Fountains originally from Rain-water. An Encomium of Nilus: *In Scripture it is call'd, The River* [illegible], *and* Schichor, *or* Niger: *By some of the ancients* Astapus, *and* Astaboras: *In the* Amharic *Dialect call'd* Abawi, *or the* Parent of Rivers; *it flows not in* Paradise, *as some of the Fathers thought. Admiration caus'd the desire of knowing its Original, that the Ancients plac'd in the Mountains of the Moon. The* Portugals *discover'd the true Fountains; their description from* Peter Pays, *not different from* Gregories: *It rises in* Sacut; *it has five Heads. It mixes with the Lake in* Dembea. *It passes by the principal Kingdoms of* Habassia, *encircles* Gojam, *rolls through* Egypt, *and so into the Sea;* Gregories *Ethiopic Description. He alledges, That all the Rivers of* Africa *fall into* Nile. *He limits that assertion. Some fall into the Sea. The true causes of the overflowing of* Nile, Jovius *blam'd. A double Channel of* Nile. Niger *the other Channel. The old Relation in* Herodotus, *explain'd. Whether the King of* Habassynia *can divert the Course of* Nile. *Rivers suckt up in the Sand.* Zebeus *falls into the* Indian *Sea. The* Habessines *unskill'd in Navigation. The* Tzanic *Lake, with its Islands.*

BUT much more excelling, and far more precious Gifts of Nature than those of Metals, flow from the Mountains of *Habessinia*, that is to say, several remarkable Rivers more profitable to the Natives, and the neighbouring Nations, than Gold it self, so much the Subject of human Avarice. For the Rain-water soaking through the pores of the Earth, and the clefts of the Rocks, is receiv'd, and, as it were, cistern'd up in the hidden Caverns of the Mountains, where, after it has pass'd through many secret conveyances of Nature, at length it meets with some hollow place, and breaks forth. Sometimes oppress'd by its own weight, it reascends, and seeks for passage at the tops of the Mountains themselves; which is the reason, that in Countries where there is little or no Rain, there are few or no Fountains; but where there are frequent Rains, the Rivers are large and swelling: The Effect demonstrating the

Cause. (c) But *Nilus*, owing to *Habassia* for its source, for plenty of Water, for sweetness, wholsomness, and fertility of the same, excells all other Rivers of the World. In sacred Writ, by reason of its Excellency, it is sometimes
Isa. 23. 3. call'd, The River absolutely, and particularly [illegible], from its black Colour, and by the *Greeks*, for the same reason, [illegible], because it runs with black a muddy Water. Some of the
Plin. 5. 9. & 7. 3. Ancients tell us, that it was then by the *Ethiopians* call'd *Astapus*, and that the left Channel of it about *Meroe* was nam'd *Astabora*, which others have understood concerning other Rivers that flow into *Nile*. But this we let pass as obscure and doubtful, whether meant of *Nilus* and our *Ethiopians* or no; for the *Habessines*, in their vulgar Language, have no other name for *Nile* than that of *Abawi*: And that, as some think, from the word *Ab*, which signifies a *Parent*, as if *Nilus* were the Parent of all other Rivers. But this derivation neither suits with Grammar, neither does (d) *Abawi* simply signifie a *Parent*, neither, if you rightly consider it, is it agreeable to Sense; for *Nilus* does not send forth from his own Bowels, but receives the Tribute of all other Rivers: So that he may be rather said to be their Captain and Prince, than the Father of them. And therefore the *Egyptians*, out of a vain Superstition, call'd him their *Preserver*, their *Sun*, and their *God*, and sometimes Poetically, *Parent*. In our *Ethiopic*, or the Language of the Books, this River is call'd *Gejon*, or *Gewon*, by an ancient mistake from the (e) *Greek* word [illegible], *Geon*, and that from the *Hebrew* word *Gihon*, because it seem'd to agree with the Description, *Gen.* 2. 13. which encompasses the Land of *Ethiopia*, whereas it only encircles *Gojam*, but only glides and passes by all the other Kingdoms of *Ethiopia*.

If you object, That *Gihon* had its source in the Terrestrial Paradise; 'tis twenty to one, but that they extol their own Country for Paradise: For you must understand, that many

(c) *No true opinion concerning the Original of Rivers.* Aristotle *quotes it in his* Meteorologics, *l.* 1. *f.* 4. *c.* 5. *but without reason dissents.* Most *Neoterics defend it.* See *Isaac* Vossius, *De Origine Nili & Fluminum. c.* 6.

(d) *It is in the form of an Adjective*, Heavenly, Golden; *So* Abawi *signifies* Paternal.

(e) *For in the time of the* 70 *Interpreters it was so called, who render'd* Shichor, *Jer.* 2. 18. *where the Prophet speaks positively of* Nile, Γηών, Gihon. *The same you shall find in the Book of* Syrac.

of the Fathers of the (*f*) Church were of the same opinion; which that they might defend, they brought the River *Nile* under Ground, and under the Sea, into *Egypt*, well knowing that no body would follow them thither, leaving their Readers to find out the way.

Certainly the Ancients never inquir'd so curiously into the Nature or Source of any River, as they did in that of *Nile*, neither were they ever so deceiv'd; for it was a thing altogether unusual for any other Rivers in the World to overflow in the most sultry Season of the year; an Inundation so wholsom and profitable to *Egypt*. So that the ignorance of the cause of it fill'd the minds of the Ancients with so much admiration, that both Princes and private Persons desired nothing more than to know the Head of that River, which was the Original of their Happiness; in so much, that there were some Emperours and Kings, who sent great Armies in quest of the satisfaction of their Curiosity, tho with ill success. (*g*) Most of the ancient Geographers, by meer conjecture, plac'd the Fountains of this River beyond the Equinoctial Line in I know not what Mountains of the Moon, to the end, they might deduce the cause of its swelling from the Winter Rains of those Regions: For they could not perswade themselves, that the Sun being in the Northern Signs, so much Winter or Rain could be so near to cause so great an increase of the Flood, tho there were (*h*) some who made it out plainly enough, but that Credit would not be given to them. (*i*) But by the Travels of the *Portugals* into *Habessinia*, and the sedulity of the Fathers, those Fountains and Spring-heads have been since discover'd, so long and unsuccessfully sought for by the Ancients. *Athanasius Kircher* has describ'd them from the Relation of *Peter Pays*, who view'd them himself. *In the Kingdom of* Gojam, saith he, *and in the Western Parts thereof in the Province of* Sabala, *which the* Agawi *inhabit, are to be seen two round Spring-Heads, very deep, in a place somewhat rais'd, the ground about it being*

(*f*) Theodoret, *int.* 2. *Gen.* q. 19. Austin, *l.* 8. *de gen.* c. 7. Ambros. *com.* 2. *Gen.* c. 13. & 26. q. 8.

(*g*) As Cambyses, Alexander, Ptol. Philadelph. J. Cæsar, Nero, &c.

(*h*) So Pliny, *l.* 17. c. 18. *Whereby Summer Rains are not as in India and Ethiopia.*

(*i*) Photius in Bibl. n. 249. *In the Life of Pythag.* Agatharchides, Strabo, and others. See Vossius, *d. l.* c. 20.

quaggy and marshy; nevertheless the Water does not spring forth there, but issues from the foot of the Mountain. About a Musquet Shot from thence, toward the East, the River begins to flow; then winding to the North, about the fourth part of a League, it receives another River; a little farther, two more flowing from the East fall into it; and soon after, it enlarges it self with the addition of several other Streams. About 10 days journey farther, by the Relation of the same Peter, *it swallows up the River* Jema; *then winding Westward some twenty Leagues, it turns again to the East, and plunges it self into a vast Lake.* This Relation differs not from what *Gregory* has discoursed to me, only he particulariz'd the names of the Countries, that perhaps were the more special Denominations of those places, of which *Sabala* was the more general Name. For as he related to me, the Spring-head of *Nile* is in a certain Land call'd *Secut*, upon the top of *Dengla*, which perhaps is the name of a Mountain. He also affirm'd, that it had five Spring-heads, reckoning in the Heads of other Rivers, which have no particular name, and are therefore taken for the *Nile*. But it passes through the Lake *Tzanicum*, preserving the colour of its own Waters, like the *Rhosne* running through the Lake *Lemann*, and the *Rhine* through *Acronius*, or the Lake *De Zell*. Then winding to the South, it washes on the left hand the principal Kingdoms of *Habessinia*, *Bagemdra*, *Ambara*, *Walaka*, *Shewa*, *Damota*, and takes along the Rivers of those Countries *Bashlo*, *Tzohha*, *Kecem*, *Jema*, *Roma*, and *Wancit*. Then on the right hand embracing *Gojam*, its Native Country, almost like a Circle, and swell'd with the Rivers of that Region, (*Maga*, *Abaja*, *Ashwari*, *Temci*, *Gult*) and *Tzul*, it turns again to the West, as it were bidding farewel to its Fountains, and with a prodigious mass of amass'd Rivers, leaving *Habessinia* upon the right hand, rolls to the North through several thirsty Nations, and sandy Deserts, to enrich *Egypt* with its Inundations, and there makes its way through several mouths into the Sea. For the more certain Demonstration of the Truth, it will be of particular moment to insert the Relation of *Gregory* himself, perhaps the first that was ever made public by an *Ethiopian*.

Epist. d. 20 Octob. 1657.

The Course of Nile *is like a Circle, it encompasses* Gojam, *but so, that it never returns back to its Head, making directly to* Sennar. *And therefore* Gojam *lies always upon the right hand of* Nile; *but all the other Kingdoms of* Ethiopia, *as well those that* lye near, as those at a distance, remain still upon the left. As it flows along, it takes in all the Rivers great and small with several Torrents, as well Foreign as Habessinian, which by that general Tribute, acknowledge him their King; who having thus muster'd together all the Waters of Ethiopia, proudly takes his leave, and proceeds on his Journey, like a Hero, according to the Command of his Creator, to drench the Fields of thirsty Egypt, and quench the drouth of Thousands.

The Spring-head of this famous River first shews it self in a certain Land, which is called Secut, upon the top of Dengla, near Gojam, West of Bagemdra, Dara, the Lake Tzana, and Bada: Rising there, it hastens with a direct course Eastward, and so enters the Lake of Dara and Bed, as it were swimming over it. Passing from thence, it flows between Gojam and Bagemdra; but leaving them upon the right and left, speeds directly toward Amhara. Having touch'd the Confines of Amhara, he turns his Face toward the West, and girdles Gojam like a Circle, but so, that Gojam lies always upon the right hand of it. Having past the Limits of Amhara, it washes the Confines of Walaka, and so on to the extream bounds of Mugara and Shewa: Then it slides between Bizamna and Gonga; and descends into the Country of the Shankelites. Whence he winds to the right hand, and leaves by degrees the Western Clime upon the left hand, to visit the Kingdom of Sennar. But before he get thither, he meets with two great Rivers that plunge themselves into his Stream, coming from the East; of which one is call'd Tacaze, that falls out of Tigra, and the other Guangue, that descends from Dembea. After he has taken a view of the Kingdom of Sennar, away he travels to the Country of Dengula, and so comes to the Kingdom of Nubia, and thence turns to the right hand, in order to his intended Voyage for Alexandria, and comes to a certain Country which is call'd Abrim, where the Stream is unnavigable by reason of the Clifts and Rocks; after which, he enters Egypt. Sennar and Nubia are seated upon the shore of Nile, toward the West, so that they may drink of his Waters; besides, that he guards their Eastern Limits, as far as he approaches near them. But our People and Travellers from Sennar, after they have cross'd Nubia, quit the River Nile, leaving it upon the right hand toward the East, and ride through a Desert of six days journey upon Camels, where neither Tree nor Water, but only Sand is to be seen; but then they meet with it again in the Country of Rifle, which is the Upper Egypt, where they either take Boat, or travel a foot in Company with the Stream.

But

But as to what he wrote concerning the flowing of great and small Rivers into *Nile*, he explains himself in these words.

All great Rivers and smaller Torrents flow into Nile, *excepting only two: The one is call'd* Hanazo, *which rises in* Hangota; *and the other* Hawash, *which runs near* Dawara *and* Fatagara.

But as if this had not been enough, he goes on with a farther Explanation in another Epistle, as follows.

But whereas I told you in a Description of Nile, *that all the Rivers of* Ethiopia *flow'd into it except two, I am not to be understood, as if I spoke of all* Ethiopia. *For those Rivers that are upon the Borders of the Circuit of* Ethiopia, *which are near the Ocean, they fall into the Sea, every one in their distinct Regions. Now the Countries adjoyning to the Ocean, are these;* Canbat, Guraghé, Enaria, Zandera, Wed, Waci, Gaci, *and some others.*

The Native Country of *Nile* being thus discover'd, the cause of his Inundation is manifest: For most of the Countries under the *Torrid Zone*, when the Sun returns into the Winter Signs, are wash'd, as we have said, with immoderate Showers. So that the prodigious mass of Waters that randevouzes from all parts, cannot be contain'd within his Channel, and therefore when it comes into the Levels of *Egypt*, it presently disburthens it self. Those Northern Winds, from their Anniversary Breezes, call'd *Errisiæ*, add little to the Increase. Tho some have written, That their forcing the Sea against the Mouths of the River, drives back the Waters of *Nile*, and augments the cause of the Deluge. A thing not likely, in regard they are the most temperate of all the Winds, and blow only in the day-time. Thus far indeed they may prevail, as they blow slacker or stronger, to render the Increase somewhat the more unequal, and that is all. Vainly therefore did many believe, that the Snow that melted from the *Ethiopian* Mountains, deluge'd into the River *Nilus*; for them, that profound Tracer of Nature, *Seneca*, has solidly refuted. Which makes it a wonder that *Paulus Jovius* should report the same, as what he had gather'd from the certain Conjectures of the *Habessines*; who at another time speaks of the very same thing, *as a great Secret of Nature*, which no Man had ever div'd into; nay, he reproves it for weakness, with an ostentatious Wit to be over diligently curious in the search of such matters.

Quæst. natur. l. 4. c. 2.

Yet

Yet tho the Fountains of *Nile* are known, the course of it is not so well discover'd to the *Habessines* themselves after it has left them. But the ancient and constant report is, that it does not fall (p) entire into *Egypt*, but that it is divided into two Channels, and that the right Channel runs to the North, as is well known; but that the left runs Westward, and keeping a long course, divides the Country of the *Nigrites*, 'till it fall into the Ocean. This the ancient *Egyptian* Priests were not ignorant of; for *Herodotus*, the foremost in History, after he has discours'd concerning the Springs of *Nile*, learnedly reports, That he had heard from an Auditor of the Money sacred to *Minerva*, That half of the Water of *Nile* flow'd Northward into *Egypt*, the other half Southward toward *Ethiopia*: Which none of our Geographers either observ'd or mended. But the *Nubian* Geographer puts me quite out of doubt, when he writes, *Clim. 1. Par. 4.*

And in this part of Ethiopia *are the two* Niles *parted*; that is, *Nilus* which waters our Country of *Nubia*, directs his Course from South to North, and most of the Cities of *Egypt* are seated on each side of his Banks, and in his Islands. The other part of *Nile* flows from the East toward the West, and upon this part of *Nile* lies the whole Country of the *Nigrites*, or at least the greater part of it.

A little after he adds concerning a certain Mountain; *And near to that, one of the Arms of* Nile *turns off, and flows to the West*: And this is the *Nile* that belongs to the Country of the *Nigrites*, many of their Provinces lying upon it. But near the Eastern side of the Mountain, the other Arm turns off, waters the Country of *Nubia*, and the Land of *Egypt*, and is divided in the *Lower Egypt* into four parts, of which three fall into the *Syrian* Sea, and the other empties it self in a Salt Lake which is near to *Alexandria*. The words are every way most clear; and very probable it is, That the separation of the two *Niles* might be caus'd by the resistance of some rocky Mountain that constrain'd the two Streams to part, since they could not undermine it. To which, the words of *Leo Africanus* relate; *The Region of the* Nigrites, *through which* Nilus *is said to flow*: Which seem to intimate, that he had heard something by report concerning this same *In Descript. Afric. l. 1. c. 2.*

(p) Jul. Solin in Polyhist. c. 43. *The Ethiopian and Atlantic Nations are divided by the River Niger, which is believ'd to be a part of* Nilus.

left Channel. Nor am I a little confirm'd by the judgment of *Gregory*, which he expressed to me by writing, in these words.

But as to what is reported, that Nile *does not flow altogether and entirely into the Land of* Egypt, *but that it is divided another way. This all those persons of whom I have enquir'd, aver to me to be truth. This I also encline to believe, for should it descend entirely thither in the Winter time, the* Egyptians *could never be safe in their Houses.* But as to what concerns its separation, they say, That Parting happens after the River has pass'd by *Sennar* in the Country of *Dengula*, before it arrives at *Nubia*: However, they say, That the greatest mass of Water flows into *Egypt*, and that the separated part runs directly to the western Ocean; yet so, that it comes not into *Barbary*, but descends toward the Country of *Elwah*, and so throws it self into the western Ocean.

Now that the River *Niger* should be the left Channel of *Nile*, is most probable from hence, for that as *Pliny* writes, L. 5. c. 8. and Experience confirms, *it partakes of the same Conditions with* it, agrees in colour and tast of the Water, it produces the same sort of Reed, the same sort of Papyr, and the same sort of Animals; and lastly, encreases and overflows at the same Seasons. Neither does the Name it self contradict the Conjecture, in regard that, as we have said, *Nilus* it self is by the *Hebrews* and *Greeks* call'd *Niger*. But as to what the *Egyptians* related to *Herodotus*, That the left Channel flow'd toward the South, that perhaps might be for such a certain distance of Land, not but that afterwards it might vary its Course, and wind toward the West. Which opinion, after I had communicated to the most famous *Bochart*, so highly skill'd both in the ancient and modern Geography, and the best Judge of these matters, he wrote me in answer, *Il est tres vray, que le Niger est une partie du Nile*; *Most certain it is, that* Niger *is a part of* Nile.

Now follows a Question, no less admirable than it is of moment; *Whether it be in the power of the* Abyssine *Kings so to divert the Course of* Nile, *that it should not overflow* Egypt? Many Writers assert the Affirmative, trusting partly to Fame, and partly to a Relation, which we shall produce out of *George Elmacin*; adding, That the *Turks* therefore pay a Tribute to the *Abyssines*. Others also upon the sight of the Geographical Map, believe it a thing easie to be accomplish'd, to turn the Stream of *Nilus* into the *Red-Sea*; which *Albuquerque*, that magnanimous *Portuguese*, Viceroy in *India*, was contriving to do. However (r) *Tellezius* denies it feasable, to turn the Course of such an immense mass of Waters, for so vast a space of Earth, through so many steep and rugged Rocks, and that the Course ordain'd by the Prince of Nature, is no way to be alter'd. Of the same opinion are (s) *Hornius*, and others; but they make no mention of *Elmacinus*: Perhaps they never read, or never consider'd his words, which we shall here expose to the Readers view, taken from the *Saracenic* History.

'In those days, that is, in the days of *Michael* the Patriarch, '*Nilus* fail'd extreamly; *Mustansir* therefore, a *Mahometan*, 'Prince of *Egypt*, sent him to the Country of the *Habessines*, 'with costly Gifts, and other things of high value. Whereupon the King of the Country came forth to meet him, 'whom the Patriarch reverenc'd publicly. After that, the 'King demanded of him the cause of his coming. Then 'the Patriarch made known to the King, how that the Waters of *Nile* fail'd in *Egypt*, to the unspeakable detriment of 'the Land and Inhabitants. Thereupon, in favour of the 'Patriarch, the King commanded the Channel to be open'd, 'through which the Water ran into *Egypt*, which was then 'stopp'd up. Which being done, *Nilus* encreas'd three 'yards in one night, and the River was so fill'd, that the 'Fields of *Egypt* were water'd and sown. So that the Patri'arch return'd with great Honour into *Egypt*.

I could wish to hear the opinions of those that deny this place. The words are clear of themselves, that the King commanded the Channel that was stopp'd to be open'd. The Historian himself is accounted a credible Author, bred and born in *Egypt*, as also Secretary to the *Mahometan* Princes of that Country. So that he could not possibly be ignorant of such an accident; and besides, he wrote his History above a hundred and twenty years after the thing happen'd: And therefore had it been an untruth, he durst not have mention'd it for fear of being contradicted, which he might easily have been. But it may be objected, That the Historian does not

(r) *Alf. d'Albuquerque, in Comment. apud.* part. 4. c. 7. *ap. Tellez abridg.* p. 20.
(s) *In Orbe Imperante, tit. Africa.* Period 2. Sect. 2.

mention by whom the Channel was obstructed, or whether it happen'd, as many times it does, naturally, when the course of a Stream is damm'd up by trunks of Trees, Mud and Stones driven by force, and heap'd together in the narrow passages of the Water. But this Objection does not resolve the doubt; for such remarkable stops rarely or never happen in such large or violent Rivers. Or if Nature could effect so much, what might not be accomplish'd by Art? *Athanasius Kircher*, a person not only generally vers'd in the Affair of *Egypt*, but more particularly in what related to the River *Nile*, in his Catalogue of the Patriarchs of *Egypt*, relates, That one (r) *Michael* was sent into *Ethiopia*, for the restoring of *Nile* to its Channel, from whence the *Ethiopians* had directed the Course of its Waters; tho it be the fault of that learned Man to write much, rather than accurately; nor does he always commend his Authors. The Question being put to *Gregory*, he did not remember the Story of *Michael*, but that he had heard from persons of great Credit, That not far from the Cataracts of *Nile*, all the Land toward the East lies level; and unless it were for one Mountain that stands in the way, *Nile* would rather flow that way, than into *Egypt* or the Northern Sea. So that if that Mountain were digg'd through, a thing to be done with pains and difficulty, the Course of the River might be turn'd and carry'd into the *Red-Sea*; which is well known to the *Turks*, and many of the *Portugals*: And for this reason have the Emperours of *Ethiopia* obtain'd those advantagious Conditions from the *Saracens*. Nay, it is said, That once one of the *Ethiopian* Emperours had an intention to have done it, and had commanded his Subjects to undertake the Work, but that he was prevail'd upon to desist at the entreaty of the *Egyptian* Christians.

I must confess, this thing has very much perplex'd my thoughts; nor are the Reasons that are brought against it to be contemn'd: For either to raise a Mole or Dam of Stones, and then to remove it again, are things requiring so much toyl and labour, that the Task does no way agree with the nature of the *Abyssines*. And it seems somewhat unlikely, that so vast a River, so long accustom'd to a declining and

(r) *In Supplement. Prod. and Lexic. Copt. p. 534. c. 2. This Michael was the 65th Patriarch of the Jacobites, and dy'd about the year 1110.*

 head-

headlong Course, should be diverted and compell'd to change its Channel. I consider'd also with my self, that if the King of *Habessinia* had the River *Nile* so much in his Power, he might have all *Egypt* easily at his Devotion, and that the *Turk* could deny him nothing whatever he demanded. Nor would he ever suffer the Christians of his own Religion, and the Patriarch, who is the Head of his Church, to groan under such a miserable Bondage. Lastly, I did not a little wonder, that the Jesuits did not insinuate it into the heads of the *Abessines* to make use of that Power which Nature had put into their hands, and that they did not use Threats, rather than Intreaties and Bribes to obtain those conveniencies which they enjoy by the favour of the *Turkish Bassa*, who commands the Ports of the *Red-Sea*. But all things consider'd, and rejecting the History of *Elmacinus*, we may answer *Tellez* from the Relation of *Gregory*, which is, That a new Channel may be carry'd on, not from those parts of *Abessinia*, which lie upon the *Nile*, and are so many Leagues distant from the Sea, but from that part which is near the Cataracts, and formerly perhaps belong'd to *Nubia*. My first Opinion was, That the Channel of *Nile* could no where be so easily alter'd as in that place where it divides it self into two Channels, for that there, by the direction of Nature her self, it seem'd, that the whole might be more easily turn'd another way, where a part runs naturally without compulsion. For tho other Rivers empty themselves into *Nile* beyond this separation, and flow into *Egypt*, yet are they not enough to make the Inundation so great as necessity requires; which would not only be the ruin of *Egypt*, but a great diminution of the *Turkish* Power. But however it be, this I believe to be certain, That the King of *Habessinia* is now no more Lord of those places where the River *Nile* ever was, or ever can be diverted from *Nile*; nor are the Princes of those places now at his Devotion, neither are they indeed *Christians*, but unhappily revolted to *Paganism*. So that whatever formerly might have been done, cannot now be brought to pass, not that the nature of the place obstructs the design, but that the Prince of the Country wants Power, or else has no inclination to the Project. Otherwise I should not think it either absurd or improbable, that some Rivers that make their way through the high Fields of *Habessinia*, might be convey'd another way by the descents of the Hill, through the sandy Levels that lye below to a vast diminution of the *Egyptian* Stream, provided that skilful Artists were employ'd to survey the declivities of the places, and the places most proper to carry off the Water. For though it be a difficult thing to alter the Course and Limits of Rivers, which Nature has settl'd, yet Examples are not wanting. We read in *Herodotus*, That *Nitocris* King of the *Babylonians* turn'd the Course of *Euphrates* several ways, by making several new Cuts and Dikes. And *Cyrus* King of the *Persians*, being in wrath with the River *Gyndes*, by reason of one of the Sacred white Horses drown'd therein, divided it into a hundred and sixty small Streams, the Summer's labour of his whole Army.

L. 1. call'd Clio.

But there are other remarkable Rivers that owe for their Springs to *Habessinia* besides *Nile*. Of these the most famous is *Tacaze*, which rising in *Angot*, not far from *Bagemdra*, out of the Mountain *Abugna*, divides *Tigre* and *Walkayt*, and so passing through the *Ethiopian Nomads*, and the Kingdom of *Dequin*, at length falls into *Nile*. *Maleg*, according to *Tellez*, takes its rise in *Damot*, and falls into *Nile* westward of *Habessinia*. As for the other Rivers, sufficiently large, which *Nile* receives from all the Kingdoms of *Habessinia*, we have set them down in our Chorographical Table, and therefore forbear to name them here.

All these Rivers, as well as *Nile*, in the Winter time swell to that height, as not to be contain'd within their own Banks.

Nor must we omit the admirable nature of two more Rivers, of which the one call'd *Hawash*, rising in the Confines of *Shewa* and *Wed*, hastens into the Kingdom of *Adel*, to quench the drought of those thirsty Soyls. Nor are the Inhabitants wanting to themselves; they gladly go to meet their welcom Guest, and bring it in several large Cuts to water their Grounds. And thus being frequently intercepted, and wasted by degrees, as if asham'd to carry a small portion of Water to the Sea, it plunges it self into the Sand. In imitation of this, the other River *Mareb*, rising in *Tigre*, not far from *Fremona*, encompasses a great part of that Kingdom; then falling into the Kingdom of the *Cafers*, as if the Stream disdain'd that Nation, it hides it self for a long space under ground; yet not so, but that it affords both Water and Fish to them that dig eight or ten spans deep, and at length disperses speries and leaves its divided Waters in the miry Fields of *Dequin*.

As for those Rivers that fall into the neighbouring Ocean, *Gregory* remember'd no more than those already recited. *Zeb* rising in *Enarea*, and embracing the adjoyning Kingdom of *Zendero*, from whence it turns to the South, and near to *Melinde* is thought to fall into the *Indian* Ocean. For as for the *Abyssines* themselves, they are utterly ignorant of Navigation, in regard that the Rivers being full of Rocks and Cataracts, will not admit of it; nor have they any Ports upon the *Red-Sea*. Only upon the Lake *Tzana*, which they call the Sea of *Dembea*, they make use of little Cockboats made of thick Water-torch, or Cats-tail, tho with great hazard and jeopardy to themselves. It is situated on this side the Equinoctial Line, in the thirteenth Degree and a half of Latitude. The length of it is thirty, the breadth twelve *Portugal* Leagues, or somewhat (x) less. It contains many Islands, of which the biggest is

1. *Tzana*, from whence the Lake derives its name, for from thence it is call'd *Bahr Tzana*, or the Sea of *Tzana*. (y)
2. *Dekstea*.
3. *Dabra-Antons*: The Monastery of *Antony*.
4. *Dabra-Marjam*.
5. *Daga*.
6. *Dek*, famous for the Exilement of great Men.
7. *Galila*.
8. *Mecraha*.
9. *Merzie*.
10. *Qebrat*.
11. *Rima*.

All which Islands, *Dek* excepted, are possess'd by the Monks. There are also other Lakes in *Habessinia*, but it is not of any importance to name them. But since we have given an account of the true Rivers, let us not omit that Fabulous Stream, which they will have to run between *Prester John*, and their own Country-men, found out among the Figments of the *Jews*. They call it *Sabbation*, or the Sabboth

(x) R. T. *says, where length 25 Leagues. Pet. Pays where it is 16 in breadth. It is more largely describ'd by Kircher, in his Oedipus.* Synt. 1. c. 8. p. 57.
(y) *In the Maps Barrens, but ill plac'd.*

River,

River, because it never runs upon that (z) day; but upon the other days of the Week so rapid, that it carries all before it. And therefore their Religion, they say, forbids them to visit their Brethren on the other side; as if they could not send some person of another Religion to bring them News from that Region, or were unwilling to put their Pidgeons upon that Employment. With so frivolous a fiction do they endeavour to comfort themselves for the loss of their Kingdom: Ignorant where this River rises, or where it ends, whether in *Asia*, in *Africa*, or in *Utopia*; nor do they trouble themselves to enquire how those miserable Souls got thither, or how they shall get out, should that unfortunate River deny them passage upon a Calm day. Yet the Story is ancient, tho not of any River in the extream parts of *Asia* or *Ethiopia*, but of a River in *Judea*. For *Pliny* writes of a River in *Judea*, which us'd to be dry'd up every Sabboth day: *Josephus* (x) also makes mention of it, and unless it be corrected, in a plain contrary sense. He reports, it was observ'd by *Titus* the *Roman* Emperour, as he march'd along. But the later *Jews*, more cunning at Invention, lest it should be found no where, have plac'd it in a corner of the World where no body shall find it.

An Addition to part of this Chapter.

What *Gregory* tells us briefly concerning the Fountains of *Nile*, *Tellez* more at large recites out of the Relations of the Jesuits, agreeable to those things which we have produc'd out of *Peter Pays*. In the twelfth Degree of Northern Latitude, to the West of *Gojam*, in the Kingdom of (m) *Sacahala*, there is a certain Field, and in that Field a certain Lake fill'd from two Fountains, about a Stone's cast distant one from another. From them, through a Subterraneal Channel (which yet the verdure of the Grass betrays) the Water flows eastward for about a Musquet shot; but by and by bends to the North, and about half a *Portugal* League farther, bursts forth into a River; and being soon after that enlarg'd with the addition of other Streams, after a Course of 15

(z) *Cinfuls, Buxtorf's Lexicon concerning this word.*

(x) *Of the Wars of the Jews*, l. 7. *Nic. Fuller, Miscel. Sacr.* l. 1. c. 9.

(m) *So write for* [illegible].

Leagues,

Leagues, the River *Gems*, bigger than *Nilus*, loses its Name, and gives *Nilus* the honour of her Torrent. Then insensibly winding to the East, and receiving two Rivers more, *Kelti* and *Branty*, it hastens (*n*) directly for *Dembea*, which it glides through preserving its own Waters entire, as if disdaining to mix more noble Waves with a viler Puddle. These things are all deliver'd by consent, that there may be no farther reason to doubt of the Fountains and Original of *Nilus* for the future.

(*n*) *A Lake by others call'd the* Tzanic *Lake*.

CHAP.

CHAP. IX.

Of the Fertility of the Soyl in general, and of the Vegetables and Plants in particular.

In Habessinia, *sometimes two, sometimes three Harvests.* Tef, *a sort of Corn unknown to us. They want Rice; despise Oats; feed their Horses with Barley; Grass always; no Hay; sundry sorts of Herbs.* Amadmagda *cures broken Bones.* Assazor *intoxicates Serpents. The ancient* Psylli *safe by the vertue of this Herb. Oyl of Saffron. They want Hops. Grapes they have, but no Wine. They abound in Sugar; want Spices.* The Indian Fig, Mana; *perhaps the* Dudaim *of the* Hebrews. *No Pears nor Apples. Citrons, &c. they have. Their Trees. Ensete, a Pot-herb. Another Tree that kills Worms in Children.*

THE fertility of the Soyl in *Habessinia* is to be admir'd; for the Land where it admits of Tillage, abounds in all sorts of Fruits. The long Summers affording that extraordinary plenty, that in the same place you shall find Seed-time and Harvest; which is in some places double, in other places threefold. For Grain and Pulse the *Habessines* have not only those known to us, as Wheat, Barley, Millet, and the like; but also another sort unknown to us, which they call *Tef*, which makes very good Bread: The Seed of it is extreamly small, less than Pepper, but longer. Rye they have none: Yet when *Gregory* smelt to a Rye Loaf, he said, It was the true *Tef*, and that it had the true smell of *Tef*. He look'd upon Oats as not worth sowing, saying, It was no better esteem'd than Cockle in their Country: For that Barley or Grass only was the general Food of their Horses. They neither sow nor mow, for the sake of their Cattel; Grass abounding in the more temperate places; by reason of the perpetual heat, and the moisture continually distilling from the Mountains: For the solid Stones not admitting the Rain, the Water falls off from them, and spreading under the fertile Turf, wonderfully recreates and enlivens the growing Plants. For which reason, the Fields are always pleasing and verdant, always smiling with a flowry Grace. From whence an extraordinary superfluity of Honey, the Trees being so plentifully fed. In the midst

of

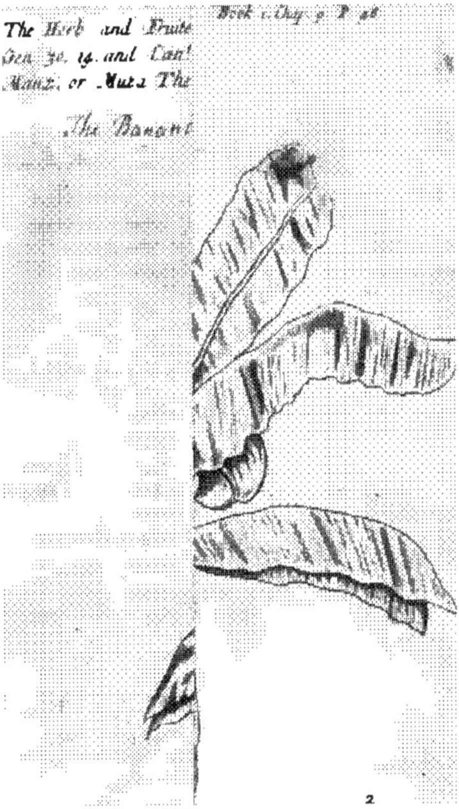
Book 1. Chap. 9. P. 48
The Herb and Fruite
Gen. 30. 14. and Cant
Mauz. or Muza The
The Banani

2

of such abundance, the *Habessines* neither lay up, nor provide against the years ensuing, whether trusting to their Plenty, or destitute of Store-houses. They never stack their Hay, tho for the sake of the Locusts it many times falls out to be very necessary. For that same pestilent Vermin devouring Corn and Grass, occasions frequent Famines, destructive to Man and Beast. *Gregory*, observing afar off certain Cartloads of Hay, compar'd them to Elephants at a distance.

Herbs of all sorts grow in this Country, not only the fragrant and medicinal Plants of *Europe*, but some more peculiar, and of admirable vertue. The *Amadmagda* cures broken and dis-joynted Bones, contrary to the *Ossifraga* of *Norway*, which snaps the Bones of Cattel that tread upon it. The Herb *Assazoe* is of that rare vertue against the biting of *Asps*, that the most hurtful Serpents touch'd with this Herb, are streight intoxicated, and lye for dead. He that eats of the Root of this Herb, may walk without danger in the midst of Adders and Water-Snakes, and for many years shall be free from the fear of them: In so much, that some of the *Habessines* have been seen, after they have eaten of this Root, to handle the most venomous Snakes like Eels, twist 'em about their Necks; and then to kill 'em, when they had done shewing tricks with 'em. So Providence ordering the most efficacious Remedies where the Poysons are most pernicious. Which makes me believe that it was not a thing peculiar, or a particular faculty in the *Psylli*, an ancient People of *Africa*, that they could cure the biting of Serpents, but got by the use of this Herb; only they kept the thing secret to render themselves the more admired. For they made a Trade of it, by carrying Venemous Animals about the World without danger, for the sight whereof, the more curious gave them Money. *Garden Saffron*, which the *Ethiopians* call *Denguelet*, is frequent in *Habessinia*; the Seed of it *Gregory* shewed me for a great Rarity: and cryed up the Oyl which was to be pressed out of it, against the *Hypocondriacal Evil*, and *Obstructions of the Spleen*. They want Hopps, and boyl their Drink without it. And therefore *Gregory* finding, that it was the vertue of the Hopps, which kept our Drink so long, took great care to carry some of the Seed along with him into his own Country. Their Vine and Grapes are most Transcendant, but they never make any Wines, whether out of ignorance, or because the Grapes being ripen'd in Summer, the excessive heat hastens the fermentation and sowers the Liquor before the Lee be setled. They abound in Sugar, but as for Pepper, Ginger, and other such like Spices they have none; rather out of carelesness to Plant, as I believe, than through the fault of the Soyl; which considering the variety of the Air, and the continual heat of some Places, seems most proper for such a sort of Husbandrie. The Indian Figg also, which the *Arabians* call *Muz* or *Mauz*, grows plentifully here, a most Excellent Fruit it is; and you shall have fifty Figgs, about the bigness and shape of a Cucumber hanging upon one stalk, of a most delicious odour and taste. They are ripe in *June*, as I learnt from the Itinerary of Prince *Radzevile*, who had seen some of them near *Damascus*, where they are rare; for they require a hotter Climate. Which Circumstances make me believe, that this same Fruit may be the [illegible] *Dudaim* mention'd in *Genesis*, which occasion'd so much discontent between the two Wives of *Jacob*. Soon after I observ'd that many others, Learned Men, lighted upon the same Conjecture, though they do not give their Reasons. For in my Opinion, it should be some rare and pleasant Fruit, that should move the Boy to gather it; yet not so much a Boy neither, as to think it worth his while to carry home a stinking *Mandrake*, which could be a fruit little worth contending for. Besides, *Rachel* might have sent her Servant as well to have gathered Amiable Flowers, (as some render the Word) that is to say, Lillies, Violets, or the like. And besides the *Hebrew* word seems to confirm this Opinion: as being in the *dual* Number, and seeming to infer a relation of more than one Fruit to one and the same Stalk.

Apples and Pears, such as grow in our Climates, they have none. For at what time they Ripen with us, Storms and Tempests rage in *Habessinia*. For the Trees, as I have heard the Habessines acknowledge, observe our Seasons, sprout forth and shed their Leaves in the same Month with ours; but with the Plants it is otherwise, which Flower there in our Winter. However, they have Pome-Citrons, Abricots, Peaches, and Pomegranates, rip'ned to their full and due Perfection. *Gregory* admired to behold our Woods of tall Firrs, some seventy, some eighty Foot high; and often call'd them *Arbores benedictas*, blessed Trees: especially, when he heard how useful they were towards the building of Ships and Houses. However we do not find but that *Ethiopia* has

its

its share of tall Trees, as well as other Countries. But the Tree which goes by the Name of *Ensete*, is not to be pass'd over without Admiration; being like that which bears the Indian Figg, two fathoms in thickness. For being half cut down, it renews again by means of innumerable shoots that spring again from the remaining Trunk, all which is fit to be eaten; so that there is no need that the Tree should bear any other Fruit, it being all Pot-herb of it self. For being slic'd and boyl'd it asswages the Thirst of the common sort of People, who bruise the Leaves and boyl them with Meal, and then eat the Composition instead of a Hasty-pudding. There is another Tree which *Godignus* praises, most excellent against the Worms in the Belly: a Distemper frequent among the *Abyssines*, by reason of their feeding upon Raw Flesh. For remedy whereof the *Habessines* Purge themselves once a Moneth with the Fruit of this Tree, which causes them to Void all their Worms.

The best Banana's grown, [illegible] at [illegible]

Chap. X.

Of Fourfooted Beasts.

Cows of a Stupendious bigness; the Cause. Bull-Elephants; their Horns. The Heards of Africa. *The Greatness of* Buls. *Generous Horses, of various Colours; Horses for War. Mules for other uses; taught to amble by Art. Camels only useful in lower Grounds. The ponderous tails of their Sheep: in Sacred Writ, in* Asia. *Flocks of Elephants: They lay the Country waste, make High-ways, they fodder upon Trees; Docile: they observe the Laws of Hospitality. The* Habessines *more properly call those things Horns which we call Teeth; they never make any attempt upon Man; they are careful of their* Lechoscety *now tame in* Ethiopia. *The* Camelopardalis, *why so called? the name in* Arabic *in the* Amharic *Dialect.* Zecora, *the most lovely of Fourfooted Beasts; difficult, high priz'd. The Lyon Magnanimous, a Terror to other Beasts. Tygers and Leopards more truculent; how they differ. Wolves Slothful. The* Hyæna *Cruel. Flocks of Apes; they greedily devour Emmets, they devour Fruit but rarely; they are a Prey to the wild Beasts, they Defend themselves wonderfully. The* Cercopithecus *concerning which, a Rythme in three Languages. Whether the* Callitrix *of the Ancients.* Arwe Haris *the Unicorn, seen by* John, Gabriel, *and other* Portugals: *the Ancient Descriptions of the Unicorn various. Many Unicorns, no Bears, but Harts, Boares, and wild Goates.*

BY reason of the Plenty of Grass, and the perpetual heat of the Country, 'tis not to be wondred at, that the Beasts should be larger and fuller grown in those Countries than in other Regions. Their Cows are of an unusual bigness, far exceeding those in *Russia* and *Hungaria*. The biggest that I could shew to *Gregory*, he called *Middle-siz'd*; for where there is Milk and Fodder sufficient, the body easily enlarges after the Birth, and extends it self by reason of the heat, which proves to be quite contrary in the Northern Climes, which justifies *Elian* in his Relation, concerning the *Ethiopic* Bulls, that they were twice as big again as ours; and this put me in mind of the Bull-Elephants, of which, *Philostorgius* Writes, that he had seen them at *Rome*, brought out of the *Southern* Countries: for it is not to be thought, that a Bull twice as bigg as ours differs much in Magnitude from an Elephant. And what *Pliny* reports concerning the *Indian* Oxen, which he relates to be as high as Camels:

L. 17. c. 45.
L. 3. 11.
L. 8. c. 45.

common; the Tayls of which are so fat and ponderous, that the least of them weigh Ten and Twelve, the biggest of

them

erence from an Elephant. And what *Pliny* reports concerning the *Indian* Oxen, which he relates to be as high as Camels :

mols, I rather believe, should be taken for those of *Abissinia*. For that *Habessinia* was by many of the Ancients comprehended under the name of *India*. And that Oxen so large should wear vast Horns, four Foot broad, is as probable altogether, as *Pliny* relates in the same place.

Africa was formerly Famous for the Heards and Droves of Cattle fed therein; and at this time there are some Nations that support themselves meerly by Grazing: of this sort are the *Alcroites*, not far from *Suaquem*, who in the *Summer* Inhabit the Mountains; in the *Winter* spread themselves upon the Plains, changing their Seats as the Tempestuous Seasons varie, and settling where they find most Fodder for their Cattel.

Their Horses are couragious and strong; but they never make use of them, unless it be in Battel, or when they run Races; so that they never take care to shooe them; for if at any time they cannot avoid passing through Stony and Rocky passages, they lead their Horses, riding themselves upon Mules. They are of various Colours, as our Horses are; bright Bay, Sorrel, cole Black, Roan, &c. but most commonly Black. *Elmacin* reports, That *Cyriacus* King of *Nubia* brought into *Ægypt* an Army of a Hundred thousand *Blacks*, all mounted upon Black Horses. *Gregory* pitied our Horses, when he saw them drawing great Carts; admiring at the Patience of the Beasts: and our Cruelty, in putting so Noble and Warlike a Creature to such base and servile Exercises. And therefore the *Abissines* make more frequent use of Mules, as well to carry their burthens, as when they travel long Journeys; for no sort of Beast treads more safely in their rugged ways: and for the greater ease of the Rider, they teach them sometimes to Amble. It was very troublesome to *Gregory* when he travell'd, to ride a Horseback; especially, if the Horse either Trotted or Gallopp'd: a vexation which he frequently complained of.

Camels are never used but in the plain Country, for they tread upon the Sand though scalding hot, without any harm to their Feet; but in Mountainous and Rocky ways, they are altogether useless.

That same sort of Sheep also, so much admired and so well known, both in the *East*, and in *Afrika*, is here very common; the Tayls of which are so fat and ponderous, that the least of them weigh Ten and Twelve, the biggest of

them

them sometimes above forty Pound, so that the Owners are forc'd to tye a little Cart behind them, wherein they put the Tayl of the Sheep, as well for the convenience of Carriage and to ease the poor Creature, as to preserve the Wooll from durt and nastiness, and being torn among bushes and stones. And it is a probable conjecture that *Exodus* speaks of this sort of

Exod. 29. 22. *Ram*, where *Moses* commands, among the rest of the fat parts of the *Ram of Impletions* that were to be cut off and burnt, the Tayl of the *Ram* אליה *Aljah* to be cut off for the same purpose; For that the Word *Aljah* seems to import as much, which signifies only the Tayl of a fat *Ram*, זנב or *Nabab* being the general word for the Tayl of all other Beasts; among which, the leaner sort of Sheep like ours are included. (*b*) As for other tame Beasts, they have the very same as are to be seen common in these parts of the World.

But as for Wild Beasts, *Abyssina* breeds more, and more bulkie than any other Region: of which, we shall give a short account, beginning from those which appear most Monstrous in their Creation. In the first place *Elephants*, conspicuous for bulk of Body and Docility, heard together in the Plain and Woody places in great Numbers. *H. Lodovic Azevedez* saw in *Tigra* a hundred of them together differing in Bigness, and he attests, that as great a Number went but a little before them. (*c*) But it is almost incredible to be told, what a havock they make in the Fields and Woods: they will shake Trees bigger then themselves in Bulk, so long, till either their Trunks break, or the whole Tree be torn up by the Roots, as with an Earthquake. Smaller Trees they snap off about a hands breadth from the Ground. As for shrubs and underwoods, and all sorts of fruit Trees, they either eat 'em up, or trample 'em under their feet. *Gregory* was wont to say, That they open'd *High ways*, and where they had gone before, Travellers would rather choose to follow, as being less cumbersom. But least Food should be wanting to such Massie Creatures, Providence has provided: For in those Places there grow certain Trees about the bigness of Cherry-Trees, full of Pith, like Elder, upon which they ban-

(*b*) Bochart in Hierozoico. *l.* 2. *c.* 45. *p.* 494.
(*c*) *The number may easily be believed by them who shall read* Nonnosus *in Bibliotheca* Photii, n. 3. *Where he writes of* Elephants, *in some Number near five thousand.*

quet,

banquet, as upon Grass. Of all the dumb Beasts, this Creature certainly shares the most of Human Understanding: kind usage excites their Ambition, contumely fires their Revenge. Of which many Examples are extant among the Writers of Natural Historie. *Gregory* told us, that where they like their Entertainment, they are very punctual in observing the Laws of Hospitality; though one of the Females would have serv'd her Host but an ugly trick after her departure from her Lodging. This Elephant had brought forth a Young one, in a certain Field which her Landlord had sow'd with Corn; who willing to dislodge such an unwelcome Guest, had resolv'd to kill the said Elephant: his Neighbours dissuaded him, assuring him, that the slaughter would not be unrevenged; but on the other side, that she would defend his ripe Harvest against all others, and therefore advis'd him to let her alone, till she had brought up her Cubb; but withal, so soon as she had done that, forthwith to reap his Harvest. The Husbandman following this Counsel, preserv'd his Harvest untouch'd, suffering no other Injury than what the Beast spoil'd in her passage to and fro. After the Female had carryed away her young ones from that Place, the Husbandman by the help of his Neighbours got in his Harvest with all speed. The next Night the Elephants came in Troops, with an intention to have Supp'd with their Landlord before their departure, but found the Table taken away, and the Buttery Empty. The People of the Country aver, that they are not their Teeth, but their Horns of which the Ivory is made; and indeed, their substance and situation demonstrate the same thing: for they grow out of the Head and not out of the Jaws: and besides that, they only adorn the brows of the Males; the Females like our Does have none at all. The Elephant never offers to attempt upon any person, unless provok'd; if he be threatn'd with sticks or cudgels, he hides his *Proboscis* under his Belly, and goes away braying; for he is sensible it may be easily chop'd off: the extream part of it being very nervous and tender, which causes him to be afraid of hard blows. At the end of it three little sharp pointed Langets come forth, by the help of which, he can take up the smallest thing that is, as men do with their fingers. They never take care to tame them here, where there is no use of them, either in Peace or War, among so many high Mountains.

The next is, the *Camelo-pardalis*, or *Panther-Camel*, which is

not

and bulkie as the Elephant, but far exceeds him in tallness. For this Beast is so very high, that a man of a just Stature, reaches but up to his knees, so that it seems very credible what is reported, That a Man on horseback sitting upright on his saddle, may ride under his Belly. He derives his Name from hence, that he has a long Head, and a long Neck like a Camel, but a Skin spotted all over like a Panther. The *Romans*, when they first beheld this Beast, called it a *Wild-Sheep*, tho being more remarkable for its Aspect, then its Wildness, or Fierceness; as we read in *Pliny*. By the *Abissines*, by reason of the smalness of his Tayl, he is call'd *Ziratacachin*; that is, *slender Tayl*: by the Italians *Giraffa*: from the Arabian word *Zurnapa*.

But there is a Beast which is called *Zecora*, which for beauty exceeds all the Four-footed Creatures in the World. They of *Congo* give it the Name of *Zebra*. This Creature is about the bigness of a Mule, and is brought out of the Woods of *Habessinia*, and the Countries possessed by the *Galans*, and easily tam'd. A present of great esteem and frequently given to the Kings of *Habessinia*. *Tellez* briefly describes him thus, *A Circle of a black Colour encompasses his Loyns like a girdle; adjoyning to which, Nature has pencill'd out several others, some broader some narrower, some black, and some of a bright shining Ash-Colour; with so much Elegancy and Order, as no Painters Art can equalize. His Eares are the only thing that disfigures him; being of a disproportionable length: for which reason he is called by the* Portugals *Burro do Matto, (though improperly) the wild Ass.* But you may guess at his beauty, by his price. For King *Susneus* having given one of these Beasts to the Turkish *Basha* of *Suaquena*, he sold the same for Two thousand *Venetian* Pieces, to a certain *Indian*, that bought him for a Present to the great *Mogul*.

The Lyon, tho he excel in fierceness and cruelty all the rest of the wild Beasts; yet he shews a certain kind of Magnanimous respect to Man. For he never injures him, unless he be ready to Famish, so that he do not betray his own (d) fear. But there is hardly any other Creature that does not tremble when he either hears or sees a Lyon. The hu-

(d) *Solin. in his Polyhist. c. 27. al. 40. allows them many mark(s) of Clemency: they sooner assail Men than Women; they never kill Infants, unless pinched with hunger.*

gest

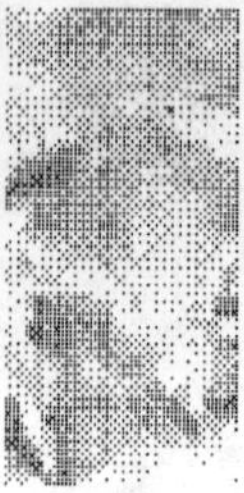

gest Bulls are so terrified that they tremble every joynt, unable to contain their Urine: and yet the *Habessines* will venture to Encounter him. *Tellez* relates a story of a Shepherd, who kill'd a Lyon, that was eight Cubits in length from Head to Foot, without the help of any other Weapon then two *Javelins*. They also use to tame their Whelps, but there is no trusting to their Education.

Tygers and *Panthers* are much more Cruel and Fierce then *Lyons*, for they never spare Mankind: yet they covet the *Ethiopians* before *White men*, as more accustomed to that sort of Dyet. These two Beasts differ only in (e) Colour; for the *Panthers* are brown spotted with black: the *Tigers* gold-Coloured, with fine black Spots, like Fiveleav'd Grass: they are Beasts of a dreadful celerity and boldness; by Night they break into Villages, and make doleful Massacres among the poor innocent Cattle: yet *Alvarez* affirms, That these Butcheries never happen in *Midra-Bahra*.

As for their *Wolves*, they are small and lazie, such as *Africa* and *Ægypt* bred in former times, as *Pliny* testifies: But the *Hyæna*, or the *Crocuta* neer akin to the *Wolfe*, is the most Voracious of all their wild Beasts; (f) for she not only by Night and by stealth, but openly and in the day time Preys upon all she meets with, Men or Cattle, and rather then fail, diggs down the walls of Houses and Stables. *Gregory* describ'd her to be speckl'd, with black and white spots. L. 8. c. 22.

Of *Apes* there are infinite Flocks up and down in the Mountains themselves, a thousand and more together: there they leave no stone untorn'd. If they meet with one that two or three cannot lift, they call for more Ayd, and all for the sake of the Worms that lye under; a sort of Dyet which they relish exceedingly. They are very greedy after *Emmets*. So that having found an Emmet-hill, they presently surround it, and laying their fore Paws with the hollow downward up-

(e) *Panthers and* Tygers *are the only Beasts remarkable for the variety of their Spots, saith* Pliny, *L. 8. c. 17. In which place, the* Panther *is taken for the* Leopard; *but when the* Panther *is oppos'd to the* Leopard, *there it is to be taken for the* Tyger. *For the Antients have not accurately enough distinguished these Beasts, as being very much like to one another, and very rarely or never seen together. They knew there were two sorts of Beasts, but to which to give the true names they either knew not, or very much doubted.*

(f) *Begot between a* Hyena *and a* Lioness; *familiar to* Ethiopia. *See* Solinus *c. 65. and* Salmasius *upon him.*

H not

on the Ant-heap, as fast as the Emmets creep into their treacherous Palmes, they lick 'em off with great comfort to their Stomachs: and there they will lie till there is not an Emmet left. They are also pernicious to fruit and Apples, and will destroy whole Fields and Gardens, unless they be carefully look'd after. For they are very cunning, and will never venture in till the return of their Spies, which they send always before; who giving Information, that all things are safe, in they rush with their whole Body, and make a quick dispatch. Therefore they go very quiet and silent to their Prey; and if their young ones chance to make a noise, they chastise them with their fists, but if they find the Coast clear, then every one hath a different noise to express his joy. Nor could there be any way to hinder them from further Multiplying, but that they fall sometimes into the ruder hands of the wild Beasts, which they have no way to avoid, but by a timely flight, or creeping into the clefts of the Rocks. If they find no safety in flight, they make a vertue of necessity, stand their ground, and filling their Paws full of Dust or Sand, fling it full in the Eyes of their Assailant, and then to their Heels again.

But there is another sort of Creature very harmless, and exceeding sportive, call'd in the *Ethiopic* Language *Fonkes*, in the *Amharic* Dialect *Gurreza*, (which is a kind of *Marmoset*) and in *Latine Cercopitheculus*. Of which the following Rhime is common in several parts of *Ethiopia*.

I put no Man to pain,
I eat not his Grain,
They hate me in vain.

They are varie-Colour'd, and skie-Colour'd mixt with gray: *India* breeds them white, and beautiful; but so tender, that unless they be wrapt very warm, and carry'd in your bosome, they cannot be brought into these Parts. Whether it be the *Calli-triches*, or *Fair-hair* of the Ancients, I leave to others to judge. Of them, after a Discourse of *Apes*, thus *Pliny*, The *Callitricks* differ in the shape of the whole Countenance. The Beard is in the midst of the face, the Tayl is broad in the fore-part; This Creature they say, lives no where but in the *Ethiopian* Clymate where it was bred. *Solinus* hath the same words, only adding; *To catch these is easie, to bring away very difficult.*

Besides these, *Gregory* nam'd to me another sort of Beast,

both

both Strong and Fierce, call'd *Arwebaris*, from the Arabic *Harish*, or *Harshan*, which signifies with one Horn. This Beast resembles a *Goat*, but very swift of Foot; whether it be the *Monoceros* of the Ancients, which as *Jeronimus Lupus* reports, is found in *Habessinia*, I leave to the Scrutinie of others. Many skilful Authors look'd upon this Four-footed Beast as a kind of *Chimera*, considering the idle Relations as if it could not be taken alive; that it was a Beast compos'd of two Creatures of different Forms: as if Writers were framing Fables concerning some Errour of Nature. However the *Portugals* tell us, that the Report was not altogether vain. For one of them was seen by *John Gabriel*, whom we have already nam'd, in the Province of the *Agaus*, in the Kingdom of *Damote*; it was a Beast with a fair Horn in the Fore-head, five Palmes long, and of a whitish Colour, about the bigness and shape of a middle-siz'd Horse, of a Bay Colour, with a Black Main and Tayl, but short and thin (though some have been seen with longer and thicker) a lively Creature, haunting the thickest Woods, and seldom appearing in the Fields. And lest there should be any doubt of the Truth of the thing, there was a young *Colt* brought to one of the Fathers of the Society, who was an Eye-witness of the reality of the thing. Moreover, several *Portugueses*, who were banish'd by the Emperour *Adamas Saghed*, into a certain high Rock in the Province of *Namna*, which is a part of *Gojam*, have attested, that they saw several such *Unicorns* feeding in the Woods that lay under the said Mountain. From whose Relations *John Bermudes*, and *Lodowick Marmolius* made their Reports concerning (*k*) this Beast. The Description of the *Portugueses* seems most agreeable to Truth: For what the Ancient and Modern Writers have written concerning (*l*) *Unicorns* are so confus'd, that some things have reference to the *Monoceros*; other things to the (*m*) wild *Stag*, or wild *Goat*; some things to the wild *Indian Ass*; and other things in reference to the *Greenland* Whale, or

[illegible] *Plin.* L. 8. c. 21. [illegible] *Solin.* *in Polyhist.* c. 52. [illegible]
(*k*) *In his Relation Translated into* English; *Tit. a short Relation of the River* Nile.
(*k*) *As Bochart in Hierozoico.* L. 3. c. 26.
(*l*) *As Carus by* Bochart, *in the place already cited.*
(*m*) *In the relation of Paulus Venetus concerning the Unicorn in Java the less.* L. 3. c. 15.

Nahrwhale; so many Beasts were required to form this *Chimæra*: however there is no question to be made, but that there are many *Unicorns* up and down the World. Only there is still some Controversie remaining, what those Beasts should be, of which the Scripture makes mention; in regard that all Interpreters, after the Seventy Seniors, agree, that the *Hebrew*

Numb. 23. 22, & 24. 8. [illegible] or [illegible], *Rim*, or *Reem* was a Beast altogether unknown to the *Israelites*. The *Ethiopic* Interpreter, whether ignorant of that Beast in *Ethiopia*; or believing some other Creature to be thereby understood, renders the Greek *Monoceros*, the

L. 3. c. 27. & l. 6. c. 12. *Beast with one Horn.* The most famous *Bochart* tells us, That the Arabian *Rim*, is a sort of wild *Goat*, or which seems more probable to me, a kind of wild *Bear*. The Word *Deb* in the *Arabic*, and *Deb* in the *Hebrew* Language, are the two words that signifie a *Bear*: yet is that Beast unknown in

L. 8. c. 36. L. 5. c. 28. those Parts. *Pliny* also Affirms, That there are no *Bears* in *Africa*; But as for *Boars*, *Harts*, and *Goats* they are granted to breed there, as in other places, contrary to *Pliny's* Opinion; unless he may be thought to speak only of *Africa* properly so call'd.

CHAP. XI.

Of Creatures Amphibious, and those that live only in the Water.

The River-Horse, *whence his Name; the* Behemoth *of* Job; *pernicious to Corn, Boats, and Men; frighted with fire; why taken.* The Crocodile. Job's *Leviathan.* The Anguieg *described.* Many Fish. *The wonderful Nature of the* Torpedo. *A cure for Feavers, and the Gout; touch'd with a wand it makes numb it self.*

WE shall now Treat of Amphibious Creatures, and such as live altogether in the Water. Among which, the first is that Monstrous Beast call'd *Hippopotamus*, or the *River-Horse*: in the *Ethiopic* Language *Bihar*, in the *Amharic* Dialect, called *Gomari*, (a) a vast

(a) So correct Bochart in Hieroz. l. 5. c. 13. for Bihr. and Gomer.

Bulk

Hippopotamus The
or the River Horse By y Indians

Bulk of Flesh, and of a Prodigious Strength. The Greeks when they invented that name for him, beheld only his Head above the Water; for his Snowt, Nose, and especially his Ears are like to those of a Horse. But the shape of his (o) Body and Feet is altogether different; and beside that, he wants a Mane; (p) as appears by the Picture; for he has very short Feet, and a short Tayl, a rough Skin without any Hair; and for bulk, twice as big as an Oxe. (q) This is that Beast, which *Job* describes by the name of *Behemoth*, making use of an old *Egyptian* Word; of which many end in *Oth* in the singular number. And that as *Bochartus* learnedly teaches, was the Language that first taught the World. Nor does *Job's* description disagree from that of the *Hippopotamus*, if compar'd. There are many of them in the Lake of *Tzana*, which infest the Neighbouring Fields, to the great dammage of the Corn. They overturn small Boats, which renders all passage by Water very unsafe to the Inhabitants, in regard they lye in wait for the Men themselves. They are afraid of Fire, as are most wild Beasts (r) with which alone a Child may scare them. Some poor People there are that make it their livelihood to hunt them, and feed upon their Flesh. Their Skins being very thick, are employ'd for several uses, especially, to make Shields.

His Companion the *Crocodile* is much more mischievous, which however does not frequent the said Lake, so much as the River *Tacazé*, that flows as we have said into the River
Nile. This is that which *Job* calls the *Leviathan*, as many c. 41.
Learned Men have (s) observed; to whom *Bochart* also gives his consent.

Water-Lizards are very frequent every where, and those very large. Among which, there is one sort call'd an *Angueg*, deformed to look upon, with a sharp Tail, and that so strong, as to be able almost to cut a mans Thigh in sunder; and therefore by the *Italians* call'd, *Caudi-verbera*. To me it seems

---

(o) *Thus Tellez Writes, They are rightly called Horses, for that their Noses and Ears are much alike.*

(p) *Otherwise than Pliny thinks, who makes them to Neigh. l. 8. c. 25.*

(q) *The Italians considering the vastness of his Bulk, call him* Bomarino, *or the* Sea-Oxe.

(r) *Ever Lovers thereof.* Solin. Polyhist. c. 27. al. 40. *And therefore the Abyssines keep Fires all Night near the Gates of their Towns.*

(s) *Beza, and Diodati, as Bochart alledges, c. 19.*

to be the *Ward* of the *Arabians*, and the *Coahh* of the *Hebrews*, and to have deriv'd its name from *Coahh*, which signifies *strength*. *Bochart* has a more copious Description of it: but that which follows *Gregory* gave me.

Levit. 11. 30.
L. 4. c. 2.

The *Angueg* lives in the Rivers; but when he comes forth, he feeds upon the Grass; he is Four footed, very deformed: shap'd like a Dragon, without any hair. His Tayl is sharp like a Sword, strong enough to cut a Mans thigh in two; as big as a Cat, but slenderer.

But setting these strange Creatures aside, the Lakes and Rivers abound with Fish; even those that run under Ground; as we have already related concerning the *Maeb*.

Among the rest, the *Torpedo* is very remarkable, frequent in *Africa*. The *Hollanders* (t) call it *Pitterfish*, or the *trembling Fish*. For it is of that Prodigious Nature, that if it be touched with the hand, it strikes a most intolerable Trembling into the Members. This (u) *Peter Almeyda* the Jesuit experimenting, paid for his knowledge. The *Habessines* cure *Quartan* and *Tertian* Agues with it. The manner thus, the Patient is first to be bound hard to a Table, after which the Fish being applyed to his joynts, causeth a most cruel pain over all his Members; which being done, the fit never returns again. A severe Medicine, which perhaps would not be unprofitable to those that are troubled with the Gout, in regard some say that Disease is to be Cured by Torment. Those *Ethiopians* would certainly believe it, who affirm, That the Vertue of this Fish will dispossess a man of the Devil himself. And yet if you touch this Fish with a Spear or Wand, the sinews of it, though very strong, presently grow numb; and the Feet of it, though otherwise a swift runner, lye as if they were bound, as *Pliny* reports. Which Modern Writers also Testifie to be no untruth.

(t) O. Dapper in his *Description of Africa*.

(u) *They shewed him, says* Tellez, *meaning* Almeyda, *the Fish, called in Latin* Torpedo, *which he had no sooner taken in his hand, but immediately he felt such a cruel pain in his hand and Arm, that he threw it presently away again, not able to endure such a tormenting experiment. More see in Codignus.* L. 1. c. 13. *See the Author himself,* L. 9. c. 42.

Chap.

Chap. XII.

Of Birds.

The Struthiocamel, *and the* Casawaw, *swifter than Horses; frequent in* Africa; *a great enemy to Doggs; the flesh of it good against Poyson.* The Ibis *and* Ophiomachus *kill Serpents.* *The* Pipi *betrays the wild Beasts to the Fowlers; the same Bird in* Guiny. *No tame* Geese; Gregory *wondred at his lying in Feather Bedds;* No Cuckows *nor* Eagles. The Ruch *and Birds of* Condura *Fabulous.*

AS the largest Four-footed Beasts are found in the Regions and Seas of *Habessinia*, so do also the largest Fowl breed in the same Places. Though indeed, they may not properly be call'd Birds, for that they never rise upon the Wing, as the *Struthiocamel* or *Ostrich*, and the *Casawaw* or *Casuarius* next to him in Bulk. However, the swiftness of their Feet compensates the slowness of their Wings; they being able to out-run a Horse upon his full speed. As for the *Ostrich*, he is so well known, that he needs no farther description. The *Casuarius*, or *Casawaw* is a Bird frequent in *Africa*; by the Inhabitants of *Guiney* call'd *Eme*, but the *Habessines*, and particularly those of *Tigra* give it the name of *Casawaw*, denoting thereby the Bulkiness of the Body. But for the *Tinshemeth* or *Mergus*, or as others Interpret it the *Swan*, mention'd *Deut.* 14. 16. The *Abessines* are in an Errour to mistake it for this Bird. For that is no more than the Greek Κύκνος or *Cygnus* in Latine, which perhaps they had heard by report was bigger than all other Birds; this Fowl has a great antipathy against Doggs, which she eagerly pursues though with hazard of her Life. I had a young one sent me out of *India* which was kill'd by a Mastive; but the Skin I still preserve. The Flesh of the Fowl whether new or smoak'd is made use of in Remedies against the biting of Serpents, which was found out by observing how eagerly they devour them without harm. But Providence has not provided one single Enemy to their Serpents only. For the Egyptian *Ibis*, and the *Ophiomachus*, from his continual Enmity to those Vermine, call'd in the *Amharic Dialect*, the *Serpent devourer*, make great havock of those Venemous Creatures. So that *Africa*, though it breed most pernicious Animals, yet it affords most excellent Remedies against those Mischiefs.

And

This is a smaller kind of Ostrich as large in the body but shorter limbs, [illegible] equally strong, covered with coarse black hair [illegible] kind of feathers, I saw one at London alive. [illegible]

And indeed, some of those Birds seem to be granted to Man for the Extirpating the Enemies of their well being, which, because they cannot vanquish themselves, they betray to those that they think more able. For there is a little Bird, by those of *Tygra* call'd from the Noise which it makes *Pipi*, which, strange to tell will, lead the Hunters to the Places where the Wild Beasts lye hid; never leaving their Noise of *Pipi*, till the Hunters follow them, and kill the discover'd Prey. *Gregory* related to me, *That as he was walking with one of his acquaintance, an Inhabitant of* Tygra; *this Bird cry'd* Pipi *over their heads; thereupon, understanding the meaning of it from his Friend, he resolv'd to try the Truth of the Story. The Bird conducted them to a shady Tree, about the bought of which, a Monstrous huge Snake had Curl'd her self; at the sight whereof, he and his friend made more hast back again, then they did in coming to satisfie their Curiosity.* And indeed, it is not safe to follow this Bird, unless a man be provided with all his Hunting Instruments: nevertheless, the Bird has her own ends in her deceitful diligence too; for she is sure to have her share of the Slaughtered Carcase where're it be. Nor is this Bird to be found only in *Habessinia*, but also in *Guiny*, in the Kingdom of *Quoja*, where they give it the Name of *Fonton*, being about the bigness of a Larke, where it is reported to betray not only wild Beasts, but also Serpents and Bees.

They have no tame *Geese*: and therefore *Gregory* observing a Flock of *Geese* once driven along by their Keeper, *pleasantly demanded of me, Whether those Birds were obedient to their Keeper?* to whom, when I reply'd *yes*, he asked me a second time, Whether if they flew, the Keeper flew too, and whether before or behind? but when I told him what profitable Birds they were, he extoll'd them for blessed Feather-bearing birds; especially, when he had layn upon their soft Down, at the Castle of *Gota*. For he had never layn upon a Feather-bed before he came into *Germany*: So that he thought that the *German* beds swelling with light Down, had been blown up with the Wind. But he Admir'd that the *Germans* were arriv'd at that height of delicacy, that Men should stoop to so much Effeminacy as to lay themselves, where it was only fit for Children, and Women in Child-bed to lye. For he did not believe they would easily take the Field, unless their soft beds followed them. As for other *European* birds, they have most of them: and for their Water Fowl

I have nothing to relate worth Remark. By the way, I have this further to add, That there are neither *Eagles* nor *Cuckows* in all these Parts; and therefore they tell Stories and Fables of their bigness and strength: such as the *Arabs* recount of their (y) *Ruch*; which as they say, lays an Egg, as bigg as a Mountain. Not to mention the winged (z) Horses of *Monomotapa*, and of other Monsters, half-birds, half-beasts, by the Ancients and Moderns either believ'd or heard to have been in *Africa*.

CHAP. XIII.

Of Serpents and Insects.

Dragons *only mischievous by biting; the biggest in* India; *their Scales and Colour.* *The* Boa. Salamander. Snakes, *and* water-Snakes *most Venomous.* Gregories *description.* *Cure from Human Excrement, which perhaps the* Panther *taught; they are kill'd with a stick beat like a Bow.* *Torrid places impassable by reason of Serpents.* *The* Oxen *put to trample upon and break their Eggs.* Locusts *most pernicious, but good to eat.* *The Food of St.* John Baptist. Bees, *some unknown to us, they have no Sting.* Emmets, *of several kinds.*

FRom hence we pass to another sort of Creatures, mischievous to Men and Beasts, of which there are divers kinds. In the first place, *Dragons* of the largest size are in *Habessinia* to be found; mischievous, only in their voracity, but not at all Venomous; Nature providing that they should not be doubly hurtful to men. However they grow to such a bigness, that *Gregory* allow'd there were some in *India* so large, as to swallow whole Infants, Piggs, Lambs and Kidds: he further said, that they were cover'd with Scales, which in Colour very much resembl'd the bark of an old Tree, and hard to be distinguish'd from the bigger boughs. Of the *Boa*, that devour'd Oxen, he had never heard; neither did he believe that ever any other person

(y) *Of which* Bochartus *in* Hieroz. *L. 6. c. 14.*

(z) P. Balthaz. *the Jesuite says, that he saw one of the smaller Feathers of that Bird, twenty Spans long, and three broad: and the Quill is as big, being three Spans long, and as thick, as an ordinary Mans Arm: as it is cited by the Most Noble* Thevenot *in his Remarks upon the relations of Ethiopia.*

would. Of the *Salamander*, *Gregory* could tell me nothing; which of all Venemous Creatures, as *Pliny* reports, is accounted the most Exquisitely Mischievous. In *Jova* the Greater, it is called (*b*) *Joke*, as some think from the sound that it makes; or as others believe, from the most pernicious Effects of its Poyson. However there are in *Habessinia* other Serpents, whose Venome is of a most searching Nature. Such are those sort of Snakes called *Hydri*, inferiour to none for their Poyson; they breed in Ponds and Marshy Puddles which are dry'd up in the Summer: and then the Serpents appearing in the same places, are by the *Greeks* call'd (*c*) *Chersydri*: at which time they are also far more Mischievous, as being exasperated by Thirst and Heat; and of these, unless I deceive my self, is the Description of *Gregory* to be understood. *There is*, said he, *a Serpent among us, about as long and as bigg as a Mans Arm, of a dark red or brownish Colour, which lurks under Bushes and Weeds: thither if any Person or Beast happen to come, the Serpent breaths forth a Poysonous Breath* (*d*) *so Pestilent, and of so noisom a smell, that in a short time proves Mortal, unless speedy Antidotes be applyed.* Which Nature has afforded ready at hand, where the mischief requires so speedy a prevention. For, as he said, *it was to be cur'd by drinking Human Excrement in Water.* Which Remedy perhaps the *Panther* taught: which Beast, if at any time he hath devoured Flesh laid for him by the Hunters rubb'd over with *Henbane*, cures himself by eating Human ordures: for many things which are beneficial to Beasts, are in like manner advantageous to Mankind. Other sorts of Serpents commonly and generally known I forbear to mention. The vulgar sort of People contemn 'em, walk among 'em, and kill 'em at their pleasure. Therefore as often as they go into the Country, they carry with them a crooked stick; for being streight, it hits only with the Point, but being bent like a Bow, it strikes with greater force and certainty. *Gregory* hearing there were a great many Serpents about *Edelburgh* in *Franconia*, belonging

(*b*) *See the Itinerarie of* Volcard Iversen, *L.* 1. *c.* 7. *It is somewhat like an* [illegible] *or* Viper. *Consult* Bochart. *Likewise* Hieroz. *P.* 1. *L.* 4. *c.* 4.
(*c*) *As much as to say* [illegible]. Ælian *L.* 13. *c.* 35. *or Water-Snake upon the Land.*
(*d*) *This circumstance induced us to believe, that* Gregory *meant the Serpent call'd* Hydrus *and* Chersydrus, *or Land-water-Snake, by reason that Authors allow them a venomous poyson breath.* Virg. *L.* 3. Georg. Ælian. Hist. *L.* 8. *c.* 13.

to the Duke of *Saxony*, provided himself with such a sort of Weapon, and when he met a Snake, never struck it upon the head, but upon the middle of the back; by which means, having disabled the Serpent from creeping any further, he easily kill'd it.

Those parts of *Africa* which are most subject to heat, are most Infested with *Serpents*; which being for the same reason uncultivated are therefore impassable. And therefore *Gregory* seeing our Boots, said they were excellent defences against the Biting of *Serpents*. Sometimes they drive their Cattle, as I am apt to believe, fortified before-hand, by feeding upon the Plant *Assazoe*, into the Fields and places that are strew'd with Serpents Eggs, on purpose that they should trample 'em to pieces with their Hoofs: otherwise, they are so Fruitful that they would encrease beyond Imagination.

But much more pernicious than these are the *Locusts*, which do not frequent the Desert and Sandy places like the *Serpents*; but places best Manur'd, and Orchards most laden with Fruit. They appear in Prodigious Multitudes, like a thick Cloud that obscures the Sun: nor Plants, nor Shrubs, nor Trees remain untouch'd: and wheresoever they feed, their leavings seem as it were patch'd with the Fire. Sometimes they enter the very Bark of the Trees, and then the Spring it self cannot repair the Damage. A general Mortality ensues, and Regions lye wast for many years; in regard the *Habessines* never take care (e) for Stores of Provision, or to stack their Hay. Indeed, for some time they may support themselves by feeding upon the *Locusts* themselves, which they greedily eat, as well to satisfie their hunger as in Revenge; for it is a very sweet and wholesom sort of Dyet: by means of which, a certain *Portuguez* Garrison in *India*, that was ready to yield for want of Provision, held out till it was Relieved another way. And therefore it is not to be doubted, but that St. *John* the *Baptist* fed upon those *Locusts* in the *Wilderness*.

Concerning other Insects, of which that Climate is sufficiently fruitful, it will be needless to say much more; only as to their *Bees*, we have this to observe; That they swarm in *Habessinia*, and produce Prodigious quantities of Honey: They are a small sort of black Earthing-*Bee*, which make

(e) Dapper in his *Description of Guiny, or the Golden-Coast*, p. 479. but in this he is deceiv'd; because he says, they came out of Arabia the Happy, so far off.

the whiteſt and the ſweeteſt Honey that is uſed in Medicaments. From their Labours the *Habeſſines* gather their wild Honey, of the ſame nature with that which fed *John the Baptiſt*; but in regard they want Stings, they ſeek for ſecurity in concealment; for they build their Architecture under Ground, into which the entrance is ſo narrow, that upon the ſight of a man, five or ſix of them will fill it, and place their little heads equal with the ground ſo like Artiſts, as to delude the quickeſt ſight.

Next to theſe their *Ants* or *Emmets* are very remarkable; of which, there are likewiſe ſeveral ſorts, not ſo bigg as a ſmall Dogg, (*f*) ſuch as *Thuanus* relates, was ſent among other Preſents, by *Thamas* the *Perſian King*, to *Solyman* Emperour of the *Turks*, but bigger than thoſe in our Climates; as the *African* and *Indian* Inſects generally are. Among the reſt, the moſt obſervable are thoſe which they call *Gundan*, for they always march in a kind of Military Array, obſerving Order and Diſcipline, leaving a kind of High-way behind them. They do not gather with induſtry, but preſently devour; and the pricks of their Stings are not a little painful. The next to theſe, are thoſe which by the Inhabitants are call'd, the *Gundan*'s Servants, being as it were Slaves to the Greater ſort; they march in Order, but carry their Proviſion in the nippers of their little Snowts, and lay it up; when it is moiſt they bring it forth again and dry it in the Sun: of theſe, by reaſon of their great Induſtry, it is thought, that *Solomon* ſpake. There are ſome that have Wings at certain ſeaſons, with which they can Fly; which happens ſometimes in *Germanie*: once I ſaw ſuch in my own Country; and theſe flying *Ants*, I remember, were eaſily devoured by the Poultrie.

(*f*) *This I rather believe, than the ſtory of Plinie, L.11.c.30. concerning Emmets among the Northern Indians, that dig up great pieces of Gold; themſelves as big as* Egyptian Foxes. Soline *alſo makes them as big as great Doggs.* Polyhiſt. *c.42. al. 27.*

CHAP. XIV.

Of the Nature and Genius of the Inhabitants.

The Habessines *of a towardly disposition. The commendations which* Tellezius *gives them. The best of all the* Africans. *Servants of the Nation priz'd all over the World.* Prester-Chan, *why so called. The* Habessines *desirous of Arts and Sciences; especially, the* Latine Tongue. *The causes of* Gregorie's *going into* Germany. *They want the Opportunities of attaining to Learning, and why? They of* Tygra *are blam'd. For shape and features the* Habessines *excell. White Ethiopians in* Guiny. *They prefer Blackness. They paint the Devill White. The Men very strong. So are the Women, and bring forth with little pain. Nor are they unfruitful, and therefore the Country Populous. The* Jews *Inhabiting among them, formerly enjoy'd their own Provinces, now Dispers'd and Exiles. They use a corrupt* Talmudic *Dialect. Mahometans mixt with Christians. Pagans innumerable, wandring; Naked Creatures, by the* Portugals *call'd Cafres, or Infidels.*

HAving thus given an account of the Beasts, Insects, and Fish, peculiar to these Regions, we are now to speak of the Inhabitants; Man being the most perfect of all the Creation, and for whose benefit the rest were designed. And first, we must confess, That there is not the same harshness and roughness in the Dispositions of the People, as in the nature of the Soyl: for the *Habessines*, as *Tellezius* Witnesses, in other things not so just to them, are well inclin'd, and of an excellent good Nature.

All the Habessines, (saith he) *are endu'd with a pregnant Wit, and goodness of Disposition; not Cruel, nor Bloody: they easily forgive Injuries; there are few Quarrels among them, or if any do arise, they are seldom determin'd by the Sword; only Boxing and Cuffing decides the difference: They are Naturally given to Justice and Equity; so that having Cufft a while, they presently choose Arbitrators, or repair to the Lord of the Place, and there set forth their Complaints in Words, without any of our Parchment Ambiguities, and hearing the Sentence which he gives, submit without any delay or tergiversation: So that they have no need of Answers and Replies, and Rejoynders, and Exceptions; but avoid the noise of the Bar, and the expences of Pleading.*

And when he inveighs against *Adamus*-Saghed, the Prince of the *Habessines*, he adds, *That he had forgot the Lenity, Truth,* and

and Christian Piety, which wonted to be almost natural to the Abessines.

But before all the rest he prefers those of *Enarea* by the Confession of the *Habessines* themselves. For (g) those he commends above all others, both for their Endowments as well of Body as Mind; and for their Courage and Fidelity. A Testimony which certainly contains a very high Applause of a Nation, otherwise rude and impolish'd; so that if they had but the advantages of Education, most certain it is, that the *Abessines*, would prove the most ingenious and understanding people of all *Africa*; which is well known all over the *East*: And therefore Servants out of this Nation, are sold for more, and more esteem'd than Slaves out of any other of the Black Nations whatever. For which cause some Learned Men are of Opinion, that the King of the *Abissines* was therefore call'd *Prester-Chan*, for that in the *Persian* Language *Prester-Chan* signifies (h) A Prince of the best Servants, being taken in War, or otherwise by Pirates, and sold to the *Mahumetans*. If they were not well grounded before in the Christian Religion, they are easily seduced to renounce their Christianity, for that there is no Circumcision exacted from them, as being already Circumcis'd: and then again, though they be Foreigners and bought with Money, yet are they often advanc'd to Dukedoms and Governments, and rise to great Preferments above the Natives and Free-men. They are most Covetous after Learning, and desirous of the knowledge of Arts and Sciences. Nor was there any other greater reason of that kindness which was shewed to the Fathers of the Society towards the beginning of this Century, in *Habessinia*, but that they were skilled in all sorts of Arts and Sciences, and therefore admir'd by the King and Princes of the Nation. For they love and reverence all sorts of Forrain Christians that are adorn'd with the Ornaments of Art and Learning. *Gregory* related to me, That when the *Portugues* Patriarch carried thither a great number of very fair Books, sundry of the Nobility, and among the rest, *Tino*, one of the King's Councellors, expressed himself with a Sigh in these words. *Oh happy he that can understand all these Books!* And many persons of full years, hearing of the excellency and large use of the

(g) *For these are his words, L. 4. c. 10. pag. 170. b.*
(h) Jacob Golius, *as* Blancard *alledges in his Notes upon* Curtius.

Latine

Latine Language, have most Ardently desired to learn it. And that indeed seemed to me to be the most prevailing reason, why our *Gregory* though stricken in years, undertook so long a journey after me into *Germany*; and why *Acoles* a young *Habessine* followed him soon after; though not being understood in *Germany* where he pronounced *Ehrfalter* instead of *Erfort* he had the ill fortune to lose his labour. Therefore they neither want ingenuity nor industry, but only Opportunity and Assistance, for they never travel long Journies: our *Europeans* are hindred by the difficulties of getting into their Country, and the tediousness of the Journey, whether by Land or Sea: and besides all this the Envy of the *Turks* joyn'd to their implacable Avarice will not permit them to suffer us to import our Arts of Peace and War, to their own and the disadvantage of the rest of the *Mahumetans*. Lastly, their continual Civil Broyls, and Forraign Wars with the *Gallans* are such as will not allow the Nobility leisure to mind the Studies of Tranquillity.

But among such a variety of people, it is impossible, that the same manners and dispositions should be in all; for Nature has brought forth nothing so good in the Universe, which has not something of Evil mix'd with it. Thus *Tellez* sets a very bad Character upon the Inhabitants of *Tigra*; who, as he says, are a People irresolute and faithless, inconstant, and false-swearer, bloody and Vindictive; so that Enmities in Families among them remain from Posterity to Posterity. *Godignus* gives the same report: saying, *That in all* Ethiopia *there is no Nation like them for their vile manner of living and ill Customs.*

But as the *Habessines* generally excell in generosity of Mind and smartness of Understanding, so do they far exceed all other *Ethiopians* in shape of Body, and symmetrie of Lineaments, the rest of the *Africans* being generally mark'd with a Blubber Lipp'd and Flat Nos'd deformity.

The Habessines, *saith* Tellez, *are remarkable for the comeliness Shape of their Bodies, of a due procerity, free and chearful Countenance, and thin Nos'd, that is not flat Nos'd, nor blubber Lipp'd, so that our* Europeans *exceed them only in Colour: in other Perfections of Proportion they differ little or nothing. They are generally Black, which they most admire; Some are Ruddie Complexioned; some fair White, or rather Pale and Wan, without any grace or wellfavouredness.*

True

True it is, there are some *Whites* among the *Ethiopians* in other places, but they look like the countenances of Dead Men, or as if they had the Leprosie: which other Authors also Testifie, but write withal, that it proceeds for some Disease in the Body, and therefore other *Ethiopians* avoid being (*i*) breathed upon, or touched by them, as believing them Contagious. Also in the Midland parts of *Guiny* there is a Nation consisting all of *White People*, which are therefore call'd Plin. l. 5. c. 8. *Leuc Ethiopes*, or *White Ethiopians*, and of these the ancient Authors make mention. However, the *Ethiopians* are pleas'd with their own *Blackness*, and prefer it before the *White Colour*. Neither would *Gregory* permit himself to be overcome with this Argument, That our Children were frighted at the sight of an *Ethiopian*; averring, that their Children were as much terrified at the sight of our *White Europeans*: they are not born Black, but very Red; and in a short time turn Black: Some Authors write, that the *Ethiopians* paint the Devil *white* in disdain of our Complexions.

Their strength of Body is extraordinary. And by reason of the admirable temper of the Air, they are extreamly vivacious and patient of Labour; nor are they easily wearied with clambering their own Rocks. They live till meerly dissolv'd by pure decrepid Age, unless they fall by the Sword, or are devoured by the Wild Beasts, as *Salust* writes of the *Africans* in his time. I am apt to think, that the *Macrobii*, or *Long-livers*, formerly inhabited some part of *Habessinia*, for that the Ancient Writers report them seat'd beyond *Meroe*. (*k*) Their Women are also strong and lusty, and bring forth with little pain, as most Women do in hot Countries. When they are in Labour they kneel down upon their knees, and so are (*l*) delivered, without the help of a Midwife, unless very rarely. And that they are Fruitful you may well

(*i*) *The Famous* Isaac Vossius *in his Book of the Original of* Nile *and other Rivers, believes that these* Ethiopians *are truly Lepers, and that the difference of Colour proceeds from the Disease: but with submission to so great a person, I should think that a Nation so Infected could not long endure: nor that the King of* Loango *would admit Lepers into his Guard.*

(*k*) Solin. in Polyhist. c. 43. *ad.* 30. *out of* Pomponius Mela. *The Long-livers, or* Macrobii, *saith he,* Honour Justice, Love Equity; they are very strong, and particularly well favoured. *But presently after he brings in the old Fable, the Table of the Sun, which* Herodotus *sets forth at large,* l. 3. *where he Treats of the Ambassie of* Cambyses *to the King of the Macrobii.*

(*l*) Thus did the Hebrew Women; *as it is said of* Eli's Daughter in Law, she fell upon her knees and brought forth.

imagine

imagine from the Multitude of People; for though *Habessinia* be not so numerously Inhabited, yet the Latine Patriarch *Alphonsus Mendez*, giving his Visitation, in one little Province, reckon'd Forty thousand; in other places, a Hundred thousand: and in other places, others of the Fathers Baptiz'd a Thousand two hundred and five. Nor is it to be question'd but that if the Kingdom were at Peace; if their Cities and Towns were Fortify'd, and that they took care of their Granaries, that the number of Inhabitants in so healthy a Country would soon be multiply'd.

Besides the *Abyssines*, several other Nations Inhabit this Kingdom, *Jews*, *Mahumetans*, with several *Pagans* mix'd amongst the rest. The *Jews* formerly held several fair and large Provinces, almost all *Dembea*, as also *Wagara* and *Samen*, stoutly and long Defending themselves by means of the Rocks, till they were driven thence by *Susneus*; at that time they also liv'd according to their own Customs; whence perhaps arose the report, already hinted at by us, That they liv'd either within the Dominions of *Prester John*, or near them, under a Prince of their own. Now they are dispers'd, though many still remain in *Dembea*, getting their livings by Weaving, and exercising the Trade of Carpenters. Others have retired themselves without the bounds of the Kingdom, to the Westward near the River *Nile*, adjoyning to the *Cafers*, whom the *Ethiopians* call *Falassan*, or *Exiles*. Most of them still keep up their own Synagogues, have their own *Hebrew* Bibles, and speak in a corrupt *Talmudic* Dialect. The Fathers of the Society never took care to enquire, when, or upon what occasion the *Jews* came first into *Ethiopia*? whether they are addicted to the Sect of the *Karri*, or the *Jews*? what Sacred Books they use, whether with Points, or without Points? whether they have any other Books, especially Histories, or whether they have any Traditions concerning their own, or Nation of the Habessines? which to know, would certainly be most grateful to many Learned Men; in regard it seems very probable, that there may be found some Ancient Books among them, since they have liv'd so long and so securely in such inaccessible holds.

Next to these the *Mahumetans* are frequently admitted into this Kingdom intermix'd up and down the Country with the Christians, employing themselves altogether in Tillage or Merchandizing; Trade being all in their hands, by reason of their freedom of Traffick which the *Turks* and *Arabians* grant them, and the liberty of Commerce which they have by their means in all the parts of the *Red Sea*, where they exchange the *Habessinian* Gold for *Indian* Wares.

There are yet many other Barbarous Nations, that wander about in the *sandy Desarts*, having no knowledge of God, and living without any Government of King or Laws; varying in Customes and Language, having no certain Habitations, but where Night compells them to rest: Savage, Naked, flat Nos'd, and blubber Lipp'd. *Agriophagi*, devourers of wild Beasts, or rather *Pamphagi*, All-eaters, for they feed upon (m) Dragons, Elephants, and whatever they meet in their way. The most sordid and vilest of Human Creatures. *Gregory* described them to me, as *Pliny* described the L. 5. c. 8. *Troglodytes*, for they dig themselves Dens in the Earth, which are instead of Houses; they feed upon Serpents Flesh; their Language being only an inarticulate Noise: the *Portuguezes* called these sort of people *Cafres*, borrowing the Word from the *Arabians*, who call all People that deny one God *Cafir*, in the plural Number *Cafrans*, Infidels or Incredulous. There are also other *Pagans* that have their peculiar Names, and Regions, as the *Agawi*, that Inhabit the Mountainous part of *Gojam*: the *Gongæ*, *Gafates*; and the *Gallans* themselves, otherwise the most professed Enemies of the *Abessines*; but being expell'd by Factions of their own; the King Assign'd them certain Lands in *Gojam* and *Dembea*; and makes use of them against their own Country-men from whence they Revolted.

(m) *For many of the* Barbarians *have been nam'd from the particular Dyet they fed upon, as the Man-Eaters, Fish-Eaters, Ostrich-Eaters*, &c. Solin in Polyhist. c. 30. al. 43. Plin. L. 6. c. 30.

CHAP. XV.

Of the various Languages us'd in Ethiopia, *particularly of our* Ethiopic, *Erroneously call'd* Chaldaic, *in the last Century.*

The Antiquity of the Ethiopic *Language; its various Appellations; formerly the natural Language of those of* Tigra; *in that all their Books written. The* Tegian *Language, what.* Joh. Potken, *first divulg'd the* Ethiopic *in* Europe, *and call'd it* Chaldee *by mistake; more like the* Arabic: *the use of it in the* Hebraics. *An Example in the words* Adama, *and* Adam; *not so called from the Redness of the Earth. What was the natural* Habassian. *It differs from the* Ethiopic, *which is much more noble: to be learnt by reading and use; for that they have neither* Grammer *nor* Lexicon. *Few understand it; difficult to pronounce. Multitude of Dialects. Eight Principal Languages. They understand not the* Greek. *The number of Languages in vain profess'd; not so numbered in* Africa.

AMong so many and such variety of Nations, it is no wonder there should be such diversity of Languages. The most Noble and most Ancient Language of this Kingdom is our *Ethiopic*, commonly so call'd by the Learned: for the Attaining of which, we set forth a *Lexicon* and *Grammer* some while since in *England*; the *Abissines* 1661
call it *Lesona Ethiopia*, the Language of *Ethiopia*, or *Lesana Gheez* and sometimes singly *Gheez*, or the Language of the Kingdom: or if you please, the Language of the Study, for that the Word signifies both: also the Language of Books; either because it is only us'd in Writing, or else because it is not to be attained without Study and Reading of Books: it was formerly the Natural Language of those of *Tigra*, when the Kings kept their Court at *Axuma*, the Metropolis of *Tigra*; in this Language all their Books, as well Sacred, as Prophane, were written, and still are written: and into this Language the *Bible* was formerly Translated. For whereas others Write, that the *Abessines* read the Scripture in the *Tigran* Language, (n) that's a mistake; for the *Tigran*, or the Language of *Tigra*, is to be understood of our *Ethiopic*.

(n) *Walton, in his Prolegomena before the Bible, c.* 15. *out of* Alvarez, *for the* r. *and the* 3. *written without a Point after the* Italian *manner, deceiv'd the Reader.*

Though it be true, that since their Kings left *Axuma*, the Dialect of this Country is very much alter'd, yet still it approaches nearest to the Ancient Language, which is as we but lately said, now call'd the *Ethiopic*: so that the *Abessines* themselves if they meet any doubtful word in this Language, presently consult those of *Tygra*, concerning the signification.

John Potken, a *German* of *Cologne*, now Ancient and Gray, was the first that divulg'd this Language in *Europe*; and then setting up a new *Ethiopic* Printing House at *Rome*, there Imprinted the first *Ethiopic* Books, that is to say, the *Psalter*, with the *Hymns of the Old Testament*, and the *Canticles*. He was deceiv'd that he gave too much Credit to certain idle *Habessines*, who Affirm'd, That as well their Language, as their *Ethiopic* Characters were (a) *Chaldaic*. I could not find out the Cause of so Gross an Errour, neither had *Gregory* ever heard it in his own Country: perhaps it fell out by reason of the likeness of the Language, though indeed it agrees with the *Chaldaic* no more than with the *Hebrew* or *Syriac*; for it approaches nearest to the *Arabic*, of which it seems to be a kind of Production, as being comprehended almost within the same *Grammatical Rules*, the same forms of Conjugations, the same forms of Plurals, both entire and anomalous; So that whoever understands either that, or the rest of the *Oriental Languages*, may with little labour understand this our *Ethiopic*. Neither is it useful alone for the understanding of the *Habessine* Books and Affairs, but for Illustrating and Expounding the rest of the *Eastern Languages*, and first the *Hebrew*, of which there is yet a small remainder in the Bible; insomuch that the genuine significations of many words are to be fetched from the neighbouring *Dialects*: and many texts of Sacred Writ borrow that Light from hence, as shall be more amply demonstrated by Examples in our Commentary. One more then ordinarily remarkable we shall here produce. The *Latines* called the most Elegant and Delightful piece of Workmanship of the Most Omnipotent God, *Mundus*, or the World; in imitation of the *Greeks*, who nam'd the same thing

(a) *Ambrose Theseus, his Contemporary, validly reproves him for it, in his* Introduction to the Oriental Languages; *for saith he, with tenderness to his age and friendship,* Thy Learning very much fails thee in this matter. *Now Theseus ... affirms,* The Habessines to be Indians, *and their Language* Indian; *perhaps the more tolerable Errour of the two.*

Kosmos,

[illegible], or Ornament; (p) assuming the same Word not from Native Invention, but from the *Phœnicians*, by whom the World, but more especially the Earth, is called *Adamah*, or Beautiful. I know it is vulgarly deriv'd from the signification of (q) *Redness*, because the *Hebrew* Root *Adam* signifies to be *Red*. But how much of the Earth can we aver to be *Red*; certainly a very small quantity; so that it is most insipid to derive the Etymologie of so vast a Mass from *Redness*. Therefore first Created Human Being himself, the common Parent of us all, deriv'd his Name *Adam*, not from the *redness* of the Earth, but from the Absolute Perfection of his Frame and Shape, as being the Masterpiece, to speak *more Humano*, of his (r) Creator. For this signification, which has hitherto been unknown to the *Lexicon-writers* of most of the *Oriental Languages*, is most apparent from the *Ethiopic*; in which Language *Adamah* signifies *Beautiful*, *Elegant*, and *Pleasant*. Nor do the *Ethiopians* understand the Word *Adam* otherwise than of a thing that is *Beautiful*. And there is no doubt, but that the City *Adamah*, before it was destroyed with *Sodom* and *Gomorrah*, seated upon the Banks of *Jordan*, which are often compar'd to the (s) *Garden of the Lord*, was so call'd, from the Pleasantness of its Situation.

But *Axuma* being relinquish'd, and the *Empire* being transferred into the Heart of the Kingdom, the Vulgar use of this our Language ceas'd. For the *Zagæa* Line failing, when they set up a *Semen* Prince, where the *Amharic Dialect* is vulgarly spoken, and that some others who were Exiles in the Rock of *Amhara*, were call'd to the Government, the *Amharic Dialect* came into request. For the new King not well understanding the Language of *Tigra*, and having advanced about his Person his own Friends that spake the same Language with him, brought his own *Dialect* into the Court and Camp; which being long fix'd there, and in the Parts adjoyning,

(p) *For the Greeks borrowed their Letters, and many other things, from the Phœnicians, as Bochart, and many other Authors, at Large.*

(q) *So most Lexicon Writers, Buxtorf tells us, that Adamah, Earth, is so call'd as being of a Red, or Clay Colour.* Schindler *affirms, True true Earth, before it is dug'd is Red, and that Adam was Form'd out of Red Earth. Which are such crude guesses; neither does* Kimchi *in his Book of Roots mention any such Derivation.*

(r) *But after his Fall, having lost his Primæval Beauty, he was admonish'd of his Mortality, by an Allusion to the Word Earth, out of which he was Created.*

(s) *Garden of* Jehovah, *the Paradise of God, according to the Vulgar Latine Version.*

ing,

ing, was seldom remov'd into *Tigre*. In imitation of whom, the rest of the Nobility and great Personages used the same Speech. Thus the *Amharic Dialect*, otherwise call'd the *King's Language*, being carry'd along with the Camp and Court over all the Kingdom, (*t*) got the upper hand of all the other Dialects, and the Ancient and more Noble *Ethiopic Language* it self; and at length became so Familiar to all the Chief of the *Abissines*, that you may easily by the use of that one Dialect Travel the whole *Empire*, though in several Parts so extreamly differing in Dialect from one another. It differs from the *Ethiopic*, both in Construction and Grammer, so that he who understands the one, cannot comprehend the other; yet he who understands the one, may easily learn the other, because that for above half the Language, as far as I can judge, the words are common to both. *Gregory* could hardly be perswaded to Translate me the Lords Prayer, and some few Texts of Scripture into the *Amharic Dialect*, by reason of the difficulty to write it. For it has seven peculiar Characters not usual in the *Ethiopic*: however the *Ethiopic* retains its pristine Dignity, not only in their Books, but in their Divine Worship, as also in the Kings Letters Patents, and Commissions, which are dispatch'd in his Council.

Therefore they are accounted Learned in *Ethiopia*, that can but Read and Write it: for it is to be learnt out of Books, and by long use, as also by the Assistance of School-masters too, though they are very rare there; for they have neither Grammer nor Dictionary, which *Gregory* beheld here, not without Admiration. At first he extreamly wondred what I meant, when I requested of him the Root of any *Ethiopic* Word, at what time I was compiling my *Lexicon*; and seeming to be much offended, asked whether I thought the *Ethiopic* Words grew upon Roots. But when he understood the scope and use of the *Question*, he cryed out, *O the Learning of Europe!* They are contented only with a *Vocabularie*, wherein according to several Classes, the *Ethiopic* Words are Explained in the *Amharic Dialect*. They call it a *Ladder*, in imitation of the *Arabians*, who call such a kind of Book, a (*u*) *Great*

(*u*) *Such is the* Great Kopto-Arabic *Scale, which* Kircher *published at* Rome.

Scale,

Scale, or *Ladder*. The more unskilfull seek for such words therein which they do not understand in the *Ethiopic*; but there are very few that speak *Ethiopic* in *Ethiopia* it self. *Gregory* was perswaded to speak it for my sake, using at first many *Amharic* Words, which I observ'd also to happen in the Writings of their more unlearned Authors, before he could accustom himself to the true *Ethiopic*. Both, but especially the *Amharic* are very difficult to pronounce, for there are Seven Letters in both [illegible], whose true Power unless it be that of [illegible], is altogether unknown to the *Europeans*, so that it is almost impossible for them to shape their Tongues to speak several words, which makes me very ready to believe *Pliny*, when he Writes, That *the Names of the People and Towns in* Africa, *are not to be utter'd but in their own Languages*. L. 5.
Besides, the sound of their Vowels is so harsh and unpleasant, that they almost scare the hearer; the obscurity of their Language and Pronunciation corresponding with the Darkness of their Complexions.

But this variety of Speech is much more conspicuous in other Kingdoms and Provinces of this Empire. *Tellezius* Elegantly Writes, *That there are as many Languages as Kingdoms; nay, that there are different Dialects and Inhabitants in one and the same Kingdom.* In Gojam, saith he, *there are some Towns not far distant one from another*, *the* Damotans, Gafatans, Shewans, Serans, Shatans, *besides the* Agawi, *the* Gonge, *and the* Natives, *whose Dialects differ as much as* Portugueze *from* Italian *or* French: *But the Nobility and Learneder sort, as we make use of* Latine, *so they speak generally* Amharic. That which follows, I had from *Gregorie's* Lips; by which the difference of their Language may be the better understood.

The Language of *Tigra* comes the nearest to our *Ethiopic*, as being least corrupted of all the rest.

To the *Amharic* Language, those of the Neighbouring Kingdoms come the nearest; though their Dialects are different one from another; for that of *Bagemdra* is peculiar; *Angota*, *Hata*, *Gojam*, and *Shewa*, use a Dialect common to one another.

Gafata makes use of many *Amharic* words, but in so difficult a Dialect as requires a long time to understand it.

Dembea speaks a Language, altogether different as well from the *Ethiopic* as *Amharic*.

The Language of *Gonga*, is the same with that of *Enarea*, but

but different from all the other Speeches of *Ethiopia*.

The Inhabitants of *Cambat* the *Gallans*, *Agaws*, and *Shankali*, have each of them their distinct Languages, so that there are Eight or more Principal Languages in this Kingdom; and many more Dialects. For an Example of some of these differences, the following Words signifie all one thing; that is to say, *Lord*, or *Dominus*.

Ethiopic.	*Amharic.*	*Tigran.*	*Dembean.*	*Enarean.*
Egzie.	Abet.	Hadani	Jeg-ja.	Donza.

Gregory left me some words of the *Gallan* Language, which I here insert, to shew the difference between the *Amharic* and *Ethiopic* Dialects.

Ethiopic.	*Amharic.*	*Gallan.*	*English.*
Semaj.	Idem.	*Kake.*	Heaven.
Maberekt.	Idem.	*Dagae.*	Thunder.
Asat.	Idem.	*Ibise.*	Fire.
Amaezea Asat.	*Anetza Asat.*	*Hise fuse.*	bring Fire.
Maj.	*Wabba.*	*Bisan.*	Water.
Ferese.	Idem.	*Farej.*	A Horse.
Kalebe.	*Wesha.*	*Sarees.*	A Dogg.
Hobaje.	*Janedjero.*	*Tiedesha.*	A Baboon.
Halibe.	*Watete.*	*Anne.*	Milk.
Negus.	Idem.	*Nekue.*	A King.
Anesate.	*Setoeje.*	*Fute.*	A Woman.
Ahuja.	*Wanrdama.*	*Abletsha.*	My Brother.
Ahuteja.	*Hate.*	*Ablete.*	My Sister.
Hubaste.	*Jaba*	*Budeno.*	Bread.

We shall say nothing of the Forrainers scattered over all the Kingdom, who being naturally *Arabians*, use their own Native Language, which at Court and among the Merchants is well enough understood; and therefore they who can speak that Language, negotiate their own Affairs with ease in any publick Place. The *Jews* make use of their own corrupt *Talmudic*, which by Converse with the Natives is daily more and more corrupted. As for the *Greek* Language, the *Habessines* are utterly Ignorant of it; though several *Greek* Words were transferred into their Country, together with their Sacred Writings, upon the Change of their Religion.

When

When I consider this great Variety of Languages, I cannot sufficiently wonder at the vanity of those People, who have presumed to confine the Languages of the World to a certain Number. (y) Whereas all the Nations of the World are not yet known; for if it be true, what I have been told by several Mariners, that upon the Coast of *Africa*, the Languages vary at every Fifteen or twenty *German* Miles Distance, it follows, that that one Quarter of the World contains more Languages then all the rest, by reason of the innumerable number of Nations which are cherish'd within the Bowels of so large a Continent.

CHAP. XVI.

Of the Neighbouring Nations; and particularly of the (z) *Nation of the* Gallans.

The Adelans *have almost ruin'd* Habessinia; *the* Turks *possess the Sea Ports; The* Gallans *more formidable; The Relation of* Gregory *concerning their Originals: Another of* Tellez; *both reconcil'd. Their Laws. Polygamy lawful among them. Incitements to Courage. Their Armies. Graziers. Their Dyet. A formidable, unquiet Nation. Their Power at present. Their Deities. Circumciz'd: capable of the Christian Religion. Their acquisitions: divided into Two Nations: The Kingdom of* Zendero *describ'd. Inchanters allow'd. The cruel Election of their King; the Kingdom of* Alabac, *&c.*

Hitherto of the People at this time or formerly subject to the Kings of the *Habessines*. Now it remains, that we speak of their Neighbours, that we may the better judge of the State and present Condition of the Kingdom.

The most cruel and bloody War which the Inhabitants

(y) Clemens Alexandrinus *believed, there were Seventy sorts of Languages.* Epiphanius *reckon'd up Seventy five upon an idle computation.* Pliny *tells a strange thing, That when the City of* Dioscurias *a City of the* Colchi *flourish'd, by the relation of* Timosthenes *it held three hundred Nations of different Languages; and that afterwards the* Romans *were forc'd to make use of a Hundred and thirty Interpreters to manage their affairs in the same place: but mistakes in Figures are easily committed.* Lib. 6. c. 5.

(z) *They are called* Galla, *briefly by the* Habessines: *we give them the name of* Gallans; *lest while we discourse the Barbarism of the* Galli, *we should injure one of the Politest and Gentilest Nations in the World.*

L of

of *Adel* wag'd in the foregoing Century under the Conduct of their Captain (a) *Granius*, against the *Habessines*, so ruin'd their Affairs, that they could never since recover their losses. From whence, as well the *Turks* as the *Gallans* have taken an occasion continually to vex them with Wars and wastful Inroades. And first, the *Turks*, after they had possest themselves of *Egypt*, and slain the King of the *Mamalukes*, sent a Fleet into the *Red Sea*, to secure the *Indian* Navigation, which is vastly profitable to *Egypt*: for that the *Portuguesses*, to the intent they might enjoy the sole Trade of *India*, took all the Ships of the *Saracens* they could meet with, pretending a hatred of their Religion. The *Turks* therefore to shut up all the Ports of that Sea, made themselves Masters of *Suaquena*, and *Matzua*, Islands that formerly belong'd to the *Habessines*, which they might the more easily do, in regard the *Habessines* having their handsful by Land, took no care of their Sea Affairs. But soon after they became sensible, how vast an Inconvenience it was to have so Powerful a Neighbour; finding what Potent Succours of Men and Fire-arms the *Turks* sent to assist their Enemies and those that revolted from them. Nor are they less frequently sensible of it to this day; in regard that neither Men nor Merchandise can be admitted into the *Gulph*, unless they request it from the *Basha* or his Deputies, with vast Expenses of rich Presents.

But the Fierceness and Cruelty of the *Gallans* is much more Formidable. For they having Subdu'd many Kingdoms & Provinces thirst after all the rest; whence 'tis very probable what *Tellezius* writes, That unless they had fallen into Factions among themselves; or that the *Habessines* were not so Invincibly secur'd within their own Rocks, they had been ere this utterly destroy'd. Therefore it seems but requisite, that I should here give an Accompt of the Original and Customs of these People: which I shall do as well from *Tellezius*, as from the Lips of our *Gregory* himself.

What time *Etana Denghel*, sirnamed *David* was entangled in that fatal War with the *Adelenses*; that other Plague brake forth about the Year One thousand five hundred thirty seven, from the Kingdom of *Bali*. A certain number of Servants being cruelly handl'd, by one *Matthew* a Noble-man,

(a) *The French read the word Gragne, the Portuguese Granhe.*

Revolted;

Revolted; and despairing of Pardon, associated to themselves all the Fugitives and Criminals that fled from the Punishment of their Misdeeds, and liv'd upon Publick Spoil and Plunder, which they did with more success, in regard the Inhabitants of *Bali* were not able to oppose 'em: And for the *Habessines*, they being involv'd in Wars with the *Adelans*, contemn'd those inconsiderable Robbers. *Tellez* affirms them a particular Nation, and the same that Inhabited the *Eastern Coast* of *Africa*, and the Places adjoyning to the *Indian Sea*: perhaps those Servants, of whom *Gregory* makes mention, belong'd to that Neighbouring Nation, and flying to their own Country-men for Aid, discover'd *Habessinia*, and those Countries which were by their Servitude well known to them.

And now the *Gallans*, puft up with their success and rich Plunder, and increas'd in their number, having Subdu'd *Bali*, over-ran the neighbouring Kingdoms; But when they saw that what was won by Force must be defended by Force, they began to make Laws among themselves, very advantageous for the Enlargement of their detestable Dominion, and the preservation of their untam'd and barbarous fierceness. They are not so unlimited, as to despise Matrimony, like the *Garamants*, nor do they live commonly with their Women; but they have as many Wives as they please. The young Men are not permitted to cut their Hair, before they have kill'd an Enemy in the Field, or some wild Beast, an encouragement of boldness and hardiness to adventure; that by such a conspicuous Mark, the sluggish and cow hearted should be distinguished, from the bold and daring. In their Banquets and Feasts the best Bit is alway set in the middle, and he that takes it, must be the first in any Perilous undertaking: nor is there any long consideration; every one prepares to win that Honour to himself, Ambition stimulating their Fortitude: but then there is a necessity of bringing some proof of an Enemy Slain, first they bring the Head, as the most modest part of the Body; but if there be any doubt of the Sex for want of a Beard, they cut off the most Obscene Parts of the Slain; a thing foul to relate: these they number, and heap up before the Army, as if their barbarous Fortitude could not be made appear without such kind of Testimony. However by those parts it is not manifest, whether he be a Friend or an Enemy that is Slain, and therefore the Head decides that Question. But their most

 prevailing

prevailing encouragement in Battle is, that because no man should be thought to Fight for base hire, or out of servile Obedience for another man's honour, but only for his own Reputation, the Plunder is equally divided among them all. They go to War, as if they had devoted themselves for Victory, with a certain Resolution, either to Overcome or Dye; from whence proceeds great obstinacy in Combat. They use but few Weapons, at a distance they fight with Lances or Darts, hand to hand with Clubs or Stakes burnt at the end; relying more upon their Courage, than their Hands: They make their Shield of the skins of Oxen, or wild *Bufalo's*; formerly they fought for the most part afoot, now more frequently a Horse-back. And though the *Abessines* are generally more in Number, and better Arm'd, as also more skilful Horse-men, yet are they not able to withstand the violence of their furious Onsets. But how they may be Subdu'd we shall then declare, when we come to the Chapter concerning the Power of the Kings of *Habessinia*.

Being thus bred up to War, they abhor all peaceful Callings, believing it much better to ravish wealth, then get it by honest Labour; they willingly eat the Bread which they find among the *Abessines*, but do not love to grind the Corn; for they neither till nor sow their Lands, never minding Agriculture, but only grazing of Cattle: their Herds they drive before 'em, as well in War as in Peace, through the most fertile Pastures, upon the raw Flesh of which they generally feed without Bread, and then drink their Milk, using the same sort of Food and Drink, both at home and in the field.

They never cumber themselves with any Baggage, nor so much as Kitchin Utensils, only wooden Cups to drink their Milk in. Such wild Nations are generally a Terror to civiliz'd People, whom Aboundance renders slothful, and Riches effeminate. Thus the *Cimbrians*, *Goths*, *Vandals*, and *Normans* over-ran the more civiliz'd Kingdoms of *Europe*. Thus the *Oriental Tartars* formerly Invaded *China*. The *Gallans*, if at any time overcome by the *Habessines*, retire with their Herds into remote Corners; Opposing only wild Deserts, and Solitudes for their Enemies to Encounter. Every Eight Years they chuse one amongst them for their Leader, as it were a kind of Master of the Horse, whom they call *Luva*; and him all the rest of the Captains obey; but that

is

is only in time of War: his first Enterprize is, to Muster the People together, and Invade *Habessinia*, for the sake of Honour and Bootie.

They have a Language peculiar to themselves, and different from all the rest of the *Habessinian* Dialects; which argues their Original both forrain and common to all their Tribes; they admit of Circumcision among themselves, whether it be by any ancient Custom, observed by many of the Neighbouring *Ethnics*, or for that they find the *Arabians* and *Abessines* to do the same.

They have no Idols, and but very little Divine Worship. If you ask them concerning God, or any Supreme *Numen*, or who it is that Governs the Earth with so much Order and Constancy? they answer, *Heaven*, which embraces in their view, all the rest; however they adore that *Heaven* with no Solemn Worship, more barbarous than the *Barbarians* themselves: nor yet are they altogether void of Humanity, for they aspire to a large share of Ingenuity, and in aptness to learn equalize the smartest of the *Habessines*. From whence we may observe, that there is no sort of Humankind so fierce and savage which may not be civiliz'd by Education and Learning. Many have submitted to the Instructions of Christianity, and persisted constant in the Faith. *Tellezius* testifies, and *Gregory* farther witnessed, That several Thousands of the *Gallans* were Converted to the Christian Religion, and submitted to Baptism under King *Basilides*. Now let me tell you, this is that formidable Nation which has ruin'd the Power and Dominion of the *Abessines*; insomuch that they have torn from the *Abessine* King above the half of those Territories which his Ancestors enjoy'd; for after their Irruption out of *Bali*, they made themselves Masters of the Provinces of *Gedman*, *Angota*, *Damara*, *Wed*, *Fatagar*, *Ifat*, *Guragea*, *Ganze*, *Cemta*, *Damota*, *Walaka*, *Bizama*, part of *Shewa*, and many Intermix'd Kingdoms. Nor had they stopp'd there, had they not, being sent into Divisions among themselves, turn'd their Arms one against another, and given the *Habessines* a little breathing time: for Concord among Equals rarely long attends Prosperity. At this time they are divided into certain Tribes, (Seventy or more,) and as it were into Two Nations; of which the more *Westerly* are by the *Habessines* call'd *Bertuma Galla*, those that lye to the *East*, *Boren Galla*: those *Easterly* and *Southerly*

thority, in a manner encircle *Habessia*, and harrase it with frequent Incursions. They have also separated *Cambata* and *Enarea* from the rest of the Body, as having subdu'd the Kingdoms that lye between; which makes it very difficult for the *Abessine* Prince to convoy home the Tribute of those Kingdoms. Thus there is a necessity for the *Habessines* to be always in War with these People; nor is there any hopes of regaining their ancient and pristine Glory, unless that Nation be first reduc'd into order. The King has prudently made use of their Intestine Discords; for he has plac'd the Revolters in *Dembea* and *Gojam*, and successfully makes use of their Arms against their Country-men: for as they are the most excellent Antidotes, which are compos'd of the most Venomous Animals themselves; so the *Barbarians* themselves are the most prevalent Force against the *Barbarians*.

Now let us take a view of the Kingdom of *Zendero*, till lately undiscovered, although contiguous to *Habessinia*, as being not above four or five days from it. The Inhabitants are but little more civil than the *Gallans*, only that they acknowledge a King, and have an awful respect for something, whether it be God or Devil. The King being dead, the next of Kin retire into the Wood, and there modestly wait the Election of the Nobility, who in quest of their King newly Elected among themselves, enter the Wood, guided by a certain Bird, of the *Eagle*-kind, which by the Noise it makes discovers the Conceal'd Person: presently they find him surrounded with a Guard of Lyons, Dragons, and Panthers, (*d*) assembled together by a sort of Incantation to the Ancients unknown: At first he makes a resistance against the Electors, and wounds those that he can, that he may seem to be Constrained to take the Government upon him: soon after, as they are going along, another Gang, to whom it belongs of ancient Custom, endeavour to Rescue their King from the other Party, claiming to themselves the Honour of being the Persons that set the Crown upon the King's Head, and purchasing the hopes of Royal Favour, by means of a seeming Sport, which oft-times proves very Bloody. *Thus instead of Inauguration, the* African *Gentiles think it Lawful to attone the Devil with humane Blood.* The King proud in the height of Poverty, not contented with the few steps to his Throne, gets upon the Beam of his House, from whence he looks down, as from a Gallery, and gives Answers to

Embassadors.

Embassadors. *Antony Fernandez*, Travelling with the *Habessinian* Ambassador into that Kingdom, having viewed this same *Lybian Soveraign*, compares him for colour and gesture to a Rampant *Monkey*. Nor does the word *Zendero*, which is the Name of the Kingdom intimate much less, in regard that *Zendero* signifies an Ape. *Tellezius* adds, That it is the Custom of those *Barbarians*, if their King be wounded to kill him, which is conformable to the Nature of *Monkeys*, who having receiv'd a Wound, tear and scratch it so long, till their Entrails drop out, or that they lose all their Blood.

The next Kingdom is *Alaba*, conterminous Easterly to *Cambat*; the Governour of which, in the Sixteenth Year of this Century was call'd *Adici*. To the East, *Habessinia* is bounded by vast Deserts, and open Solitary level Wildernesses, and therefore altogether unknown. Southward, it joyns to the Kingdom of *Sennar* or *Fund*, Govern'd by its peculiar King, formerly a Tributary to the *Abessines*, but now Absolute. He Possest a part of the ancient *Nubia*, near to which adjoyn'd the Kingdom of *Balou*, whose Inhabitants are by the *Portuguezes* call'd *Balous*: their King was formerly Lord of *Suaquem*, and in friendship with the *Abessines*; now he only receives the half of the Maritine Tribute from the *Turks*. From what we have said, it may be easily gathered, with how many Adversaries and Enemies *Ethiopia* is surrounded; so that the *Abessines* may not improperly compare their Country to the Flower of Saffron *Dragalia*, set [handwritten in margin: Carthamus or Safflower] about with Thorns. For being perpetually struggling with their Foes, they rather apply themselves to the Arts of War, then Peace; which seldom thrive amidst the Noise of War and public Contention.

An Addition.

It remains to speak of the *Portugals* in *Habessinia*, who are neither *Africans* nor Forreiners; for that some time since they have submitted themselves to the *Habessine* Jurisdiction. For of the Four hundred, which *Christopher Gamez* brought to the succour of the *Abissines* in the *Adelan* War, about One hundred and seventy surviving, in the space of one Age multiply'd so fast, that when the Fathers of the Society came thither, they were able to Muster Fourteen hundred

Fighting

Fighting men: a small handful, but very considerable to the Party to which they adhere, as retaining their ancient Courage and dexterity in handling their Arms; for the use of Fire-arms superiour to the *Habessines* or any of the *Barbarians*.

When the War with the *Adelenses* was ended and *Granius* slain; having certain Lands and Possessions granted them by *Claudius*, they chose themselves Wives, got Children, and being furnish'd after the manner of the Country with Mules and Servants and other necessaries, began to live comfortably; for while the success of their assistance was fresh in memory they were courted, and every where kindly entertained, and had the free liberty of their Religion: but these Priviledges were abridg'd by *Menas* successor to *Claudius*. They impatiently brook'd to see their kindness so ungratefully retaliated, it being the nature of Soldiers rather to do, than receive injuries. However, their Lands were taken away, (for jealousie began to Rule) or else exchang'd for worse, and those bordering upon the Enemy; so that at length the Kings of *Portugal* were forc'd to allow them Twelve hundred Patacks a year to maintain them. In this last Century while the Fathers of the Society flourish'd they wanted for nothing, but liv'd in great Prosperity: but the Fathers losing their Credit, they were again reduc'd to the extremity of Misery. So that it was the fear of *Mendez*, lest in that miserable Poverty, forgetful of their Native Language and their Ancestors, they should revolt to the Religion and Customs of the *Habessines*.

The End of the First Book.

CONCERNING

Their Political Government.

BOOK II.

Chap. I.

Of the Kings of the Abessines, *their Various Titles, their Names and Arms.*

The King of the Abessines *why called* Prester John: *The King of* Portugal *sends to discover the* Indian *Trade, and to find out* Prester John; *One of them not finding him in* India, *causes a false Report in* Europe. *The true* Presbyter John *in* Asia. *Why so call'd: Ridiculous Expositions of his Name. The true Title of the Kings of* Abessinia. *They have a double Name relating to their Baptism, and the Government; sometimes treble, which renders the Story uncertain. Their Arms. Their Titles. The Queens Title, retain'd during Life. The Title of the Noble Women.*

THE King of the *Habessines* has been hitherto known to the *Europeans* by no other Title than that of *Presbyter John*, which was first given him by the *Portuguezes*. The Occasion thus: *Peter* the Son of *Peter*, Prince of *Portugal*, returning home from *Venice*, carried along with him a Treatise of *Paulus Venetus*, being a Discourse of the Affairs of *India*; wherein many things were more especially and magnificently written concerning *Presbyter John*: which as the *Portuguese* Chronicles witness, was the chief Motive to prosecute the Design of the *Indian* Navigation, that *Henry* the Son of *John* the First had begun. He being induc'd into a certain belief that there might a Compass be fetch'd about *Africa*, by which means the Passage would be open into *India*, as having read in the Relations of the Ancients, that *Hanno* the *Carthaginian*, sailing out of the Streights of *Gibraltar*, came at length through the Ocean into the Red Sea, and sent a Navy into the unknown Atlantic Sea, to discover the Shore of *Africa*. Whose Design *Ramus. c. 53.*

John the Second pursuing, to bring the Discovery to Perfection, sent two *Portugueses*, Skilful in the Arabic Language, *Peter Covillian*, and *Alphonsus Payva*, to try what they could do; among other things, giving them more especially in charge, to find out that so much celebrated *Presbyter John*, that most wealthy King as he was reputed, either in *Asia* or *India*, hoping easily to obtain a League and Friendship with him, as a Christian Prince. They Travell'd through *Egypt* several ways into *India*, and after a long and vain Search for *Prester John*, *Payva* came home, but *Peter* more inquisitive, at length in some of the Ports of the Red Sea, heard much talk of a most Potent Christian King of the *Abessines*, that us'd to carry a Cross in his Hands; as also of his Subjects, who were great favourers if not Followers of the Christian Religion. Believing it therefore to be of little moment whether this famous Monarch liv'd in *Asia* or in *Africa*, he certainly perswaded himself, as being Ignorant both in History and Geography that this was the Prince so much sought after; and thereupon gave Intelligence thereof to his own King, while he himself continu'd his Journey into *Ethiopia*, with a resolution to take a view of this Celebrated *Presbyter* Emperor, who was look't upon as another Pope. These glad Tidings the *Portugals* sooner believ'd, than consider'd; and so spread the News all over *Europe* for real Truth; Credulity gaining easily upon those that are ignorant of Foreign Affairs and Kingdoms. And now the Learned Men began to enquire into the Cause and Original of this same Appellation. As it is the Custom generally to search for true Originals of feigned Names, and wrest them after a strange manner to make good their own Opinions.

We find among the most Eminent Historians, that formerly there was a certain Christian Prince, that reign'd in the utmost Parts of *Asia*, not far from the Kingdom of *Tenduc* toward (a) *Cataya*, who being of great Power and Fame, was by the Neighbouring *Persians*, to signifie his remarkable Sanctity, call'd *Prester-Chan*, or Prince of the Adorers; that is to say, Christians; or as *Scaliger* will have it, *Frestegiani*, the *Apostolic* Prince. However the Name is to be pronounc'd, we shall not contend; but this is certain, that the

(a) *The most Skilful Geographers teach us, That* Cataya *is no peculiar Kingdom, but a Part of North* China. *See* Nieuhofius's *China Embassy.*

unskilful

unskilful Vulgar having learnt the Name from the *Italians*, who at this time were great Traders into the *East*, call'd him by the *Italian* Name of *Preste*, or *Pretegianni* or *Giovanni*: after which, the same Name prevail'd with all the People of *Europe*.

This his Name and his Fame continued for some Ages, though under much obscurity. For few understood, that that same Asiatic *Prester Chan* was (*b*) driven out of his Kingdom by *Cecchi* or *Cingis*, King of the *Tartars*. Therefore for this reason, because the *Portugueses* were greatly mistaken, first in the Name, and secondly, in the thing it self; that Name was given to this *African* King, which belong'd to a King reigning some Ages since in *Asia*, some Thousands of Miles distance.

Now after this *Sir-name* prevail'd among the *Habessinians*, and yet there could be found no Cause or Signification of the same, they began to find out (*c*) words Foreign, and altogether from the purpose to uphold their own Vanity, as *Gian-Belul*, *Beldigian*, *Tarasta-Gian*: one among the rest super-exquisitely Critical, perswading himself that *Prete-Janni* was faulty, would have it to be *Pretiosus John*, as a Title more becoming the Person of a King. This Epithete the Pope once assum'd, and that he might not be thought to be in an Error, many there were that obstinately maintain'd it; L. [illegible] so that *Tellezius* had much ado to instruct them better. It would be too tedious to rehearse the Originals of these Chimera's: only we must take notice of this by the way, that *Beldi-gian*, and *Taras-ta-gian* were the figments of Men of no Credit; but *Gian-Belul* derives its Original from the Cries of Petitioners, with which they address themselves to the King. But setting aside all these idle Derivations, and Surmises, which are ridiculous even to the more ingenious sort of *Habessines* themselves, most certain it is, that the Name of the King of the *Habessines* is no more in the *Ethiopic* Language than Negus, *King*; But in the Titles which both he himself, and all the *Habessines* use, he is call'd Negusa Nagast (*e*) *Zaitiopia*, King of the Kings of *Ethiopia*,

(*b*) Scal. in his Notes ad Comp. Ethiop. but by what Authority he writes that the Habessines were driven out of Asia by the Tartars, I cannot apprehend.
(*c*) [illegible] of [illegible] Wolves.
(*d*) [illegible] Urrean, and Tesserrus.
(*e*) Erroneously Negusa Nagasta in Tellezius, L. 1. c. 2. p. 5.

in Reference to some Rulers of Provinces, and Viceroys that are under him, who are also dignified with the Title of *Negus*, or *Nagash*. In the *Amharic* Dialect he is saluted *Hatzeghe*, which they render *Supream Prince*; and given to none but to the Prince, as the *French* in their Address use the word *Sir*. Hence the *Arabian* word *Asjelabasi*, or as *Ortelius* pronounces it, *Asielabasir*; compounded from the forementiun'd word, *Hatzeghe*, the *Arabic* Article *El*, and the National name *Habesh*, *Hatzeg-el-Habesh*; or Supream Prince of the *Habessines*. When they add the Proper Name, they cut the word short, *Hatze*, as *Hatze-Susneus*, *Hatze-Jacob*; *Hatze-Basilides*. The *Persians* and *Indians* honour him with the Title of *Padeshah*, which is given to none but the greatest Kings in the Empire; as to our *German* Empire; the Kings of *India*, *Persia*, *Turky*, and *China*, who have several Governours and Princes under their Subjection, which the common People call Emperors; and as this King by *Tellez* is call'd in the *Portugal* Language, *O Emperador Abexim*, Emperor of the *Abessines*: which his Title seems to intimate, in regard a King of Kings may not unproperly be call'd an Emperor. Neither shall we derogate in the least from his Title, as being so highly Eminent above all the Barbarous Kings of *Africa*, both for his Power, and the Honour of being a Christian. Among the Ancient *Arabians*, the Kings were always call'd *Najashi*, as the Kings of (*f*) *Ægypt* were call'd *Pharo's*; and the *Roman* Emperors *Cæsars*. But as to the Proper Name of the King; it was the ancient Custom, that at his first coming to the Crown, he was saluted by the Souldiery with a new Name, for lucks sake; and generally the change was made of the Christian Name. However they do not cast it quite off, as the Popes do, but assume both together. Thus *Zar-a-Jacob* in an Epistle to the Tome of Councils, writes himself *Zaraa Jacob*, and our *Imperial*, or *Inauguration* Name *Constantine*. This Name design'd for a good Omen, generally signifies Reverence and Veneration, as *Atznaf-Saghed*, Venerable to the Ends of the Earth; *Melec-Saghed*, a venerable Ruler. Sometimes they take the Names of Gems; as *Adamas-Saghed*, the venerable Diamond. *Encua-Saghed*, or *Waug-Saghed*, a Precious Gemm. This was the

(*f*) Pharao in the Egyptian *Language signifies a King*. Joseph. L. 8. c. 3. & c. 1. Bochart in Hieroz. *P. II. L. 1*.

Name

Name of *David*, the Son of *Naod*, the Father of *Claudius*. Whence I believe it came to pass, that his Embassador *Tzagazabus*, being sent into *Portugal*, call'd him *Precious John*, instead of *Prete Gianni*, as judging that the Person could not but be precious, that bare the Name of a Precious Gem. Sometimes several Names, and those variously pronounc'd are clapp'd together. For that same *David*, besides the two Names already mention'd, was Baptiz'd *Etana Denghel*, *The Virgins Incense*: or as others will have it, *Lebna Denghel*, The Virgins *Storax*. But this multitude and variety of Names often renders the History imperfect, while many times that is spoken of many Persons, which should be only said of one. Thus that famous King *Caleb*, that ruin'd the Kingdom of the *Homerites*, was by the Greeks call'd *Elesbaas*.

The King's Seal which they use in Sealing their Letters, is a Lion holding a Cross, with this Motto: *The Lion of the Tribe of Juda hat won*.

Ridiculous therefore are those Arms which are set forth by a certain *French* Author in the Fabulous History of *Tzagazi*, and which the Impostor himself assum'd in his Epistles to *John Wisling*, a Physitian of *Padua*.

King *David's* Titles which are vulgarly published, are very tedious and corrupted; but here by us amended.

I Etana Denghel, *The Virgins Incense, by my Name in Baptism; by my Inauguration Name call'd* David, *beloved of God, the Pillar of Faith, descended from the Tribe of* Judah, *the Son of* David, *the Son of* Salomon, *the Son of the Pillar of* Sion, (Amda Tzeonis) *The Son of the seed of* Jacob, Zar-a-Jacob. *The Son of the hand of* Mary (Baeda-Mariami) *the Son of* Nahu, *or* Naod, *according to the Flesh.* Here some have interlarded (*The Son of St.* Peter *and* Paul, *according to Grace*) that there might be something to oppose the Flesh. *Emperor of the Upper and Lower* Ethiopia, *and of many other Kingdoms and Provinces*; *King of* Shoa, Gafata, Fategara, Angota, Bara, Dawara, Hadea, Bali, Ganza, Vanga, Gojam, *where are the Fountains of* Nile, Amhara, Bagemdra, Dembea, Vagna, Tigra, Sabaim, *whence the Queen of* Sheba, *Midre Bahr*, &c. Methinks I am now writing out not the *Abissine*, but the long Scroll of *Russian* Ostentation. But the *Portugals* taking the Advantage of the *Abissine* Simplicity, swell'd up the Title for them, or else over-perswaded the *Habissines* to do it themselves, that after the *European* manner, their Epistles, which *Alvarez* was to (g) carry to the Pope and the King of *Portugal*, might render his Negotiation more formidable and magnificent. For neither before nor after did the Letters which the *Habessinian* Kings sent to the Princes of *Europe*, appear with any such tumid Style or ostentatious Loftiness.

The first Letter from *Helena* brought by *Matthew* into *Portugal*, began with onely a bare Salutation without any Title; to omit the false and forgotten names of Kingdoms in those other forged Titles. Again, how nonsensical it is for a Prince to mention such an uncertainty as the Queen of *Sheba's* Country, or the Fountains of *Nile* among the Titles of his Empire; as if the Fountains of *Nile* were such a Miracle to the *Abyssines*, as they were to the *Greeks* and *Latines*. What a pleasant thing it would be if any one should add to our Emperour's Titles, the Fountains of the *Danau* in the Dukedom of *Schwaben*, which were also unknown to the ancient Philosophers? How idly are those proper names of *Son of the Pillar of Sion*; *Son of the Seed of Jacob*; *Son of the Land of Mary*, turn'd into Appellatives? Then for *Naod*, *Alvarez* reads *Nahu*; which makes me believe him to be the Author of that surreptitious Title; because he mistakes the word all along in his Itenerarie. But to insist no longer upon these figments, the Genuine stile of the *Ethiopic* Letters, which was made known and attested to me by *Gregorie* is also to be found in *Tellezius*, where the King writing to the Pope, uses only this Introduction;

Let the little book of the Letter from Malec-Saghed, *King of the Kings of* Ethiopia *come to the hands of the Holy Roman Patriarch.*

In the same manner, writing to the King of *Spain*.

Let the little book of the Epistle or Letter from Atznaff-Saghed, *King of the Kings of* Ethiopia, *come to the hands of our Brother, the Lord* Philip, *King of the Kings of* Spain.

Thus he also writes to his Subjects.

Let the Codicile of the Letter sent from Sultan-Saghed *King of the Kings of* Ethiopia *come to the hands of our Servant* N. N. *Hear what we say to thee, and what wee write to thee.*

But

But *Tellezius*, a Person of a more excellent Wit, condemns and laughs at this Catalogue, of which, he accompts *Dungaleus-Geez* to be the Author. He himself produces another, as appears by the Order of the Kings, and the years of their Reigns, wherein he has traced the Succession as far back as from King *Solomon*, trusting to the Credit and Tradition of the Habessines. So that he numbers ninety and nine Kings, but does not name them all.

He also omits all the Kings of the *Zagæan* Family, as unlawful Successors, though it be the part of a Historian, to recount as well the evil as the good, the unjust, as well as the just Princes, in honour of their Virtues, and in detestation of their Vices. Moreover he says, *it is not the least part of that Glory which belongs to the Abessines*, that they *have such a long and ancient Series of Kings*. Nor is it to be question'd, that though they cannot fetch their pedigree from *Solomon*, yet they are able to deduce it from *Abreha* and *Atzbeha*, two Brothers, under whom the Christian Religion was first received among the *Axumites*; and may contend for antiquity of descent, with the most ancient Royal Families of *Europe*: not to speak of the diuturnity of the Monarchy, which is much more ancient. Formerly the (i) *Egyptians* boasted the antiquity of their Kingdom, before that of all other Nations. The (k) *Chineses* extend the Pedigree of their Kings beyond the *Flood*, *Johannes Magnus* reckons up Kings of *Swedland* from the Deluge. Others in other places take the same liberty, whether out of love to flatter or fiction I cannot tell: as if there were more pleasure in deceiving the Credulous, then shame in being deceived by the Wise. For no wise men will contaminate their works with such Fables; or if indeed such Kings had ever been, what does it signifie to them, or their posterity, if nothing more be known of them but only a monstrous kind of a name? Our *Gregorie* had never (l) heard of that same *Cusus* nor his Nephews, whom these Genealogy Writers put in the Front. But being ask'd concerning King *Arwe*, he made answer, that there was an ancient Tradition among them that the most

(i) See the learned *Egyptian* Cronical Canon of Sr. *John Marsham*, and the Authors by him cited.
(k) See *John Nieuhoff*'s description of *China*, c. 8.
(l) See the Catalogue annexed to *Tagaun*'s fabulous History, and *Jonas* [illegible]

ancient *Ethiopians* worship'd for their God a huge Serpent, in that language called *Arwe-midre*. Whence it came to pass that some would have *Arwe* for the first King: but however that he was slain by one *Angab*, who for that bold attempt was created King, and had for his Successors *Sabanut*, and *Gedur*. *Tellez*, omitting all these *Ethnic* Kings as fictitious, begins from the Queen of *Sheba*; whom we shall follow, rejecting that fabulous and corrupt Catalogue which numbers up a hundred seventy and two.

Chap. III.

Of the Salomonean *Family, which is said to have its Original from* Menile-heck *the Queen of* Sheba's *Son, who came to visit* Salomon.

The Ethiopians *derive their Kings from the Queen of* Sheba. *The relations of* Tellez *and* Josephus: *Both reconcil'd. The Tradition of the* Arabians *Their Contention with the* Abessines. Mendez *his Arguments for the* Abessines. *The Opinions of* Tellez *and* Gregorius. *The Author suspends his judgment for several reasons.*

WE find in Sacred Writ (that we may begin at the Fountain of *Antiquity*) that the Queen of *Sheba* came to *Jerusalem* to hear and behold the Wisdom of *Salomon*, and that she brought along with her, precious Gifts, as Gemms, Gold, and Spices. Our Saviour tells us, A Queen of the South, [illegible], that came from the ends of the Earth to hear the Wisdom of *Salomon*. The *Ethiopic* version renders the *Queen of the South Nagasta-Azeb*, (m) *which signifies the same thing.*

Her therefore the *Ethiopians* assert to be their Queen; and have her History written at large, but mix'd with sundry Fables. We shall transcribe the Summ of it out of *Tellez*, who saith, *That the Queen of* Ethiopia *Maqueda*, understanding from her Merchant *Tamrin* the certainty of the Report which had bin spread abroad concerning the great Power and Wisdom of *Salomon*, with a great train of her Nobility, and Royal

(m) *Tellez* erroneously takes *Azeb* for a proper name, p. 63.

presents

presents gave him an Interview at his own Court; where she learnt from him the true Worship of God: And at her return, after a certain space of time she brought forth her Son *Menilehec* begot by *Salomon*, and whom he had nam'd *David*. This young Prince was afterwards sent to *Jerusalem*, to his Father, where by his order and care he was Exactly instructed in the Law of God. Being grown up, he was anointed King of *Ethiopia*, and sent back into his own Kingdom, accompany'd with several noble *Israelites* and Doctors of the Law, who were joyn'd with him, as Friends and Companions, and Ministers of State; among the rest went also *Azaria*, the Son of *Zadoc* the High Priest. And this is that Prince from whom all the *Habessine* Kings and the chiefest of the Nobility derive their Pedigrees to this day.

But then follows a Tale no less insipid, then misbecoming the new King. *That these noble Jews, nefariously and Sacrilegiously took away with them the Ark of the Covenant, together with the Tables of the Ten Commandements, the Temple being carelessly lookt after, and the Gates being left open as it were by the Providence of God.* Presently the Mother, upon his return, resign'd her Kingdom to her Son *David*, obliging him and all the Nobility of the Nation, That they should never for the future admit a Woman to rule over them, but onely males of the Line of *David*.

But it has bin the Long and Serious Enquiry of the Ancients, of what Countrey and of what Progenie this same Queen of *Sheba* was. *Josephus*, while he writes the Antiquities of the *Jews*, an Author not to be contemn'd; tho in Forraign matters not so well vers'd, affirms her to be one *Nicaule*, mentioned by *Herodotus*. And yet in the Modern Editions of *Herodotus*, there is no such Name to be found, unless she should be the same whom he calls *Nitocris*. That *Nicaule*, according to *Josephus*, was not onely Queen of *Ethiopia*, but of *Egypt*; in which 'tis to be fear'd he is foully mistaken. However, that she came out of *Ethiopia*, many of the Ancients agree, as *Origen*, *Austin*, and *Anselm*, whom Cardinal *Toletus* Cites. Others on the contrary, declare her to have come out of *Arabia*, as *Justin*, *Cyprian*, *Epiphanius*, *Cyril*, *Alexandrinus*, Cardinal *Baronius*, *Suarez*, *Lorinus*, and at large *Pineda* in his Treatise of the Acts of *Salomon*; where he labours by ten Reasons to confirm his Opinion. Of which, those that seem to carry most weight are these: *That* Saba *is seated in* Arabia *to the South of* Judea. *That Camels, Spice, Gemms and*

Gold are more consistent with Arabia *than with* Ethiopia. But these different Opinions are easily reconcil'd; if as many of the Old Writers held, the ancient *Ethiopia* extended it self into *Arabia*. For they assert the *Sabeans* and *Homeritæ* to have bin Nations of *Ethiopia*, which without question were formerly seated in *Arabia the Happy*. That Region which the *Hebrews* call by the Name of *Cush*, by the 70 Interpreters is rendred *Ethiopia*. From hence *Moses* chose his Wife, who is call'd the *Ethiopess*; and yet that Country is a part of *Arabia*, according to the Common acceptation now adays, whence the *Arabians* are call'd *Cushites*. Therefore was the *Ethiopia* of the Ancients two-fold, *Asiatic* and *African*, or Oriental and Western. For the Ancients did not limit the principal Parts of the World as we do now; while they extended *India* into *Africa*, and brought *Ethiopia* into *Asia*, and believed that the *Indians* inhabited beyond the *Ethiopians*. Nor did they think that *Asia* and *Africa* were distinct parts of the Orbe of the Earth, but onely particular Regions. *Egypt* seemed to belong sometimes to *Asia*, sometimes to *Africa*; and others made *Nilus* to be the bounds between those two Continents. And, which is most remarkable, the Antient *Arabia* was not of so large an Extent, as now the Modern is. For the *Sabeans* and *Homerites* were plac'd beyond the Limits of *Arabia*. The *Arabian* Gulph was also taken onely for a part or Bay of the Red Sea. All which things the Geographers of later Times have much more distinctly reform'd. So that altho by Us, the *Sabeans* are accounted to be a Region of the Southern *Arabia* that lyes upon the *Indian* Ocean, and consequently toward the utmost Limits of Land there, yet may the Queen of *Sheba*, according to the Opinion of the Ancients, be said to come out of *Ethiopia*. Nor does it argue any thing of absurdity to conjecture that she might at the same time command that part of *Ethiopia* which lay upon the Opposite Shore, and at so near a distance.

The *Arabians* made no question, but that she was descended from the Line of the Sons of *Homer*, or the *Homerites*, and that she was the daughter (n) of King *Hod-hadi*. They call her *Belkis*, and affirm her to have bin, not the Concubine,

(n) He was the twenty first, as is to be seen in the Catalogue of the *Homerite* Kings, which the learned Pocock set forth in his Specimen of an *Arabian* History, p. 59.

but

but the (o) wife of *Solomon*: from whence we gather, that they themselves believ'd that Tradition to be true, that she had a Son begotten by *Solomon*. The *Arabs* and *Ethiopians* contend about this, to this very day, as if the Modern Franks should contend with the *Germans* about *Charles* the *Great*. *Alphonsus Mendez* the Patriarch adheres to the Tradition of the *Abessines*, (p) mov'd thereto by their Arguments: because the continuation of Officers both Civil and Military, and other customes and Ceremonies made use of in the Hebrew Common-wealth so long since, are still observ'd there to this day. So that *Ethiopia* seem'd to him to be a certain lively representation of the Ancient Hebrew Government. And his other reason was, for that he understood many places of Scripture much better since he came into *Ethiopia*. *Tellezius*, none of the mildest Censurers of the *Ethiopic* Traditions, in this thing agrees throughout with the Patriarch, adding, That it ought to seem strange to no Person, that *Solomon*, who took to wife the Daughter of *Pharaoh*, and also lov'd the *Moabitish*, *Ammonian*, *Sidonian* and *Hethic* Women, should desire to tast the *Ethiopic* Variety. The *Habessines* also call'd the Posterity of their Kings *Israelites*: neither do they think any other persons worthy of the Scepter but the Male Issue of *Menilehec*; who for that reason bear the Lyon in their Royal Coats, with this Impresse, *The Lyon of the Tribe of* Judah *has overcome*: to demonstrate that they are descended from the Tribe of *Judah*, and the Line of *David*: nor that *Candaces* Eunuch learnt the Orthodox Religion from any other then from the *Israelites*. *Gregory* also aver'd to me the same things, and that the Book wherein those things were recorded, was call'd the *Glory of the Kings*, and was of great authority among them; and that no person in *Ethiopia* doubted of the Truth thereof. He added, That all the Offices, both Civil and Military, of which the Patriarch discourses in his Letter, (q) are still continu'd in the same Families, and that they who Enjoy them, can make it appear how long those Employments have been officiated by their Ancestors, from Generation to Generation. However, I do not think it con-

(o) *Arabian* Geographer, speaking of the City *Marde*. There, saith he, was *Belkis* born, the Wife of *Solomon* the Son of *David*.

(p) In his Epistle to *Tellezius*.

vement, to augment or lessen the Credit of these things, untill those *Ethiopic* Institutions, Offices, Customs and Manners, of which the Patriarch speaks in general, shall be more particularly made known to me; that I see the Genealogies of those public Ministers, whom *Gregory* mentions; and that I hear the answers to such doubts as I shall propose. I find indeed the Consent of the Nation, and the affirmation of their Kings; for *Claudius* calls his Ancestors *Israelitish Kings*: and at the time of Inauguration, they proclaim the Creation of the *Israelitish King*: and they who are kept in the Rock *Geshen*, bear the Name of *Israelites*: And lastly, I find some Rites and Customs agreeing with those of the *Jews*. Nor is it any wonder to me more than to *Tellezius*, or disagreeable from *Solomon's* practice, that after so many profound and knotty Riddles unloos'd, he should unty the Queen of *Sheba's* Marriage Girdle. Again, if the *Habessines* are Colonies of the *Sabeans* and *Homerites*, it may as well be granted that the *Queen of the South* deriv'd her Pedigree from them. Yet there are many things that seem to perswade the contrary. For as to the *Israelitish Rites*, we shall hereafter shew, that they might have bin introduc'd long after *Solomon's* time upon other grounds; and that they were common as well to the Gentiles as to the Christians. For if the true Worship of God began from this time, how came it to be preserv'd without Synagogues, and the Sacred Volumes? But they have them not, either in the Hebrew Language, nor translated into their own. Nor does the Appellation of *Israelitish Kings*, argue the Verity of their Descent, no more than if any one should assert our Emperours descended from the Ancient *Romans*. But if, as the Posterity of the *Israelites* they continue in their Offices, or are so sollicitous to preserve their Posterity; why not as well in preserving the Histories of their Ancestors? and in perpetuating Kindnesses between their Relations and those of the same Tribe or Family? why not more choice in their Marriages? more earnest in Visiting the Temple of *Jerusalem*? and in giving mutual assistance to their Brethren? Especially when *Rehoboam* the Brother of *Menelec*, suffer'd that great Loss of the revolt of the Ten Tribes? and when he was invaded by *Sisack* King of *Egypt*, whom no man better than the King of *Ethiopia* could have diverted? when the *Jews* were oppress'd by so many Enemies; when they were carry'd away Captive to *Babylon*? when ruin'd by the Kings of *Assyria*? and

when

when subdu'd by the *Romans*? For then the Passages were free thorough *Arabia* or *Egypt*; and the *Red Sea* was open. Lastly, which is of most moment, if the *Ethiopians* receiv'd their divine Ceremonies and Religion from *Salomon*, why not his human Learning? For Learning and Religion generally go together, as may be prov'd by the Examples of many Nations. But as to this, their manner of writing and reading differs very much, though some of their letters seem to be borrow'd from the *Samaritans*. Lastly, the *Jews* inhabiting up and down all over *Ethiopia*, it would be of great Concern to put these Questions to them, When? and how they came thither? What they think of these Traditions of the *Habissines*? and what they find in their Books concerning them? it not being probable that all their Books should be lost in a Country so well defended by nature? But we have made too long a Digression: now let us return to *Menilehec*.

CHAP. IV.

Of Menilehec, *the Son of* Makeda, *and of his Posterity, to the interrupted Succession of the* Salomonians.

Menilehec *first King; the interpretation of his name: nothing certain of his Son or Posterity. Christ born in the Reign of* Bazen. *No mention here of Queen* Candace. *She reign'd in* Meroe, *not in* Habessinia. Abreha *and* Atzbeha, *Brothers and Kings; first Christian Kings: A* Triumvirate *of Kings. Their Successors. The Subversion of the Kingdom of the* Homerites *by* Caleb. *He restores* Nagra *to the Christians. His Successors:* Saif ibn-dhi-Jezen *advanced by the* Persians; *Slain.* Ibn *the last, submits to the* Mahumetans. *The* Greek *Historians Confuted.* Caleb's *Encomium. The Martyrdom of the* Nagranites. Caleb's *Successors: The* Salomonean *Line interrupted.*

NOW then they acknowledg *Menilehec El-Hagim* to be the first King. Which name some interpret, *As He*. Others, *As God created him like me*. Neither of which interpretations can be pick'd from the *Ethiopic* Language. However, *Ebn-El-Hagim*, is apparently in Arabic the *Son of Wisdome*, or of *Salomon*. *Tellezius* gives to his *Son* the name of *Zadgur*; whereas *Gedur*, in *Marianus Victor*'s Catalogue precedes

cedes Queen *Makeda*. Then, saith he, four and twenty Kings succeeded, till *Bazen* reign'd; and yet in the next Chapter, writes him to be the Twentieth from *Menilek* the Son of *Solomon*: but neither does he name them, neither will we detain the Reader amidst these uncertainties.

There is less doubt, that Christ our Saviour was born in the time of *Bazen*, more particularly in the Eighteenth Year of his Reign. Here is no mention made of *Candace*, whom some of the *Ethiopians* acknowledg for their Queen: in this contradictory to themselves, while they will not admit a Female to the Throne. And therefore it is more proper, that we should in expounding that place in the *Acts*, c. 8. v. 27. which speaks of the Queen of *Ethiopia's* Eunuch, find out some other more probable part of *Ethiopia* bordering upon *Ægypt*: which with some probability we may conjecture to be the Island of *Meroe*, in regard that *Pliny* testifies, That in that Iland reign'd a Certain Woman call'd *Candace*, and that the succeeding Queens assum'd that name afterwards for many Years. After *Bazen*, for the space of 327 Years *Ethiopia* was govern'd by Thirteen Kings, as *Tellezius* records it. But he mentions not one of their names, perhaps because he found there was nothing of certainty. From the time that (1) *Abreha*, and *Atzbeha* held the Scepter, the Ethiopic History has afforded much more clearness and light, and the names of the Kings are more certainly recited. Of these and several other Successive Kings, there is mention made in the Ethiopic Liturgy, and otherwhere. For in *their Commemoration of the Dead*, there is this Ejaculation,

> *Remember, Lord*, Abreha, *and* Atzbeha, *Kings of* Ethiopia.

My Ethiopic Poet also gives them this Encomium,

> *Peace be to* Abreha, *and* Atzbeha,
> *They in one Kingdom did the Scepter sway*;
> *And yet in Love, and yet in Concord still*,
> *They liv'd as Princes with one Heart and Will*;

(1) *Abreha is an Arabic word, corruptedly spoken.* Alius: *Erroneously taken for* Abraham, *which they pronounce* Ibrahim.

Like

Like those good Men, that with Religious awe
Walk'd in the Precepts of Mosaic *Law,*
Their Lipps the words of Christ's own Gospel taught;
To build him Temples with their hands they wrought.

They are applauded for their Concord; rare among Brothers, who are partners in Royalty; yet that it may so happen, is clear by that great Sentence, *A Kingdom may endure Colleagues in Kingship, so They can but endure themselves.* But much more were they to be Extoll'd, for embracing the Christian Religion, at what time *Frumentius* Preach'd; of which more in due place. But more then this, the *Habessines* give us another Example of a Concording and Unanimous *Triumvirate.* These Royal *Triumvirs* were *Aezsa, Aizfed,* and *Amey,* who govern'd the Empire long and prosperously by turns, as they agreed. A thing which the *Habessines* will hardly perswade most people to believe; unless it were in reference to the hearing such businesses as afterwards requir'd common Consultation, or the executing such Decrees as were made by Common Consent; tho in such Transactions likewise there must be harmony and agreement. To them succeeded *Arado, Aababa* and *Alamid,* at what time several Monks went out of *Ægypt* into *Ethiopia,* to propagate the Gospel. To *Alamid* succeeded his Son *Tacena,* and after him *Caleb* his Nephew, who flourished in the time of the Emperour *Justin,* about the Year 522. The Greek and Latin Authors call him *Eles baan.* Perhaps from the Ethiopic name of Baptisme, *Aczbeha,* with the Arabic article *El. El-Aczbeha,* from whence *Eles baan.* He was famous for the Subversion of the Kingdom of the *Homerites,* and revenging the blood of the Christians slain by that Impious *Dunawas*: for which he was placed in the Kalendar of the Saints. It is a Story most worthy remembrance; wherein the Arabic and Ethiopic Historians very punctually agree with the Greeks and Latins. This (*) *Dunawas* was the Last King of the *Sabaeans,* who were afterwards call'd *Homerites,* in opinion a *Jew*; and therefore one that afflicted the Christians with a most dire Persecution. For he caus'd large Pits to be digg'd, and then commanded the Christians

(*) You have the History at large in *Baronius* Annals, who, sayes he, had the Story from an Author of an unsuspected Credit, and the Writings of that time.

the

to be burnt therein in heaps, as it were for quicker dispatch. Three hundred and forty perish'd in this manner in the City of (x) *Nagra*, together with *St. Areta*, entomb'd in Fire. *Caleb*, being admonish'd by the Patriarch, would not endure so much barbarous Cruelty; but with an Army of a Hundred and twenty thousand Men, and a Navy of 423 Vessels, he cross'd over into *Arabia*, and having vanquish'd *Dunawas*, he he utterly destroy'd the Kingdom of the *Homerites*, restor'd *Nagra* to the Christians, and made *St. Areta*'s Son Governor of the place. To *Dunawas* succeeded *Abreha Elashram, Jacsum F. Masruk F.* but their Kingdom remain'd Seventy two years under the Yoke of the *Habessines*. After these, *Saif ebn-Di-Jazan*, of the race of the *Homerites*, by the assistance of *Anusherwan*, King of the *Persians*, recover'd the Throne of his Ancestors, but was soon after slain by the *Abessines*. However, the *Persians* at that time prevalent, set up over the *Sabeans* other Kings, whom the *Abessines* oppos'd, and some they slew. And thus this Kingdom harrass'd with continual Wars between the *Persians* and the *Habessines*, at length, when the *Saracens* began to grow powerful, under *Bazan*, the last King, became tributarie to *Mahomet*. And by this perhaps we are to understand what *Abdelbachides* writes concerning a *Nagash* of the *Abessines*, whom he calls *Atzhama*, as if he had revolted to *Islamism* at the invitation of *Mahomet*. But these things are confused and imperfectly delivered by the *Arabes*, *Greekes* and *Latins*, and besides that, the diversity of names adds obscurity to the History. For as to those Acts which *Procopius* attributes to *Hellesthiaeus*, King of *Ethiopia*, as if he, having slain the King of the *Homerites*, (of which many were Jews) set up another in his place, *Esimiphaeus* by name, and a Christian, those things are proper to none but *Caleb*; in regard that Kingdom being destroy'd by *Caleb*, could not be again subverted by *Ellesthiaeus*. But as for those things which are reported by *Cedrenus* and *Nicephorus* of *Adad* or *David*, a certain *Ethnic* King of the *Indian Axumites*, who demolish'd the Kingdom of the *Homerites*, and by occasion of a former vow, became a Christian, they are altogether false. For that there is no other History than that which we have related of *Caleb* to this purpose, we shall hereafter

(x) *Negra* by *Niceph. Callisto. l.* 18. *c.* 6. by others *Najran*

declare,

declare, when we came to discourse of the Original Christianity in *Ethiopia*. For that the corrupt names of *Damian*, of *Damnus*, from *Dimnus*, or *Dunawas*, and other Circumstances demonstrate. But 'tis no wonder the History of the *Homerites* should be so confus'd among Strangers, when the *Arabians* themselves complain, that among all other Histories that of the *Homerites* is the most imperfect.

Our Poet before cited thus praises *Caleb* in the following Lines.

Peace be to Caleb, *who with the Laurel wreath'd,*
Behind him left such Monuments of his Power.
To Salem *he his Royal Crown bequeath'd*
An Offering to his dreaded Saviour.
For he, great Hero, from his mighty deeds,
Vain glory scorn'd, that proud ambition feeds.
The dismal Slaughter of Sabean *Host,*
So dismal that not one alive remain'd,
Swell'd not his thoughts of Victory to boast;
Yet glad to see his Sword so nobly stain'd.
Glad that by him the Homerites *enslav'd,*
Martyrs were now reveng'd, and Christians sav'd,

Concerning the Martyrs of *Nagra*, the same Poet goes on thus.

Your beauteous Stars of Nagra *I salute;*
Such Themes would force loud Language from the Mute.
You brightly shine before the Mercy-Seat,
And like rich Gemms the world illuminate.
Oh may your Lustre reconcile my Sin
Before the Judge of what my Crimes have bin.
Shew him your blood which you for him have spilt,
And beg Pacification *for my Guilt.*

To *Caleb* succeeded *Gebra-Meskel*, or *the Servant of the Cross*, so nam'd at his Baptism, whom the Poet thus honours.

Peace to thee also, King of high renown,
That in the Strength of God so much hast won.
Yet with thanksgiving, to thy heavenly Lord
Didst still ascribe the Trophies of thy Sword.
Concord and Peace adorn'd thy happy daies

Gg Thy

Thy reign resounded only Hymns of praise,
Glory to God thy Pious Cares obleged;
And Peace on Earth from fear of thee proceeded.

The next to him in the *Ethiopian* Liturgy are *Constantine*, and *Fresenna*, or the good Fruit.

Then followed an Interruption or discontinuance of this Line, in the time of *Delnoad*, who reigned about the year of *Christ* 960. But then the Scepter was usurp'd by another Race, of which we are next to discourse.

Chap. V.

Of the Zagæan *Line, and the Kings that descended from that Race.*

The Zagæan Line originally from the wickedness of a woman: the Successors uncertain: yet some of them very Famous.

Upon the Death of *Delnoad*, the *Zagæan* Family invaded the Kingdom, and enjoy'd it Three Hundred and Forty years. They first obtain'd it by the devices of a wicked Woman, (*b*) *Essat* by Name, Stigmatiz'd for Unchastity, Sacriledge, and Avarice in the highest degree. Her Successors are uncertain, and the Names which *Marianus Victor* produces, together with the several years of their Reigns are very much to be suspected, to omit what *Tellezius* learnedly writes, *That the Queens are never inserted in the Catalogues of those that Reign*. Nevertheless, *Victorius* nominates one *Tredda Gabez*, who Murder'd all the Posterity of the *Salomonean Family*, that he might Establish the Kingdom to his Son. Yet in the midst of the Slaughter, there was one young Lad of the Royal Blood, who making his Escape to the Lords of the Kingdom of *Shewa*, most passionately zealous for the *Salomonean* Line, was there privately preserv'd. The Kings of this Line are very enviously traduc'd by *Tellezius* as unjust, and unworthy to be remember'd; tho it has honour'd *Ethiopia* with many Renowned Monarchs: of whom there is still a happy Memorial both in the *Ethiopic* Li-

(*b*) *The word signifies Fire.*

turgy,

turgy, and among the Encomiums of my Poet; as *Degna Michael* and *Newaja-Christos*, or the *Wealth of Christ*, who never appears in *Victorius*'s Catalogue: However he is thus Praised by the Poet.

Peace to Newaja, *from whose Royal Loins*
Illustrious Princes born for high designs,
Ennobling more their high Descent, his Praise
Advanc'd, and thence their own Renown did raise.
No wonder he dy'd Poor; his Zeal was such
He stript himself, his Temple to enrich.
Himself had built the House of God, and scorn'd
To leave God's House behind him unadorn'd.

But the most famous, and most renowned for his Magnificent Structures was, (c) *Lalibala*, whose future Greatness was portended by a Swarm of Bees, that while he was an Infant newly born, lighted upon his tender Body, without doing him the least prejudice. Of him the Poet thus sings:

To mighty Lalibala *Peace,*
Who stately Structures rear'd,
And to adorn the Pompous piles
For no Expences spar'd.

By vast Expence and hideous pains,
The Rock a Church became:
The Roof, the Floor, the squared Sides
All one continu'd Frame.

No stones in blended Mortar lay'd
The solid parts divide;
Nature has carved all without,
Within the Workman's Pride.

But newly born, and hardly swath'd,
The tender Infant lay,
When strait a Wonder, that portends
The Honour of that day.

(c) *Alvarez* makes mention of him, c. 54. and 55. where he relates the same Story of the Swarm of Bees.

A Swarm of Bees, Prophetic swarm!
His Princely Head surround,
Thus Jove *himself on* Ida *Mount*
The Martial Insect Crown'd.

It was their Errand thus to shew
The grandeur of the Child;
That he should Conquer and Command,
And yet be wondrous mild.

That done, as if by sight the face
Of Majesty they knew,
With such a fear as aw'd their stings,
Away again they flew.

This great Monarch when he came to Rule, sent for Artists out of *Egypt*, and after a wonderful and unheard of manner of Building to that day, he did not cement Stones or Bricks together with Lime, or Lome, nor joyn the Roof together with Rafters, but hollow'd whole solid Rocks, leaving Pillars for Ornament where Pillars were requisite, the Arches and Walls being all of the same Stone. Nor do the Rocks of *Ethiopia* withstand that kind of Structure, for that most of them advance equilaterally toward the Sky, as if they had bin squar'd by Art; and besides, the Stone is so soft and tender, that the Tools of the Artists easily make their way. *Alvarez* gives an accompt of Ten Temples fram'd after this wonderful manner, which were Four and twenty years finishing. He saw them all, and gives you a draught of them in Picture, and lest any one should doubt of the Truth of what he says, he confirms his Relation with an Oath. This Magnificent King reign'd Forty years; and after him his Son *Imra* rul'd as many. The last of this Race was *Naacueto-Laab*. Of him the Poet thus,

Hail Naacueto-Laab, *thy Renown*
I sing, and all the Glories of thy Crown
In Peace and Love, which thou didst love, thy Reign
Concord and Peace did mutually sustain.
And that no fear of Death might him dismay,
God plac'd him where there is no end of Day.

CHAP.

Chap. VI.

Of the Salomonean *Line, restor'd again by* Icon-an-lac.

The Salomonean *Family restor'd. The Successors of* Icon Am lac. Etana-Dengiel *preferred before his Elder Brother.* Helena *a Woman of a great Spirit.* David's *various Fortune.* Claudius *succeeds him; who restores his ruin'd Kingdom by the Assistance of the* Portugueses. *His Encomium and miserable Death. The Succession decided by Arms.* Menas *succeeds; his Cruelty.* Bahrnagassus *revolts.* Malac-Segued *succeeds; better than his Father; Prosperous in War, not in Marriage. He designs his Brother his Successor; but repents, and Prefers his Natural Son* Jacob: *He recommends his lawful Son to the Nobility upon his Death-Bed; but they Imprison him.* Susneus *in the same Danger, but Escapes. They make* Jacob *a Child King; afterwards Depose him, and place* Za-Dengel *in his room; his Mildness and Fortitude; a bold act of his. His Kindness to* Pays, *and the* Latins *cause him to be hated. A Conspiracy against him; he Consults the* Portugueses; *despised the Counsel of* Pays: *He loses the Day, and dies in the Field.*

THE *Zagean* Family being thus Extinct, about the year of Christ 1300. The Nobility of *Shewa* restor'd *Icon-imlac*, a Prince of the *Salomonean* Race to the Scepter of his Ancestors; whose Posterity have continu'd in *Habessinia* to our time. *Tellezius* reckons up Sixteen Kings to *Zar-a-Jacob*, (*d*) which we shall insert out of *Vecchietti*, adding the *Ethiopic* Names of them which we have found mention'd in the Liturgy, or elsewhere. *Icon-amlac*, or as the *Ethiopians* write him,

1. *Ayzana-zaniat.*	7. *Vdimrad.*
2. *Jegera-Tzegan.*	8. *Ande Tzegon.*
3. *Bihar Sarda.*	9. *Scifaarad.*
4. *Esbraad.*	10. *Vdmanssan.*
5. *Cadim-Sagbed.*	11. *David.*
6. *Zera-Sagbed.*	12. *Theodorus.*

Of whom the Poet thus makes mention in his 29 *Encomium*, June 3.

(*d*) *In his Abridgm. of Sacred Times, L. VI. Ult. Success. c. 44.*

Hail Theodore, *wide* Ethiopia's *King*;
Thee, by thy Name Anbasa, *must I sing.*
For thee thy Mother Tzejon-Mogusa
T' adorn thy great Inauguration Day,
Whole Heards of Sheep, and fatted Oxen slew:
And not she only, for the Clouds to show
Themselves contributary to thy Feast,
Rain'd Fish from Heaven, to supply the rest.

13. *Isaac.* 15. *Hezbinaani*, whose Son was,
14. *Andreas.* 16. *Amde-Jesus.*

To him succeeded *Zara-Jacob*, by the Name of his Inauguration, *Constantine*. An Emperor of great Renown, and inquisitive after Foreign Affairs: for he sent his Ambassadors to the Council of *Florence*; of which more in due place.

Bueda-Marjam, as I Collect out of *Alvarez*, came to the Crown, about the year 1465, and dy'd Ten years after, leaving his Widow *Helena* behind him, of whom more anon.

Alexander ascended the Throne about the year 1475, and dy'd in the year 1491. At what time *Peter Covillian* found the way into *Ethiopia*; the first *Portuguese* that did so.

Amda-Tzejon (e) his Son, reign'd but a short time, and dying without Male Issue, made way for his Uncle.

Naod, The Son of *Baeda-Marjam*, who while his Brother *Alexander* possess'd the Government, was shut up in the Rock *Ghesben*; but the Male Issue failing, he was call'd forth by the Nobility, and reign'd Thirteen years. He dy'd about the year 1505.

Etana Dengel, or *Lebna-Denghel*, call'd afterwards David, by his Inauguration Name. Some few years expir'd, he assum'd a third Name, *Wanag-Saghed*, which *Tzagazab* interprets,

(e) *This Succession is taken out of* Tellez, *and agrees with the vulgar Order of the Ethiopic Kings, which* Gregory *himself did not contradict.* Alvarez *here err'd very much, or else forgot himself: for he apparently leaves out* Amda-Tzeon, c. 59. *and makes* Alexander *the Father of* Naod, c. 98. and 89. *when he was really his Brother. He also calls* Helena *the Mother of* David, *when she was his Grandmother; but only look'd upon as his Mother in respect of her care. Neither is* Tellezius *without his Mistakes, for* L. 1. C. 4. *He omits* Amda-Tzion, *and writes that* Helena *never had any Children.*

Eskua-

Eskan-Saged, or the Precious Gem. He was the second Son of *Naod* by his Wife *Mogesa*, the Nephew of *Bada-Maryam*. For the Eldest, whom *Naod* begat in the Rock of *Amhara*, *Helena* and *Marcus*, the Metropolitan, who had then the Government in their hands, did not think worthy to Rule, by reason of his Pride and Cruelty; adding, That he was born when his Father was but in a private Capacity before he came to the Crown: unless it were, that they thought that they should carry a greater sway during the Minority of the young Prince. For then was *David* but Eleven years of Age; as he himself declares in his Letter to King *Emanuel*.

Helena therefore his Grandmother, took upon her the Management of Affairs, as his Tut'ress, being preferr'd before the Mother; in regard the Junior Queens always give place to the Senior, and then too she is always look'd upon as the King's Mother. A Woman of great Prudence and Courage, that has left a great Fame behind her still in *Ethiopia*; insomuch, that King *Susneus* would often praise her for her Virtue and Moderation. She is famous among the *Europeans* for her Letters sent to *Emanuel* the First, King of *Portugal*, of which we shall hereafter speak more at large. *David* at the beginning of his Reign very prosperous in his Undertakings (for he had won several Victories from the *Adelans*) after his Grandmothers Decease, as if he had now the Curb in his teeth, giving himself up to Luxury, and the love of Women, was very Unfortunate toward the end of his days. For being driven out of all his Kingdoms and Territories, he was forc'd to betake himself with some few Soldiers to the Rock *Damo*, where he dy'd in the Forty sixth year of his Age. In this the more unhappy, that during his Reign, the Nation of the *Gallans*, the Scourge of *Habessinia* made their first Incursions out of *Bali*. He had four Sons; of whom, the first *Victor*, dy'd before the Father; of the other three we shall have occasion to speak in due place. He was very well vers'd in Holy Writ, and in the three first Councils, as may be understood by his Discourses with *Alvarez*.

Claudius, by his other Name call'd *Asnaff Saghed*, the Son of *David*, came to a Kingdom miserably shatter'd, and overburthen'd with Calamity; and lurking in the utmost Confines of his Dominions, there attended some miraculous assi-

stance

stance from Heaven; which soon after answer'd his Expectation; *John* the Second, King of *Portugal* sending him Succour, under the Conduct of that most Valiant and Noble Portuguese *Christopher Gama*, who with a small Band of Four hundred *Portuguese* Foot Soldiers, overthrew vast Armies of the *Barbarians*, and laid the Foundations of regaining the *Habessinian* Empire. *Claudius* was a man of a most Princely Port. For besides the outward Grace of his Person, he was endu'd with many Virtues of the Mind, which made him judg'd by all worthy of the Royal Dignity. The Fathers of the Society applauded him for a most Prudent Prince, though otherwise not so well pleased with him, because he had not shew'd that Affection to the *Roman* See, as they requir'd; though he did not prohibit the Divine Worship of the *Latin* Church; nor hinder'd the *Roman* Priests from the free Exercise of their Religion. He was also Learned, and well instructed in Ecclesiastical Antiquity. So that, as *Tellezius* witnesses, his Teachers seem'd illiterate in comparison of their Scholar. For in Disputes with the Fathers of the Society, he himself for the most part would argue, with so much vehemence, that sometimes he put them hard to it to make him an Answer. And when he observ'd that the *Habessines* were blam'd for retaining certain *Judaic* Rights contrary to the Christian Laws, he put into Writing a succinct Confession of Faith, by which he clear'd all Objections, and excus'd himself and his Subjects. That Confession we formerly (*f*) set forth, and shall publish again in our Commentary: So that the Fathers of the Society could object nothing but Schism against so great and famous a Monarch. He reign'd Eighteen years and some Months, with great toil and trouble, by reason of his continual Wars with the *Adelans*, who mindful of the overthrows they had receiv'd, frequently attempted Revenge. The King stout of hand and indefatigable, never refus'd Battel, till at last in the Month of *March*, 1559. fighting against *Nurus*, the Captain of the *Adelans*, his Army being vanquish'd, guarded only with Eighteen *Portuguezes*, and Combating more furiously than warily, he fell by an Immature but not unrevenged Death. He left no Children behind him, whence it came to pass,

(*f*) In England, Anno 1661. It is also added to our Ethiopic *Lexicon and Grammar*.

that the Right of Succession being very ambiguous in *Ethiopia*, the Contention was long dubious between his Brother *Menas*, and *Tasfar*, the Natural Son of *Jacob*, the second Brother deceased. For this claim'd the Kingdom in right of his Father, while he liv'd, the Elder Brother, the other alledg'd himself to be the nearest in Blood, than he who was Illegitimate. The Controversie being decided by the Sword, *Tasfar* was taken in the Battel, and thrown headlong down a Rock.

Menas, otherwise (g) *Adamas-Saghed*, having obtain'd the Kingdom by Arms, being of a Cruel Disposition, degenerated altogether from the Lenity, Sincerity, and Piety of the *Habessines*; as if he had learnt the savageness of the *Turks* and *Arabians*, among whom he had been long a Captive. For he hated the *Portugueses*, as minding their own Affairs; and forbid the use of the *Roman* Religion, not suffering any of the *Habessines* to go into the *Latin* Churches. He also revok'd the Liberty which his Predecessor *Claudius* had granted to the Wives and Families of the *Portugueses* to frequent the *Roman* Chappels; which caus'd many to wish again for the Clemency of *Claudius*, with which they were not contented however before. He despis'd the Romish Bishop *Andrew Oviedo*, who in the Reign of *Claudius*, was sent to make way for the new Patriarch; and for some Months kept him in Prison. Nor was he much more kind to his own Subjects. For which reason, out of an aversion to his Proceedings, they revolted from him in several Parts. Among the rest, *Isaac Bahrnagassus*, a man in great Power, and skill'd in Military Discipline, calling the *Turks* to his Assistance upon the Twentieth of *April*, 1562. overcame the King in Battel, and slew him: to the great detriment of *Habessinia*. For ever since that time, the *Turks* have been Masters of the Coast of the Red Sea. He left three Sons, *Sarza-Denghel*, *Lesanax*, and *Tazcar*. Of which the last dy'd without Children.

Sarza-Denghel, taking the Government upon him, call'd himself *Malac-Saghed*, and was Inaugurated after the ancient manner at *Axuma*. His Fortune was equal to his Vertues; for he was stout of Hand, and wise in Counsel. And first he drave the *Turks*, who were Masters of *Dobarwa*, the Me-

---

(g) *Erroneous here, some Historians ignorant that the word signifies a Gem, read here Adam.*

tropolis of the Maritime Province, out of *Tigra*. He would also have driven them out of the Port of *Arkiko*, and the Isle of *Mazua*, had he not been recall'd to defend his Upland Dominions from the Incursions of the *Gallans*. These People by the Rapines and Plunder of five and twenty years, while the *Habessines* were busied in so many other Wars increased to that power, that now they over ran *Habessinia* not with scattering Troops, but with compleat Armies. So that all the time of his Reign, though otherwise prosperous in War, he was forc'd to struggle with them. However he subdu'd *Enarea*, and caus'd the Prince thereof to turn Christian. For he carefully observ'd the Christian Religion, according to the Constitutions of the Church of *Alexandria*. The *Latin* Rites he left indifferent. And for the Fathers of the Society; he often commended their Conversation of Life, and their Studies, but despised their Doctrine, saying, That their Manners, and not their Doctrine was to be imitated. Certainly Manners and Doctrine do not always accord. And therefore, *sometimes the Doctrine is to be approv'd, where the Manners are not Correspondent; and sometimes the Manners are to be imitated, where the Doctrine is not to be follow'd.* But tho he were Prosperous in his Affairs of Government and War; yet in his Marriage he was unfortunate; for his Wife *Mariamsena* brought him many Daughters, but not one Son. He had two Natural Sons, of which one was call'd *Za-Mariam*, and the other *Jacob*; but they could not succeed by the Laws of the (*b*) Kingdom. And therefore it fell out with him as with many others, who are more addicted to illicit Concubinage, than lawful Matrimony, that they want Successors from their own Loins; and frequently expose their Kingdoms to War and Bloodshed upon Disputes of Succession. First, therefore he shew'd to the Nobility *Za-Denghel*, his Brother Lecanax's Son, as the Son of a Prince adorn'd in Royal Habit. Then again, some few Months before his Death, he began to change his mind, either envying a greater Adoration to the Rising than the Setting Sun; or whether it were that *Za-Denghel* himself, certain of the Succession gave the less re-

(*b*) Tellezius tells us, l. 2. c. 14. *that the Ethiopian Laws will not allow Bastards to succeed. Which nevertheless is not agreeable with what he says in another place,* l. 3. c. 29.

spect

spect to his Uncle, or whether his Disposition were not grateful to the Nobility. However it were, *Jacob*, a Child of Seven years of Age, never seen before to the King, came to Court; which was no obscure intimation, that he would be preferr'd before *Za-Denghel*, as being of the King's own Blood. The Grandees, whether they durst not admonish the King; or whether they had an intention to usurp the Government, under pretence of being Guardians to the Minor, consented to the King: But soon after they taught us to understand how uncertain the Tranquillity of Kingdoms is, where the Right of Succession is uncertain, or that there are no Rules; but that the grand Affairs of a Kingdom are at the disposal of Courtiers, intent upon their own Interest. Nevertheless, most wonderful to relate, when the King upon his return from the War with the *Gallans*, fell sick, and found himself near his end, Right and Justice more prevail'd with him, than Hatred against his Brother's Son, or love to his own Illegitimate, and therefore calling before him the chief of his Nobility, he is reported to have spoken thus:

Seeing that the end of my life Approaches, I thought that next the Care of my Soul, that of my Kingdom was the chiefest, the safety of which I have always held no less dear to me, than the Salvation of my own Soul. True it is, that having none Legitimate, I always lov'd Jacob *as my own. And I have observ'd in him Endowments of Mind not unworthy so fair an Inheritance; so that I could not have had any reason to repent, had I Establish'd him my Successor, nor you, had you yielded him Obedience. But now I prefer the Love of my Country, and the Laws of the Kingdom before my private Affection. Therefore it is, that I recommend to your Allegiance* Za-Denghel *my Brother's Son, my nearest Kinsman, stout in War, Mature in years, conspicuous for his virtues, and one that by those virtues Merits the high Dignity which is due to him by Birth.* Having thus said, in a short while after he expir'd. An. 1596.

But as it was a thing absolutely unexpected by the Nobility, that the King would change his Mind; so the Management of Affairs among themselves during the Minority of the King, was that which they had already deeply fix'd in their minds; nay more, they had under-hand already divided the great Offices of the Kingdom. And therefore repining to find the Power thus as it were ravish'd out of their hands, they perfidiously enter into a Conspiracy. To which purpose they conceal the Death of the King, and sending away some few Bands of Soldiers drawn together in hast, they cause *Za-Denghel* to be apprehended, and carry'd away into the Island of *Wdeks*, lying in the *Tzanic Lake*; and then changing his Imprisonment from Rock to Rock, carry'd him up and down to prevent his Conspiring with the Neighbouring People. The same Trap was lay'd for *Susneus*; for that they fear'd least he being youthful, and brave, seeing the Order of the Succession so disturb'd, should put in for a share and assert his Claim; as afterwards he did. But he escap'd in good time to the *Gallans*, where he fix'd himself among them against the threatning Danger, resolving if need requir'd to make use of their Assistance. The Chiefs of the Faction were *Ras-Athanateus*, a man of high Authority, and *Kesflawahed*, Viceroy of *Tigra*, who having cajol'd into the Conspiracy, the Queen Dowager his Mother-in-Law, covetous of preserving her Power, by means of her Son's nonage, as it were under colour of lawful Power, they presently set the Crown upon the head of *Jacob*, then a Child of Seven years of Age, and therefore call'd the Infant King; reserving the management of Affairs to themselves. A *triumvirate* unusual with a Woman, and therefore not like to endure long. For, seven years after *Jacob* coming to be of Age, impatient of so many Tutors, assum'd the Reins of Government into his own hands, perhaps more imperiously than might become a Lad of 15 years of Age. The Guardians therefore taking it ill to be so soon depriv'd of their Power, seeing their Obedience would immediately follow, chose rather to obey their lawful King, and render themselves deserving of his new Favours. Therefore before *Jacob* could fix himself in his Throne, as it were induc'd out of Repentance, that they had preferr'd an Infant and Illegitimate before a lawful Successor and of ripe Age, they recall *Za-Denghel* then lurking in the most remote Mountains of the Kingdom, and salute him King by the Name of *Atnaff-Saghed*; which they did the sooner, and that with the more speed, that they might have the less reason to give an Accompt of what was done, to the new King.

Jacob with only Eight of his Guard, for the rest had deserted him with his Fortune, hastens to *Samena* to his Mothers Kindred; but being known in his flight and taken, he was brought back to *Za-Denghel*, who shewing the Effects of a strange Compassion, receiv'd his Rival with a singular Affe-

ction

ction and Clemency, and trusting to his own Right, would never incur the censure of being Cruel in cutting off his Nose and Eyes, which was usually done to others in the same Condition, and to which he himself was advis'd. For he scorn'd to pollute himself with a Crime after the manner of Tyrants, who distrustful of their own Right, or the Peoples Affections, count it a piece of Policy to cut off their Rivals in Empire, how innocent soever, imputing to them before-hand the future Crimes that may happen to be committed not by them, but any Promoters of Sedition: However he sent the degraded King into *Enarea*, the most remote Kingdom of *Habessinia*, under a strict Guard, in a short time to be restored to the Kingdom to his own Ruin.

Za-Denghel, for Grace of Utterance and Majesty of Countenance was equally Venerable (as are most of the Princes of the Royal Blood of *Habessinia*) in the most flourishing years of pleasing Youth; and through his Experience of Adversity and Prosperity worthy of the high degree, to which he had arriv'd; and which was more than all, mild and ready to Forgive. For among all the crow'd of so many Enemies, he never punish'd any, as by Law he might have done: but without any disgrace, suffer'd them to continue in their several Offices, and in the same degrees of Honour even the Queen her self: so mild and gentle even to a fault is the Disposition of those Kings, saith *Tellezius*. Moreover he behav'd himself with an undaunted Courage in all sorts of Danger: For he had hardly grasp'd the Helm of Government in his hands, when the *Gallans* understanding the Divisions at Court fell into *Habessinia* with three Armies, and overthrew the Governor of *Gojam*, who presum'd to fight against the King's Command, whereupon the King arriving soon after, leading an Army tir'd by a long March, with a greater Courage than Force, he assail'd the Enemy, who puft up with Victory, bore down the *Habessines* with so much Violence, that the Captains finding their Battalions recoil, perswaded the King to betake himself to an early flight. When he, disdaining the motion, as arguing Effeminacy, leapt from his Horse, and advancing with his Sword and Buckler, cry'd out, *Here will I die; you if you please, may flye; perhaps you may escape the fury of the* Gallans, *but never the Infamy of deserting your King.*

The

The *Habessines* mov'd with such a Speech, and the Countenance of their Prince, cast themselves into a Globe, and with a Prodigious fury, like Men prepar'd to dye, broke in among the *Gallans*, and constrain'd them to give back; which the Fugitives perceiving presently return'd, and renewing the Fight, gain'd a glorious Victory with such a Slaughter of the Enemy, that a greater had not been made among them at any other time. The King believing that the Advantages of such a Victory were not to be let slip, did not indulge himself to be as soon overcome with Banquets and Luxury, under pretence of Refreshment, but with a swift March, led his Army over Mountains and Rocks, against the other Body of the Enemy, which with the same success he put to Flight; The third Army, not daring to withstand the force of the *Habessines*, retreated into the Fastnesses of their Country. Of these, Four hundred thought themselves secure with their Prey, in a steep, and almost inaccessible Mountain. But the *Habessines* now contemning their Enemies, already terrify'd with the Slaughter of their own People, couragiously drave them from their Holds, and slew them every Mothers Son.

About the same time *Peter Pays* a Jesuit, arriving in *Habessinia*, at the Request of the King went to Court, and so oblig'd him with several Discourses concerning Matters as well Ecclesiastical as Civil, that at first privately, then publickly he embrac'd the *Latin* Religion, which he testify'd by Letters as well to the Pope, as to the King of *Spain*, then *Philip* the Third; and preferr'd the *Portugueses* before his own *Habessinians*. But this same Kindness of his to Strangers, and a Foreign Religion, begat him the Hatred of his People, and caus'd his own Destruction. For the Nobility of the Kingdom took it in great disdain to see their Ancient Religion chang'd, and that the Patriarch of *Alexandria* should be deserted: And they were the more enflam'd out of their Envy to the *Portugals*, and the Rancour which they bore to *Laeca-Marjam*, the King's principal Friend. Therefore they Conspire against him among themselves. The Head of the Faction was one *Saslac*, born of mean Parentage, but of great fame for his Experience in War, and for that reason proud. He was exil'd by *Jacob*, but recall'd by *Za-Dengbel*, and made Governor of *Dembea*; consequently ungrateful, and out of an inbred Stubborness, frowardly disdaining Obedience. *Ras-*

Athanatius

Athanasius was drawn into this Society, a famous Captain, and a Man of great Conduct; and being first in Dignity, frown'd to see that he was but Second in the King's favour; and therefore he proves a Traitor to a most excellent King, as one that had forgot who set the Crown upon his Head. But the Cause of Religion was the main pretence; the most prevalent to put the Minds of People into disorder: for they were not ignorant what Preparations were making at Court for the introducing of the *Latin* Religion. Frequent Complaints were therefore divulg'd abroad, *That the King was Revolted from the Church of* Alexandria, *the Common Mother Church; and that there was nothing intended by his frequent Discourses and familiarity with the Jesuits, but the Abrogation of the Institutions of their Ancestors, and the Introduction of new Ceremonies and Foreign Priests into the Kingdom. That the* Portugals *would come in and establish their Religion by force of Arms; and when they had done that, would endeavour also to take the Kingdom from them. That it behov'd them to succour their Distressed Country, and that such a King was not to be endur'd, who had first deserted the True Worship of God.* These things were easily inculcated into those that were of the same mind before. But there was nothing which alienated so much the minds of the People, as that the *Portuguezes* had been heard to say, *That the Reduction,* so they call'd the *Conversion* of Ethiopia, *was but vainly attempted, if it could not be upheld by force of Arms.* The King, having detected the Conspiracy, calls the *Portuguezes* together, confiding in them, as Foreigners and Men of the *Latin* Religion; then marching with all speed toward *Gojam*, he was deserted by the way, first by *Ras Athanasius*, whom tho he suspected, he durst not apprehend; then by *Jonael*, one of his Principal Captains. Their example many others following, forsake the King. The King seeing himself left with a slender Guard, applying himself to *Peter Pays*, spoke these words, *This therefore befalls me, because I am desirous to shew them the way of Truth, and to set free the Weak from the Oppression of the more Powerful.* Thereupon *Peter*, and the Commander of the *Portuguezes*, *John Gabriel*, advis'd him to *Protract the War, till the heat of the Rebels fury waxed cool; that his Friends with his Innocent Subjects would repair to his Assistance; that the rest would in time come to themselves, and repent their folly:* That *Sedition was like a Torrent, violent at first, but that it abated by degrees.*

But

But the King impatient of delay, look'd upon Protraction as a Diminution of his Honour; and being too full of Courage, and in his boyling Youth, resolv'd to try the Fortune of War, that rarely accompanies rashness, before the Rebels should encrease their Numbers. So he Marches with a small Army of scarce Twelve thousand Men, thinking to fall upon them e're they were aware of his coming. This over-hastiness had but ill success. For most of his Adversaries were Men experienc'd in War, who did not follow their business negligently; and besides they were as eager to come to a Field decision, before the King should gather Strength.

In the mean time the Enemies of the new Religion Rendevouz'd together from all Parts; and among the rest *Abuna Peter*, the *Alexandrian* Metropolitan, and chief Head of the Rebellion; who by an unheard of President in *Ethiopia*, contrary to the Laws of God and Man, absolv'd the Rebels from the tye of their Oaths which they had Sworn to their lawful Prince, which they themselves had already broke, by virtue of a detestable Excommunication of his Prince. Thus more and more embold'nd, and contemning the Majesty of the King, they turn'd their Veneration into Hatred. And so with mutual Animosity they joyn Battel. The *Portugueses*, who fought in the right wing, maintain'd their ground a long time, believing the Kings and the Cause of Religion to be their own. But in the left Wing, of which the King himself took charge, all things went to rack; for many fled over to the Enemy, many look'd on without striking a stroke, resolv'd to follow the Fortune of the Day. Thus the King forsaken by his own, fought bravely for a long time, till *Laeca-Marjam*, and the rest of his Guard being slain, he was himself struck down from his Horse with the fling of a Lance. After that getting up again to renew the Fight, he was stuck through the body, and slain with several Darts thrown at a distance; reverence of his person not permitting them to come near to hurt him. The third day after the Fight, he was taken up and buried without any Funeral Pomp in a little Chappel hard by the Field of the Battel. Such was the end of the short Life and Reign of this Famous and Lawful King of *Ethiopia*. A doleful Warning to admonish us, that the Cause of Religion ought to be moderately and prudently handled. And that it behoves a Prince

not

not to thrust himself rashly into a Battel, especially when there is no certain Successor. For proof whereof, the fatal Example of *Sebastian* King of *Portugal* may serve among the rest.

CHAP. VII.

Of the Kings of this Centurie, To our Times.

Susneus *aspires to the Crown; acknowledg'd by* Ras-Athanasius. *He requests the same from* Zaslac. *Who refuses at first; then submits. But* Jacob *appearing, he takes his part: So does* Ras-Athanasius. Jacob *again made King. He desires an agreement with* Susneus, *but in vain. They take Arms.* Zaslac *beaten; he goes over to* Susneus. *A new War.* Jacob *and* Abuna *slain. The Victor's Clemency.* Zaslac *imprison'd; he escapes; invades* Walaka *and* Gojam. *Kill'd by the Pagans.* Ras Athanasius *dies.* Susneus *kind to the* Portugals *and Jesuits. He submits to the Pope. A Counterfeit* Jacob; *but dares not stand the coming of* Susneus. *An Impostor of the same kind comes into* France. *His Conditions; his Epitaph.* Melca *boasts himself the Son of* Arzo. Susneus's *Nativity, Conditions, Vertues, Vices, and Death. His Son* Basilides *drives the Jesuits out of* Ethiopia. *He kills his Brothers. A General Table of the last Kings of* Habessinia.

King *Zadenghel* being thus slain, the War indeed ceas'd; yet Peace did not presently ensue. For the Rebels not dreaming of such a speedy Victory, had not consider'd of a Successor. Wherefore, as it were stupid with Emulation, *Ras-Athanasius* departs for *Gojam*, and *Zaslac* for *Dembea*, without ever holding any common Consultation. Thereupon *Susneus*, hearing of the King's death, and believing that the Kingdom was now fallen to Him, as being the Son of *Basilides*, the Nephew of *Jacob*, and Grandchild of *David*; and then being also a Young man, train'd up in the *Gallan* Wars, belov'd and surrounded with the choicest of the Military Bands, he conceiv'd no small hopes of his design. First therefore he sends before one of the Faithfullest of his Friends to *Ras-Athanasius*, with instructions to declare to him in short, *That whereas the Kingdom belong'd to him by right of Inheritance, he should come presently and joyn Forces with his.* In the mean time, *Susneus*, not expecting an Answer, follows the Messenger with the nimblest of his Army, and writes to *Athanasius* as if

 already

already made King. That *he was at hand, and that therefore he should come to meet him and pay him the accustom'd honours due to him.* *Athanasius* amaz'd at the unexpected approach of *Susneus*, void of Counsel, the Danger being Equal on both sides, either to refuse or admit him, at length, finding all assistance far distant, and no hopes of delay, to give him time to consult with *Zaslac*, he rather chose to be before-hand with the new King's Favours, than to hazard the uncertain Fortune of a Battel. So that *Susneus*, being honourably receiv'd into the Camp, was saluted *King*. Which done, he presently writes to *Zaslac*, *That by the Providence of God he had recovered the Throne of his Ancestors; and was now marching for* Dembea: *therefore he should take Care that there might be Forces there ready to receive him, and those deserved Favours which he was ready to bestow upon them.* But he, tho astonish'd at the suddain News, was unwilling to acknowledg him for King, whom he had not made himself; and therefore consulting with his friends, return'd for answer, *That he would then obey him, if* Jacob, *to whom he had already by Message offer'd the Kingdom, did not come before* June; *and therefore begg'd that short delay.* *Susneus*, no way pleas'd with the Condition, wrote back to him again, *That he was King already, and therefore would give place neither to* Jacob, *once before adjudg'd unworthy, nor to his Father* Malec-Saghed, *though he should return from the other World.* *Zaslac*, having receiv'd this surly Answer, equally mettlesom and diligent, turns his Arms upon him, and comes on briskly to meet him. *Susneus* finding himself prevented with the speedy March of his Adversary, and perceiving himself over-match'd, and, which was worse, not well in health, retir'd to the Craggy Mountains of *Amhara*. *Ras-Athanasius* also, whose precipitancy *Zaslac* had upbraided, retreated into other Fastnesses to avoid the Fury of his Associate. In the mean time there being no News of *Jacob*, the other Captains and Commanders of the Army began to scatter words of discontent, *That they would not be without a King, that if* Jacob *would not come, there was no Person fitter than* Susneus, *neither would he be at rest, till he had obtain'd by force, what they would not give him by fair means.* *Zaslac*, fearing the Inconstancy of his own People, and consequently a Revolt, orders Commissioners to be sent; and by them surrenders the Scepter to *Susneus*, who presently sent a Person to whom Allegiance should be sworn in his Name. Which being done, Ten of the chiefest Peers ride forth to

meet

meet the new King, and to conduct him with a Pomp befitting into the Camp. And now Shouts and Acclamations are to be every where heard. Neither were Banquets wanting, with all other Solemnities usual at the Inaugurations of their Kings; when on a sudden new Commissioners from *Jacob*, quite disturb'd their mirth, with such a suddain alteration, as with which Fortune never more odly mock'd before the hopes of those that thought themselves in the possession of a Throne. For *Jacob* twice Depos'd, twice restor'd, between the Highest and the Lowest, (which is most rare) had twice Experience of the Mean betwixt both. While the Promoters of these Troubles exercis'd their Hatred and their Love without fear of punishment, that one might think it the sport of Scenes, rather than a serious possession of Royalty. For immediatly *Zaslac*, without any hesitation, rode forth to meet *Jacob*, as if he had bin *Susneus* himself, to whom he had but just before sworn Fidelity, and receiv'd him with the usual Honours due to *Ethiopic* Majesty, and with his whole Army saluted him King, the Commissioners, sent to *Susneus*, being privately recall'd. *Susneus*, knowing Time was to be watch'd, once more gave way to Fortune, and retir'd to his former lurking holes, and hid himself again in the Natural Fortresses of *Amhara*. For he had learnt from the Example of *Zadenghel*, to give way to Popular Heats and Tumults, till they cool'd of themselves: for that the People after their first Passions are spent, resume their former Modesty, and return repenting to their duty. *Ras Athanasius* also, tho so great a Person, yet accustom'd to follow Fortune, rather than his Faith, he, I say, with the same Easiness that he had acknowledg'd *Susneus*, fell at the feet of *Jacob*.

And now *Jacob*, did not think it prudent to suffer a Rival in his Dignity, and therefore resolving to try what might be done by way of agreement, he commanded *Susneus*'s Mother to go to her Son, and offer him the Kingdoms of *Amhara*, *Walaka*, and *Shewa*, as also all the Lands which his Father possess'd, and he had hitherto claim'd in vain. But *Susneus* bearing a lofty Soul, deny'd, *That what he had receiv'd by the Gift of God, could be taken from him by Men. That the whole Kingdom was his due, which he would not relinquish but with his Life; That* Jacob *would deal with more Justice and Uprightness, to quit his Diadem, than to hasten Ruin to himself and his Country.*

 This

This haughty answer being deliver'd, *Jacob* desired to decide the business not with Messages, but by the Sword. However, *Susneus* Expert at delays, by the assistance of the Rocks and Mountains, avoyded the pursuit of *Jacob*, watching for those Opportunities which soon after presented themselves. For *Zaslac*, whether out of a vain-glory to behold the Event of the Battel, or out of any private Indignation, did not joyn his Forces with *Jacob*; but on the contrary, and as it were in despight of Military discipline, acted all things carelesly and remisly; believing his fame a Terror sufficient to the Enemy. This was not conceal'd from *Susneus*, who taking a shorter way came upon *Zaslac* so of a suddain, that his Souldiers had not time to handle their Arms, much less to put themselves into order: so that they were slain like sheep, and utterly routed, and *Zaslac*, having lost his Army, was forc'd to entrust his Safety to an ignominious flight. Which Victory as it dejected *Jacob*'s Friends, so it rais'd the spirits of *Susneus*'s Party. *Zaslac* himself had lost the Kings favour, and began to be suspected. Thus the business began to work; for *Zaslac* jealous of these disparagements, notwithstanding *Jacob* had heap'd so many favours upon him, for he had created him *Legate Royal*, began to Enter into a Correspondence with *Susneus*, using Treachery as the hire of those that valu'd him most. *Susneus* standing in need of his Power, accepted his Propositions, and dissembling his Hatred, made him a Confederate in the War, to lessen the force of his Enemy. *Jacob* hearing of his Revolt, judging that it behov'd him to make hast, before the rest should follow his Example, resolv'd to put it to the hazard of a Battel; well knowing that he far exceeded *Susneus* in number of men: nor did *Susneus* refuse him, tho inferior; however, he cunningly kept the rough and hilly Grounds, watching like a Lyon when to take his fatal jump.

The Enemy judging his delay to proceed from his fear, and confiding in their multitude, began to act more daringly, and to provoke *Susneus* with upbraiding Language, until he had brought them into a narrow place where he could not be surrounded by his Enemies. Then Exhorting his Souldiers, *Now*, said he, *the day is come, that You may make me King of* Ethiopia: *and for Your selves, You are to be either Masters or Slaves, as You behave Your selves. I will not be onely the Companion of Your*

Victory,

Victory, but your Dangers: Victory is in your own power, so that you do not turn your backs to your Enemies, before you see me begin to flye.

Having thus Encourag'd his Souldiers, he gave the Signal of Battel. Which seen, they gave so furious an Onset, that the Enemy was every where beaten down, without resistance, amaz'd and astonish'd, to be so subdu'd by those whom they reck'ned for fugitives. The slaughter was great, with little loss on *Susneus*'s side. *Jacob* himself, together with *Abuna Peter*, who had in vain thunder'd out his Anathema's against the Enemy, were both slain. Which *Susneus* understanding, sounded a retreat, that by his clemency to the Common Soldiery and his own Country-men, he might win to himself the Reputation of Gentleness, necessary for the Establishment of a New Prince.

But such was the Terror that possess'd the hearts of the *Jacobeans*, forc'd on by the croud of Fugitives, ignorant of the Country, tho there was no pursuit, that they threw themselves headlong in the night time from a Rock dismally steep and cragged. Among the rest, there was a certain Portuguese, by name *Emanuel Consalvo*, who betimes perceiving his Horse as it were flying in the Air, quitting his Stirrups, left him, and taking hold by chance of the branch of a Tree, made a shift to recover a Seat in the bough, where he sate all night. Nor did he well understand his danger, till day appearing, he discovered, not without horror, at a prodigious distance underneath him, a vast heap of Men and Horses with their Limbs and Members broken all to shitters.

Susneus having obtain'd so great a Victory, exercis'd no so sort of Severity or Reveng against any Person; only *Mahorbin* he commanded to be beheaded, as being a follower of the sect of *Islamism*, and the Person that had first wounded *Zadenghel*.

After that he departed for *Coga*, there to, settle the Affairs of his Kingdom, where *Zaslac* whom he could not endure to see, was still in his Eye, the grand promoter of all these troubles. He was the first that went over to *Susneus*'s Party, and therefore was look't upon by *Susneus* as one that would be constantly casting in his Dish the kindnesses he had done, and pride himself to be the setter up of kings. And indeed in one of his vain-glorious humors, of which

which deserving Soldiers are generally too much guilty, he had unwarily given out, That it was foretold him, *That he should pull down three Kings, which was fulfill'd in Two.* So that the New King seem'd only to be wanting for the third. It being therefore a Maxim, *That jealousie and friendship cannot long remain in one and the same Brest, and that the fruit of Treason being reap'd, there is no further need of the Traytor*, the King commanded him to be apprehended and carried away into the steep Mountain of *Guexan*, in the Kingdom of *Gojam*. He would not put him to death, as not believing it became a noble Prince to take away a mans life for fear of a future crime. But he making his Escape, about a year after, invaded *Waleka*, where having gather'd together some Troops of Vagabonds and dissolute Persons, he supported himself by Robbery and Rapine; till at last, making his Incursions into *Gojam*, he was there slain by the *Pagans*. His head being brought to the King, was fix'd upon a Lance, and set up before the Royal Pavillion, to be view'd by all the World; no man pitying his misfortune, in regard that all people knew his advancement had cost the loss of so many innocent lives.

Not so inglorious was the end of *Ras-Athanateus*, and yet sufficiently miserable. For he every day losing more and more of the Kings favour, was at length the contempt of all men; Insomuch that his wife, the daughter of *Malec-Saghed*, unaccustom'd to brook indignities, forsook his bed. Thus once the next to Supream authority, now the next to most dejected misery, not able to overcome the anguish of his mind, he fell into a Fever, of which he dy'd.

But *Susneus*, to establish himself in his Dominion by all ways, courted the friendship of the *Portuguezes*, as being skilful in the art of Gunnery and Fire-arms, the chiefest terror of those Nations: hoping, & that not without reason, by their assistance, to defend himself as well against his own Subjects, too much addicted to Tumults and Seditions, as the Kindred and Friends of the slain Kings. And not only so, but to render himself formidable to the *Gallans*. To that purpose he kindly receiv'd the *Fathers of the Society* then living in *Dembea*. He sent for *Peter Pays*, and most courteously gave ear to him; and treated him as his familiar Friend.

And

And as he was favourable and bountiful to them; so did he dayly afford many testimonies of his kindness to the rest of the *Portugueses*, and the more to oblige them he set up the Latin Religion; nothing terrify'd by the example of *Zadenghel*. And indeed the Fathers had such a power over him, that at length he surrender'd himself to the Pope, and together with his Son, sware obedience to him as Universal Bishop, and Vicar of Christ, abrogating the Religion of *Alexandria*. Which was afterwards the occasion of horrid uproars, bloody wars, and the slaughter of many great Personages.

But the possession of a Kingdom won by the Sword, seldom enjoys a perfect tranquility, especially when the death of the Predecessor comes be in question. For presently, that is to say, the very next year, up starts a counterfeit *Jacob*, who alarum'd all *Habessinia* with the fear of a new War. Some there were, that acknowledg'd they both knew and saw the dead body of King *Jacob*, after the blood was wip'd away, but no man durst assert himself to be the Person that kill'd him. The Counterfeit therefore addresses himself to the Monks of the famous Monastery of *Bizan*, in the prefecture of *Bahrnegassus*; where he remain'd, and to hide the fraud, as if his face had bin disfigur'd with his wounds, went always vail'd. Nor was it long before his Story was believ'd. Not so much out of respect to his own Person, as out of malice to *Susneus*, whom they hated as a Person that was unknown to them, and by his exilement inur'd to the Savage Customs of the *Gallans*. Neither were they pleas'd with *Ras-Seelach*, his brother by the Mother's side, whom he had made Viceroy of *Tigra*, whom they look'd upon also as a forraigner. So that he not being able himself to quell the Disturbances, the King was forc'd to advance himself. But the Rebels having intelligence of his coming, fled several ways, to avoyd fighting. Their Captain, with only four of his Associates, and some few Goats, which he carry'd with him for their milks sake, secur'd themselves by a painful Pilgrimage through the most wild and uncouth concealments of Nature, that the Rocks could afford him, where it was impossible to trace him. So that the King dispairing, after a tedious search, to find him out, return'd to *Dembea*, and having solemniz'd his inauguration at *Axuma*, after the anci-

ent

ent Custom of the Country, he made *Ausalax* Governor of *Tigre*, in the room of his Brother, who afterwards by the help of two Noblemen that counterfeited themselves their friends, having apprehended the Rebels, put them to death.

But what was more strange, our *Europe* it self could not, some time after, discern an *Æthiopian* Counterfeit of the same name.

For in the Year 1632. a certain Impudent Counterfeit, by the names of (*i*) *Tzagax*, assuming to himself to be the Son of *Jacob*, came into *France*, and producing several Recommendatory Letters, and Certificates from the Credulous Monks of *Palestine*, was taken for a Great Prince, and expell'd Heir to the Kingdom of *Ethiopia*, and Entertain'd with a large Pension from the King: after the Example of some of the Princes of *Italy*, which is, to consider what may be Correspondent with their Munificence toward an Exile of so great Dignity, rather then to enquire who he really is. Which was to be admir'd: For that both at *Rome* and in *Portugal* there were at that time extant several annual Relations, by which it was apparent that *Jacob* was slain in Battel, Young, and never marry'd, above Twenty years before. But that which added to the Credit of the Impostor, was his graceful Presence, with a Countenance wherein Seriousness and Frankness were wonderfully intermix'd, that while he kept company with other Princes, (as *Bochart* himself told me) he seem'd to excel them all both for beauty of form, and sweetness of disposition; and particularly that his Majestick Aspect strook all his beholders with admiration. Whether that Beauty were really in his Person, or whether the Novelty of the thing, or the Opinion that he was of the Race of *Salomon*, byass'd their Judgments. Tho otherwise, no reason could be given why he acted the part of the Son of an *Ethiopian* King, unless it were to contend with (*k*) *Hercules* or (*l*) *Messalina* for the prize of most enormous Lust: And indeed it may be thought,

(*i*) For so the *Ethiopic* word *Tzaga Christos* is pronounced. There is a Relation of this Person extant, Entitl'd, The Strange Accidents of the Travels of His Highness Prince *Zaga-Christ* of *Ethiopia*, &c. very abfurd, and full of Fables.

(*k*) Relating to the Daughters of *Thespius*.

(*l*) See *Suetonius in Claud. Juvenal. Sat.* 6. *Tacit. Annal. l.* XI. *Plin. X.* 23.

that

that fearing his Impusture should be discover'd, he rather chose to bring himself to his end by the pleasing debauches of Luxury, than to fall under the Hangman.

Being dead, he was branded with this Epitaph,

*Cy gist le Roy d'*Ethiopie,
L'Original, ou la Copie.

Here lyes the King of *Ethi opie*,
Th'Original, or else the Copie.

Gregory being question'd concerning him, made answer, *That the Report of him reach'd* Egypt, *and the Countries next adjoyning; and he had heard from the Governess of* Ruma, *being a Woman of noble descent, that* Tzagaz *came to her, and told her he was the Son of* Arzo, *who was the Brother of* Zadenghel, *the Son of* Lesana, *and Grandchild to* Menas. The same thing he affirm'd to his Countrymen in *Egypt*, and to those that liv'd at *Jerusalem*. For to them he did not dare to counterfeit himself the Son of *Jacob*, in regard they well knew that *Jacob* was slain in the Eighteenth year of his Age, or thereabout, without any legitimate off-spring. But for *Arzo*, he liv'd an obscure life, and whether he had any Children or no, there was no body knew. Let us now therefore return to *Susneus*.

Susneus, descended from the Royal Line, bigg, tall, and strong Limb'd; and in such a Body a large Soul. His Countenance affable and pleasing, with a high Nose and thin Lips, nothing different from the *Europeans*, but only in colour. He was Prudent, Courteous and Liberal, and well read in the *Ethiopic* Books; and which is most necessary to him that will ruffle for a Crown, he was Warlike, Patient of Labour, and had among the *Gallans* learnt to be Content with any sort of Dyet. However he was unhappy during his Reign, by reason of his continual Wars, and the frequent Rebellions of his Subjects, whom he sent to compel by force to submit to what he thought convenient to enjoyn them. He swore obedience to the Pope; before he had weigh'd what benefit he might get by it. And therefore toward his latter End, he was forc'd to indulge that Liberty, for the maintaining of which, many Thousands had already lost their Lives. He dy'd in *September*, in the Year 1632. leaving several Sons and Daughters behind him.

Basilides, by his Inauguration name *Seltan Saghed*, after the Death of *Marc* his Eldest Brother, succeeded the Father, Who to quiet the Minds of his Subjects, Exterminated the *Jesuits*, together with their Patriarch, out of all his Dominions; so that he would not permit the *Portugals* a Priest to say Mass, which the severity of *Menas* allow'd them. All the rest of his Brothers, if the Fidelity of *Tellezius* do not here give way to his Passion, he put to death, upon bare allegation of Crimes committed. Neither do we know any thing more of certainty concerning him, he refusing any farther Commerce with the *Europeans*, for fear of the Forces, for which he heard the Fathers were sollicting both at *Rome* and in *Portugal*, to revenge the Indignities he had put upon them.

After this I saw certain Letters, which the King of *Abyssinia Af-Saghed*, the Son of *Alam Saghed*, sent to the Governour of *Batavia*, written in Arabic; of which we shall have occasion to say more in another place, for I am not certain whether or no *Basilides* did not make use of a double Sirname, nor whether he were the Father of that same *Af Saghed*. I have here inserted a Genealogic Table of the Last Kings of *Habessinia*, which I had from *Gregory*, but now more Corrected out of *Tellezius*.

CHAP.

[illegible]

[illegible]

[illegible] Dank.

[illegible] Opposition [illegible]

[illegible]

[illegible]

[illegible]

from BAEDA-MARJAM *Son of* Zara-Jacob; *Grandchild of*
gn of Basilides, 1632, &c.

rjam,
year 1465. whose Second Wife was *Helena*.

'd in the year Reign'd Six

3. *Naod* fetch'd from the Rock of *Ambara* to the Crown, dy'd in the year 1504. leaving his Widow *Moghesa* behind.

na-Denghel, and *Wanag-* made King 1504. dy'd *ghel* behind.

3. *Romana Warck* wife 1. to N. N. 2. to *Abuder*.

4. N. N. who Escap'd from the Rock of *Ambara*.

ly'd be- Brother

4. *Menas*, Sirnam'd *Adamas Sagbed* made King 1559. Slain in Battel, *April* 20. 1562.

5. N. 6. N. 7. N. three Daughters of whom *Alvarez*, c. 61

a- h,

3. *Zertza-Denghel*, otherwise *Malech-Sagbed*, made King 1562, and dy'd 1579. His Wife was *Marjam-Sena*.

AQUIETER, ABALE *Lecanaxos*.

orn 1589. of Age, , depos'd lain March

Za-Marjam, another Natural Son.

Za-Denghel alias *Atznaf-Sagbed*, Born 1577, Slain in Battel by his own Son, *Octob.* 13. 1604.

Arzo whose Son *Tzaga-Christus* called himself,

Wife to the Viceroy of *Tigra*, with others whose Names are not known.

Table in the Second Book, between Folio 192, 193.

Chap. VIII.

Of the Royal Succession, and the Imprisonment of the Kings Children in the Rock Geshen, *now quite out of use.*

Certain Succession the Safety of Kingdoms. Two Bonds of Government. How far Prudence, how far Nobility and Power prevail. Election not always to be preferr'd before Succession: more agreeable to Liberty. The Males only succeed in Abassia. *Their Claim dubious: hence Wars. The Inconveniencies of Hereditary Kingdoms. The ill Events of uncertain Succession. The Imprisonment of the Kings Children.* Tellezius's *Relation of it. The Custom for 300 Years, abrogated by* Naod. Alvarez's *Relation; it disagrees with* Tellezius: *reconcil'd. No president for half a Century. The pleasantness of those Rocks fabulous. The severe usage of those Princes there. The severity of the Governour displeasing to the Prince: pleas'd him when King.*

FRom what has bin said, it appears that the Succession of the Kings of *Habessinia* is uncertain; and that there is no great difference made between the Legitimate and the Illegitimate. However, the most assured Safety of Kingdoms consists in a Constant and Establish'd Settlement of Succession. But if in Hereditary Kingdoms, it may be lawful either for the King to choose one of his Sons; or if it may be lawful for the Nobility, not so much to regard the order of birth, as the disposition and conditions of him that is to govern, or to respect the favour of the People, War and Sedition must of necessity follow.

They that are set aside will never be quiet, nor shall they want Factious Abettors and Associates. The Grand Pretence, more Especially in Elective Kingdoms, is this, *That Conditions cannot be distinguish'd by Nativities; but the best may be taken by Election and Judgment.* A specious pretence in words, but vain in Reality; while the Imbecility of human Nature prevails, which is guided by the affections, and obeys rather Favour and Hatred, than Virtue; which usually happens in great Assemblies. But there are two Pillars which sustain the Safety of great Monarchies, Reverence and Authority, which they that Govern never can reconcile to themselves either by Wisdom or Probity alone. For there are many who will esteem themselves if not their Superiors, yet their Equals: and men very unwillingly obey their Equals, much less their Inferiours: so that it is altogether vain and pedantic, what *Plato* writes concerning the Felicity of Kingdoms, *That they should be Govern'd by Philosophers*, while other Aids are wanting. A Philosopher, how wise soever, would hardly find a Subject that would obey him three days together for his Philosophies sake. There ought to be something External and Visible, which as well the vulgar and ordinary sort, as the prudent, Equally acknowledg, which is not subjected to the fluctuating and inconstant determination of Men. For this reason in the Election of Kings and Princes, *Nobility* and Power are preferr'd before Wisdom and Sanctity of disposition. Yet the one requires the assistance of the other. The one is the cause that the Subject willingly and freely obeys; the other compels the refractory to submit. And therefore because Election does not bring much more advantage to a Kingdom, than the chance of birth, but is rather liable to Tumults and Seditions, many People have (w) abandon'd it of their own accord. However, it approaches nearest to Liberty, because the Electors may prescribe Laws and Conditions of Government to the Person that is to be Elected; tho that same wariness proves many times ineffectual: Because the Prince, upon refusal, either positively cannot, or else will be very unwilling to be brought to an accompt. So impossible it is, that there should be a compleat happiness in this World. And therefore it is the part of a good and prudent Statesman to prefer that form of Government which he finds (x) Established.

But I return to the *Habessines*, among whom there is this most prudent Constitution, That only the Male Issue shall govern, or the Male kindred nearest in blood; But because the Determination of the Fathers and Mothers, and the chief Nobility happens frequently to be intermix'd; and that the natural Issue is likewise, if male, allow'd the same Priviledge for want of Legitimate Off-spring: hence it comes to pass,

(w) The *Swedes* in the last Century. The *Danes* in our memory; The *Chineses* of old. *Joh. Nieuhof*. Descript. Chin. c. 18.

(x) That the Wise call *[illegible]*, to preserve the present state of the Republic. *Isoc.* against *Callimach.*

that

that their Successions are most unhappy and turbulent ; the chief cause of all their Calamities.

We have already declar'd, how *Icdena*, with the consent of *Marc the Metropolitan*, preferr'd *David* the second Son before *Naod* the Elder Brother, as having nothing else to advance him but a meer brutish strength. The Civil Wars between *Menas* and *Tazcur* his Brothers Eldest Son ; between the Illegitimate Son of *Malec-Saghed*, and *Zadenghel* his Legitimate Kinsman ; and lastly, between *Jacob* and *Susneus*, and all about the doubtful right of Succession, are sufficient Arguments to prove what we assert. *Telleqius* indeed declares, That according to the Lawes of *Ethiopia*, the natural Sons do not succeed. But in another place, he so discourses concerning their Law, alledging the Example of *John* the First, King of *Portugal*, that the Reader may perceive, that he varies in this, from his other Relation. But the chiefest Inconvenience which uses to arise in hereditary Kingdoms, where the Succession is ty'd to a certain Family, proceeds either from the sence of Rivalship and a jealousie which they that rule have of them that are nearly related in blood ; or from their Ambition, which always animates the Factious. Dismal are the Examples among the *Barbarians*, where there are no Laws or Rules for Succession, but all things are at the Will of them that bear sway, or else of Fortune her self. What ruin'd the Family of the *Cæsars* ? What the *Roman* Empire ? but onely that the Creation of the Emperors was inconstant and unfix'd, and at the Will of the Souldiery. Certainly it was a great Oversight in *Augustus Cæsar*, after he had vanquish'd all his Rivals, and had all the Power in his own hands, that he ordain'd no certain Settlement of Succession. The Emperours of the *Turks*, to prevent the Crimes of their Brothers, more impiously put them to death, and punish that Disloyalty which perhaps was never intended. The Ancient Kings of *Abyssinia* to rid themselves of these Fears, were wont to shut up their Brothers under safe Custody, where they might abide unknown to turbulent Spirits ; and so be uncapable of attempting any thing against the raigning Prince ; and yet, be ready to supply the want of Successors. The Rocks of *Geshen* and *Amhasel* were set apart to this end. The whole Story from the Relations of *Antonio d' Almeyda* runs thus. The Emperour *Icon Imlac* had five Sons (others say nine) which he lov'd all alike. Out of which affection he most imprudently

advis'd

advis'd them to raign all with Equal Power; or which was worse, to govern by turns. The Youngest impatient of the delay of so many Years, design'd with himself not to part with the Scepter, when once he had got it into his hands, but to send away his Brothers to some distant Rock, and so continue the Kingdom to his own Posterity. But being betrayd by one of his peculiar Friends, who rather chose to accept of a reward from the raigning Prince, than to expect a guerdon from him that was to raign, he was taken in the same snare which he had laid for his Brothers, and sent to the Rock *Geshen*. But lest the King might seem to have consulted more for his own than the Security of the Kingdom, he also shut up all his own Sons, which he then had, in the same place. After which this Custom continu'd as a Fundamental Law in *Ethiopia*, for above Two hundred and thirty Years, by which means the raigning Kings were secur'd from danger of Civil Wars among Brethren; till in the Year 1590, at what time King *Naod* was sent for from the Rock to ascend the Throne. He had a Son, about Nine years of Age, whom he dearly lov'd; which Child, one of his chief Courtiers steadfastly beholding, *Certainly*, said he to the King, *this Child grows apace*. The Boy was of an acute Wit, and understood what the Courtier drove at, and therefore fixing his weeping Eyes upon his Fathers Face, *Oh Father*, said he, *Have I grown thus fast, to be hurry'd from your sight to the Rock* Geshen? Which word strook his Father so deeply to the heart, that having assembl'd the Nobility of his Court and Kingdom, he told them, *That such a wicked and inhuman Custom was to be remov'd*. Which was immediatly done, neither he nor his Councel considering that private affections are not to be preferr'd before the Safety of a Nation. And thus it came to pass, through the Kings unseasonable tenderness, that this same Custome receiv'd and continu'd in *Habessinia*, so much to the Health of the Government, was abrogated to the unspeakable detriment of the Kingdom: And from that time never any Prince was Exil'd to those Rocks.

Alvarez writes, *That* David *being advanc'd to the Throne, his Younger Brother, with the rest of the Sons of* Naod, *were sent away to the Rock*; and afterwards, *That one of the Younger Sons Escap'd, but was taken and sent back; and that he saw him there.* From whence it may be objected against *Tellezius*, That this Custome continu'd after *Naod's* time. But we have some rea-

son

son to believe, That he foresaw this Objection, because he binds it with an Asseveration, saying, *The thing is certainly true, and is easie to be confirm'd as well by the Fathers of the Society, as by the Example of* Susneus, *who tho he had several Sons, yet never went about to send any of them to the Rock.* But then again when he sayes *Alvarez* is to be believ'd in all things that he saw, there is some need of Reconciliation: That is to say, That the Sons of *Naod*, the Brothers of *David*, were then carry'd to the Rock, and that one of them after an Escape was taken and sent back. So that the new Constitution might not help them, tho it were a kindness to the Sons of the succeeding Kings. The Reports concerning the Pleasantness of those Rocks, and the splendid attendance upon those Royal Exiles, are all ridiculous Falsities. The Rocks we have describ'd already. And as for the splendidness of Attendance, when the Custome was in force, most certain it is, that those Princes were kept close Prisoners, and they that either attempted to Escape, or were assisting to their Escape, lay under great Penalties. The Princes themselves were harshly us'd; Neither was any person permitted to come at them, so that their Education could never fit them for a Crown, but was rather to put them out of Hopes of having any thing to do with the Affairs of this World.

It is reported of one of the Keepers, that one morning observing one of his Royal Prisoners putting on a Garment somewhat neater than ordinary, he not only chidd him, and tore the Vestment, but gave notice of it to his Father; all which the poor Prince was forc'd to take patiently. Afterwards the same Prince coming to be King himself, did not onely forbear to revenge the Injury, but hearing that his Keeper was gone aside, as dreading some heavy punishment, caus'd him to be sought out, and being brought before him half dead for fear, both prais'd and rewarded him; Exhorting him to continue in his Office as Faithful to Him, as he had bin to the King deceas'd. And thus we generally impose upon others, what we are very unwilling to endure our selves.

CHAP.

Chap. IX.

Of the Priviledge and Power of the King in Ecclesiastical and Civil Affairs.

The Kings Power absolute: Experienc'd by the Jesuits. Alphonsus the Patriarch offends the King. He claims the Ecclesiastical Jurisdiction. He abrogates the Latin Religion; calls Synods. He forbears the right of Nomination: not bound by the Secular Laws. He has no Estates. The benefit of them; He enjoys all Royal Priviledges, but makes no use of all. Hunting Lawful for all. Private persons have nothing proper. The King takes and gives as he pleases; Certain Families excepted.

THe Power of the *Abyssinian* Kings is absolute, as well in Ecclesiastical as Civil Affairs. Of which the Fathers of the Society have had sufficient experience; in whose favour, and to whose disadvantage he has exercis'd his supream Ecclesiastical Authority, without ever consulting the Patriarch of *Alexandria*: First when he put forth several Edicts, for receiving the *Roman* Religion, and abrogating the *Alexandrian* Ceremonies: which was done with the consent of the Fathers. Afterwards the state of Affairs changing, when he dispenc'd by public Edict with certain Ceremonies that were indifferent, *Alfonsus* the Patriarch reprov'd him. *It is not lawful*, said he, *for a King to put forth any such Edict, as being purely Ecclesiastical, and belonging to the Priestly Office: and You ought to remember what the High Priest said to King* Uzziah. *It belongs not to thee, O King* Uzziah, *to offer incense to the Lord, but to the Priests, the Sons of* Aaron, *who are consecrated to that Ministry, get thee forth out of the Sanctuary, for it will not be imputed to thee as an honour by the Lord God*; to which the Patriarch added the Punishment that follow'd. The King for that time gave way to the Patriarch, and publish'd the Edict in another manner and form. But not brooking the Comparison made between him and *Uzziah*, among other things he gave the Patriarch this answer. *Wherefore didst thou bid us be mindful of* Uzziah, *and wherefore didst thou compare us with him? He was therefore punish'd by God, for usurping the Office of the Priest which did not become him; and because he offer'd Incense and Sacrifice to God, which We never attempted to do; only We commanded an Edict to be publish'd about those Indifferent things which were agreed on between Us both.*

Nothing more incens'd the King, but that he saw his Prerogative call'd in question, which for so many Ages had bin enjoy'd by his Ancestors, and which was never deny'd by the Patriarch of *Alexandria*, even before the Schisme. Nor was he ignorant what the ancient Emperours after *Constantius* had done in the same Cases. Nor was he so dull of apprehension, as not to be able to distinguish between Episcopal rules, and Kingly Jurisdiction, which he thought belong'd to himself. Which Prerogative, tho he had a great Reverence for the Patriarch, he would not part with, but rather chose to publish another Edict, which tended manifestly to the Diminution of the Patriarchal Power. For the Patriarch had order'd a certain Monk to give some part of his Ecclesiastical Revenues to a certain Parish. The Monk would not obey; but complain'd to his Superiour, one *Iteg*, who obtain'd a Decree from the King, wherein the Patriarch was enjoyn'd to keep to the Rules of the Metropolitans of Ancient *Ethiopia*, and that *Iteg* should enjoy his due Priviledges.

His Prerogative in Ecclesiastical Affairs was most apparently made manifest, by the making of that severe Decree for the abrogating the Latin Worship, and restoring that of *Alexandria*. Moreover, the King summons the Synods of the Clergy, as often as need requires; he sends for the Metropolitan out of *Egypt*, exercising plenary Jurisdiction over him and all the rest of his Clergy; and punishing them according to the nature of their Offences, which the Examples recited by *Alvarez*, sufficiently demonstrate. In one thing however he differs from our *European* Kings, that he never nominates to Ecclesiastical Benefices. For the Patriarch of *Alexandria*, sends a Metropolitan, at the request of the King indeed; but he knows not who or what he is. He also admitted the Patriarch, whom the Pope sent, tho not he but the King of *Portugal* nam'd him.

Neither are there in *Ethiopia* any other Ecclesiastical Dignities; and therefore the Prerogative of nominating Bishops and Archbishops, signifies little or nothing. In Seculars he acknowledges no positive Laws. And well it were that he did not think himself also altogether free from the Fundamental Laws of his Realm, upon which the Safety of the Kingdom depends.

For *Naod* dispenc'd with the wholesome Constitutions of his Ancestors, by vertue of which the Kings Children were sent to the Rock of *Ambora*. And *Malec-Saghed* would have preferr'd his natural Son *Jacob* before his Brothers Legitimate Son *Zadenghel*; both which prov'd very disadvantagious presidents to the whole Nation.

But such things frequently come to pass, where the Kingdome is without Estates. For they are the most Trusty Guardians of the Law, and the true Bulwarks of the Peoples Liberty against the Encroachments of the Ambitious. For they have a more vigilant eye and tender care over the Commonweal, of which they are themselves Members, than the Friends of Princes, whose Fortunes hardly descend to their Heirs; so that a man may admire at their Counsels, who taking away the Priviledges of *Estates*, endeavour to assume the whole Power into their own hands, as deeming every slight bend of the Law, to themselves heavy and intollerable. So that they are forc'd to distribute those Favours and Kindnesses which are due to their fellow Citizens, among the Souldiery, whose fidelity is brittle and inconstant: not caring who are poor, so they be rich: and many times the Souldiers turn those Arms which were put into their hands for the defence of their Prince, against him, being put upon the ferment either by the Ambition or the Wealth of some particular person. Which in *Habessinia*, as in all other absolute Goverments, frequently happens to the destruction of those that bear the sway.

He has also the sole disposal of Peace or Warr, and indeed all the Prerogatives that a King can claim (both the greater and the lesser *Regalia*) are solely at his devotion; tho he makes no use of many of them, merely because he is ignorant of them; as the Prerogative in reference to Metals, Coyning of Money, and the like. As for the liberty of Hunting, he grants it to all; in regard there are such multitudes of Wild Beasts that breed up and down in the over-grown Woods and high Mountains, that it is not onely troublesome but dangerous to find out their haunts: by which means that

which

which in other Countries is a Pleasure, to the *Abessines* becomes a Toyl and Detriment.

One thing is much to be admir'd, and rare ev'n among the *Turks*, which is, that no private person, whether Peasant or Lord, except some few can call any thing his own. All the Lands and Farms in the Country belong to the King, and are held by the Subjects onely at the Kings pleasure, so that no man takes it amiss, if the King takes away their Lands and bestowes them upon another as he pleases himself; and that not onely after two or three years, but also the same year they were given: So that it often happens that one man ploughs, and another man sowes. Whence it comes to pass, that they are more submissive to their Kings, then a Servant to his Master, or a Vassal to his Lord; they serve him in Peace and War; and bring him Presents according to their Ability, in hopes of obtaining new Farms, or for fear of losing those they have. For being commanded out of possession, they never grumble, but presently obey without the least distast against the King, or envy to the person that succeeds in their Room. Custome and long use prevailing, while they see the same happening to others. However there are some ancient and Illustrious Families, especially in *Tigra*, who enjoy by right of Inheritance not only Lands and Possessions purchas'd by their Ancestors, but some certain Prefectures also, retaining their ancient Title; as *Bahr-Nagash*, *Sham Seraue Sird*, *Tembea*, and others; as also *Cantiba* in *Dembea*; over whom the King claims no other Authority, than to confer the public Employments every two year, or yearly, or as he pleases, upon others; yet so as that they be of the same Family.

Chap. X.

Of the Power and Revenues of the Habessine *Kings.*

The Power of the Habessine *Kings formerly great; Formidable to their Neighbours; it fail'd after the* Saracens *came in Play. Yet strong at home till the* Adelan *War, and Incursions of the* Gallans. *Easie to be restor'd. The wayes and means. Our Princes unkind to Forraign Christians. Demonstrated by Examples. They took no care of their Sea Ports. The Kings Revenues the Natural Commodities of the Country; what they are. His Tribute, Farms; Herds; the Prices of things low. The King has enough to supply him both in Peace and War.*

SO great and so absolute a Power, and so uncontroulable a Dominion over their Subjects, one would think should render the Kings of *Ethiopia* vastly Potent: and so no doubt it would, if other things were correspondent. Certainly of old it was vastly great, when they kept their Courts at (o) *Axuma*; for there was no considerable Empire near them to withstand their Fortune: and for that cause the adjoyning petty-Princes were all at the devotion of the *Habessinian* Kings. But as to what several have written, through mistake or misapplication of the name, (p) of their Expeditions into the *North* parts of *Asia*, they are all meer fables and figments. Yet this cannot be deny'd, but that formerly they were very terrible to the neighbouring Nations: for they made several Expeditions into (q) *Arabia*.

We have already mention'd the Famous and Successful War with *Caleb* made against the *Homerites*. With no less Renown, King *Cyriacus* hearing of the Christian Persecution in *Egypt*, led a very numerous Army against the (r) *Muslims*. Wherefore *Merwan*, Captain of the *Saracens*, upon promise

(o) *Nonnosus* in *Bibliothec. Phot. n.* 3. calls the *Ethiopians*, the *Homerites* and *Saracens* τὰ ἐξοχώτατα τῶν τότε ἐθνῶν, the stoutest of the Nations at that time.

(p) *Scal.* in his notes *ad Comp. Eccl. Ethiop.* but I know not by what Authority.

(q) The *Arabians* wont to use this Computation. From the Invasion of the *Abessines*. For so [illegible]. They computed their years from the *Arabians* invading *Abessina*.

(r) So the *Mahometans* call themselves.

of

of mitigating his severity, besought the Patriarch of *Alexandria*, to perswade the King to desist from his design; which he did, and stopp'd the Progress of the King, till he (s) heard that the Christians were better us'd. Which, tho it be reported of the King of *Nubia*, yet several Authors attribute the same to the King of the *Abissines*; in regard that by the Nubian Geographer, *Nubia* (r) extended to the Fountains of *Nile*. *Gregory* also affirm'd the same, and that the History was to be seen in his Country. But when the *Saracens* grew stronger, and had invaded the Neighbouring Kingdoms, the *Abissines*, relinquishing *Axuma*, and turning the force of their Arms against the more upland parts of *Africa*, enlarg'd their Empire by the Overthrow of several weak and effeminate Nations, no more regarding forraign Countries, or the subduing of far distant Regions: which was the reason that after that, they perform'd nothing that was memorable abroad. However they were Potent at home, and had under them several petty-Princes that were their Tributaries. And in this Greatness they flourish'd, in the time of *Helena* and *David*, till it was not only shaken by that Dreadful War with the *Adelans*, but so overturn'd, that it never could recover it self afterwards. For about that time the *Gallans* also breaking out, and never after that subdu'd, layd wast and harrass'd the most Opulent and most Noble Provinces of the Empire: and still to this day every year gain upon the rest with their continual Incursions. However, that Power which yet remains is so considerable, that if they would but make use of the Arts and Arms of the *Europeans*, they might not onely subdue those *Barbarians*, but also recover their Lost Dominions. For a Kingdom well order'd within, under such a Monarch, where the People are under so much subjection; so large a liberty to do well or ill; if Concord and Unity attended these Opportunities, together with a constant method of Counsels, it is impossible, but that they must soon prevail over a wandring Nation, divided among themselves into so many Tribes and Factions. All their truculent and savage fury would be in vain, if the Streights of the Mountains were but well forti-

(r) *Elmacinus* Hist. of the *Saracens* l. c. 17.

(s) *Bochart's* Sacred Geography l. 2. c. 23. However most certainly *Cyriacus* had another name.

fy'd

fy'd and guarded with Field-Pieces. They should also send forth several Colonies, and give them a tast of the Blessings of Peace, by which the wildest of Nations oft-times grow tame. But which is more than all, and which the *Habessines* most earnestly desire, Towns should be built, and replenish'd with people, and an increase of Wealth be permitted by the Encouragement of Arts and Arms. Lastly, if the King would remit something of his Prerogative which he has over the Estates of the Subject, and reserving those Lands which are already till'd, to himself, would distribute to his Souldiers and the rest of his People such Lands as should be won from the Enemy, every one his proportion, and grant them an irrevocable Inheritance of such Lands; setling also Dukedoms and Earldoms in fee-simple out of the Conquer'd Countries, upon his Nobility, and best deserving Captains, no doubt but in a short time, it would prove the most flourishing Kingdom in *Afric*, greatly to the propagation of the Christian Religion.

And it seems but reason, that in the setling and ordering his Kingdom, the *Habessinian* Prince should be advis'd and assisted by the *European* Princes, not onely out of Christian Charity and hopes of propagating Christianity over *Africa*, but also to lessen the Power of the *Turk*, which would follow, were the Dominion of the Red Sea but wrested out of his hands, and the Commerce of *Egypt* spoyl'd. Ah! what pity it is, that we should be so ill affected towards other Christian Nations, that unless they are of the same Opinion with us in all points of Divinity; or unless they promise us large Rewards, or an ample share of their Profits, we can patiently look on, and see them perish, while the most inveterate Enemies of the Christian Faith are enrich'd with the spoyls of their Wealth; not considering that in the end the mischief will redound to our selves: and that we shall one day, unless God in mercy prevent it, dearly pay for our Dissensions.

Thus we forbore to assist the *Grecian* Emperours, and several of the Eastern Princes, till they became at last a prey to the *Ottomans*. Thus, while none of Us lay'd it to heart, *Egypt* was reduc'd under the Power of the *Turk*; a vast addition to their Empire: as if it were a Crime to breed up Doggs to hunt the Wolves. Now the reason why the *Abissines* do not court with greater ardour the Alliances of the *Europeans*, is

plain:

plain: for it is to be attributed either to their ignorance, or their difference in Opinion from the *Latines*. Moreover, they fail very much in this, that they permit the *Turk* to be Masters of the Ports and Ilands of the Red Sea, whereby it is absolutely at their pleasure what Persons or Commodities shall pass in and out. But they understand not, that there is no Nation can be truly Powerful and Great, that does not Command some Sea-Towns.

As for the Revenues of the King, they are not paid in ready money, but in the natural Productions of the Countries, the most equal sort of Tribute. For some Provinces afford Gold; others Horses, Cattel, Sheep, Corn and Ox Hides, and some few, where Weavers live, send him Garments. They bring their Gold rough and unrefin'd, as they gather it up among the Sands of the Rivers, or digg it out under the Roots of Trees, or else with less Labour find it loose upon the Earth. For they know not how to coyn money, but after the ancient manner, weigh their Metal, wherein they are many times gull'd by forraign Merchants, who frequently deny the Gold to be pure; and therefore change it for the meanest of their Commodities. How much better might the King provide for himself and his Subjects, should he with Money of his own Coyn, buy up all the Gold in his Kingdom, to his own and the great advantage of his People. *Enarea* (*a*) pays a Thousand and five hundred Ounces of Gold: formerly much more. To *Susneus* it pay'd but a Thousand, and sometimes but Five hundred, when the *Enareans* were either at Wars with the *Gallans*, or else embroyl'd one with another. *Gojam* pays every Year Eleven hundred Ounces, and some Garments, to the value of 3000 *German* Dollars, together with Two hundred Fustian Tapestries, very broad and close woven. Formerly they also pay'd a Tribute of Horses, but *Melec-Seghed* remitted that, to the end they might be the better able to withstand the *Gallans*. Out of *Tigra* he receives Five and twenty thousand Patachs. Out of *Dembea* Five thousand. As much out of other Kingdoms, or sometimes less. There are also several *Tolls* pay'd, but generally granted to the Nobility for their subsistance; except those of the high Mountain, *Lamalmona*, over which all the Merchants and Merchandize must pass from the Red Sea into *Habessinia*, which the King reserves

(*a*) 15000 *Patacks of Portugal* or *German* Dollars.

to

to himself. He also has his Lands and Farms, from whence he is serv'd with Provisions for his Table, ten or twelve Horse-Loads at a time. Lastly, *Dembea*, *Gojam*, and *Bagemdra* find him Corn and Flesh. That which he receives out of *Dembea* is distributed among the Souldiers which have no Land, or else among the Poor. But his chief Tribute is from the Graziers, who are bound to pay him every Tench Oxe or Cow every Three Years: which is as much as if they should pay the *30th* every Year. And the whole Empire is so divided, that every Year he has his certain Tribute of Cows and Oxen. Besides, every Year every Christian Weaver pays him a fustian Garment; Every Mahumetan a *Drim*, or Parach, which amounts to a Thousand *Imperials* every Year.

Most certainly the Revenues of this Empire seem to be very small, if we consider the Extent of so many Large Provinces. But on the other side we are to observe, That the Prices of all things are very low. A huge Oxe may be bought for half a Dollar. The Souldiers live upon Flesh and Fish without bread; and Servants Wages are paid in necessary Commodities not in money.

Again, if we consider the plenty of all things; the *Abissine* Emperour has enough and to spare: not that his Diadem glisters with Gemms or Pearls, or that his Treasuries are full of Money; or that his Cupboards shine with Silver and Gold Plate; or that his Table is spread with Forraign Banquets while his Subjects are in want, his Courtiers poor, and his Souldiers under penury. But he has that which suffices to afford him moderate Dyet, and slender Cloathing. Then for his Souldiers and his Warlike Subjects, that is to say, his poor People, they, detain'd at home by no delicacies, are ready still to gird on their Swords. Which they who dexterously and courageously know how to weild in a good Cause, need never want Gold nor Silver, nor what ever Mortals esteem pretious and desireable.

CHAP.

CHAP. XI.

Of the Royal City of Axuma, *and the Inauguration of the King.*

Axuma *the Metropolis of* Habessinia *formerly. Now more like a Village. Thus the* West *forsak'n by the* Greek *Emperours. The Situation good. The King there formerly Crown'd. The Ceremonies of Inauguration. Some other Towns of* Habessinia: *They live in Villages. No Forts nor Castles. They wonder great Cities can last.*

THE Royal City of the *Abissines*, and formerly the Metropolis of the whole Empire, is by the (x) *Habissines* call'd *Ascum*: from whence, as we have already observ'd, they were formerly call'd *Axumites*. Of old this City was adorn'd with most beautiful Structures, a fair Palace, and a Cathedral proudly vaunting her Obelisks, Sculptures, and several sumptuous Edifices. Some of the Pillars are still to be seen, with Inscriptions of unknown Letters, remaining arguments of their Antiquity, now demolish'd by the Wars, or deface'd with Age. The City it self, now totally ruin'd, looks more like a Village, than a Town of Note; *So fading and inconstant are those things which men account most durable.* How many Cities, how many Monuments now lye in ashes, whose Founders are well known? and how many are yet in being, whose Founders are unknown? As for this, it began to fall to decay by degrees, presently after that the Kings of *Habessinia* relinquish'd it, and remov'd their Court from thence, as being depriv'd of those advantages that attend the abodes of Princes. Thus the Seat of the Empire being Translated to *Byzantium*, the *West* was neglected. And the same Fate, no doubt, had certainly befallen *Rome*, had it not bin sustain'd by the Care of the Bishops, now the *Roman* Pontiffs. In the time of the *Adelan* Warr, the Revolt of the Vice-Roy of *Tigra* in the Raign of King *Menas*; and lastly, when the *Turks*

(x) Of which *Nonnosus* in *Biblioth. Phot. n.* 3. *p. m.* 2. [illegible] *Axuma* is a very great City, and as it were the Metropolis of all *Ethiopia*; erroneously *Chavano* in *Abissin.* c. 17.

invaded that Country, it was totally lay'd wast, and now can scarcely shelter a hundred Inhabitants: onely the Ruines still remain, to testifie that once it was great and populous. It is Seated in the Fourteenth degree and a half of Northern Latitude, Encircled with pleasant and fertile Fields which afford a Prospect becoming a Royal Mansion. It lies distant from the Red-Sea Five and forty *Portugal* Leagues, or six or Seaven tiresom days Journey by reason of the Mountains that lye between. The antient Kings of *Ethiopia* were wont to be here inaugurated; nor would *Susneus* admit of his Coronation in any other place, though when he related the particulars of the Ceremonies to the Commander of the *Portugueses*, he could not but laugh at them, as ridiculous himself, *For many things are to be done by Princes to please the Vulgar, which to others may seem superfluous.* Such as were for the most part the *Solemn Ceremonies of the Antients invented by mean Capacities, but retain'd by the more prudent.* *Tellezius* thus sets them down. When *Susneus* was to be Crown'd, first the Masters of the Ceremonies, read to the King out of their Memorandums, how and in what order every thing was to be perform'd. The Army being drawn up, the Foot march'd first: then follow'd the Horse with their Trappings: after them the Courtiers Comb'd, and neatly habited: presently appear'd the Emperour himself upon a stately Prauncer, clad with a close Purple Damascene Tunic, and over that a magnificent *Attalic* Vestment, with narrow Sleeves hanging down to the ground. When they came to a great Stone engraven with Forraign Characters, not far from the Church of *Axuma*, next to which the Solemnities of the Inauguration us'd to be perform'd, the Emperour with all the Courtiers alighting from their Horses, stood upon the Ground that was spread with rich Carpets. At what time the Virgins of *Axuma*, holding a Silken Cord cross the Street, stopp'd the Way, and as the King press'd to go forwards, they hindred him, and ask'd him, *Who he was?* who answering, *I am the King of the Israelites.* They reply'd, *Surely thou art not our King.* Which said, he retir'd smiling. At length being ask'd a third time; he reply'd, *I am the King of Sion:* and drawing forth his Cimitar, cut the Cord: which done, the Virgin cry'd out, *Of a certainty, thou art our King of Sion.* Presently all the Guns they have are fir'd, and the neighbouring Mountains rang with loud Acclamations; the Drums beat

to

to the noise of the Flutes, and the Trumpets fill'd the Air with harmonious Levets. Which done, the *Metropolitan Simeon* accompany'd with all the Ecclesiastical Orders of Clerks, Monks, and Canons, singing several Songs and Hymns, conducted the King to the first Porch of the Church, and there set the Diadem upon his Head. The King being crown'd, if it may be so call'd; proceeded forward into the Temple, and there receiv'd the Eucharist; which having done he rode back to the Camp with his Diadem upon his head. For in *Ethiopia* they use no Scepter. Nor is the Crown any other than a Hatt twice doubled, with an Azure colour'd Silken broad brimm trimm'd with Gold and Silver Plates, in the likeness Lillies; with a row of false stones glistering between every Plate.

Besides *Axuma*, there are no Cities in *Habessinia*, and but few Towns. In the Kingdom of *Tigra*, *Dabarva* is the Seat of the Vice-Roys: *Fremona*, the first Residence of the Fathers of the Society, enlarg'd by the *Portugueses*. *Guhay*, a Town in *Dembea*, where the Queen resides. *Nanina* in *Gojam*, long inhabited by the *Portugueses*. *Macana celace*, in *Ambara*. To reck'n up more is not worth the while; neither is it certain whether those already mention'd are standing or no. For in regard of the meanness of the Building, there is nothing of invitation to hinder their being deserted and layd wast by the Inhabitants themselves; in regard the *Habessines* choose rather to live after the manner of Villagers, not caring that their Houses should joyn one to another; which saves them many Suits in Law. For they never fear any Actions about Party-Walls, stopping up of Lights, or Nusances of Water-Courses. In places that are fertile and till'd, you shall see the Fields, as it were, planted with Houses, which affords no unpleasant Prospect. They have neither Castles nor Forts. The Celebrated Mountains of *Ambara* are their onely Citadels, where the Kings Children were formerly committed to Custody. The *Habessines* wonder to hear of so many great Cities among Us. For they do not believe the Country can afford Timber and Food sufficient for so many Houses, nor the Cattel that must support such Numbers of People, remaining so long in one place. For they pitch their Tents up and down the Country, and cut down and make havock of whatever they have need of, without any consideration of the dammage, or regard to the future. For they neither Navigate their own Rivers, neither do they know what belongs to Carriage or Stores; living without any care of to Morrow.

Chap. XII.

Of the Kings Court, his Titles, and his Court-Officers.

The Kings live in Tents: P. Pays built a Palace. The Kings Table. Women attend: Plain dyet. The King and the Nobility crown'd. They drink after they have done: They read the whole Psalter before meals. The ancient manner of receiving Ambassadors: now chang'd. Formerly two Court Officers: discontinu'd. The Rasnm chief Minister in Peace and War. Officers beside.

AFter the Kings of *Habessinia* lost *Axuma*, they never had any constant Mansion, nor any Palaces, but contented themselves to live in Tents. But at length *Peter Pays* built the King a Palace after the *European* manner, which cost him an incredible deal of Labour and Industry; for that in regard of the want of Artists, he was forc'd to teach them every thing, and to look after the Work like a Master-Builder. He chose to build this House in a most commodious and delightful place call'd *Gorgora*, being a kind of Peninsula, almost surrounded by the *Tzana* Lake, where the King was wont to take up his Winter-Quarters, and contriv'd it very spacious and beautiful, with Rooms of State, Bed-Chambers, Galleries, Battlements and Balconies, which yielded a most pleasant Prospect over the Lake, and the Neighbouring Fields. Insomuch, that it was not inferiour to the Country Palaces of some of our *European* Princes. The *Abessines* were amaz'd when they saw one story rais'd above another, which they thought could never have bin done: and call'd it *House upon House*. Nor till that time did they believe the Fathers, when they told them of the numerous and splendid Palaces, Sumptuous Cathedrals, and Stately Monasteries in *Europe*. For those things they related to the *Abessines*, to make them in love with the Magnificence and Majesty of the *Roman* Church.

The Garniture of the Kings Table is much different from ours.

ours. For no person is admitted into the Room while the King is at Dinner; or if any of the Nobility be invited, they must stay till the King rises: then they take their places at the same Table, and eat the Kings Leavings, which is look'd upon as a very great Honour. Yet the Fathers of the Society were admitted to Dine by themselves, in the same Room next to *Susneus*'s Bed-Chamber. To which purpose there were two low little round Tables, about Eighteen Spans in Compass, brought in to the Room and plac'd upon the Ground which was spread with Carpets; one lesser for the King, another bigger for the Fathers, but without Table-Cloaths or Napkins: instead of which they made use of thin Wafers made of Wheat or Rie past. So that their Table-cloaths serv'd them for Bread, which there was no need for the Servants to take away, fold up, or wash: no Trenchers, Knives, Forks, nor Spoons: no Salt-seller, no Pepper or Sugar-box; nothing of Extravagant was there to be seen: A great Ease to them in time of War; to us an impediment, while so many Carts, so many Waggons are requir'd to carry Kitchin Utensils, and Kitchin Officers, to pleasure our Luxury. The Meat is serv'd up by Women, not in Gold or Silver Dishes, but in broad Earthen Platters, which would never tempt an *European* Thief. They are made of black Clay, with covers of Straw neatly woven and painted. The meat is very ordinary, Flesh and Broths of several sorts boyl'd after their fashion. So soon as the Dishes are marshall'd, the Hangings are presently let down, lest any one should see the King while he is eating: and truly there is good Reason why. For, the King and the chief Nobility, a thing you would think almost incredible, account it a great trouble to lift their hands to their mouths. And therefore the Children belonging to Court, take the meat and put it in their mouths, and if the Gobbets be too bigg, they thrust 'em in, as they do that cramm Capons. The crumms that fall, sometimes they put again i'their chopps after they are well soak'd in the Broth. A way of eating that may well deserve a good thick covering: as being a sight, that would certainly cause our squeamish Stomachs, that will hardly eat off of one anothers Trenchers, to rise a hungry. But this is common both to Lord and Peasant, that they never drink till they have done feeding.

One

One thing we must not omit, which is, that they always read Prayers both before and after meals; a thing that some of our Courtiers are in a manner asham'd of, who will hardly tarry to hear a short Grace; while here you shall have the whole *Psalter* repeated at their great Feasts, without any inconvenience to the Guests: For he whose Office it is, distributes to every one a part. The King and they that are accustom'd to it, know their proper time. The larger *Psalmes* are divided among more, the shorter to one singly. And thus by several, the whole *Psalter* is read, as it were, in a moment. For the *Psalter* is made use of by all: neither have they any other Book for dayly Prayer.

Their manner of giving Audience to Ambassadors is different from what it was in former times. For *Alvarez* relates how that after long waiting, and a deal of haughty formality, the *Portugal* Embassadour, *Lodowic Limaus*, was four times ask'd *From whence he came?* and that he receiv'd no other answer the first day, but that *They were Welcome*: nor were they admitted to the King; and yet Presents were to be left. Nor was the Embassadour to be Visited by any one, before he had kiss'd the Kings hands. At length, after he had bin several times call'd, he was first admitted to discourse the King, the Hangings being let down between them; and at last, with much ado, to see and salute the King. Of which the chief Reason was thought to be, because he had brought no Present (for it is not lawful to appear before the Eastern or *African* Kings, without an acknowledgment) or else because he wanted the Kings Credentials. Which superbness is now adays layd aside; for that being humbled by so many Losses and Calamities, they begin to reckon Urbanity and Civility among the rest of the Vertues.

Among the Court Employments, the chiefest Dignity was that of the Person who was call'd *Behtudet*, of whom one was of the *Right* hand and the other of the *Left*. They were the chief Ministers of State, and manag'd all Affairs, and were entrusted with all the Kings Secrets; with them alone the King consulted: few others being admitted into his Presence: as if Majesty were more Venerable when conceal'd. But afterwards so much Greatness in Subjects began to grow irksome

irksome to the Kings; and some there are also that abuse their Power: few men being able to contain themselves within those Bounds of moderation, to be able to do all things, and yet not to covet all things. For there are many Examples of those, who out of a desire of preserving their Greatness, have requited their Masters with ill Turns for Favours of the highest nature; making use of that authority which they receiv'd from their Princes, to their mischief. By which means *Kings* have bin overwhelm'd by the hatred of the People; or else have bin forc'd to pull down that Greatness with extream hazard, which they themselves advanc'd. Those Princes act more prudent that keep the Power in their own hands, never trusting to the Management of one single Person. Neither are they less provident Ministers, who never affect it: For the Grand Affairs of a Kingdom are more safely and easily manag'd by Plurality.

To these succeeded another Chief Officer whom the *Ethiopians* call *Ras*, from the Arabic word which signifies a *Head*. The reason of whose institution at first, was for the Command of the Army. But as Warlike Command, and Martial Fame excell all other accomplishments, it came to pass in a short time, that these chief Generals advanc'd themselves above all others, to govern the Kings Counsels, and so by degrees to be the chief Ministers of State for the management of all Affairs, both Forraign and Domestic, such a one was *Ras Athanasius*, who first deposed *Zadenghel*, and then *Jacob*, so that *Susneus* did not hold it convenient to confer so great a dignity upon any person, unless it were by his Brother by the Mothers side, by name *Ras-Selach*. Next to him, there are two Comptrollers of the Court. The upper Comptroller, who is called *Bellatenot-Gueta*, as much as to say Master of the Officers, whose jurisdiction reaches all Inferior Vice-Roys, Prefects, Governors of Provinces, and Judges. The other is called *Dahaka Bellatenot-Gueta* who controles the Houshold Servants, the Grooms and such like, who are generally of mean Condition, and of several Nations. Slaves also set free are admitted to Dignities and Offices. For the Kings believe their Slaves, when freed, will be most faithful, as owing to their Fortunes to none alive besides.

Next

Next in Dignity to the Court Officers, are the Vice-Roys, and Princes, Camp-Masters, Senators, and Kings-Counsellors, who are called the lesser Judges and Magistrates without any distinction of Superior or Inferior Judges; for they have equal Jurisdiction and Cognizance of all Crimes. The Captain of the Kings Guard they call the *Guardian of the Fire*, not without reason comparing the King to Fire. *For that they who are Servants to Kings and Princes, receive heat and warmth from them as from the Fire; though if they act not prudently, they may chance to be cruelly burnt.*

Chap. XIII.

Of the King's Camp.

The Kings Tent described; The Camp pitch'd in great order. The same always. It consists of four parts; formerly in Sewa, *now in* Dembea. *How large. As it were a Marching City; the great Power of the Camp-Masters.*

WHatever others have feign'd concerning any other Royal City or Metropolis, besides *Axuma*, are meer Fables. For the Kings of *Habessinia* live continually in Tents, whether it be that they are not accustomed to Houses, or that their frequent Wars and tedious marches will not admit of long rest. The Kings Pavilion is a very large one, of white colour placed in the middle of the Camp; there being a large space of Ground left void round about it; as well to prevent the Casualties of Fire, as also to receive the Horses of the Nobility and those that bring Provisions. Next to him, the Grandees, the Friends and kindred of the *King* and the rest of the Courtiers pitch up their Apartments. The whole Camp consists of four parts, every one of which has his Camp-Master. The first part is call'd the *Front*, and the Camp-Master is call'd *Fit-aurari*. The Hindmost part is call'd *Chuala*. The First Camp-Master goes before to take up convenient Ground where there is store of Wood and Grass, chiefly near some River or Lake, to prevent want of Water. Having chosen out his Ground, he fixes a Pole in the Earth with the Royal Banner at the Topp; upon the sight whereof, they that measure for the Nobility, set up their

their Masters Lodgings. After them the Common Souldiery, and others that follow the Camp either for Victuals, or else upon business. And thus in a few hours time the whole Camp appears in the same Order as it was before. For every one knowes his place and his proportion, there being never any alteration of the Order, but the same Streets and Lanes, the same distance of Tents, so that were it not for the variation of the Prospect, other Mountains, other Rivers, and another Face of the Country, you would think your self still in the same place. When the Cryer has once proclaim'd the day of Removal, they presently know how to pack up their Baggage, and in what order to march without any more ado; who are to march in the Front, who in the Rear; who on the Right, who on the Left hand: so that all things are done without Noise or Tumult.

Neither is there any thing which more commends the Industry of the *Abyssines*. For what they have acquir'd by long use and continual War, they still retain; never pester'd with confusion either marching or sitting still. The constant disposal and largeness of the Camp may be understood from hence, that the same Dialect and the same words continue in the same Streets and Quarters: in other Quarters another sort of words, and a different Dialect: as for *Dala*, a word used in the Front of the Camp, which signifies to *put in*; the Vulgar in the Rear Quarter say, *Tikummara*. Of old, before the *Gallans* conquer'd it, the Camp was pitch'd in *Shewa*, a fertile and most plentiful Countrey. But for the most part in *December*, and that for three or four years together in one place. In the beginning of *Susneus's* Reign in the year 1607, they pitch'd at *Coga*. Thence they remov'd to *Gorgora*, in the year 1612, from thence to *Dancaza*; and lastly to *Guendra* which place, *Bernier* because he had heard perhaps that it was the Residence of the King, calls the Metropolis of *Ethiopia*; of which perhaps in a few years there will be nothing to be seen.

These Camps take up a vast deal of room, as well in the Summer as in the Winter, for they do not onely contain the Souldiers, but their Wives and their Children, whose work it is to bake their Bread, and make their Hydromel. So that the weak and helpless multitude far exceeds the number of the Souldiery. Nor are they without Merchants and Trades-men of all sorts, besides Slaves and Lackeys, necessary for such a Multitude: So that the Camp looks more like an Ambulatory City, and moving Houses, then a Martial Camp. So many Tents and Pavilions seeming a far off to represent the Prospect of some great Town. But less wonderful is that which is reported out of *India*; That near the Island of *Sumatra*, there are certain Cities, if they may be so call'd, which are always swimming, and yet great Markets and Fairs are kept therein; and many People live there who have no other Country or Habitation.

Now for the Camp masters whom the *Ethiopians* call *Sebra Catim*, they carry a great sway in managing the Succession of the Kings, and affairs of greatest moment. The Kings also themselves are guided by them in making and abrogating Laws; and generally they are the first springs of Faction and Sedition. And as formerly the *Pretorian* Bands gave Laws to Prince and People, so among the *Habessines* the effect of all Consultations good or bad derive themselves from the Camp.

CHAP.

Chap. XIV.

Of the Military Affairs of the Habessines.

Continual War. The Winter causes a Truce. The Habessines *good Souldiers, Strong and active. They serve without pay. They plunder the Countries as they march. The* Gallans *secur'd by their Poverty. The* Habessines *ignorant in Fire-Arms. Few Muskets, and fewer Musketeers. Their Armies chiefly made of Foot. Light Armour. Drums us'd by the Horse. Their Weapons. Bad Discipline; because they count it as shame to fly. Their Onsets furious. Their Rocks are their Fortresses. The King Commands in chief. Traytors unpunish'd.*

THat the *Habessines* are a Warlike People and continually exercis'd in War, we have already declar'd: neither is there any respit but what is caus'd by the Winter, at what time by reason of the Inundations of the Rivers, they are forc'd to be quiet. For they have neither Ships nor Boats: neither do they know how to make Bridges to command a passage over their violent Streams. Concerning which, *Gregory* wrote to me in these words.

There is no making War in Ethiopia *in the Winter time; neither does the Enemy attack us, nor we them; by reason of the great falls of Rain and the Inundations of the Rivers.*

Tellezius also further testifies, That the *Habessines* are good Souldiers. They ride and manage a Horse well; and readily take Arms; as well in obedience to their Soveraign, as for other causes already mention'd. They are strong, They endure hunger and thirst beyond belief, and with little sustenance can brook any unseasonable sort of weather. They serve without pay: contented with honour and applause, and such Lands, as the King after the Roman Custom bestows upon the well deserving. Therefore they must certainly be thought to fight much more generously and faithfully in the defence of their Countrey then Hirelings. They expect no part of the Enemies Booty, nor no redemption, and therefore never serve them in the Field, and because they know not the art of protracting a War, therefore they never are sparing of themselves to return home rich. However the Poverty of the Souldiers impoverishes the Countries through which they march. For in regard it is a difficult thing to carry Provisions over such steep and rugged Mountains, and long wayes, they take by force what is not freely given them; and by that meanes lay wast their own Countries no less then their Enemies: whereby the poor Countrey people are constrain'd to turn Souldiers, and so taught to deal by others, as they were dealt with themselves. For which reason they neither can vanquish nor make any long pursuit after the *Gallans*; who being retir'd with their Droves, the Pursuers find nothing left behind but Lands untill'd, and empty Cottages. So invincible a Fortress is Poverty to withstand the stoutest Enemy. But, as we have said already, Those *Gallans* might easily be vanquish'd, did but the *Habessines* know the use of Muskets. *Tellezius* writes, that they have among them about fifteen hundred Musquets, but not above four Musquetters, and they but very bad Firemen neither; neither do the Commanders know how to place and order them to the best advantage: and therefore after they have once discharg'd, the Enemy rushes on so furiously before they can charge again, that they they are forc'd to to throw their Musquets away: and then another thing is; they have but very little Powder.

The biggest Army which the King brings now into the Field hardly amounts to Forty thousand Men, among which he has not above Four or Five thousand Horse, the rest are all Foot. Their horses are couragious and mettlesome, but they never get upon their backs till they are ready to charge the Enemy: at other times they ride their Mules, and lead their Horses. They are slightly arm'd after the manner of the antient *Velites*; and tho their Stirrups are no bigger then onely to thrust in their great Toes, least if the Horse should fall, their feet should be hung in the Stirup, yet they sit very fast. Their Weapons are Swords and Darts, as also Launces and short Javelins, with which they fight at a distance; after which they dispute it hand to hand with their Swords or Launces, and Bucklers. Their War like Musick for the Horse are Drums much bigger then ours, and the King's, which are the biggest, go by the name of the *Bear* and the *Lyon*. Besides which, several Hornes and Fifes march before Him. They for the most part, are

arm'd

arm'd with two Spears, of which they dart away the one at a distance, and maintain a close fight with the other, defending themselves with their Bucklers. The Horse never fight afoot, nor the Foot a horseback: a practice very necessary in such a Country, where many times there is no use of Horse. In brief, the Military Discipline of the *Habessines* is very irregular; rather the fault of the Captains that know not how to command them, than of the Souldiers. For they run away without any fear of Infamy or Punishment: neither do they know how to rally when they are once disorder'd; so that the first array being broken, the rest are carry'd away like a Torrent: neither do they strengthen their Wings with Reserves; neither do they separate the Veterans from the Raw Souldiers, disheartning the Courage of the one, by the unequal mixture of the other. The fury of the first Onset for the most part wins the Field: for which reason, the *Gallans* surpassing the *Habessines* in heat and violence, have so often vanquish'd them. They are not easily perswaded to avoid the Combat, believing it slouthful and dastardly to tire out an Enemy by delay, and wait for opportunities. Which has bin the Ruin of many of their Kings, that have joyn'd Battel with more Courage, than Prudent Advice. The Kings themselves, for the most part bred up in the field, command their own Armies themselves; or else they create a *Ras*, to command in their stead.

One thing more remains behind, That this Country is very much infested with Robbers as well as Enemies; who many times robb in Troops like Souldiers, and very much infest the Roads; and this without any searching after, or care taken to punish them, by reason that the King and the Governours being wholly busied with continual Wars, have no time to ridd the Nation of these Vermin, who being pursu'd, presently shelter themselves among the Rocks and Mountains.

CHAP.

Chap. XV.

Of the Wars in the last Century, Especially of the Fatal War of the Adelans.

Their ancient Wars uncertain; the distance between Egypt, *and our* Ethiopia. Caleb's *Expedition into* Arabia. *The Wars of the last Century; First the* Adelan *dreadful. The Lamentations of the* Ethiopians *at* Rome, *Caus'd by the sloath and voluptuousness of their Princes. The assistance of the* Turk, *and Fire-Arms; The* Portugals *assist the* Habessines. *The Enemies vanquish'd by* Gomez. *His Fame; His Fidelity tempted by* Graïnus: *but in vain: They both act warily.* Graïnus *fights, and his Horse shot under him. A second Battel. The Enemies Camp taken.* Gomez *forces the Jews Rock.* Gomez *wounded, kill'd, his death reveng'd by* Claudius. Graïnus *overcome and slain. The Kingdom at quiet. The* Adelans *recover strength, vanquish and kill* Claudius. *To whom* Menas *succeeds, who is also slain in the Field.* Sertzadenghel *vanquishes the* Turk. *Civil Wars after his death.*

WE shall forbear to set down over-ancient or uncertain Relations, concerning the Expeditions of the Kings of *Ethiopia* into *Egypt*, in regard it does not appear to us, what part of *Ethiopia* those Writers mean; or how far the Empire of the *Axumites* of old extended. For those things which Historians have deliver'd to memory in reference to the *Ethiopians* adjoyning upon *Egypt*, are not presently to be apply'd to the *Ethiopians*. For that the distance between *Egypt* and our *Ethiopia*, comprehends Eight or nine degrees, or a hunder'd *German* Miles and more. In which wide space, *Nubia* was seated, so that there might be Kings of other *Ethiopick* Nations next to that. And therefore till we see the Histories themselves of the *Axumites*, we are unwilling to publish Incertainties for Certainties. But that the *Habessines* did make several Famous Expeditions into *Arabia*, is a thing not to be question'd; insomuch, that some of them have made a Computation of their Years from thence: and that the Kingdom of the *Homerites* was totally subdu'd by *Caleb*, we have already declar'd. To omit then several other Wars wag'd with their Neighbours, the Stories of which are to us unknown: as for example, that with the *Nubians* in the 15*th* Year of the former Century; recorded by *Alvarez*; the most lamentable and most fatal was that War which they enter'd

into

into with the *Adelans* their Ancient Enemies. True it is indeed, that in the beginning of his Reign, *David* vanquish'd them in several Battels. But after the *Turks* had vanquish'd *Egypt*, and some Ports of the *Red Sea*, the *Adelans*, strengthen'd by their assistance, turn'd the Scale of Fortune, and were always Victors. For King *Adelu* sent one *Ahmed*, a *Mahometan*, vulgarly call'd *Grainus*, or *Grannus*, that is to say, *Left-handed*, with an Army to invade *Habessinia*, and revenge the Losses of the *Adelans*. He, about the Year 1526, subdu'd all *Fatagara*. For the first two Years the War was carry'd on with various Success; but the next Twelve Years to the Year 1540, at what time King *David* deceas'd, the *Habessines* had the worst of it. The King having lost the choicest of his Kingdoms, and his Second Son *Menas*, who was taken Prisoner, languish'd out the rest of his days in the Rock *Damo*. And indeed the *Habessines* were brought to that low and miserable Condition, that they began to despair of their Countrey. For such are the Lamentations which we find made by those that liv'd at *Rome*, in the Epilogue printed after the Gospel of St. *John*.

Not without reason do we weep, when we call to mind the Captivity of our Brethren, our Countrey layd wast, Our Temples Burnt, our Books and our Sanctuaries consum'd with Fire, and the Profanation of our Monasteries by that wicked and impious Grainus, *a Companion for Goats, a Persecutor and Invader of the Sheep, from* Waipaci, *to the Red Sea.*

Among the Causes of such a Torrent of Calamities, these may be reck'nd not to be the least: for that the King, vanquish'd by his own sluggish humour, had given himself wholly up to the Temptations of Pleasure; so dedicated to Women, that he permitted some of them to have their Idols in his Palace. Next, the *Turks*, out of their inbred hatred to Christianity, had supply'd their *Mahometan* Friend with Fire-Arms, and such as knew well how to use them; whose Thunder, then by the *Abessines* first heard, they were not able to endure; nor did they know how to cure the Wounds which the Bullets made, as not being accustom'd to them: besides, that on the other side, the *Mahometans* so numerously abounding throughout *Abessinia*, favourably every where entertain'd those of their own Sect. Many also of

the

the *Abessines* themselves, following, as is usual, the Fortune of the Victor, forsook their Native Soveraign: So that now every thing threaten'd utter destruction and desolation, when the King, lurking among the Rocks, began to bethink himself of craving Succour from the *Portugals.* To that purpose in the Year 1535, one *John Bermudes*, a *Portuguese*, was sent. Who first arriv'd at *Rome* in the Year 1538, where he was made Patriarch joyntly of *Ethiopia* and *Alexandria*, and afterwards went into *Portugal* in the Year 1539, and there obtain'd a Commission from *John* the Third, to the Vice-Roy of *India*, to send Assistance to the *Abessines.* Their Commander was *Christopher Gomez*, a Person of great Valour, who in the Month of *July*, in the Year 1541, enter'd the Kingdom with Six small Field-Pieces, and Four hundred and fifty Musqueteers. At first they had a very severe March: for they wanted Horses and Teams; the Country being so wasted, that they were forc'd to carry their Luggage and Conveniencies upon their shoulders over most rugged and steep Mountains. Nevertheless, these Souldiers, few in number, but all choice men, and coveting the honour to restore the King of *Habessinia* to his Kingdom and his Liberty, patiently underwent all sorts of hardship. This caus'd a change of Fortune, so that now the late Victors were every where put to flight, astonish'd at the Execution of the Guns. In the first place, *Gomez* assail'd the Rock *Anba Sanet*, which was thought invincible, and forc'd the Enemy to quit it. Whereby he won to himself great Fame, and highly Encourag'd the *Habessines.* First therefore the King's Mother, confiding in this small Force, left a certain Rock, which gave access to none, nor permitted any to ascend, but as they were drawn up or let down with Ropes, and cheat'd them with her presence. *Claudius*, who lay sculking in the Kingdom of *Shrwa*, had writ word he would be suddainly with them, but durst not adventure through so many Numbers of the Enemies that lay in the way. So that *Gomez* with some few of the *Habessinians*, was constrain'd to bear the whole burthen of the War with a most incredible Courage. The *Barbarians* were not ignorant of the Gallantry of the *Portugals*, nor did they believe their own People had hearts sufficient to withstand the Fury of the great Guns. And therefore thinking it convenient as well to try the Disposition of *Gomez*, as to spie what Force he had, they sent certain Commissioners to him, pretending to blame

 in

blame his rashness, and to offer him safe Conduct, as being deceiv'd by the *Abessines*, if he thought fit to return. But *Gomeus*, as it were provok'd with the indignity they had put upon him, gave them an answer that savour'd both of fierceness and contempt, telling them, *That he was sent by the most Potent King of the* Portugals, *to revenge the Injuries done to the* Habessines; *and that his coming was not to return again, but to fight* Grainus. The Enemies Force in that place was 15000 Foot, and 1500 Horse, together with 200 *Turkish* Musqueteers, whom *Gomeus* had most reason to fear. But he confiding in the Courage of his own men, tho but a small parcel, resolv'd upon a Battel. However, he keeps within his Camp. On the other side, *Grainus* would not stir, well knowing the *Portugals* had Provision but for a few days; which being spent, they would be forc'd to forsake the Hill where they lay Encamp'd, and so might be easily environ'd by his Numbers. Nor did that cunning in part fail the *Barbarian*; for the *Portugals* were forc'd to forsake their Camp, but could not be surrounded by the Enemy, in regard their Field-Pieces and Musquets struck such a Terror into the *Mahumetans*, that they, contemning all Orders of their Captain, would not stir. And it so happen'd, that *Grainus* himself, riding about to force his men on, was wounded in the Hips with a Musquet Bullet, and had his Horse shot under him. The fall of the Captain quite damp'd the Courage of the Souldiers; so that they presently retreated, and the *Portugals* keeping the Field, look'd upon themselves as Victors. Twelve days after the *Barbarians* renew'd the Fight, for which the *Portugals* were prepar'd. While both sides fought at first with equal Success, an Accident happen'd, lamentable in sight, but yet the cause of the Victory. For while the Souldiers went with their lighted Matches to fetch Powder, a Barrel took fire, the noise of which so terrify'd the *Barbarians* Horses, that their Riders not being able to rule them, they disorder'd the Body of the Army, which the *Portugals* observing, lay'd all their force upon the *Turks*, who being put to flight, the rest easily follow'd. However, they could not pursue them far, because they had but Eight Horses. Nevertheless the Enemies Camp was taken and plunder'd. This was the work of that Summer; for the Winter coming on, put an end to farther Action. The Winter now declining, the *Portugals*, who thought nothing too difficult for them to undertake, attack'd another steep Rock in *Samen*, call'd the *Jews Rock*, which was kept by the *Adelans*, with a Garrison of 1500 men. For it was large, and contain'd many Fields, Meadows, Fountains and Streams. The attempt was occasion'd by a *Jew*, who had bin formerly Governor of the Rock, who hearing of the Courage of the *Portugals*, advis'd the taking of it, in regard there were many Horses in it, which the *Portugueses* principally wanted: and the more to encourage them, he promis'd to shew them such by-ways, that they might be able to surprize the Garrison; adding withal, That there would be no safe Passage for *Claudius*, so long as the Enemy held that Pass. *Gomez* understanding by the Queen that the *Jew* spake truth, undertook the Enterprize with prosperous Success: for having slain all the *Barbarians*, he got a Booty there of Fourscore brave Horses, Three hundred Mules, several Slaves, and other good Plunder beside. After which he restor'd the Rock to the *Jews*, understanding they had always bin faithful to the *Habessines*.

In the mean while *Granius* finding there was no good to be done against the *Portugals* without Guns and Fire-Arms, sent for immediate Assistance from the Neighbouring *Turks*, and petty Basha's of *Arabia*. So that he obtain'd from the Bashaw of *Zebid* a fresh Supply of Seven hundred, some say, Nine hundred Musqueteers, and Ten Field-Pieces. Some noble *Arabians* also that were his Friends came to his assistance. *Gomez*, either knowing nothing of this, or else heighten'd by his two former Victories, never staying for *Claudius*, as he ought to have done; in regard he delayed somewhat longer than was expected, nor yet tarrying for some of the *Portugals* who brought Horses along with them: Or whether it were, that he was constrain'd to it, as having no place of Retreat, and did not believe that *Granius* himself would appear before the Winter was over, gave the Enemy the opportunity of a Battel. But being over-powr'd by the *Turks*, he was wounded with a Musquet Bullet in the Thigh. He himself, having lost many of his own Souldiers, and the stoutest of his Commanders, by the help of the Night escap'd to a Rock. The wounded and weary were all slain, the rest dispersed themselves into the Woods, while the Camp became a Prey to the Enemy. Fourteen only accompanied *Gomez*, the most of them wounded; who void of all assistance, without food or medicaments, refresh'd themselves by the Fountains

which

which afforded but small relief. There they were apprehended by the *Turks* and *Arabians*, and carried to *Granius* exulting for joy of his Success. He causing about a hundred of the heads of the *Portugezes* to be brought and laid down before him, upbraided *Gomez* for his madness in undertaking a War against him: and then after he had receiv'd a stern answer from his Captive, caus'd him to be tormented to death.

After that misfortune, the King came up, sad for the loss of *Gomez*, whom he desired most earnestly to have beheld with his Eyes. Nor were they less sad to whose assistance he came, as well for the loss they had receiv'd, as because he had brought so few Forces with him. Therefore they lay still three or four months, till they could raise more. They being come, the *Portugals*, who were now reduc'd to a hundred and twenty, and yet zealous to revenge the death of their Captain, were very urgent with the King to fight, giving him great hopes of Victory. For they had intelligence that the *Turks* were return'd home, leaving only two hundred behind them: whether by Command of their *Bassha*, or taking it ill that *Gomez* was not deliver'd to them. The King, though he had not above Eight thousand Foot, and Five hundred Horse, resolv'd to follow the Inclinations of the *Portugals*. And first in a slight skirmish he routed some of the *Barbarian* Forces that marched before; Then sets upon *Granius* himself, who led an Army of 13000 men, and vanquish'd him; *Granius* himself, the Terror of *Habessinia* for so many years, was shot with a Musket Bullet by a *Portugueze*, who reveng'd the death of his Captain. All the *Turks* but fourteen were slain. The head of *Granius* was exposed to the view of the People in several Provinces and Kingdoms of *Habessinia*, to the great comfort of the beholders. For upon the sight of it, the *Abissines* recover'd Vigour and Courage; They congratulated their Kings Success; and they who had revolted, return'd to their duty, pretending necessity for the fault committed. The King considering the condition of those times, thought it convenient to pardon all, to confirm the wavering, to win the hearts of his People by Clemency, to rally his scatter'd Forces, and to do all those things which were necessary for the re-establishment of his Kingdom. Onely one of the principal Commanders, to whom the King had granted his pardon, the *Portuguezes* put to death as laying to his charge the Murder of *Gomez*. His perfidiousness was thought to have deserv'd death; and so justice prevail'd, without any further notice being taken of it. In the mean time, the *Gallans*, till then an obscure Nation, were neglected, tho they had invaded many Provinces already laid wast by the *Adelans*; not being look'd upon as such as would have encreas'd so much to the future dammage of the Kingdom. There was still a greater fear of the *Adelans*, who having in time repair'd their Losses, onely waited an Opportunity to make a New Invasion. Soon after their Spies returning with intelligence that the *Habessines* were grown secure, and consequently carelefs, under *Narus* their Captain, they again broke into *Habessinia* with a mighty Force; overthrew *Claudius* who advanc'd to oppose them, and slew him. After his Death, *Menas* obtain'd the Crown, hated by the People for his Cruelty. From thence Intestine Wars ensuing, the *Turks* being call'd into the Kingdom, overthrew the King in Battel and slew him; which gave them an easie advantage to make themselves Masters of the Port of *Arkiko*, and the Iland of *Matzua*. His Son *Zerza-Denghel*, much more fortunate than his Father, perform'd many brave Atchievements, and beat the *Turks* of *Tigra*, but could not regain *Arkiko*, nor the Iland of *Matzua*. He raign'd Thirty Years continually vex'd with the *Gallans*, or harrass'd with Intestine Broyls. After his Death, Civil Dissentions, and deadly Strifes between the Royal Off-spring about the Crown, so weakn'd the *Habessines*, tormented at the same time with the *Gallans*, that from that time to this day, they could never Master that Potent Enemy. As to their Wars about Religion, that arose in the time of the Fathers of the Society, we shall speak more hereafter.

CHAP.

CHAP. XVI.

Of the Leagues and Embassies of the Habessinians.

To the Portuguese. Helena *sent* Matthew *an* Armenian, *and wherefore. After a long stay in* India, *he Arrives in* Portugal, *Suspected. From* Portugal, Odoardus Galvan *sent Ambassador. To whom* Rodericus Limaeus *Succeeds.* Alvarez *his Priest. Are after six years dismiss'd with* Tzagazaabus *to the Pope. Which Letters* Alvarez *carried to* Rome. *Read at* Bononia, *and with what effect. Upon receiving the* Portugueze *Succour, they do not refuse the* Latin *Religion. Whence hopes of their Embracing the* Roman *Faith. Letters sent to the Pope. An Embassie appointed, without Effect. Commerce with the* Europeans *interrupted: nor admitted unless try'd by Merchants. Embassies rare in* Habessinia, *unless to* Constantinople; *or to* Batavia. *Embassadors Forrainers. A League with the* Persians.

AT what time the *Portugueses*, making several Voyages into *India*, made War upon several Nations, their fame reach'd the *Abessinians* also; who glad that the Power of the *Saracens* was brought low, and that *Egypt* and their Patriarch of *Alexandria* was restor'd to freedom, were in hopes that the Passage to *Jerusalem* would be open. At the same time also was *Peter Covillian* among the *Habessines*, who had given them more certain Relations concerning the *Portugueses*. Therefore *Helena*, the Grandmother of *David*, and Governess of the Kingdom, as we have said, sent an Embassador into *Portugal*, one *Matthew* an *Armenian*, skilful in Foraign Affairs, and one that understood the Arabic Language, joyning with him a Young Nobleman of *Habessinia*. She was willing to employ a Forraigner, either because she could find none among her own People that were fit for such an Employment; or that she believ'd none of that Nation could get safely into *Portugal*, that Kingdom being hated by the Neighbouring Nations, by reason of the Pyracies of the *Saracens*. *Matthew* was certainly in danger, and sometimes detain'd a Prisoner among the *Arabians*, out of whose hands he us'd many devices to escape; and at length got safe to *Goa*, to *Albuquerque*, Vice-Roy of *India*, together with his Colleague. By whom, tho he were nobly there entertain'd, yet he question'd the sending him into *Portugal*: Because such

an

an Embassie seem'd no way Correspondent to the Dignity and Grandeur of the famous *Presbyter John*. And therefore he resolv'd first to expect the Kings Pleasure. Thereupon *Matthew* being detain'd Three Years in *India*, at length in the Year 1513. he arriv'd in *Portugal*. The (z) Letters which he brought from *Helena* being written with the *Ethiopic* plainness, without any bombast of gaudy Titles, seem'd to contain more than they that sent them were able to perform. For they freely offer'd safe Conduct, and a Thousand other necessary Conveniences for Ships, which was look'd upon as a piece of boasting Vanity by the *Portugals*, who perhaps thought the Queen had spoken of the *Indian* Vessels of those Nations that lay upon the *Red Sea*. *Matthew* himself an ordinary Merchant, without any Magnificence of Train, was hardly thought worthy so high an Employment; and they were afraid of future shame for having acknowledg'd a false Embassadour. After many and long delays, at length they were satisfy'd; and in return, another Embassie was decreed to the *Habessines*, and *Odoardus Galvan* was sent upon that Employment. He dying by the way, *Roderick Limez* was sent in his room, whose Priest was *Francis Alvarez*, who left behind him an Itinerary, written in the *Portugueze* Language in a plain and ordinary style, tho afterwards, for Curiositie's sake, translated into several (a) Languages.

Six Years *Roderic Limez* resided in *Ethiopia*, before he was dismiss'd by the King, that he might be in a Capacity to make the same return of Kindness to the *Portugals*. At length he sent him back, joyning with him *Tzagazabus*, with Letters to the Pope and the King of *Portugal*, flourish'd at the beginning, with those usual Titles, which we have already recited. But what is to be admir'd at, *Tzagazabus* arriv'd not at *Rome*, till the Year 1539, being detain'd at *Lisbon*. Certain other (b) Letters were also recommended to *Alvarez*,

(z) They are to be found after the Preface of *Alvarez*'s Itinerary, as also in the Treatise of *Damianus a Goes*, concerning the Great Emperour of the *Indians*, to *Emanuel*, King of *Portugal*, first printed at *Dordrecht*. But *Tellezius* forgot himself, where he writes, That *Matthew* brought *David*'s Epistle full of Titles; for that is to be attributed to *Alvarez* or *Tzagazabus*.

(a) By *Michael de Selves* into *Spanish*; by others into *Italian* and *Dutch*: *Jovius* promis'd also to do it into *Latin*, but fail'd.

(b) Extant in *Alvarez*. *Damianus a Goes*. of the *Ethiopian* Customes. and Tom. 11. *Mission. Illustrat.* p. 1252.

who

who carry'd them to *Bononia*, and made a long Discourse of the Respect and Reverence which the Kings of *Habessinia* had to the See of *Rome*. They were read before *Clement* the Seventh, and the Emperour *Charles* the First, with the general Applause of the Court of *Rome*; but with no Success. For that *Claudius* the King plainly deny'd to ratifie either those things, or what *John Bermudes* afterwards related at *Rome* to the same effect; as if never given in Command, nor so understood, but that the business of the Embassie, and consequently the Letters themselves had bin faign'd and contriv'd by the *Portugals*. However, the *Habessinians* being reduc'd to very great streights, at the intercession of *Bermudes*, had an assistance of Four hunder'd and fifty men granted, and sent into *Habessinia* by the Command of *John* the Third. But *Peter Pays* positively writes, That this was done at the request of the Queen of *Ethiopia*. And that *Stephen Gomez* who sail'd into the *Red Sea* to burn the *Turkish* Ships, and by chance came to an Anchor before the Iland of *Matzua*, after he had consulted his Councel of Warr, resolv'd to send the said Supply, as seeming to be for the honour of God and the King. Of which Consultation there had certainly bin no need, if the King had Commanded the Supply before. However it were, that Succour was not onely very necessary, but very advantageous to the *Habessines*. From which time the *Habessines* were not onely gratefully, but honourably receiv'd among the *Habessines*: nor did they then refuse the *Latin* Religion, but frequently went to the *Portugueze* Chappels, and admitted Them into Theirs. Moreover, they also gave Liberty to the *Habessinian* Women that were marry'd to the *Portugueses*, to go to Mass with their Husbands, and to partake of the same Ceremonies with them. So that during the Raign of *Claudius*, there was great Hopes both at *Rome* and at *Lisbon*, that the *Habessinians* might be perswaded to embrace the *Romish* Religion. But that Hope proving vain, there was for some time a Cessation of Embassies, and the *Abessinian* Friendship with the *Lusitanians* was almost interrupted; untill by the Artifices of the Fathers of the Society, the Minds of the later Kings were somewhat more inclinably dispos'd to give Obedience to the See of *Rome*.

Upon that, Letters were written to the Pope and the King of

of *Spain*, who was then also King of *Portugal*, and answers upon them, which gave an Occasion to *Susneus* to decree an Embassie into *Europe*. To that purpose (*e*) *Fecur-Egzie* was chosen, and with him *Antonio Fernandez* was joyn'd, who were commanded by unknown and by-ways to Travel *Southward*, till they reach'd *Melinda*, upon the Shore of the *Indian Ocean*, from whence the Passage was more Easie and Safe into *India*. Thereupon setting forth out of *Gojam*, they Travell'd through *Enarea*, from thence into the Kingdom of *Zendero*, and so to *Cambata*, the Last Kingdom under the *Habessine* Dominions. Thence Travelling into *Alaba*, they were forbid to go any farther, by the Governour of the Province, who was a *Mahometan*. He apprehended the Embassador with his Train; and had not the Law of Nations bin of some force among the *Barbarians* (for they had about them to shew both their Letters and Presents from the Emperour) they had bin put to death, with the Law in their own hands. Being by that means set at Liberty, after a Years and seven Months time spent in hard Travel, after many sad Experiences of Savage Barbarity and a Thousand Jeopardies, they return'd home without effecting any thing. Nor can any reason be certainly given, why those unknown and dangerous Ways were chosen, thorough so many Barbarous Nations, so many Wild and Desert Countries, when the **Road** lay so plain through the Kingdom of *Dancale* in Friendship with the *Abessines*, to the Port of *Baylur*, which the Patriarch of *Portugal* afterwards securely made use of: as if so tedious a Journey had bin impos'd upon the Undertakers, not so much to go upon an Embassie, as for the Discovery of Forraign Countries, and By-Roads, for the Direction of Travellers.

After that, there happening a difference between them and the See of *Rome*, all manner of Commerce and Communication with the *Europeans* ceas'd: Insomuch, that now they would with great reluctancy admit those whom before they so highly admir'd, and with great difficulty would dismiss, out of their affection to Arts and Sciences; especially, if they suspected them to be Clergy-men, or under Religious Vows,

(*e*) Misfortunes *Fecur-Egzi* in *Tellezius*, l. 2. c. 1.

For

For which reason they try'd them first, by offering a Wife to every Stranger.

Otherwise, they rarely send any Embassadors abroad, unless it be into *Egypt*, when they have need of the Metropolitan. For they are not onely ignorant of forraign Affairs and Languages, but of the Ways and Roads of other Countries. By reason of their Vicinity to the *Turks*, and thence their frequent Commerce one with another, sometimes they are forc'd to send Embassadors to *Constantinople*, as in the Year 1660. So in the Year 1661, one *Michael* was sent thither with the wonted Presents; a living *Zecora*; several Skins of dead ones; Pigmies and the like, as *Thevenot* writes. In the Year 1671, another Embassador was sent, with some of those painted Beasts, and Letters to the *Dutch* Governour of *Batavia*. But they who are sent, are generally Forrainers, *Maronites*, *Armenians*, or else *Arabians*. But as for what *Leonardus Rauchwolf* writes in his Itinerary, it is altogether vain and false: That *Presbyter John* having made a League with the *Persians*, sent a *Persian* Bishop with so many Priests, that in Two years time they converted Twenty Christian Cities to the Christian Religion. It seems to be an old and confus'd Relation, and to be understood of that same ancient *Asiatic Prester Cham*, Neighbouring at that time upon the *Persians*. But he ascribes this passage to the Emperour of the *Abessines*, and that it came to pass Twelve years before his coming. *Philip Nicolai* believ'd him, and inserted this Figment into his Book concerning the Raign of Christ, adding the Year 1562, at what time the Affairs of the *Habessines* were in their most afflicted Estate.

Chap. XVII.

Of the Vice-Roys, Presidents and Governors of Provinces.

The various Titles of Vice-Roys and Governors. Ded Azmat *the Common Title of Presidents. The cause and Original of this Variety; And of the Imperial Title.*

THE Vice-Roys, Presidents and Governours of Countries which the King appoints and layes aside at his pleasure, are not call'd by any common sort of Title: but according to the several Kingdoms which they govern, derive to themselves particular Appellations. Some there are who are honour'd with Royal Titles; as,

Negus Gan, King of *Gan*,
Enareja Negus, King of *Enarea*.

Others are thought worthy the ancient appellation of *Nagasi*, in the *Amharic* Dialect, *Nagash*; which word signifies a Ruler, Commander or Lord. And was formerly more especially attributed to the *Ethiopian* Kings by the *Arabians*, as has bin already said: as,

Bahr-Nagash, Ruler or Regent of the *Sea Coast*.
Gojam-Nagash, Regent of *Gojam*.
Walaka Nagash, Regent of *Walaka*.

The word *Ras*, put absolutely, or with the proper name of the person signifies the Chief Commander or General of an Army: but if the name of the Kingdom be added, it signifies the Governor thereof; the same with the *Germans*, *Hauptman* or *Lands-Hauptman*; as,

Angot Ras, Captain of *Angot*.
Bugna Ras, Captain of *Bugna*.

This Title *Tzagazaabus* assum'd, altho he were but a Monk, while he subscrib'd to the Confession of Faith by him set forth, as followes.

Bugna

Bugna Ras, Arch-Presbyter, *Tzagazeab*, Embassador from *Jan Beluli Hatze Lebna Denghel*.

Some suffice themselves with the Title of *Shum*, which is otherwise common to all the Governors of *Guraga* and *Cambata*.

Guraga-Shum, Governor of *Guraga*.
Cambata-Shum, Governor of *Cambata*.

whom at other times they call the King of the *Hadians*.

The Vice-Roy of *Tigra*, is call'd *Macuenen*, as *Tigre Macuenen*, President or Judge of *Tigra*.

The names of the rest are not to be expounded out of the *Ethiopic* Language; being perhaps words significative in the vulgar Dialects; as,

Ambara, } *Tzasaldam*.
Damota, }
Shewa, }

Dembea Cantiba.
Bagemder Azmat.
Gedma Kyeen.
Ifata Walasma.
Fatagar Aguan.
Samen Aga-fari.

The Governor of *Dibai* is call'd *Ded-Asmat*, which is properly the common Title of all Presidents, and signifies the Captain of a Provincial Militia, or a Colonel. This diversity of Titles seems to arise from hence, for that the ancient Possessors of these Kingdoms, before they came to be reduc'd under the Power of the *Habessines*, assum'd those Titles of Dignity to themselves, which afterwards the Vulgar People gave to their several Governors in their distinct Idiomes. Or else the Governors themselves retain'd the ancient names; the Kings of *Ethiopia* conniving at it, as esteeming it for their Honour to have so many Persons of several Dignities at their devotion. For because the Governors and Vice-Roys of Provinces assum'd to themselves the Titles of *Negus*, and *Nagasi*, therefore the *Ethiopic* Kings took an occasion to give themselves the Title of *Negusa Nagast*, or *King of Kings*.

Chap. XVIII.

Of the Princes that are Tributary to the Kings of Ethiopia, *and of others subject to him, that claim absolute Dominion in their own Territories.*

Tributary Princes were Forty, much less Sixty; Gregory *acknowledg'd but Four: appointed by the King for a time. That Dignity hereditary to some few. The next equally Subject. The reason. All call'd Servants, even the Queen her self which seem'd very severe to the* Portugals. *The same Custom among the* Russes. *The Kings Pavilion sacred. The strange behaviour of Supplicants: and various manners of supplicating. How the King carries himself toward Supplicants. The Ceremonies of Supplicants among the* Turks *and the* Indians. *The gentleness of the* European *Princes begets them love.*

THat the Kings of *Ethiopia* formerly had several Tributary Kings under them, we have already declar'd. (*f*) *Matthew* the *Armenian* reckn'd them up, tho untruly, to the number of Fifty, tho most erroneously. Nor did they write with more Truth, who tell us of Fifty or Forty; whenas they have not so many *Vice-Roys*. *Gregory* knew but Four, that is to say, the Kings of *Sennar*, *Dancala*, *Gorgea*, and *Enarea*. As for the *King* of *Sennar*, he has often revolted and made Warr upon the *Abessines*. The *King* of *Dancala* is a firm Allie, but oblig'd to no sort of Tribute. All the rest, whether *Kings* or Governors, are by the *King* himself appointed to govern such and such *Kingdoms* and *Provinces*, and are only *pro tempore*. Some few there are, that claim a supreme Dignity by right of Inheritance. But all of Royal descent; and all other of the Nobility, who are reputed to derive their Pedigrees from the *Israelitish* Race, are equally subject to the *King*; without any distinction of Dukes, Earls, Marquesses and Barons, as (*g*) *Matthew* fabulously asserts. For the *Kings* of *Ethiopia*, as most of the Eastern *Kings*, deem it not a

(*f*) This *Dam. de Goes.* relates of him, in his Book, concerning the State and Kingdom of *Presbyter John*, n. 11.

(*g*) *Ibid.* n. 13. There are, saith he, in *Abassia*, Lords, Dukes, Earls and Barons innumerable. I would be willing to know how they are call'd in the *Ethiopic* Language.

decent

decent thing to command Illustrious Families. Not believing that Servitude can be expected from those that are accustom'd to Command themselves. Moreover, they presume that Hereditary Dignity is an obstruction to Vertue; that Men are more certainly made, than born great; and that they will prove more faithful, whom they have rais'd from the Dust, then such as claim their Fortunes from their Ancestors. Therefore the *Kings* of *Ethiopia* accompt themselves onely Lords; all others they look upon as Servants: in that particular not sparing their Brothers or their Kindred. So that when they bestow any Government upon them, they use this form, *We have created our Servant such a one Governour of this, or that Province.* Nor do they ever discourse them but in the singular number, *Thou*: whereas we generally make use in our Language of the second person plural. No other Epithite do they afford their own Queens, tho of the highest Rank of Nobility. *We have caus'd to Raign*, that is, *We have taken to Wife our Servant such a one.* Nor do they disdain these Titles: but on the contrary call themselves reciprocally *his Servants.* This word *Servant*, was very ill digested by a generous *Portuguese*, as looking upon the title of *Slave*, to be a disgrace to him that was a *Freeman.* And therefore he offer'd a good Summ of Money to him, that, according to Custome, was to proclaim the Government conferr'd upon him, to leave out the word *Servant*, and onely to proclaim his bare name; but could not obtain it. Nor is the *Negus* of *Ethiopia* to be tax'd for this alone, seeing all the Princes of *Africa* and *Asia* use the same Custom. The same Soveraignty is claim'd and maintain'd by the *Russian* Emperour; whose Grandees never call themselves any other then *Golop*, his *Servants*, nor in their Letters which they write to him do they subscribe their names any otherwise than in the (*h*) *Diminutive.* We are also to understand, That the word *Gabar*, or *Servant*, has a more diffusive signification among Them than among Us. For it extends not to real Slaves alone, but their Subjects and Domesticks. And indeed, to say truth, they differ but little from Slaves, who are bound to observe their

(*h*) As for Example; *Hanseku*, *Stephanul*, *Lavrentik*, thy Servant. *Olear.* his Itinerary.

King

King at all times with Body, having nothing at all of Property, to which they can lay the leaſt claim. Nor are the Ceremonies leſs ſervile by which they teſtifie their Submiſſion and Reverence to their *King*. The *Bah-tu-ded* himſelf the Chief of his Miniſters, as *Alvarez* relates it, ſtood before the *King*'s Pavillion, naked up to his Thighs, with his Head and his right hand almoſt touching the Earth, and a poor Linnen ſwath-band about his forehead, crying out thrice, *Aheto*, or *moſt merciful Lord*. Being ask'd according to Cuſtome, *Who he was*? he anſwer'd, *He was the meaneſt of the Court, that Saddl'd the Kings Carriage Horſes, ready prepar'd to obey all Commands*. When the Kings Meſſenger, whom they call *Kal Hatze*, the King's Voice, declares the *King*'s Commands afoot, it behoves all that hear to be afoot. Neither is it lawful to ride up to the *King*'s Pavillion, no more than if it were to ſome Altar, but the perſon muſt always alight at a diſtance.

Suppliants having occaſion to make their Petitions to the *King*, ſtand in a certain place, and inſtead of Petitions which they know not how to write, betimes in the Morning with loud Voices and different Tones, whereby they may be ſeverally diſtinguiſh'd by their Countries, they wake the ſleeping King, beſeeching him to hear their complaints. They of *Ambara* and *Shewa*, and thoſe that uſe the ſame Dialect, redouble theſe following Exclamations as faſt as they can ſpeak, *Shan Hoi, Shan Hoi, My King, My King*. Some add *Belul Hoi, Shan Hoi, Belul Hoi*; *My Apple of my Eye, My King, My Apple of my Eye*.

Hence *Tzaga-za-abus* compos'd his ridiculous *Shan Belul*, (by others more corruptly *Beldigian*) *King Apple of my Eye*, much more ridiculouſly render'd (1) *High* or *Precious John*.

The *Tigreans*, in their Supplications, cry out, *Haduelje*, *My Lord*.

The Inhabitants of *Dambea* and *Dara*, *Jegja*, or *Our Lord*.

Thoſe of *Gaſats* and *Gojam*, *Abkaw*, *O Father of Orphans*.

The Mahometan implores his own *Ja Saddi*, or, *O my Lord*.

(1) In his Confeſſion of Faith above mention'd. *Tom. 2. Miſſion. Illuſtr.* p. 1311.

Those of *Gonga* and *Enarea*, *Donzo*, *Lord*.

The *Lusitanians* in their own Language make use of their own *Senhor*, *Senhor*, *Senhor*, till they are heard. The *Barbarians*, the more savage they are, so much the more harsh and obstreperous in their Tones. For the *Gallans*, like so many Wolves, howl out their *Hu*, *Hu*, *Hu*. Others bark like Doggs, or imitate the inarticulate noises of Wolves, Apes, and other Wild Beasts, to the end they may be thereby the better distinguish'd. But the more Civiliz'd, and those that belong to the Camp use no other exclamation, but that of their *Abeto*, *Abeto*, *Abeto*, or *Lord*, *Lord*, *Lord*: which Appellation of Honour is attributed not onely to the King, but to all those whom we call (*k*) mild and merciful Lords. Others addressing themselves for relief, make use of other expressions, by which they think the King may be most honour'd; saluting him by the name of Sun, or Lord of their Hearts. But the Monks, unless access be permitted them, sing a certain *Hymn*.

These particular Tones of Suppliants are taken notice of; and as soon as day appears, such and such are commanded to be admitted, and heard: or if it be a business of moment, the King himself gives them audience and returns them their answer. And surely it is the chief Office of Kings to hear the Complaints of their Suppliants, and to administer timely Justice to their Subjects. Of which the *Barbarian* Kings not being unmindful, gave opportunity to poor and miserable people, to whom their Court was shut up from access, to convey their Complaints to the Kings Ears. Among the *Turks*, the Suppliants always carry a lighted fire upon their heads before the Window of the *Sultan*. In the Bed-Chamber of the Great *Mogul*, there always hangs a Bell, which it is lawful for the Suppliant to ring, standing at the farthermost end of the Palace, but he is taken into Custody by the Guards; and if afterwards he do not make good his Accusation, he loses his Life for his presumptuousness. Our Princes after a more noble manner receive Petitions from the hands of their Suppliants, and thereby greatly win the love

(*k*) See the Relation of *Jerome Lupus*, Printed in *English*, Entitl'd a short Relation of the River *Nile*. p. 40. See more in *Sandoval de Rebus. Æthiop.* Salut. 250.

of

of their Subjects. They who despise that sort of Clemency,
or whip out at their back doors to avoid the sight or giving
Ear to the miserable, do but onely procure Sadness to their
People, and Hatred and Contempt to themselves.

CHAP. XIX.

Of their Judiciary Proceedings and Punishments.

Their Judicial Proceedings very plain. Witnesses slightly and cursorily examined. Appeals rare. Their Punishments, Stoning, Drubbing, and Banishment. Homicides how punished. A Discourse of Like for Like.

THe manner of their Judicial Proceedings is very plain
and ordinary. For all Controversies are determin'd by
word of Mouth, without any noise of Process, without any
Writs, or Writings, of which the most part of the Nation is
ignorant. The Plaintiff has liberty to produce his Witnesses, which the Defendant may refuse, if he have any reason
to suspect them. But in regard of their ignorance of the true
Proceedings by way of Interrogatory and proof, nor understand how to examin a Witness, it must of necessity follow,
That Justice is but ill administer'd, where the Witnesses are
so cursorily heard. It is lawful to appeal from Inferiour
Sentences either to the King or the Court-Tribunals: but
that is seldom done, by reason of the Poverty of the People,
and the tediousness of Travelling: and partly out of the
Little hopes they have of redress. For the Governours and
Judges of Provinces are offended with appeals, as seeming
to them an accusation of Injustice; and therefore the wrong'd
Parties fearing their displeasure, rather choose to lose their
right, than the favour of the Judges. Neither does the resigning of Office afford any relief against an unjust Sentence.
For either through Favour or for Money they obtain a Pardon for all things done amiss in their Magistracy.

Among the sorts of Punishments inflicted upon Offenders,
besides *Beheading* and *Hanging*, the most ready at hand is
Stoning to death: the Soyl affording sufficient materials for
that sort of Execution. The next is *Drubbing*, if the Crime
be not Capital.

The

The punishment of the Nobility, is Exilement into the *Zanic* Lake, or into their high and steep Rocks, which are in a manner like Ilands; from whence however they frequently escape by reason that the People are easily corrupted by Bribery.

Homicides are deliver'd up to the next of (*l*) Kin to the Party murder'd, at whose free will it is, to pardon the Malefactors, sell them to forraign Merchants, or put them to what death they please. If the Homicide escape unknown, the Inhabitants of the place and all the Neighbourhood are oblig'd to pay a Fine; by which means many Murthers are either prevented or discover'd.

Most certainly the Law of *Like for Like*, was always and still is accompted the most just, and plainest among several Nations. Hence that of *Moses*, *An Eye for an Eye, and a Tooth for a Tooth.* But because there is not the same use of all members among men, some men according to their various Callings having more use of one Member than another; some being better able to lose their Hands than their Leggs: others their Leggs than their Hands: therefore among the Civiliz'd Nations this Law grew out of custome. And it seems unjust to surrender the Offender to the Malice and Fury of the Offended Party, when they may have unbyass'd Judges, to give Sentence without Favour or Affection.

(*l*) A Custome still us'd in *Persia*, as you may read in *Tavernier* and *Olearius*.

The End of the Second Book.

OF THE Ecclesiastical Affairs OF THE ABISSINES.

BOOK III.

Chap. I.

Of the ancient Religion of the Abissines, *and their Judaic Rites.*

The Ecclesiastical History of the Abissines *corrupt; and why. The first Relation of* Matthew *the* Armenian *false;* Tzagazaabo's *Confession as little to be credited. Those of the Fathers, and* Tellezius *more certain. Ecclesiastical History commended. The Tradition of some concerning the Original of the Judaic Rites. Circumcision us'd by many. How it differs from the Judaic. No place of holy Worship among the* Habessines. *Females circumcis'd. Why the* Abissines *abstain from Swines Flesh. The Various Customs of Nations concerning Meats. The Sabbath observ'd in the Primitive Church; Different from the Lords Day, and how. Whether lawful to marry a Brothers Wife. They abstain from the shrunk Sinew. What to be thought of* Candaces *Eunuch.* Menilehec's *Posterity revolted from the true Religion.* Claudius *disclaims the Judaic Religion.*

NOw we proceed to the Ecclesiastical History of the *Habessinians*, then which there is not any other more corrupt. For whatever we find scatter'd in our Relations, were neither collected out of the Books which are publickly authentic in *Habessinia*, nor taken from the report of any persons there skill'd in the Ecclesiastical Affairs of that Country, but partly ill related through the Rashness of the Writers themselves; partly by the same persons or others ill understood through their ignorance of the *Ethiopic* Language.

The

The first Relation concerning the Religion of the *Habessines*, was set forth by *Damianus a Goez*, a noble *Lusitanian*, from the Report of *Matthew the Armenian*, First *Ethiopic* Embassador to *Emanuel* King of *Portugal*; which Narrative of his (*a*) contains many things ambiguous, many other things altogether false. Insomuch that *Zagazabus*, the second *Habessinian* Embassador, plainly tax'd the Author of it, (*b*) for his ignorance. Tho he himself in the Confession of his Faith, which the same (*c*) *Goez* set forth, did not much excel him either for truth or probability, for which reason *Tellezius* not undeservedly reprehends him. Certainly *Gregory* was very much offended with him; And when he heard his following Doctrines,

1. *That Jesus Christ was the Son of the Father, and the beginning of himself: in the same manner that the Holy Ghost, was the Spirit of himself, and proceeded from the Father and the Son.*

2. *That he descended into Hell where was the Soul of Adam, and Christ himself, which Soul of* Adam *Christ received from the Virgin* Mary: and toward the latter end of the Book, *That Christ descended into Hell for the Soul of* Adam *and not for his own.*

3. *That the Souls of men piously deceas'd are not crucify'd in Purgatory upon the Sabath and Lords Day.*

4. *That by the Decree and Commandment of Queen* Maqueda *the Women were also to be Circumcis'd, as having a certain glandulous piece of Flesh, not unfit to receive the Impression and mark of Circumcision.*

I say, when *Tellezius* heard these things, and many other of the same mixture, in no small heat and Passion, he cry'd out, *That they were Fictions, Dreams, my Sweet Lyes*: frequently repeating those words; *If he said this, he was a Beast of the Field.*

Yet out of these Books most of those Stories have flow'd, which our Writers have made public, concerning the Reli-

(*a*) In a little Treatise often quoted, *Of the Embassie of the Great Emperor of the* Indians.

(*b*) For thus he sayes in his Confession of Faith, *Matthew, in regard he was an Armenian, could not so perspicuously understand our affairs, especially those that relate to our Faith. And therefore he reported many things to King* Emanuel, *which are not to be believed. Which he did not out of desire to tell an untruth, because he was a good man, but because he knew little concerning our Religion.* But in my opinion, that good man *Matthew* spake many things, which he knew much better.

(*c*) Extant in the 1. Tom. of *Spain* illustrated, p. 1304.

gion of the *Abessines*. But the Fathers of the Society, having bin conversant so long in *Ethiopia*. and view'd the *Habessine* Books, after several Disputations and Discourses with them, have bin able to afford us more Truth, whose Acts and Writings being free for the perusal of *Tellezius*, we shall cull the choicest of his accurate Relations, and what he has reported more ambiguous or more partially, out of his dislike of the *Alexandrian* Religion, we shall correct out of their own Writings, or from the Discourses of *Gregory* himself.

Certainly to Christians, no History can be more pleasant than that of Ecclesiastical affairs; especially if we look back to the Primitive Church. For whom would it not ravish into a high admiration of the wonderful Providence of God as well in founding as preserving his Church; when he shall consider that it grew up, and increas'd, not by the Propagation of Arms or human Arts, but by the Oppression of Heathenish persecution. To whom can it be unpleasing to consider with a Pious Contemplation, the undaunted Courage of the Martyrs, the Constancy of her Doctors, the Sincerity of the Christian People, the Purity of the Faith, the Strife of Good Works, the Patience of the Weak, the plainness of the Rites and Ceremonies? Which when they once began to be alter'd, with the reverence to the Church be it spoken, then also enter'd in Pride instead of Modesty, Ambition instead of Charity, together with Faction and Contention. As if our leisure and our Quiet were therefore granted us by Heaven to consume that time in making Scrutinies into all the misteries of Faith, and moving such impertinent Questions, which ought to be spent in exercises of Charity and Piety.

But I return to the Religion of the *Habessines*, concerning the Original of which, there are various Opinions of sundry Authors. They that admit the Tradition of the *Habessines* concerning Queen *Maqueda*, are of Opinion, that the *Abessines* had the true knowledge of God, ever since the Raign of King *Solomon*, and that their Judaic Rites, such as *Circumcision, abstaining from meats forbidden, Observation of the Sabbath, Marriage of the Brothers Wife, and the like*, had their Original from thence. But in regard these things were commonly practis'd as well in other Nations, as among the Primitive Nations, who conform'd to the *Jews* in several things, It is not a thing to be easily affirm'd, that these were the footsteps of those Ceremonies receiv'd so many Ages before from the

the *Jews*. For not onely the *Jews*, but several other Nations made use of Circumcision, and still so do to this day, tho not out of any knowledge of its Original, or any Consideration of Divine Worship. The most (*d*) ancient Historians tells us, That the *Egyptians* were the first that instituted that Ceremony, or else learnt it from the *Ethiopians*. From thence it came to be in use among the *Colchi*, *Phenicians*, and *Syrians*. They of *Anajah*, an *Ethiopian* Nation, circumcise with sharp Stones. And *Ephinanius* expresly mentions the *Homerites*, from whence the *Habessinians* are descended, for the same Custome. We omit the *Troglodytes*, *Nigrites*, and other innumerable Nations, which either do not understand the cause of it, use it for (*e*) cleanliness; or else pretend it to be conducible (*f*) to generation; or that they have a longer *Preputium*, and therefore thought it convenient to have it cut away, as (*g*) *Thevenot* writes; for fear those more pure *Musulmen*, should be polluted with their own Urine.

Neither did *Mahomet* recommend it to his *Arabians*, as learnt from the *Jews*; but left the Custom as he found it; nor does he make any mention of it in all his Alcoran. Besides, there is a great difference between the Circumcision of the *Jews* and that of other Nations. For other Nations onely round the Skin with the Knife, but the *Jews* slit the Skin with their nailes, till the *Preputium* falls down, and leaves the Nut altogether bare; for unless there be *Periguah denudation*, they do not think the Circumcision accomplish'd. For so their Doctors teach, *Who circumcises and does not lay bare, is as one that never circumcis'd*. So that if the Skin should happen to grow together again, it must be again dissected. Whence it is easier to understand what is meant by those Places in Scripture which mention the (*h*) drawing over of his *Preputium*. For being cut off, it can never be restored by any Art, but being onely slit or torn, it may be sowed together again. Whence

(*d*) Herodot. in *Thalia*.

(*e*) τῆς καθαρότητος ἕνεκα for cleanliness sake. *Idem*.

(*f*) *Philo Judaeus* in his peculiar Chapter of Circumcision, brings these and many more reasons.

(*g*) In his Oriental Itinerary. *c.* 52, *p.* 1.

(*h*) If any one be Circumcised, let him not draw over, *&c.*

is

it is easie to find that the *Habessines* do not use the same manner of Circumcising with the *Jews*. Neither is it performed with any signal Ceremony or Commemoration. For it is done privately by some poor woman or other, without any Standers by, not so much as the Father himself. But the Confession of *Claudius* King of *Ethiopia*, takes away all doubt, who to clear himself and his people from all Suspition of Judaisme, says thus.

But as to the Custome of Circumcision, we do not Circumcise like the Jews, *For we understand the words of* St. Paul, *the Fountain of Wisdome, who saith,* It profits not to be Circumcis'd, *nor doth Circumcision avail: but rather the new Creation, which is Faith in our Lord Jesus Christ. And then to the* Corinthians *he sayes, again, who hath taken upon him Circumcision,* (i) *let him not keep his Preputium. All the Books of* St. Pauls *learning are among us, and tell us of Circumcision and the Preputium; but our Circumcision is done according to the custom of the Country, like incisions of the Face in* Ethiopia *and* Nubia, *and boaring the Ears among the* Indians.

This puts us in mind of the Circumcision of Females, of which *Gregory* was somewhat asham'd to discourse, and we should have more willingly omitted it, had not *Tzagazabus* in his rude Confession of Faith, spoken of it as of a most remarkable Custom introduced by the command of Queen *Maqueda*; or had not *Paulus Jovius* himself, Bishop of *Como*, insisted in the same manner upon this unseemly Custome. This same Ceremony was not onely us'd by the *Habissines*, but also familiar among other people of *Africa* the (k) *Ægyptians*, and the *Arabians* themselves. For they cut away from the Female Infants something which they think to be an Indecency and Superfluity of Nature. The most impudent women that inhabit about the *Cape of good Hope*, still retain this Custome, and for a small matter, expose themselves to the Sea-men. *Jovius* calls it, *Caruncula*m, or a little *piece of Flesh*. *Golius*, an oblong Excrescence. The *Arabians* by a particular word called it *Bedhron* or *Bedhara*, beside which they have many other words to

(i) The Printed Copy varies from this, where the words are more obscure. *If any one goes in uncircumcised, let him not go forth.*

the

the same purpose. Among their Women it is as great a piece of reproach, to revile a woman by saying to her, *O Bonkarom*: that is, *O uncircumcis'd*, as to call a man *Arel*, or *uncircumcis'd* among the *Jews*. A strange thing, that onely in *Africa* and some Parts of *Asia*, the Women should be noted for those exuberancies: for the Jewish women in *Germany*, being acquainted by their reading with this Custome, laugh at it, as admiring what it should be that should require such an amputation.

Nevertheless this seems to have some reference to the forbidden use of Swines Flesh, and other Meats not allow'd by the Mosaic Law, as the same King *Claudius* manifestly gives us to understand in his Confession.

But as to what relates to the Eating of Swines Flesh, we are not forbid it, out of regard to the observance of the Mosaic Law, as the Jews *were. For we do not abhor him that feeds upon it; nor do we force him that does not, to make it his diet, as our Father* Paul *writing to the* Romans *hath written. Who eats, let him not contemn him that eateth not, for the Lord accepts all. The Kingdom of Heaven consists not in meat or drink. But it is not good for a man to eat to the scandal of another: And* Matthew *the Evangelist sayes, Nothing can defile a man but that which goeth out of his mouth. For whatever goeth into the belly, and is retain'd in the stomach, that at length is cast into the Draught. And thus he pronounces all meat clean. Now while he spake those words he destroy'd the whole structure of the* Jews *Error, who were learned in the Books of the Mosaic Law.*

Most Nations have a particular Dyet, some by custome, some through superstition.

Not to speak of the *Mahometans*, who abstain not only from Swines flesh, but from Wine, is not the custom of the *Banians*, not much different from the ancient *Pythagoreans*, to be strangely admir'd? who onely feed upon Herbs and Meats made of Milk, which we hardly believe sufficient to sustain Nature. Others there are that devour all sorts of Creatures which the flesh consuming Beasts themselves refuse, and otherwise nauseous to the most part of Men. The Oriental *Tartars* feed upon Camels, Foxes and all sorts of wild Beasts. Some of our *Europeans* indulging their appetites, please their palats with a sort of Dyet abominated by all other People, as Frogs, Cockles, and I know not what sort of Insects. *Gregory* had an utter aversion to Lobsters, Crabbs, Crayfish and Oysters, which we accompt our chiefest Delicacies: and it turn'd his stomach to see Turkies, Hares, and several other Dishes to which he was unaccustom'd, brought to our Tables. Being ask'd, why he abstain'd from Swines flesh? he retorted still, and *why we from Horse-flesh?* And most certainly were we to banquet with the *Tartars*, there are but very few of us that would easily be induc'd to eat Horse-flesh with an Appetite, tho it be one of their principal junkets. Nay their Embassadors to our Princes desire fat Horses for their Kitchins.

However they abstain from blood and things strangl'd,not out of any observance of the *Mosaic* Law, but an Apostolic Decree always in force in the Eastern Church: which was also for many Ages observ'd in the Western Church, and reviv'd in some Councils. They also rebuke us, for that we suffer'd that Decree to be laid aside.

Nor do they allow the *Jews* Sabboth out of a respect to Judaism, or that they learnt it from some certain Nations that kept the Seventh day holy. But because the ancient Custom of the Primitive Church, who observ'd that day perhaps out of complacency to the *Jews*, being long retain'd in the East, was at length carry'd into *Ethiopia*. For thus we find it written in some *ancient Constitutions* which they call the Constitutions of the Apostles.

Let the Servants labour five days, but let them keep the Holydays, the Sabboth, and the Lords Day in the Church for the sake of Pious Instruction.

The Council of *Laodicea* decreed that the Gospels with other parts of Scripture should be read upon the Sabboth; when before the Paragraphs of the Law of *Moses* were onely read upon the Sabboth,and the *Gospels* upon the Sunday: the Texts of the old Law being thought most agreeable to the Old Sabboth, and the Texts of the New Testament, to the New Sabboth.

Socrates also farther testifies that the People us'd to assemble at Church upon the Sabboth and Lords Day.

And *Gregory Nyssen*, whose Writings the *Ethiopians* have among them, saith,

With what Eyes dost thou behold the Lords Day, who hast defil'd the

the Sabbath? Know'st thou not that these two days are Twins, and that if thou injur'st the one, thou dost injury to the other?

But *Claudius* makes so much difference between both days, that he prefers the Lords day before the Sabaoth.

But as to what pertains to our Celebration of the ancient Sabaoth, we do not celebrate it, as the Jews did, who Crucify'd Christ, saying, Let his blood be upon Us and our Children. *For those Jews neither draw water, nor kindle fires, nor dress meat, nor bake bread; neither do they go from house to house. But we so celebrate it, that we administer the Sacrament, and relieve the Poor and the Widow, as our Fathers the Apostles commanded us. We Celebrate it as the Sabaoth of the first Holiday, which is a new day of which* David *saith,* This is the day which the Lord made, let us rejoyce and exult therein. *For upon that day our Lord Jesus Christ rose: and upon that day the Holy Ghost descended upon the Apostles in the Oratory of Sion. And in that day Christ was incarnated in the Womb of the Perpetual Virgin* St. Mary; *and upon that day he shall come again to reward the Just, and punish the Evil.*

Gregory also testify'd, That the *Habessines* abstain from no sort of Labour upon the Sabaoth, but from the most servile sorts of Labour. This Custom continu'd long in the Church, till it was abrogated by degrees; for by the 22d *Canon* of the said *Council* of *Laodicea* the Christians are forbid to work upon the Sabaoth. Nevertheless the Sacred Lectures were continu'd for a time, as appears by the Canon above mention'd, till at length those were also lef off, perhaps because that the People having a licence to work, there were but few that repair'd to Church.

Moreover, according to the Custom of the *Jews*, it is lawful in *Abessinia* to marry the Widow of the Brother deceas'd, as *Alvarez* testifies. Adding, That the *Habessinian* defend their so doing by the Laws of the Old Testament. But *Gregory* positively deny'd that it was lawful, but onely conniv'd at by the Magistrate. However, that such Wives are also prohibited from coming to the Holy Communion, wherein *Alvarez* agrees with him. However it does not therefore follow, that this Custom was translated from the *Jews* to the *Habessines*, no more then if any one should assert that the Laws of Polygamie and Divorce were deriv'd from the *Jews*. And yet this is somewhat strange, I must confess, that they abstain from that Muscle, which the *Hebrews* call *Ghid Hanesheh*, or the Sinew mutilated: the *Ethiopians*, *Serrje Beson*, *the forbidden Nerve*: the *Amharits*, *Shalada*. Which very probably they might learn from the *Jews* in their own Country, of which Nation there are several Colonies in *Ethiopia*.

But as to what is reported concerning Queen *Candaces* Eunuch, we have already shew'd that she was not Queen of *Habessinia*, but of the *Ethiopians* that inhabited the Iland of *Meroe*: and if the Eunuch were a *Jew*, it does not follow that his Lady the Queen shall be so too. Others there are who tell us, That *Menilehec*'s Successors in a short time return'd to the worship of Idols. Which if it be true, the assertion of the Continuation of the Jewish Religion till the time of the Apostles, will prove altogether vain: tho in *Europe* most certainly the *Habessines* were long suspected of Judaisme, and so are many to this day. Which King *Claudius* observing by his Disputations with *Gonsalo Rodriguez*, and the Writings which he compos'd to refute the Errors of the *Habessines*, set forth a Confession, of which we have already cited several parcels, as they related to our business. The chief Scope of which was, to remove that Suspition of Judaism from himself, and his Subjects, which in my opinion he very effectually did.

CHAP.

CHAP. II.

Of the Conversion of the Habesines *to the Christian Faith.*

The Conversion of the Habessines *attributed to* Queen Candace's *Eunuch; but contrary to authentic Histories.* Candace *no* Habessinian. *Other Traditions nothing better. Demonstrated when, and by whom. To which the* Book *of* Axuma *agrees. The Reasons of doubting and deciding.* Frumentius *how call'd. His Encomium.* Cedrenus *and* Nicephorus *refuted.*

IT is the Common Fame among the *Europeans*, That the Conversion of the *Habessines* to the Christian Faith was begun by that *Ethiopic* Eunuch, *Acts* 8.27. And perhaps the *Habessines* themselves, believing it to be for their Honour, were the authors of the Story: confiding in the Credit of the Book of *Axuma*, where, the same history is set down as in the *Acts of the Apostles*, and without any other Circumstances: by which it may seem this story had not its first original among them but was transcrib'd. Neither was *Tzagazaabo* better inform'd, as appears by his Confession of Faith. Nevertheless it seems very strange, that King *David* should either assert or give his assent to *Alvarez* affirming the same thing: whereas the Credit as well of the *Ethiopic* as *Greek* History absolutely tells us the contrary. Some endeavour a Reconciliation of this difference, as if the first dawnings of Christianity, tho but very dark and obscure, began at that time first to glimmer. But then this should have bin demonstrated by solid Reasons relating not onely to the *Ethiopic* Nation in general, but to the *Habessinians* in particular. Whereas the Testimonies which we shall cite by and by do not speak of the Conversion of those that were half Christians before, but either of the *Jews*, or *Heathens*. For we have already shew'd that *Candaces* was never Queen of the *Habessines*. Neither is her Proper Name *Lacasa*, which we find in the Vulgar Catalogues to be found in *Tellezius*. For *Hhendaque* or *Hindaque*, is a quite different word from *Candace*, from whence others casting away the Aspirate, derive the name *Judith*: others, as if they would correct the Error, have strain'd it to *Judith*. Nor was the name of *Candace* ever known to the *Habessines*, tho familiar to the Inhabitants of *Meroe*. Others refer the Conversion of the *Habessines* not to *Candace*'s Eunuch, but to the times of the Apostles, and particularly ascribe it to St. *Bartholmew*; others to St. *Matthew*; or because there is no such thing to be found in his life, to St. *Matthias*. Of all which Fancies the *Habessines* knew nothing, who hearing such Whimseys from our Countreymen, not without reason answer'd, *That perhaps these things were to be understood of the Lower* Ethiopia, *that lyes between* Abassia *and* Egypt. However we can never find out what the Success of those Apostles Preaching was: what Kings or People withstood that Conversion: what Pastors, what Ceremonies, what Books they made use of: what form of Discipline, or what was the Doctrine of that time. Concerning all which things, in regard there is so deep a silence, we cannot acknowledg any such beginnings of the Christian Religion in *Habessinia*.

However this is certain, That both the *Habessine*, *Grecian*, and *Latin* Writers, Especially *Ruffinus* and his followers, agree with one consent, That the Conversion of the *Ethiopians* happen'd in the time of St. *Athanasius*, Patriarch of *Alexandria* under *Constantius* the Great, about the Year of Christ 330, or not long after, and that in this manner. One *Meropius*, a Merchant of *Tyre*, (*Ruffinus* calls him a Philosopher) intending for *India*, put into Harbour upon the Coast of *Ethiopia* in the Red Sea, which at that time was also call'd the *Indian* Sea. There dying, or, as *Ruffinus* will have it, slain by the *Barbarians*, he left two Young men, *Frumentius* and *Ædesius*, *Fremonatum* and *Sydracum* the *Habessines* call them, who being taken and brought to the King, became highly favour'd and caress'd by reason of their Ingenuity and Industry; and at length being made free of the Country, were preferr'd by the King to keep his Books and Papers. The King dying, they remain'd in the same Imployment under the Queen Regent, till the Young King came of age.

All this while they entertain'd the Christian Merchants that Traffick'd into those Parts, with all kindness, and did them all the good offices imaginable, and made themselves so remarkable for their Vertue and their Integrity among those Nations, that the Christian Religion was highly esteem'd by all. Which foundation being laid, *Frumentius* took a Journey to St. *Athanasius*, Patriarch of *Alexandria*, and was by Him, for his great parts, and Constancy in the Faith,

created

created the first Bishop of *Ethiopia*. Thereupon returning into *Ethiopia*, he initiated the Inhabitants in the Christian Religion by Baptisme, then he ordain'd Presbyters and Deacons, built Churches, and so introduc'd the Christian Religion into *Ethiopia*. Agreeable to this, are those Relations which the *Ethiopians* have in their Book of *Axuma*, onely that there is this addition to the Story of the Conversion made by *Candace*, that these *Tyrian* Young men admir'd, that the *Ethiopians* should believe in Christ and adore the Holy Trinity, and that the Women wore Crosses upon their heads, seeing that the Gospel had bin preach'd among them by none of the Apostles. We wonder much more, that *Ethiopia* should be converted in the time of the Apostles, and yet have no Bishop, no Baptism, no Priests nor Deacons, and that all these things should be first setled in the time of St. *Athanasius*. Besides, no man can be easily perswaded that such a beginning should remain so long time without a farther progress, and that the *Ethiopians* themselves, or the Bishops of the Neighbouring Christians should be so neglectful as not to lend their helping hands to the advancement of such fair Beginnings, Especially at such a time, when the Christians over the whole *Roman* Empire, chiefly in *Egypt*, suffer'd a most dreadful Persecution under *Dioclesian*. How came it to pass that they did not seek for refuge in this Kingdom out of the reach of their Enemies, where they were sure of Sanctuary and Protection from a Prince of their own Religion? Could all the Ecclesiastical Histories, and the Annals of the Patriarch of *Alexandria* have forgotten a Prince, the first in all the World that had receiv'd the light of the Gospel? Were there no Martyrs, whose memories the *Habessines* are so sollicitous to preserve? No War, no Seditions upon the change of Religion, but so great an Alteration without any noise? To assert a thing of so much moment, and yet to bring no Circumstances, no particular Events and Casualties, seems very discrepant from the Truth of History.

It is sufficient that the *Ethiopians* agree with us in the principal matters. For whether *Meropius* dy'd or were slain, whether *Frumentius* and *Edesius* were call'd *Fremonatus* and *Sydrac*, signifies little. Yet in that Place *Ruffinus* was strangely deceiv'd. For he seems with others to have meant *India* properly so call'd, when he neither knew the Bounds or Situation of it, where he sayes, That the Hithermost *India* adjoyns to *Ethiopia*:

Ethiopia: Between which and *Parthia* he places the farthermost *India*. So that he makes the farthermost *India* nearest to *Ethiopia*, and *Parthia* more remote. This was the reason that *Baronius* believ'd there were two *Frumentius's*; and that one was a Preacher of the Gospel at *Axuma*: whereas it was but one and the same person, that was Apostle and Bishop of the *Habessines*, call them *Indians* or *Axumites*, which you please.

This reconciliation of differing Writers was not known till this time, nor does he undeservedly give the honour of the discovery to the Jesuites: and that then and not before the Christian Religion was first introduc'd in *Form*, as he calls it; as being led by tradition also, that Christianity had some kind of bloomings before in *Ethiopia*. But what it was, or to what growth it arriv'd, there is no man that can unfold. Neither does *Ruffinus* make mention of any Jewish Religion, or any other deformed Sect that preceded. On the contrary, to use his own rough expression, he sayes, *That this Land* (meaning *Abassia*) *was never broken up with the Plough-share of perfunct Preaching*. In short, *Gregory* affirm'd to me, that there was not any other Preaching of the Gospel in *Habessinia*, then what was first begun by *Abba Salma*, in the time of St. *Athanasius*, and in the Reigns of *Azbeha*, and *Abreha*, Brethren. And this *Abba Salma* was *Frumentius*. He is celebrated among the Metropolitans of *Ethiopia*, in the *Ethiopic* Liturgie, as also by our *Ethiopic* Poet, as being the first that display'd the light of the Gospel in those Parts; for which he gives him this Encomium.

Peace with the Voice of Gladness I pronounce,
The fair Renowned Salama, *for he at once*
Did open wide the Gate of Mercy and Grace;
And Ethiopia *shew'd the splendid Face*
Of Truth and Zeal by which we Christ adore,
Where onely Mist and Darkness dwelt before.

Where we are to take notice of the words *Mist* and *Darkness*, which the Poet would not have made use of, if, according to the Tradition aforesaid, there had bin any knowledg of Christ in *Habessinia*, before that time.

Moreover the same Poet makes this addition upon the same subject.

Peace

Peace to thee Salama, *who didst obey*
Divine Command, His Doctrine to display;
That Doctrine which in Ethiopia *shone,*
Like the bright Morning Star, and which alone
To Ethiopia *first by Thee conveigh'd,*
Still makes the Grateful Ethiopian *Glad.*

Which Story of the first Conversion of *Ethiopia* being grounded upon a firm foundation, must of necessity overthrow what (z) *Cedrenus*, and after him (a) *Nicephorus Callistus*, a Historian of little credit, have deliver'd concerning the Conversion of the *Habissines*, as happening a long time after this. For they write, That *Adad, King of the Axumites,* (who are no other than our *Abessinians*) *about the Year of Christ* 541, *and the* 15*th Year of* Justinian's *Reign*, made a Vow, *That if he overcame the King of the* Homerites, *he would Embrace the Christian Faith.* Whereupon succeeding in his Enterprize, he sent Embassadors to *Justinian*, and desir'd him *to send him certain of his Bishops, who were the first that divulg'd the Doctrine of Christianity in those places.* But we have already shew'd, that the Kingdom of the *Homerites* was utterly subverted near Seventy Years before by *Caleb*, Emperour of the *Ethiopians*: afterwards it fell under the Dominion of the *Persians*, the *Habessines* who were then Masters of those Territories, and the defenders of Christianity, in vain contending with the *Persian* Power, which not long after was also constrain'd to yield to the Victorious Arms of the *Saracens*. How then could it happen, that the King of the *Homerites* should be overthrown by *Adad*? Neither is it likely that *Adad*, if there were any such King, would send for Bishops so far off, altogether ignorant of the Language and Customs of his Country, which he might have had at that time, much nearer at hand, either from *Alexandria* or *Jerusalem*. Besides that, if it had bin so done, *Justinian* would not have sent *Jacobites*, but *Melchites*; and so the *Habessines* would have follow'd the Opinions of

(z) In the 15 year of *Justinian*. N. 14.

(a) Many famous men were deceiv'd by their Authority, as *Joseph Scaliger*, in [illegible] Calvisius in Op. Artco. *John Lact* in Compar. Hist. Univers. & Cheret. in Hist. Univers. in *Justinian*.

the *Melchites*, whereas they always were and still are known to be *Jacobites*. Not to mention the (*b*) 36. *Nicene Canon*, in which the Seventh Seat of Dignity in the Council, is assign'd next after the Prelate of *Seleucia*, to the Prelate of *Ethiopia*. Which may certainly teach us, That our *Ethiopians*, at the time of that Council, were most certainly Christians, and were under a Christian Superintendent or Metropolitan. And therefore it is apparent that these Historians were false in all their Circumstances.

Chap. III.

Of the Increase of Christianity in Habessinia; *the Original of their Monastical way of Living, and of their Saints.*

After Frumentius *many Monks. Some out of the* Roman *Empire and some out of* Egypt. *Nine, more remarkable, nam'd. The first* Aragawi *Extoll'd by the Poet for destroying the Kingdom of* Arwe. *What that Kingdom was.* Pantaleontes *Cell, his Sepulchre and Encomium. The Encomium of* Likanos, *another of the Nine. Other Doctors and Martyrs. Portentous Miracles of their Saints. Their Austerity.* Gabra Mondes Kaddus, *the restorer of Monastical Living, which began in* Egypt *by the Institution of* Anthony. *Imitated by several* Anchorites. *Their Spontaneous torments.* Anthonie's *Successors. The Tradition of the Monastical Scheme.* Iyasus *the Abbot——His Habitation.* Abba Eustachius *famous for Miracles: He left Successors, but no Institutions.* Habessinia *full of Monks. Their Institutions and Habits different from the* Greek *and* Latin. *They practice Husbandry, and bear Civil Offices.*

THe Conversion of *Ethiopia* being thus begun by *Frumentius*, many Pious men, partly call'd by him to his assistance, and partly of their own accord, repair'd thither to Him. We find in the Chronicle of *Axuma*, that in the Raign of King *Amiamid*, the Son of *Saladoba*, many Monks came from *Rome*, and grew very Numerous in the Country. But by the name of *Rome*, the *Ethiopians* mean the *Roman Em-*

(*b*) So in the Edition of *Turrian*, but the 84. In the Version of *Abrahamus Ecchellensis*. They are both in the *Arabic* and *Ethiopic* languages, and brought into *Europe* in the last Century.

pire.

pire. For in Imitation of the *Arabians* they call the (c) Greeks *Errum*, who at that time were most prevalent in the Eastern Parts. Nine of these Persons were more Famous than the rest, who seated themselves in *Tigra*, and there erected their Chappels. It is most probable that they came out of the Neighbouring Parts of *Egypt*, which at that time was under the *Greek* or *Constantino* Politan Emperours; but their names were all chang'd by the *Habessinians*, except that of *Pantaleontes*, by whom they are number'd in this Order.

1. *Abba Aragawi.*
2. *Abba Pantaleon.*
3. *Abba Garima.*
4. *Abba Alef.*
5. *Abba Sahama.*
6. *Abba Afe.*
7. *Abba Likanos.*
8. *Abba Adimata.*
9. *Abba Oz*, who is also call'd *Abba Guba.*

I find the most of them mention'd by my Poet, who highly applauds them for their singular Piety, and their extraordinary Miracles.

Of *Aragawi*, otherwise call'd *Michael*, he has this Encomium,

Peace be to Michael, Aragawi *nam'd,*
Wisdom his Life, his Death true Prudence fam'd.
With him was God, the Holy Three in One.
To all those Saints an everlasting Crown,
Who by their Prayers true Concord did enjoy,
That they might Arwe's *Kingdom quite destroy.*

By *Arwe*, which signifies a Serpent, he either means in general the *Kingdom of Satan*, which was destroy'd by the propagation of Christianity; or in particular the *Ethiopic* Gentilism. For, as we have already said, the most ancient *Ethiopians* worship'd a Serpent, as their supream Deitie, to which the Poet seems to allude. There are to be seen to this day the Cells wherein those holy Men sequester'd themselves, by the names of *Beta Pantaleon*, the Domicil of St. Pantaleon

(c) *Frequent in the Saracen History of* Elmacin, *where by the Latin Language, the* Greek *is still meant.*

in *Tigra*: where his Sepulcher also remains. Of whom the Poet thus,

> *Peace to* Pantaleon's *Bones, who study'd here,*
> *In th' inner Cell, next to his Sepulcher.*
> *Who by the aid of Heavens most precious Word,*
> *Speech to the dead miraculously restor'd,*
> *Who by his Prayers, and his Soul saving Voice,*
> *Made the afflicted Widow soon rejoyce.*
> *Her Sons were dead, but he unlock'd the grave,*
> *And freed those Souls which Death did late enslave.*

He also makes mention of the Nine Saints in his Hymn to *Likanos*.

> *Peace be to* Likanos, *who of the Nine*
> *Makes one, who did their Lives to God resign;*
> *With lasting wreaths would they my Temples crown,*
> *How should I then set forth their high renown!*
> *Like lighted Lamps his fingers burn'd in prayer,*
> *His Hand was pierc'd, when he the Staff did bear.*

Besides these, there are several other great Doctors among them, who have highly merited for propagating the Christian Religion; as also many Martyrs, frequently celebrated by the *Ethiopians* and *Copticks* in their Religious Panegyricks. But as to their Saints, they relate of them, several Miracles more than Extraordinary: as the *removing Mountains, appeasing the rage of most Tempestuous Seas; raising the Dead; causing Water to spring from smitten Rocks, and walking over Rivers*, which are reported for common Miracles among them: so that if the Truth of the *Ethiopic* Church were to be grounded upon such Wonders, there could be no purer Religion in the World. For tho we have a *St. Martin*, that gave a piece of his Cloak to one in necessity, they have among 'em a Saint, that parted with his whole Garment to relieve the distressed. There are among them not onely several Stories of persons *that have walk'd upon the Asp and the Basilisk, and trampled upon the Dragon and the Lyon*; but also those who have rode upon those Beasts, as upon Horses and Mules. Never were the *Ascetæ* more austere. There are some who have liv'd for whole days together upon three little Dates, others upon no more than one poor little dry Bisket.

But there is not one more renowned for Sanctity among them, then *Gabra-Menfes-Keddus*, or the *Servant of the Holy Ghost*, in honour of whom they keep a Holyday every month.

Next

Next to him is *Tecla-Haimanot*, or the *Plant of Faith*, who restor'd the Monastical way of Living, in *Ethiopia*, about the Year of Christ 600. Whom the *Ethiopic* Poet extolls in a most singular manner.

All hail to thy Nativity, great Saint,
It was at first thy Mothers great Complaint,
That she should barren dye, till th' Angels Voice
Declar'd thy Birth, and made her Soul rejoyce.
Then Tecla-Haimanot *Thou didst appear*
Like to the Sun, that rules the Day and Year:
Thy Glory fill'd the Earth from end to end,
And to the Heavens thy Lustre did ascend.

This Austere way of Living was first practiz'd in *Thebais*, a Desert of *Egypt*, whither many Pious men had retir'd themselves from the Persecution of the Heathen, that through abstinence and temperance they might be more intent upon the Duty of Prayer. Among the rest, St. *Antonie*, as it were the Captain of the Hermites, prescrib'd certain Lawes to be observ'd by the Professors of this sort of severity: for which reason, next to *Paul*, he was look'd upon as its first Institutor. The Affairs of the Church being settl'd, many *Anchorites*, in imitation of him, voluntarily chose a solitary way of Living: for that reason call'd *Monachi*, *Monks*, or People that liv'd alone by themselves. Some meerly out of a Pious and godly end; some out of an opinion of merit; some out of vain-glory and a desire of worldly fame; because they found that austerity of life, as being a thing hard to be undergone, was vulgarly much admir'd and highly applauded. Many also did not think it sufficient to abstain from lawful enjoyments, or to bridle and restrain the ordinary desires of Nature, but voluntarily tormented themselves with new invented Tortures, or macerated themselves with hunger and famine. This Custome spread it self also into *Ethiopia*, where some without any advantage to themselves or others, invented several ways of afflicting their own Carcasses; as for example, *To stand whole days together in cold water, to gird their Loyns with a heavy Chain, to feed onely upon Pot-herbs and Roots,* and that very sparingly too. Nay, which is hardly to be credited; some there were, who would thrust themselves into the clefts of Trees, and so as those clos'd together again, suffer'd themselves to be bury'd alive.

To *Antonie* succeeded *Macarius*, after whom liv'd St. *Pachom*, to whom in *Ethiopia* succeeded *Aragawi*, the first Abbot or Ruler over Monks among the *Abyssinians*.

His Successors were

Abba Christus Bezana.
Abba Mesket Moa.
Abba Johanni,

Who left bequeath'd his *Asquema*, that is, the *Badge of his Abbotship*, or his Monastical Habit to *Tecla-Haimanot*. For the Tradition is among them, That the Arch-Angel St. *Michael* brought that Habit to St. *Antonie*, for which reason it was afterwards deliver'd from Successor to Successor, as it were from one hand to another. The Greek word it self is σχῆμα, *Scheme*. *Alphonsus* the Patriarch compares it to a *Scapulary*. The Life of this Saint is extant in *Ethiopia*, written at large, and stuft with several Miracles, and render'd famous for several Apparitions and Pilgrimages. Mention is also made of him in the *Ethiopic* Church Registers after this manner.

> *Remember Lord the Soul of thy Servant our Father*, Tecla-Haimanot, *and all his Companions*.

This *Tecla-Haimanot* gave new Rules and Precepts to his Monks, and order'd them to submit themselves to a Governour, who is call'd *Itegue*, and is always of highest authority and dignity next to the *Abuna*. He either Visits his fellow Monks himself, or sends some one in his stead to reform Errors and punish transgressions. Before the Kingdom of *Shewa* was won by the *Gallans*, he had his habitation in a place call'd *Debra Libanos*, or the *Mountain of Libanus*, which was afterwards translated into *Begemdra*. And hence it is, that *Tesfa-tzeyon*, who set forth the *Ethiopic* New Testament, in the Epilogue to St. *Matthew*, thus speaks of himself and his fellow Monks.

> *We are all the Sons of our Father* Tecla Haimanot, *of the Monastery of Mount* Libanus.

The

The other Abbot or Governour of the Monks call'd *Eustathius*, is no less famous than he, nor is his Memory less esteem'd in their Sacred Registers, while they cry,

> *Remember*, **Lord**, *our Father* Eustathius, *with all his Children*.

Of him the *Ethiopic* Poet thus sings:

> *Hail to thy precious Mantle, once the Boat,*
> *Which with thy Burden on the Sea did float;*
> *Thy Pilgrimage a mighty Wonder shew'd,*
> *Th'Obedient Ocean smooth and smiling flow'd*
> *And Rocks remov'd, abandon'd ancient Rest,*
> *To give free Passage where thy footsteps prest.*

He also prescrib'd Laws to his followers, but impos'd no Governour upon them, neither are they very solicitous about that neglect; pretending, *That* Eustathius *went into* Armenia, *having nam'd no Successor; and that therefore it is not lawful for them to appoint any one.* Every Abbot therefore is Supreme in his own Monastery; and if any one dye, another is chosen by the Suffrages of the rest of the Monks. *Habessinia* is full of these sort of people, to the great burthen of the Commonwealth, to which they are no way profitable; as being useless in the Field, and free from Tribute. However their Rules and Orders are very much different both from the *Greeks* and *Latins*. For excepting their *Skorms* and Crosses which they carry, you can hardly distinguish them from the Laitie: in regard they neither wear any *Coat* or Monastical Habit. Nor do they live in Monasteries, but in some Village in scatter'd Cottages near to some Church or Temple. They have certain Prayers of which they say such a number, believing their Piety fully satisfy'd if they finish their Task; which that they may make the more hast to accomplish, they huddle over the Psalms of *David* with such a dextrous celerity, that I who have heard 'em at *Rome*, holding the same Copy in my hand, could never follow them with my voice, and hardly with my eyes. Every one manures his own Ground, and lives upon the product of his Labours, of which they are also very liberal. Otherwise they go and come, every one without controul, as they please themselves. So that by no means

their

their Farms can be call'd Cloysters, nor they be said to be really Monks, but onely unmarried Husbandmen, and that onely while they preserve their Continency intire. However they are branded with infamy, if they forsake their Monastical way of living to marry Wives. Nor are their Children capable of being admitted into the Clergy; and it is taken for an affront to call any man the Son of a Monk. Nevertheless they bear Civil Offices, and are sometimes made Governors of Provinces, as is apparent by the Example of *Tzagazaabus*; who was a Monk, as appears from *Alvarez*'s Itinerary. Of such as these the Question may be ask'd with St. *Jerome*, *If thou desirest to be accompted a Monk, what doest thou do in the Cities, what in the Camp, or why dost thou undertake Civil Employments?* They could not choose but highly displease the Fathers of the Society; which is the reason, that they have always spoken of them with contempt: on the other side, the Monks have bin the main Obstacles of the Fathers Successes; for which Reason, *Tellezius* calls them Persecutors of the Catholic Faith. Their Monasteries (if we may so call their Villages) are very numerous and dispierc'd over all Parts of the Kingdom: and commonly go by the name of *Daber*, a Mountain; in the plural number *Adebarat*, Mountains: as, *Dabra Bizen*, *Dabra Hallelujah*, *Dabra Damo*, *Albamata*, and the like, as being formerly built upon steep Hills: Beside which, they possess all the Ilands in the *Tzane Lake*, except *Deka*.

An Addition to the Third Chapter, concerning their Nuns.

THat there are also Nuns in *Ethiopia*, I gather from *Tellezius*. But they are very ignorant, and therefore the more obstinate in their devotion. For proof of which, the same *Tellezius* produces a very remarkable Story of one, who by chance becoming blind, was admonish'd by one of the *Fathers*, to make Confession, and embrace the *Latin* Religion, unless she intended to go headlong to Hell. To which the Nun made answer, *That she was willing to go thither of her own accord, for that she found there was no Room for her in Heaven, as being a person with whom God was displeas'd, and had therefore depriv'd her of her sight, without any cause of offence by her committed.*

Upon

Upon which the Father press'd her the more urgently, in hopes to deliver her from that more dangerous blindness of her Mind. But finding her to continue obstinate after all his pains. *Since then*, said he, *thou refusest Heav'n, get thee to Hell with all the Devils*, *with* Dathan *and* Abiram: *But I would not have thee take thy Religious Habit along with thee, which is only proper for those that desire the Joys of Heaven.* And so saying, he presently order'd her to put off her Nuns Vestments, and to put on a sordid Vulgar Habit, which wrought in her such a sadness and contrition, that she soon after made her confession, and reconcil'd her self to the Church of Rome.

Chap. IV.

Of the Sacred Books of the Habessines.

The Ethiopians, *together with the Christian Religion, receiv'd the Holy Scripture, according to the Version of the 70 Interpreters.——The New Testament from an Imperfect Copy and ill Printed. The Old Testament divided into four parts. The New Testament into as many. The* Revelation *added as an Appendix. To the New Testament are added the Constitutions and Canons of the Apostles, as they call them, divided into Eight parts: Therefore they reckon several Sacred Books. Three Oecumenical Councils. A fair Manuscript of the Councils at* Rome. *Books therein contain'd. A Counterfeit Book of* Enoch. *Magical Prayers. Whimsical Monstrous words seeming to be taken from the* Jews. *The Form of the* Jewish *Anathematizing.*

Divine *Worship* is seldom found among any sort of Nations in the World to be without Books, by which we apprehend from whence every particular kind of worship derives it self, and by what means it got footing among the People: for the words and the worship generally go together. Which is the reason there are so many Hebrew and Greek words in all the Versions of the Bible, and that we have so many Latin words in our Theologie.

The *Habessines* together with the Christian Religion receiv'd the holy Scripture. And this Scripture was translated into that Idiom of the *Ethiopic* Language, which was at that time more peculiar to the Inhabitants of *Tigra*, from the Greek Version of the Seventy Interpreters, according to a certain Copy us'd in the Church of *Alexandria*; which the innumerable

numerable various Readings, that are inserted into the *English Polyglotton* Bibles, from one of the same Copies, plainly demonstrate, with which the *Ethiopic* Translation perfectly agrees, Especially in the 35 & 39 Chapter of *Exodus*, which in other Copies are wonderfully mutilated. Nor is it without reason that a Colonie, as it were, of the *Alexandrian* Church, should follow the sacred Copies of their *Metropolis*. As for the Author and Time of the Translation, I find nothing certainly deliver'd concerning either: however it is most probable that it was begun at the time when the *Habessines* were (*f*) converted, or a very short time after, and not in the time of the Apostles, as some have reported; and brought to perfection by several; because the more rare and difficult words, such as are the names of Gemms, are not all alike in all the Books. For example, the *Topaz* in the 118 *Psalm*, 127 *Verse*, is call'd *Pazyon*, in *Job* 28. 19. *Tankar*, in *Revelations* the 21. 20. *Waraus*: and so in many other words the same difference is observ'd.

But for the *New Testament*, they have it Translated from the Authentic Greek Text, tho as yet it has not bin brought into *Europe* pure and intire. For the *Roman* Edition is printed from a lame imperfect Copy, so that I was forc'd to fill up the Gapps which *Tesfa-Tzyon* had left, from the *Greek* and *Latin* Exemplars. This was observ'd by some Learned Men, but not understanding the Cause, it made them think that the *Ethiopic* Version had bin drawn from the Vulgar Latin. Perhaps they did not understand these following *Ethiopic* Lines.

These Acts of the Apostles, for the most part, were translated at Rome *out of the Latin, and Greek, for want of the* Ethiopic *Original. For what we have added or omitted, we begg your pardon, and request of You to mend what is amiss.*

More then this, the Publisher of the Book beggs pardon, and excuses the defect of the Edition, in regard of the ignorant Assistants which he had to help him.

Fathers and Brethren, be pleas'd not to interpret amiss the faults

(*f*) There is one who has written a certain *Ethiopic* Martyrologie, who affirms, That *Frumentius*, otherwise *Abba-Salama*, was the Author of the first Translation; but before I see it, I will not undertake to affirm it.

of

of this Edition; for they who Compos'd it could not read; and for our selves we know not how to compose. So then We help'd them, and they assisted us, as the blind leads the blind; and therefore We desire you to pardon us and them.

This Excuse he also repeats in other places, as being conscious of its being defective in several other places. Nevertheless the same Edition was afterwards printed in *England*, as an addition to that famous *Poly Glotton*; of which there is no other reason to be given, but that there was no other to be procur'd.

However they enjoy the holy Scripture entire, and reck'n as many Books as we do, tho they divide them after another manner. For they distinguish the Old Testament, which contains 46 Books into four Principal parts; to which they joyn certain other Books of a different Argument, consulting more, perhaps, the Convenience of the Volumes, then the Dignity of the Matter. They also mix the *Apocryphal* with the Canonical, whether out of Carelesness or Ignorance is uncertain. And as for *Gregory*, he plainly confess'd he had never heard of any such word as *Apocrypha*.

The first Tome is call'd *Oreth*, or the *Law*, and the *Octateuch*; for it contains Eight Books, which are call'd

1. *Zasteret*, or the Creation, call'd also by another name *Kadami Aret*, or the First Book of the Law, or *Zaledate*, or the Generation or *Genesis*.
2. *Zatzat*, Exodus.
3. *Zalewawjan*, of the Levites.
4. *Zahulekue*, or *Numbers*.
5. *Zadabetra*, of the Tabernacle.
6. *Ejashu*, *Joshua*.
7. *Masafenat*, of the Dukes.
8. *Rate*. Ruth.

The Other Tome is call'd *Nagaste*, or *Kings*, and is divided into Thirteen Books.

9, 10. 1 *Samuel*, or *Samuel* 2. } Which nevertheless they call
11, 12. *Ebrewejen*, of the } after the manner of the
Hebrews. II. } *Greeks*, the 1. 2. 3. 4 of *Kings*.
13, 14. *Hazzazan*. Of the Lesser, or Inferior. II. Thus they seem to understand the Greek word *Paralipomena*.

15, 16. *Ezra*, or *Ezra* II.	19. *Ester*. Ester.
17. *Tobed*, Tobia.	20. *Ijob*. Job.
18. *Judit*. Judith.	21. *Mesmare*. Of the *Psalmes*.

The Third Tome is call'd *Salomon*, and contains Five Books.

22. *Masle*, the *Proverbs*.
23. *Maqebeb*. The Sermon. Properly a Circle, or an Assembly of Men Assembled together in a Ring.
24. *Mahaleja*, *Mahaleje*, the Song of Songs.
25. *Tebeb*, the Book of Wisdom.
26. *Sirach*. Sirach.

The Fourth Tome is call'd *Nabijat*, or the Prophets, and contains Eighteen Books.

27. *Esajas*, Isaiah.
28, 29. *Eremjas*. *Tanbitu*, *Wakhakibu*. The Prophesie of *Jeremie* and his Lamentations.

30. *Baruch*.	32. *Daniel*.
31. *Ezechiel*.	

The next that follow, as among us, are *Nesan Nabyat*, or the Minor Prophets.

33. *Hoseas*.	39. *Nahum*.
34. *Joel*.	40. *Habacuc*.
35. *Amos*.	41. *Saphonjas*.
36. *Obadijah*.	42. *Hag*, or *Hagjah*.
37. *Jonas*.	43. *Zacharias*.
38. *Michejas* or *Micah*.	44. *Malaqjas*.

To these they add,

45. *Maqabejan*, the two Books of *Maccabees*.

Of all which there are at *Rome* in Manuscript, the

1. *Pentateuch*.	4. *Ruth*.
2. *Joshuah*.	5. Four Books of *Kings*.
3. *Judges*.	6. *Isaiah*.

In Print are Extant

1. The four first Chapters of *Genesis*.	2. The Book of *Ruth*.
	3. The *Psalter*.

4. The

4. The *Song of Songs*.
5. *Joel*.
6. *Jonas*.
7. *Sophoniah*.
8. *Malachi*.

With the Hymns of the *Old Testament*.

The *New Testament* contains Four and twenty Books, and is also divided into Four parts, of which the first is call'd *Wengkel*, or the *Evangel*, comprehending the Four Evangelists.

1. *Matthew*,
2. *Mark*,
3. *Luke*, and
4. *John*.

The second the *Gober*, or the *Acts*, viz. *of the Apostles*.

The third call'd *Paulus*, comprehends the 14 Epistles of St. *Paul*.

6. To the *Romans*.
7. To the *Corinthians*, II.
8. To the *Galathians*.
10. To the *Ephesians*.
11. To the *Philippians*,
12. To the *Colossians*.
13, 14. To the *Thessalonians*.
15, 16. To *Timothy*, II.
17. To *Titus*.
18. To *Philemon*.
19. To the *Hebrews*.

The fourth *Hakarja* or the Apostle, containing the Seven Books of

20. St. *James*.
21, 22. St. *Peter* II.
23, 24, 25. St. *John*, III.
26. St. *Jude*.

To which they add as a Supplement, the *Vision of John*, sirnam'd *Abukalamsis*: A word corrupted out of the Greek *Apocalypsis*, which they ignorantly took for the Sirname of St. *John*, as compounded of the Arabic word *Abu* & *Kalamsis*. Here we are to observe, that in the written Eastern Copies, the Epistles of St. *Paul* are found single by themselves, and this is the reason that in the *Roman* Copy of the *Ethiopic New Testament*, they were Printed apart, and not in the Order by us observ'd.

To the *New Testament* they generally annex a Volume, which they call, according to the Greek word, *Synodum*, or the *Book of Synods*. It contains those most ancient Constitutions, which are call'd the *Constitutions of the Apostles*: in their Language *Tazazate*, *Precepts*, or *Canons*, being an Explanation of the Primitive Rites and Ceremonies, written by the Industry of St. *Clement*, but they are very much different from those that are dispers'd among Us under the name of the Apostles. These the *Habessines* divide into eight parts, adding withall to the Canonical Writings of the Evangelists, and Apostles, as it were certain *Novels*, as if they were of the same Authority, and the most absolute Pandects of Christianity. Hence it was, that King *David* said to *Alvarsius*, That he had Fourscore and one Books of Sacred Scripture; that is to say, Six and forty of Old Testament (reck'ning the *Lamentations* by themselves), and Thirty five of the New Testament, adding to the *Twenty seven*, those Eight Books of Constitutions and Canons, which the Ethiopians call *Mandr & Abtelis*, the Signification of which were unknown to *Gregory*, as being words altogether Exotic. This was also the reason why *Tesfa Tzejon* has this Expression in the Title of the New Testament, *I have caus'd a New Copy to be Printed, but without a Synod*, because he did not Print together with the said Copy, those Canons and Institutions before specify'd. Next to this Book which is also call'd *Hadas*, or absolutely *New*, the chiefest Reverence is given to the three Oecumenic Councils, the *Nicene*, *Constantinopolitan*, and *Ephesine*, with some other Provincial Councils, which were receiv'd in the Church till the *Schism of Chalcedon*. But we are to understand, that beside the Twenty Nicene Canons, always receiv'd by the Greek and Latin Church, they also admit of Eighty four other Canons, which are extant among the Copies in the Arabic Language. And these in the foregoing Century, *Baptista* the Jesuit Transcrib'd and brought to *Rome*, where they were Translated into Latin. They were all formerly fairly written in Parchment, and by *Zara Jacob* or *Constantine*, Emperor of the *Habessines* in the year 440. sent to *Jerusalem*, and thence brought to *Rome* in the year 1646. where I saw it in the *Habessine* House, in the year 1649. It contains the following Books;

The Synod of the Holy Apostles for the Ordering of the Church of Christ, together with all the Precepts Decrees and Canons, which Clement *the Disciple of* Peter *wrote.*

The First Synod is that of the Council of Ancyra.

The Second Synod is that of the Council of Cæsarea.

The Third the Council of Nice.

The Fourth of Gangra.
The Fifth of Antiochia.
The Sixth of Laodicea.
The Seventh of Sardis.

Afterwards follow the Acts of 318 Orthodox Holy Fathers. Then a Treatise of the Sabbath Compos'd by *Retua-Humanot*. Next a Declaration of the Doctrine of the Law, by Constitutions and Exhortations. Lastly, a Decree and Canon of Penitence. The Book was written at *Axuma*, with a Preface of the Kings written, dated from *Shewa*.

Adjoyning to this Book are the Liturgy, or the Publick Prayers for the Use of the whole Ethiopic Church. They call it *Kanone Kedasi*, the Canon of the Eucharist, as being the Rule of *Administration*, and of all the other Liturgies. They are Printed in the Roman Copy of the New Testament, before the Epistles of St. *Paul*, but intermixed with Foreign Insertions. For there we find it written concerning the Holy Ghost, *who proceeds from the Father and the Son*; which latter proceeding neither the Greeks nor Ethiopians admit.

Besides this General Liturgy, they have several other Liturgies, which are appropriated for several Holydaies.

Kedasi Za-gezen, the Liturgy of our Lord.
Kedasi Za-Ebezetoi, the Liturgy of our Lady.
Kedasi Za-Warjat, the Liturgy of the Apostles.
Kedasi Zawedus Martium, the Liturgy of St. *Mark*.

Which Inscriptions have deceiv'd some Learned Men, who have branded them with the Characters either of *Apocryphal* or *falsly Titl'd*, for that they were not call'd so by the Composers of them, both the Text it self, and the Name of the Author sometimes added to the Title, demonstratively evince; as for Example.

The Liturgy of our Lady Mary, *which Abba* Cyriacus, *Metropolitan of the Province of* Behens *compos'd*.

Of this Nature, they have also sundry other Manuscript Liturgies, which the Ethiopians call *Equeti Korban*, or the *Thanksgiving of Oblation*: It being their Custom to use Eucharistical Prayers and Homilies in the Administration of the Sacrament.

But

But their Symbolic Book, or Compendium of the whole *Habessine*, Religion, is call'd *Hajmo Monoto Abau*, *The Faith or Religion of the Fathers*; of which *Tellez* writes, That it is a Book among them, almost of great Authority and Credit, as being as it were a Library of the Fathers: it being Collected out of the Homilies of St. *Athanasius*, St. *Basil*, St. *Cyril*, St. *John Chrysostom*, and St. *Cyril*, as also *Ephrem* the *Syrian*, and the St. *Gregories*, of which there are Four whom they acknowledge and highly esteem.

Gregory of *New-Cesarea*, the Wonder-worker.
Gregory Nazianzene.
Gregory Nyssene, and
Gregory the *Armenian*.

Tellez adds St. *Austin*; but of that I very much doubt the Truth, the Writings and Names of the Latin Fathers, being utterly unknown to the *Abessines*. And indeed had that Book been Compos'd out of the Writings of the Fathers above-mention'd, it might have been easily admitted by the Jesuits as an equal Judge between both Parties in their Disputes concerning the two Natures in Christ. They have besides these several other Books that treat upon Sacred Subjects, as Books of Martyrs, and Lives of Saints, which are call'd *Synaksar* in the Ethiopic Idiom; Among the rest,

The History of the Fathers.
The Combats or Wrestlings of Martyrs.
The History of the Jews.
The Constitutions of the Christian Church.
A Book of Mysteries, which Treats of Heresies, written by St. *George*.
A Book of Epiphanius *upon the same Argument.*
The Spiritual Old Man.
The Harp of Praise, in honour of the Trinity and the Virgin Mary.
Padab Tzahje, The Splendor of the Sun, which Treats of the Law of God.
Wedase Ambatzi, The Praise of God.
Marzehse felsit bezzeten Marjam, The Book of the Death of our Lady *Mary*.

In whose Praise and Honours there are several Hymns and Verses, among which, the most extoll'd is that which

is

is call'd *Organon Denghel*, *The Virgins Musical Instrument*, Composed by *Abba George*, an *Abyssine* Doctor, a Book not very ancient, but in high esteem by reason of the great number of Similitudes and Allegories; as also for the Elegancy of the stile and words. But as to what *Egidius* the Capuchin writes to the famous *Petreskius*, concerning the Prophesie of *Enoch*, as if such a thing were extant in the Ethiopic Language, in a Book call'd *Matzhafe Henoch*, the Book of *Enoch*, the Story is altogether fabulous. So soon as that noble Gentleman heard of this Book, he spar'd for no Cost to get it into his hands; till at length the Knavery of those he employ'd, impos'd upon him another Book with a false Title. The Book was afterwards lodg'd in Cardinal *Mazarine's* Library, and the Preface, Middle and End being Transcrib'd by a Friend of mine, was presented to me, but there was nothing in it either of *Enoch* or his Predictions; only some few Notions there were, and some very clear discourses of the Mysteries of Heaven and Earth, and the Holy Trinity, under the Name of one *Abba-Bahaila-Michael*.

There is another little idle and impertinent Pamphlet, hardly worth taking notice of, were it not so frequently currant in *Europe*, *Gregory* call'd it *Tzalot Betzet*, or a *Magical Prayer*, and averr'd, That it was not only not esteem'd, but rejected in *Ethiopia*; tho by us charily hoarded up in several Libraries. It is writ with so much stupidity, that you shall find therein many Prayers of the Virgin *Mary* to her Son, stufft with monstrous words, to which are attributed Vertues and Efficacies more than Divine; as,

Alnael,	*Tilelmesjos,*
Ahtavi,	*Cutrcutrjam,*
Alotael,	*Flaslaslaque,*

With many others more horrid to Pronunciation. But from hence it is apparent how much the *Habassines* resemble the *Jews*, as affecting words of uncouth and unheard of insignificancy, by which they thought to command both Heaven and Hell, which carrying a kind of a dreadful sound, the *Habessines* also use them in their forms of Anathematizing, they cry,

And let him be accurs'd by Addirion *and* Actariel, *by* Sandalphon,

phon, *and* Hadarmel, *by* Anficiel, *and* Parchiel, *by* Seraphiel, *and* Zeganzael, *by* Michael *and* Gabriel, *and by* Raphael *and* Meschartiel, *and let him be interdicted by* Tzamzeviv, *and* Hauchevi*v*, *He is the great God*; *and by the Seventy Names of that great King*; *and on the behalf of* Tzortak, *the great Ensign-Bearer.*

Chap. V.

Of the Religion of the Habassines *at this Day.*

The Reports of Matthew *the* Armenian *and* Tzagazaab *false or uncertain. The Fathers have omitted their soundest Opinions---And fix'd their several Errors upon them. The Confession of* Claudius *Genatne. The great Authority of the Synodal Writers. They admit the* Nicene *and other Councils till that of* Chalcedon. *They acknowledge the Trinity, one Person of Christ, and his sufficient Merit. The Proceeding of the Holy Ghost from the Son they deny.* Gregorie*'s Dispute and Opinion. The* Ethiopian *interpretation of the word* Proceed. *The Sacraments, Baptism, Communion under both Kinds. The real Presence. The words they use in Reference to it.* Gregorie*'s Opinion of Transubstantiation. Of the Soul after Death. They pray for the Dead. Deny Purgatory.* Gregorie*'s Opinion concerning it. The Original of Prayer for the Dead. They pray to Saints and Angels. Their Catechism for Children and* Neophytes.

WEre the Symbolical Book of the *Habessines*, which they call *Haymanot Abau* to be found in *Europe*, we might easily Collect from thence, the true and genuine Sence and Doctrine of the *Ethiopic* Church concerning the Heads and Articles of the Christian Faith: for hitherto we find the most of them uncertainly deliver'd, and for the Confession of Faith set down by *Matthew* the *Armenian*, and *Tzagazaab*, we have already taken notice of the failings in it. The Fathers of the Society, that have been conversant among the *Habessines* both in this and the former Century, and frequently discours'd with their Learned Men, passing by their sound and serious Opinions, tax them of many Errors which they have receiv'd from the *Greeks* and *Jews*. As for Example,

That the Spirit proceeds only from the Father.

That the Human Nature of Christ is equal to his Divinity.

They

They acknowledge but one Will and one Operation in Christ; for which reason they believe that we affirm Four Persons in the Godhead, seeing that we confess two Wills and two Natures in Christ.

They repeat the Ceremony of Baptism every year upon the Feast of the Epiphany.

They believe that the Souls of the Just shall not be receiv'd into Heaven before the end of the World; nor do they think them to be Created, but produc'd out of Matter.

They neither confess the Number, nor the particular Species of their Sins, but cry in general, I have sin'd, I have sin'd.

They use not the Sacrament of Chrism, nor Extream Unction upon the approach of Death; nor do they mind the Consolation of the bread of life. Insomuch that many of them stick not to say, Thus they who follow the Roman Religion, *are not only* Hereticks, *but worse than the* Mahumetans.

They reject the Council of Chalcedon, *casting many reproaches upon* Leo *the Great; but highly applauding* Dioscurus.

They deny Purgatory.

These things I chose to deliver almost in the very words of *Godignus*, who Collected them out of the Relations and Letters of *Gonzalez Roderic*, *Alphonsus de Franca*, *Emanuel Fernandez*, and others of the Society. Neither do they seem to be improbable, but how they evade or excuse them, we shall shortly declare. As to what is said that some of them believe the Followers of the *Romish* Religion to be worse than *Mahumetans*, I could not hear any such thing from *Gregory*: neither did he think it was to be understood in reference to their Doctrine, but their Tyranny over their Subjects; it being the Custom of the *Mahumetans* only to vex and oppress all those who are under their Power, professing a Religion contrary to theirs, but never so rage against them with Fire and Sword.

In the mean time we have a Confession set forth by King *Claudius*; but the scope of that Confession was only to clear himself and his Subjects from the Imputation of *Judaism*, which he found to be the only reason that impeded the Amity between him and the *Portugals*. Therefore leaving this Confession, by what we can gather from their Publick Liturgies, and the Writings and Sayings of Persons, both Publick and Private, the sum of the *Habessinian* Doctrine seems to consist of the following Heads.

Qq First,

First, They acknowledge the *Holy Scripture* to be the sole and only *Rule* of what they are to believe, and what they are to do! insomuch that King *David* said to *Alvarez*, That if the Pope should impose upon Him or His Subjects, any thing what the Apostles had not written or permitted, he would not obey him; nor his own *Metropolitan* if he should attempt to do the like. But with the Scripture they are so much in love, that there is nothing more delightful to their Ears, than the repetition of it. Therefore saith *Tellez*,

Nothing more pleas'd the Habessines *than to hear the Scripture often quoted in Sermons; and the more Citations a man brings out of Scripture, the more learned he is accompted.*

Nor do they give much less Credit to the Three Occumenical Councils, as appears by the Confession of *Claudius*.
They generally make use of the *Nicene Creed*, which they
call *Tzalot Haymanot, the Prayer of the Faith.* That which we
use they have not, no more than all the rest of the Eastern
Churches; a strong Argument, that it was not compil'd by
the Apostles, tho' in regard of the Doctrine which it con-
2. tains, it may be truly call'd *Apostolic.* For certainly the *Nicene* Fathers would not have stifl'd such a Creed, or set forth
another of their own, had the Apostles left such an Epitome
of their Doctrine behind them. The Ancient Greek Councils then are the Councils which the *Habessines* have in reverence, together with the Eighty four ancient Canons added
to those of the *Nicene* Council, till they come to that of *Chalcedon*, which they do not only utterly reject, but also Crimi-
nally reproach.

Whatever therefore the Catholic Church admitted and believ'd before that Council, concerning God, Three in one; the Three distinct Persons in one Essence, the Eternity of the Son of God, the Existence of the Holy Ghost, and other Articles of Faith, all those things the *Habessines* willingly consent to and allow, condemning those that Dispute against them. By the way, we are here to observe, that the Ethiopic words, *Sabsata Gaz Gaz Egzi Bahr*, Three Persons and one God, are vulgarly ill Translated, being to have bin render'd, *Three Faces, One Lord*; for the word *Gaz*, signifies as well the *Face* or *Countenance*, as it bears the force of the Greek word *Hyposasis*, or *Person*.

The

The Nestorian Heresie asserting two Persons in Christ, they so abhor, that for that very reason they will not admit of his two Natures, and two Wills, tho they positively acknowledge his Divinity and Humanity. For they affirm Christ to be true and perfect God, and also true and perfect Man, and to consist in one Individual Person of Divinity and Humanity, without Confusion and Commixtion.

Furthermore, They acknowledge the most Sacred Merits of Christ, to be most sufficient and efficacious for the Sins of the whole world, and consequently of all Mankind; and this *Gregory* himself affirm'd to be true: nor have I found in any of their Books which I have happen'd to see, any thing that contradicts what he asserted. However, as the Greeks do, they deny the *Proceeding* of the Holy Ghost from the Son; yet all this while they acknowledge him to be equally the Spirit of the Father and the Son, and to be a Person subsisting of himself. For thus they declare in their Liturgy.

We believe the Father sending, that the Father is in his own Person. And we believe the Son who is sent, that the Son is in his own Person, and we believe the Holy Ghost who descended upon Jordan, *and upon the Apostles, that the Holy Ghost is in his own Person; Three Names, One God. Not as* Abraham *who is elder than* Isaac, *nor as* Isaac *who is Elder then* Jacob. *It is not so, The Father is not Elder than the Son, because he is the Father, nor the Son Elder than the Holy Ghost, nor the Holy Ghost lesser or Younger than the Father and the Son, nor is the Son Younger than the Father, because he is the Son. Not as* Abraham *who commanded over* Isaac *in respect of Generation, because he begat him, nor as* Isaac *who commanded* Jacob. *It is not so in Divinity; The Father does not command the Son, because he is the Father; neither is the Son greater than the Holy Ghost, because he is the Son. The Father, the Son, and the Holy Ghost are Equal; One God, one Glory, one Kingdom, one Power, one Empire.*

But concerning the *Hypostasis*, or Person of the *Holy Ghost* really distinct from the *Father* and the Son, the Author of the *Orgnon* thus discourses.

But least any one, from what has been already said, should infer, that the Holy Ghost is not a perfect and distinct Per-

 son,

ſon; therefore ſaid Chriſt to his Apoſtles, *I will ſend you another Comforter.* By which we know that the Holy Ghoſt doth exiſt together with the Father and the Son, and alſo together in his own proper Subſiſtance or Perſon. Not that the Holy Ghoſt is partly in the Son, partly in his own Perſon, but one and the ſame, exiſtent in his proper Perſon, and exiſtent with the Father and the Son.

Gregory being ask'd, whether this were the unanimous and conſtant Opinion of all the *Ethiopian* Doctors? reply'd, *It was.* I thereupon urg'd, *Why they deny'd that the Holy Ghoſt proceeded from the Father? ſeeing they aſſerted, that he was equally the Spirit of the Father and the Son? He deſir'd, That I would firſt expound what was meant by Proceeding from the Father*, and then he would give the reaſon of the Denyal; and that for his part, he kept to the words of the Scripture, *John* 15. 26. and 16. 14. *Who goeth out from the Father, and takes from the Son*; and that he ſought no farther. For that it was not lawful in Diſputes concerning the moſt abſtruſe Myſteries of the Holy Trinity, to argue by Conſequences; but to ſtick cloſe to the very words and Expreſſions of Scripture themſelves. That I ſhould conſider what would follow, if we ſhould argue from the Unity and Equality of Eſſence to the Characteriſtical Proprieties of the Perſons. As if any one ſhould undertake to avert, *That Chriſt is the Son of the Holy Ghoſt, becauſe the Holy Ghoſt is one and Coeternal God with the Father.* Some ſuch kind of Argument his Countryman *Tzagazaab* may be thought to have had in his Brain, when he wrote, That Chriſt was the Son of himſelf, and the Beginning of himſelf, becauſe he was coeſſential with the Father, whoſe Son he was. By the way we are to underſtand, That the *Ethiopians*, inſtead of the word *Vazzaa, went forth or proceeded*, and in the Preterperfect tenſe, uſe the word *Saraz*, to *bud* or *ſprout forth*. Thus *Claudius* in his Confeſſion.

I believe in the Holy Ghoſt, reviving Lord, Zafraz em Ab, *who proceeded or ſprung from the Father.*

They never add from the Son, altho the Liturgy Printed at *Rome*, and *Tzagazaab*'s Confeſſion runs thus, *Zafraz em Ab-wawalde*, who ſprouted forth or proceeded from the Father and the Son. Where 'tis much to be doubted, that *from the Son* was inſerted by another hand

We proceed to the *Sacraments*, of which they neither have the common name nor number. For they are utterly igno-

rant

rant of *Confirmation* and *Extreme Unction*. They make use of the word *Mistar*, for a *Mysterie*, whenever they go about to intimate the Mysterie of the Participation of the Body and Blood of Jesus Christ. Otherwise they do not think it necessary, to signifie the *Seals of Faith*, by any other Vulgar name not us'd in Scripture, or to make much dispute about the Number. Only said *Gregory*, They make use of *Baptism* according to the Institution of Christ, and with the Ceremonies anciently made use of by the Church. But the Fathers of the Society reported, That the Ceremonies of Baptism were so deprav'd and corrupted among the *Habessines*, that they were constrain'd to Rebaptize great Numbers under a Condition.

As for the *Holy Communion*, they Administer it indifferently to all, both Layety and Clergy, as it is the Custom in all the Churches of the East. Neither has any thing more alienated their minds from the *Fathers*, than their finding the Layety to be depriv'd of the Cup by the Latins. *Gregory* being demanded what he thought of the real Presence of the Body and Blood in the *Lord's Supper*? made answer, That he acknowledged it. Adding withal, according to his manner, when any Discourses arose of Matters more difficult and abstruse than ordinary, *Retzizcz nagare ver*, 'tis a nice business; or, *Mistar ver*, *It is a Mystery*. When I produc'd him these words in the Liturgies.

Lord now lay thy hand upon this Dish, Bless it, Sanctifie it, and Purifie it, that so thy Body may be made holy therein.

Again,

Lay thy hand upon this Cup, and now bless it, sanctifie it, and purifie it, that thy Blood may become holy therein.

In another place.

Lay thy hand upon this Spoon of the Cross, to prepare the Body and Blood of thy only Saviour Lord and God.

And in another place,

Convert this Bread, that it may become thy pure Body, which is joyn'd with this Cup of thy most precious Blood.

And out of the Eucharistic Prayer, which bears the Title of the 318 *Orthodox Divines*, these following words:

Let

Let the Holy Ghost descend, and come and shine upon this Bread, that it may be made the Body of Christ our Lord, and that the taste and savour of this Cup may be chang'd, that so it may be made the Blood of Christ our Lord.

And when I ask'd him withal the Exposition of the words *Majete rvac rvalto*, *to be chang'd or converted*; and then demanded of him, *Whether he did not think that the substance of the Bread and Wine was not chang'd and converted into the Substance of the Body and Blood of Christ?* He made answer, *That no such sort of Transubstantiation was known or understood by the Habessines. That his Countrymen were not so scrupulous, nor us'd to start such thorny Questions. Nevertheless it seem'd to him probable and like, that the vulgar Bread and Wine was chang'd into the mysterious Representation of the Body and Blood of Jesus Christ*; and so was alter'd from Prophane to Sacred, to represent the true Body and Blood of Christ to the Communicants. *Tellez* confesses his dissatisfaction touching their Consecration, it being their Custom to say over the Body of Christ, *This bread is my Body*; and over the Wine, *This cup is my Blood*. Which words have not in them the true force of Consecration. For the Doctors of the *Roman* Church are of Opinion, That whoever speaks those words, does nothing: These words, *This is my Body*, being only of Efficacy to operate a true Transubstantiation. Which being true, no man can pretend that the *Abessines* acknowlege Transubstantiation, especially seeing they do not attribute those Divine Honours to the Sacraments, which the Consequences of real Transubstantiation require.

Concerning the state of the Soul after Death, there are several Opinions among the *Habessines*, every one having free Liberty of Opinion in those things that do not directly concern Eternal Salvation. So that it is no wonder that so many various Sentiments of private persons are brought away by our Doctors, as the publick Opinions of the *Habessines*.

Some of them believe that the Souls of Men piously deceased, shall not behold the Beatifical Vision of God before the Resurrection of the Body; which is also the Opinion of many of the Ancient Latins: as if the Soul remain'd in Expectation of the Body in some certain third place. Others, convinc'd by the Authority of the Scripture, *acknowledge only two Mansions of the Souls, Heaven and Hell; believing no Damnation to those that are in Christ, and dye in his Faith.*

Which

Which they gather from the Example of the Penitent Thief, and the words of Christ, thus Translated by the *Ethiopians*,

Verily I say unto thee, firmly believe, that thou shalt be with me in Paradise.

Therefore, as for those that Piously sleep in Christ, they believe them not to be in a worse Condition than this Thief, who at the point of Death was sav'd through Penitence actuated by Faith, without any satisfaction given for his Thieveries. Now to prove that the Soul of Man is not created, they produce this Argument, That God perfected the whole Work of his Creation upon the Sixth day. Nevertheless they believe it to be in its own Nature immortal, as being inspir'd into Man by God, at his first Creation. But on the other side, they think it very absurd that God should be ty'd to create new Souls every day for Adulterate and Incestuous Births.

However the first Opinion seems to be the more vulgarly receiv'd among them, in regard of their Prayers for the Dead: As for example.

Remember, Lord, the Souls of thy Servants, and our Father, Abba-Matthew, *and the rest of our Fathers,* Abba-Salama; *and* Abba-Jacob.

And a little after,

Remember, Lord, the Kings of Ethiopia; Abreha; *and* Atzbeha, Caleb, *and* Gebra-Meskah, *&c.*

Then they add,

Release, O Lord, our Fathers Abba Antony *and* Abba Macarius.

Remember, Lord, the Soul of thy Servant, our Father Tecla-Hajmanot, *with all his Companions.*

From whence it may be fairly justify'd, that the *Abessines* admit of a *Purgatory*. And yet *Gregory* constantly deny'd it. And *Godignus* confesses, *That there are no sacred Services said for the deceas'd among the* Habessines. The same thing *Tellez* confirms. However he derides them, as not constant to themselves; for that, *to pray for the Dead, and distribute Alms*

to

to the Poor, is no other than to assert Purgatory. Nor do I see how they can reconcile their Praying for the Rest of happy Souls; and at another time, their imploring the Intercession of the same Souls.

But they nothing mov'd with these Arguments and Inferences, affirm them to be *the Pious Conception of their good wishes, and only a Commemoration of the happy Estate of the deceas'd; and that it is none of their business to make any farther scrutiny into the Traditions of their Ancestors.* *Gregory* added, That *many Prayers* of the Christians were so conceiv'd, that many times those things were Petition'd for, which were *already perform'd and answer'd. That the Lord's Prayer contain'd Petitions of that kind. For that it would be a thing but badly inferr'd, that the Name of God was not Hallow'd, or that his Will was not done both in Heaven and Earth, because we daily put up those Prayers: besides we all begg every day for Daily Bread, when most of those that make that Prayer, do generally live in wealthy abundance.* He had heard perhaps among us our general good Wishes for the departed, That *God would vouchsafe to grant the Interr'd Body a Quiet Repose, and at length a joyful Resurrection.* And thereupon, said he, *Do not you your selves wish the same good wishes for the Dead? Do not you believe that the Carkasses of the Dead may be vexed with Spiritual Evils? or that a happy Resurrection may be obtain'd by your Prayers.* And he took so heinously the suspicion of his belief of Purgatory, that he cry'd out, *Would it not be an irreverent Injury to so many Kings and Fathers, should we interpret the Commemoration of their Souls to that height, as to think they should be tormented for so many Ages in Purgatory, and want the aid of our indefatigable Prayers to release them after so long an Imprisonment!* For those Kings and Fathers were men among the *Habessines* most Innocent, and had bin dead above a Thousand years since or more. So that whether they be in Paradice, or remain in any other place, expecting the Resurrection of their Bodies, in both cases Prayers of that Nature seem superfluous.

Besides, were there any Question to be made of the happy Condition of Men Piously deceas'd, we should rather pray for those whose lives were more loose and vain, than for those whose Conversations were without blame. And therefore what has bin deliver'd about the Opinions of the *Habessines* concerning Purgatory, leans rather upon Conjecture than any sufficient Authority, they being ignorant of the very Name. Insomuch that *Jacob Wemmers* the *Carmelite*, in his *Ethiopic* Lexicon, was constrain'd to forge a Word, by calling it *Manzeli Hatate*, the Purger of Sin. But we are to understand, that it was the most Ancient Custom of the Church first of all to read the Names of the Holy Martyrs out of the Public Registers, as being a Duty owing to the memory of the invincible Testimonies for Christ. Which the following Ages strain'd another way, as if they had need of our Intercession; and others, as if we could not be without their Intercession, made it a pretence to invoke the Holy Saints, as if they were present and heard them. To which we may add, That the Ancient Christian Orators, and Writers of Homilies, making use of their Rhetorick, by vertue of that Figure commonly call'd *Prosopopœia*, bespoke the blessed Saints, and introduc'd them as it were returning Answers; from whence it is not improbable that Suspicion might introduce the Custom of giving the same Adoration to them as to God himself, and worshipping them with Temples, Altars, and other Divine Honours. Which nevertheless the *Habessines* do not do; for though they keep Holydaies in memory of their Saints, they do not call them *Bagnabat*, *Solemnities*; but *Tjabarat*, *Remembrances*. They also invoke them, tho they know not after what manner they may be able to hear them; and beg their Intercessions also, especially of the most Holy Virgin *Mary*, to whom they bear such an affectionate Reverence, that they think whatever the Church of *Rome* has invented to her Honour, all too little; and yet they erect no Statues to her memory for all that, being contented only with her Pictures. When they were in a rage against those of the *Roman* Religion, and pursu'd 'em in their fury with Sticks and Stones, they cry'd out, *Kill, Kill; whoever is not an Enemy of* Marie, *let him take up a Stone to stone her Enemies to Death.*

But more than this, they many times invoke the Angels, as having for that perhaps a more specious pretence, because they have bin frequently said to appear to good Men and Women, and hear their Prayers.

Of these the *Ethiopians* reckon no less than Nine Orders, which they borrow from their Names and Epithites given them in Sacred Scripture.

Malaaket, Angels particularly so call'd, or by another Name, *Manfsat*, *Spirits*; *Bitom Malaekt*, *Arch Angels*.

Agaezt,	*Lords*, κυριότητες.
Saltanat,	*Magistracies*, ἀρχαὶ.
Manaberet,	*Thrones*, θρόνοι.
Hujebat,	*Powers*, ἐξουσίαι.
Majimenet,	*Princes*.
Qirubil,	*Cherubims*.
Surafel,	*Seraphims*.

Some there are who give them several other Sirnames, as *Bikanat*, *Primores* or *Chieftains*, and *Arbabe*, or *Arbab Asar*, as much as to say *fortie Myriads*.

Others there are who affirm, That first of all there were *Ten Orders*, of which the first, whose Chieftain was *Satanael*, together with his Associates, revolted from God; and that the Blessed hereafter shall succeed into their places; which they assert to be the cause of the Devils inveterate hatred toward Man.

As to their forms of Catechizing Youth and Neophytes, the following Accompt may afford very great Satisfaction; as being written by *Gregory* with his own hand, and all that he could then call to mind.

A Brief Accompt of the Heads of the Ethiopic *Faith, in which they usually instruct their Youth and Neophytes. They are Extant more at large in* Ethiopia, *but more succinctly, as follows.*

What God dost thou Worship?

The Father, Son, and Holy Ghost, three Persons, but one Deity.

Of these Three Persons, which is the first, which the last? which the greatest, which the least?

There is no Person first or last, no Person Superior, or Inferior; but all equal in all things.

How many Persons?

Three.

How many Gods?

One.

One.

How many Deities?

One.

How many Kingdoms?

One.

How many Powers?

One.

How many Creators?

One.

How many Wills?

One.

Is God limited by time?

No, *For he is from all Eternity, and shall endure to all Eternity.*

Where is God?

Every where, and in all things.

Is not the Father God?

Yes.

Is not the Son God?

Yes.

Is not the Holy Ghost God?

Yes.

Dost thou not therefore say there are Three Gods?

I do not say Three Gods, but Three Persons, and One only God.

Who begat the Son?

God the Father. But the Holy Ghost proceeds from Father, and takes from the Son.

Pray shew me some Similitude how Three Persons can be in one Deity?

The Sun, tho he be but one in Substance, yet in him are found three distinct Things, Rotundity, Light and Heat. Thus we also believe that in *one God there are three Persons, the Father, Son, and Holy Ghost, equal in all things.*

Of those Three Persons, which was born for our Redemption?

The second Person, viz. The Son of God, our Lord Jesus Christ.

How many Nativities had he?

Two.

Which were they?

His first Nativity was from the Father, without Mother, without time; The second from the Virgin Mary *our Lady, without Father, in time she always remaining a Virgin.*

Is Jesus Christ our Lord a Man, or is he truely God?

God and Man both, in one Person, without Separation, and without Change; without Confusion or Commixture.

In the same manner do the Habessines *Believe and Teach all matters of Faith; viz. Concerning the Baptism of Christ, his Fasting, his Passion, his Death, his Resurrection, his Ascention into Heaven, and sending of the* Holy Ghost. *Moreover, That he shall return in Glory to Judge the Quick and the Dead. That he is present in the Holy Sacrament. That the Dead shall rise at the last Day. That the Just shall inherit the Kingdom of Heaven; but that Sinners shall be condemn'd to Hell. They also believe the Catholic Church, according to the Creed compil'd by the* 318 *Orthodox Fathers, that met at the Council of* Nice.

We shall not add more at present, till more and those Publickly approv'd Books shall come to our hands, that we may not imprudently attribute, as some have done, the Opinions of private persons to the whole Church.

CHAP.

Chap. VI.

Of the Rites and Ceremonies of the Ethiopic *Church, as also of the* Habessine *Temples.*

Sacred Rites often an Occasion of Disturbance in the Church. The Prudent Decree of the Apostles. Paul's *Condescension necessary.* Judaick *Rites retain'd. Many new Ceremonies invented by the Pope, by the* Alexandrian *Metropolitan none. The most ancient Ceremonies retain'd by the* Abessines. *Their Churches dark, like the Synagogues. The Divisions of them, and Quires. The Nobility made Deacons. The Bishops Lodgings. Much honour'd. They admit of Pictures. They sign with the Cross. Baptism of grown People. Undertakers why so call'd. The Eucharist given to baptiz'd Infants. Some erroneous forms of the* Habessines *constrain'd the Fathers to Rebaptize. The Custom of Annual Bathing not effectual for Baptism. The abuse of it. The State of Ecclesiastical Affairs miserable in* Habessinia. *The Reasons. General Confession. Absolution. Before 25 years of Age they believe themselves Innocent. Much Preaching.* Gregorie's *Opinion of their Sermons. They Read Homilies, &c. The Sacred Vessels for the Eucharist. Why the Stone Consecrated by the* Romans *is call'd a* Chest *by the* Habessinians. *A particular Discourse of the Author. Leavened Bread. The Wine distributed in a Spoon. The defect of it supply'd. The time and place for the Holy Supper. Two Sabbathdaies in a Week. They want Bells. Their Mass unpleasing, yet they Dance about. Fastings, and fourth and sixth Holydaies silence. None during* Easter. *Of the Fasts of the Protestants in* Europe. *The beginning of the year. Their manner of Computation. Nuptial Rites. Polygamy. Marriages of Cousin Germans, or first Cousins. Divorces. Burials.*

Hitherto we have set forth what the *Habessines* believe concerning the *Trinity*, & the Principal Articles of the Christian Faith. The order of our Story now requires that we should say something of their Rites and Ceremonies. For tho it nothing avail at what time or in what manner sound Doctrine be Preach'd, so that all things be done decently and in order; nevertheless these Rites and Ceremonies have begat great Disputes, and produc'd great Disturbances in the Church.

For indeed from the very Infancy of the Gospel, various were the Contentions of Holy and Pious men about Ceremonies. Some believ'd that the *Judaic* Rites, not being expresly abrogated by Christ, were of necessity to be observ'd, together with the Doctrine and Sacraments of the New Testament,

stament, even as helps to Salvation. Others there were who judg'd that they might be profitably retain'd, though not of absolute necessity, as well in remembrance of the ancient Church of God, as to gain the Souls of the *Jews*. The first Opinion the Apostles themselves Condemn'd. In other things using Apostolic Prudence and Moderation, they made a distinction between *Jews* and *Ethnics* newly Converted. For they not only permitted the *Jews* to retain their ancient Rites, but perswaded *Paul* to comply with so many Millions of unbelieving *Jews*, who were Zealous Admirers of the Law, and accus'd *Paul*, for teaching a Defection from the Law, for forbidding Infants to be Circumciz'd, and for not living according to the *Jewish* Customs. *Paul* obey'd, and purify'd himself with his Companions, shav'd his Head, and so entring the Temple together, offer'd up an Offering for every one of them. Nay, more then this, what would be now accompted a heinous Crime, he caus'd *Timothy* to be Circumciz'd, being induc'd thereto by the Necessity of those times. Yet at another time he condemn'd Circumcision, if it were done with a *Judaic* Intention.

Thus an Action in it self indifferent, becomes bad or good, from the Reason and Intention of the Agent. But then, what what was to be done with the *Gentiles* that embrac'd the Faith of *Christ*, the Apostles took into their Deliberation. Nevertheless they would not oblige them to the Observation of the *Mosaic* Law, but only in answer to their Doubts, they commanded them only to abstain from those things, which might not only create in the *Jews* a dislike of the Gospel, but also very much scandalize those that were already Proselytes, and disturb mutual Charity and Friendship in daily Converse and Society. For the *Jews* would not Dyet with those who eat things *Sacrific'd to Idols*, or *strangled*, nor the *blood* it self. From that time some of the *Judaic* Rites prevail'd as indifferent among most, who did not contend against Piety and Christian Doctrine. Till at length by degrees they were either abrogated by the Church, or worn out of Use. Nor had the most ancient Institutions of the Christians any other Originals, as the *Building of Churches*, *Plunging the whole Body in Baptism*, Two *Fast Dayes* in a Week, Festivals and the like. However there were but few Ceremonies in the troublesome times of the Church; but in the times of Peace, they increas'd to Infinity: and the worse the state of the Church

was,

was, the more Ceremonies; insomuch that St. *Austin* complain'd in his time, *That the most wholsom Precepts of Divine Books were not so much regarded, as the fictitious Comments and Inventions of Men upon them.* The Church of *Rome*, by how much more opulent and powerful than the rest; so much the more sedulously and industriously it compos'd all things to Splendour and Pomp. The *Roman* Pontiff being the sole Judge of all things, whether convenient; or not commodious, and what he thought fit to Abrogate or Establish. But the *Patriarch* of *Alexandria*, whom the *Ethiopians* obey as their High Pontiff, what with the unhappy Contentions between the *Melchites*, and *Jacobites*, and the Persecutions of the *Saracens*, has had enough to do to keep his own Station, not being at leisure in the midst of so many Storms, to think of divulging new Ceremonies. Nor would the *Habessines* out of their wonted simplicity and plain-heartedness, the best Preserver of ancient Custom, attempt to alter or abrogate any thing without his leave or Command. Whence it comes to pass, that many of the most ancient Customs of the Primitive times, in other places out of date or abrogated, are still retain'd to this day among them. Which makes us hope that our Labour will not be ungrateful to the Reader, curious of Ecclesiastic Antiquity, if we compare the Old with the New. First, only their Churches are briefly to be describ'd, which formerly were sufficiently Magnificent, and by King *Lalibela* hewn out of the Bodies of the Rocks themselves. Some were also Built by the Succeeding Kings; but *Granius*, out of his hatred to Christianity, ruin'd the greatest part of them. There are yet remaining some Footsteps of that famous Cathedral, which *Helena*, *David's* Grandmother Built; In which there is more want of Light than of Gold or Silver. The Structure of most resembles the Ancient Architecture. For the ancient Christians, when first they had obtain'd the Opportunities of building Churches for Public Use, choosing rather to imitate the *Jews*, than the *Gentiles*, Built them in imitation of the ancient Temple of *Jerusalem*, or of the *Jewish* Synagogues; nor did they give them the heathenish Names of Temples; but call'd them *Kyriaca*, as it were dedicated to God, or else *Oratories*, or *Martyria*, Places of Public Testimony. Now as the Temple of *Jerusalem* being encompassed with a spacious Wall, consisted chiefly of three parts; that is to say, the or the

wide

wide Porch, היכל or *the body of the Temple*; and lastly, דביר or the *Holy of Holies*, so the Cathedrals of the Ancients, had a Porch before the great Folding Dores surrounded with a Wall, where the *Excommunicated*, and *Penitents*, and *Novices* were oblig'd to tarry, till the latter more fully instructed in Christianity, were admitted to Baptism; or the former brought forth the real fruits of Amendment. Then there was the Body of the Church, in the middle of which was a *secret* Place, screen'd with a Curtain, which was call'd the *Sanctuary*, as also the *Suggestion*, or place where the Pulpit stood, in Greek *Βῆμα*, which represented the *Holy of Holies*. Such a *Suggestum*, or Place of Ascension is still to be seen in the *Jewish* Synagogues, and call'd in imitation of the Greek word *Bimah*. But this the *European* afterward thought more convenient to remove to the farther end of the Church; we call it now the *Quire*, for the most part separated with Iron Lattices from the Body of the Structure. These Antique Forms of Building were accommodated to the ancient Ceremonies. For as the *Jews* were admitted no farther than the Dores, and the Priests only suffer'd to pass beyond the Threshold, so here none but the Baptiz'd were admitted as it were into the Bosom of the Church, the rest, like the *Gentiles* among the *Jews*, prohibited from approaching nearer than the Dores. The Quire none but the Ecclesiastical Persons enter'd, which was so rigidly observ'd by the Ancients, that St. *Ambrose* commanded the Emperor himself *Theodosius*, to withdraw; whereas the Greek Church allow'd that Priviledge to their Emperors, and gave them Liberty to enter the Sanctuary when they offer'd to the Sacred Table. After the same manner, the more famous Churches of the *Ethiopians* were Built; and they have also the same sort of Sanctuaries, which they call by the Hebrew Name, *Heichel*, at the entry whereof the Layety stand and receive the Communion. Least therefore their Nobility and their Children should be forc'd to stand among the Vulgar Croud, or they be constrain'd to break their Law and Custom, Prohibiting the Layety to enter their *Heichel*, and participate of their Sacred Mysteries, they have found out a new Evasion, by Creating the Nobility and their Children, tho' ne're so young, or under Age, *Deacons* or *Sub-deacons*; in that only deviating from their ancient Simplicity. The King's Children assume that Dignity of course, carrying a Cross, as a

badge

badge of their *Deaconship*, which they ne'r leave off when they came to the Crown. Which the *Portugueses* looking upon as an Ornament of *Priesthood*, it gave them an occasion to give the *Habessine* Emperor the Title of *Presbyter John*. There is also a little Chappel adjoyning to the Eastern part of the Church, in which the Bread and other Necessaries belonging to the Eucharist are prepar'd. Such little Chappels or Rooms were Built of old near to the great Church, where the Bishops were wont to put on their Vestments; now they are small Apartments made within the Walls of the Church, call'd by the Name of Vestries. They have no Seats in their Churches, for they neither sit nor kneel, but always stand during Divine Service; according to the ancient Canons, which the *Greeks* and *Russes* observe to this day, as believing it more becoming the Reverence due to the Place, and more proper for Attention than to sit. The next Age providing more kindly for Infirmity, permitted sitting, least Attention should be tyr'd by weariness. But the *Habessines* have found out a way between both; that is to say, little Crutches to lean and rest their Bodies, which when they go away, they leave in the Church Porch. If there be any who out of weakness chance to sit upon the Ground, they are in the midst of Prayers commanded by the Deacons to rise, in these words, *Ab Tocber, Tanse*; You *that sit, Rise*. Nay, such is their Reverence to their Churches, that tho at this day they are only poor low dark Buildings, thatch'd with Straw or Reeds, yet when they approach near to any of them in their Travels, they alight from their Mules, and walk a foot till they are past them: They also put off their Shooes at the Door, and never spit upon the Pavement. No Females are admitted during their Impurities, nor Wives that have known their Husbands, all the day following. In this none more Rigid then the Ancients, who only admonish'd such to Abstain from the Holy Communion.

Pictures they admit into their Churches; but as for Statues or Sculptures Engraven or Cast, they abominate them, with the same antipathy as they do Idols. Perhaps because they never had any in the Primitive times of the Church. For it was the Saying of the Ancients, *Why should Men go about to make any likeness of God, when Man himself was his Image, and no better could be made?* And therefore it is a hei-

S f nous

nous Offence for any one to carry about them the Picture of Christ Crucify'd. However the Clergy carry bare Crosses in their hands, which they who meet them, reverence with a Kiss; thereby Professing themselves Christians. For they often sign both themselves, and the things that belong to them, with the Sign of the Cross, after the Custom of the most ancient Christians; who were wont so to do.

We shall now proceed to the Sacred Ceremonies of the *Habessines*, beginning with the first initation into Christianity, *Baptism*. The Priest being to Baptize a Person or Persons of full Age, which there many times happens, by reason of the frequent Conversion of the Heathen, begins with the 51 *Psalm*, then having Perfum'd the Persons with a Censor of Frankincense, he enquires the Names of them that are to be Baptiz'd. Then after the Recital of certain Prayers, the Deacon at the same time frequently Exhorting the Hearers to joyn with the Priest, he Anoints several parts of the Body with the Holy Oyl, and lays his Hand upon the *Neophyte's* Head. Which done, the *Neophytes*, lifting up their right Hands, and looking toward the West, abjure *Satan*, as the Prince of Darkness. Then turning to the East, as to the Sun of Justice, and lifting up again their Right hands, they make as it were a kind of Vow to Christ; which don, they say over the Creed after the Priest, who putting the Question, They answer, *They do Believe*. Which ended, the Parties again are anointed, and some certain pieces of Chapters are read out of the Gospel of St. *John*, the Acts of the Apostles, and the Epistles of St. *Paul*. At length the Oyl is so pour'd into the Water prepar'd for the Baptism, as to resemble in falling the Signature of the Cross, and after the Rehearsal of several other Prayers, the Priest descends into a certain Pool, made on purpose before the Doors of the Church, whither the Persons being conducted by the Deacon, the Priest takes them, and plunges them three times over Head and Ears, saying, *I Baptize thee in the Name of the Father, Son, and Holy Ghost.* At the same time the Men have Men, the Women Women to assist them, who lending their Hands and Arms to their Friends, support them in going out of the Pool, and were therefore call'd *Susceptores* or *Upholders* by the Ancients. Being thus wash'd, and once more anointed, they are first

clad

clad with a White Under-garment, to signifie the Purity of the Mind; and over that, with a Red Vestment, in token of their Salvation purchas'd by the Blood of Christ; and so introduc'd into the Church, where, being intermixed with Christians, they are made Partakers of the Holy Communion. At their departure they are presented with Milk and Honey, and so the Priest laying his Hand upon their Heads, dismisses them with this Benediction, *Sons of Baptism, go in Peace.* For the *Habessines* frequently call the Christians *Velda Tenque, Sons of Baptism.* All which Circumstances are agreeable to the Rites of the Ancients. *Let us thrice be plung'd,* saith *Tertullian, and thence supported, let us tast the Society of Milk and Honey.* These are the Ceremonies observ'd toward those of ripe years.

The Ceremonies of Baptizing Infants are much shorter. Males were formerly never Baptiz'd before the Fortieth day, Females before the Eightieth day, unless upon imminent danger of Death. But now they hasten Baptism much sooner, especially if the Infant be weak and sickly. The Godfathers and Godmothers make answer to the Priest in their behalf. Nor are they plung'd in the Water, but only Sprinkl'd and Dipp'd, and that at the Entrance only of the Church, there being no admittance for them into the Church before Baptism. Lastly, Because the Holy Communion is given to those of riper years presently after Baptism, therefore least Infants should be in a worse Condition, in former times they dropt two or three drops out of the Sacred Cup, having crumbl'd a little piece of the Holy Bread into it before: to shew there was the same regard to be had to them, as to those of riper Age. Which being long observ'd in the Latin Church, the *Ethiopians,* together with the *Armenians,* observe the Custom to this day. *Gregory* told me, That they did no more than only dip the top of one of their Fingers in the Wine, and moisten the Childs tongue. Now that they use the same form of words with us, *Alvarez* is Positive, that is to say, *I Baptize thee in the Name of the Father, and of the Son, and of the Holy Ghost.* Nor could I apprehend any otherwise out of their own Liturgies.

Which makes it more to be admir'd, what the Fathers of the Society, making no mention at all of this Form, have written into *Europe,* That several partly unwonted, partly frivolous Forms, and quite altering the Essence of Baptism, were made use of by the *Habessine* Clergy: For Example, *I Baptize thee in the Name of the most Holy Trinity*; *I Baptize thee in the Name of Christ*; *I Baptize thee in the Name of the Holy Ghost* only; *I Baptize thee in the Water of* Jordan; *The Lord baptize thee*; *Let God wash thee*; *Let Baptism wash thee*; *Blessed be the Father, the Son, and the Holy Ghost*, with several others of the same Nature. For which reason they were constrain'd to Rebaptize many People, not permitted by the Catholic Church, but upon extraordinary occasions. So that at length they promiscuously Rebaptiz'd all the *Habessinians*, tho with this Condition, That the first Baptism was not rightly perform'd, which drew upon them the Hatred and Envy of the *Habessinian* Clergy.

Many Writers have believ'd, and reported, That the *Ethiopians* were branded with a Mark after Baptism, in order to the fulfilling the words of St. *John*, *He that cometh after me shall Baptize you with the Holy Ghost, and with fire*. But *Gregory* himself deny'd any such Custom, nor do the Fathers of the Society make any mention of it in their Writings. But this is certain, that the People of *Africa*, as well *Gentils*, as *Mahometans*, do cauterize the Temple-Veins of Children newly Born, to preserve them from *Catarrhs*. Which being perhaps done by some of the *Habessines* to the same end, was by some ignorant Foreigners taken for a Religious Ceremony. As having heard that formerly there were a sort of silly Heretics, who misinterpreting the word *Fire*, properly so taken, and wresting it to the improper signification of Baptism, preferr'd the Caustic Signature of Fire, before the Ceremony of washing in Water.

But now for what concerns their *Anniversary* Baptism, with which the *Abessines* are so much reproach'd, we are to give this Light. Upon the XI. of *January*, which with us is upon the Sixth, in the mid'st of their Summer, and the Feast of the Epiphany, they keep a most joyful Festival in Commemoration of the Baptism of our Saviour, which with many of the Ancients, they certainly believe, was perform'd upon that day. By the first Dawn of the Morning Light, the Clergy begin the Solemnity with certain loud and chearful Hymns. The King with all the Nobility of the Court, the Metropolitan with the Clergy, Nobles and Plebeians, Old and Young, before Sun-rise, throng into the Rivers and Ponds, and there delight themselves in the Water, plunging and diving over Head and Ears. As they meet any of the Priests, they crave a Blessing from them, who return them generally their desires in these words, *God bless thee*; or, *God the Father, Son, and Holy Ghost bless thee.* Hence it was that many believ'd that the *Ethiopians* renew'd their Baptism every year. But as excess of Joy frequently begets wantonness; so is it frequent for the Young men upon this day to leap, and dance, and swim and duck one another; and by and by to fill the neighbouring Fields with Hoopings and Hallowings, the usual Consequences of such kind of Sports. So that they make of it rather a day of Jollity, than a Pious Christian Festival. All this I relate from *Gregory*'s own Lips. The Relation of *Alvarez* is quite different, as if it were a real Baptism, and that the Men and Women were at that time promiscuously rebaptiz'd. Whether they did so, or whether *Alvarez* rightly understood the words of the Baptizer, I very much question. And yet I cannot but very much wonder at what *Tellez* reports, That at other times, and for slight causes, both Men and Women cause themselves to be rebaptized, and that after a most indecent manner. For should such a thing have been customary, King *Basilides* would never have upbraided the Fathers with their reiteration of Baptism, so frequently as he did. For my part, I never read or heard of any such thing. However, if any such thing were ever practis'd, it is to be attributed rather to the stupid ignorance of the Priests, then to allow'd Custom.

For in the last Century such was the most miserable Condition of the Ecclesiastical Affairs in *Habessinia*, that nothing could be more deplorable: at what time, by reason of the continual Invasions and Irruptions of the *Gallans* and *Adelans*, the People were dispers'd and scatter'd up and down the Mountains and Rocks, like a Flock without a Shepheard, without Law, and almost without either King or Metropolitan; all Sacred Worship ceas'd; their Clergy were dissipated, and their Temples and Monasteries every where ruin'd and burnt. What wonder then that *Ignorance* and *Sloth* should grow upon them! and that the illiterate Priests, for want of Books, not to be supply'd by Printing, and through the scarcity of Learned Men, should rashly obtrude many things altogether Foreign from the Rites of their Ancestors. For such Accidents frequently happen in great

Cala-

Calamities, when Bishops and Princes cannot perform, or else grow careless of their Offices; when little regarding their own Eternal Salvation, they leave that to fate, or the pleasure of every private Person, which should be their chief and principal care. Such was the Sluggishness that overwhelm'd all *Greece*, in the time of *Maurice* the Emperor; so that neither *Gregory* understood Greek, nor any one at *Constantinople* could understand Latin, such was the misery of that Age, in the Latin Church, as *Baronius* testifies, when nothing but meer Barbarism and Ignorance Triumph'd, when all Arts and Vertuous Studies were Exil'd, and only Vice prevail'd in Church and State. At that time there was a certain Priest, who neither like a Latinist, nor a Christian, had Baptiz'd several Infants in *Nomine Patria, & Filia, & Spiritua Sancta*, which Baptism was however confirm'd by *Zacharias* the Pope, by reason of the good intention of the *Baptizer*.

That Sinners after Baptism are reconcil'd to God and the Church, they make no Question: However they teach that there must be a Repentance for these Sins, and that Repentance to be made known by Confession. But to enumerate all and singular their particular Sins, with all their circumstances, they think it neither commanded of God, nor at all necessary. And therefore, they only say in general words to the Priest, *Absan, Absan, we have Sinn'd, we have Sinn'd.* So that when the *Roman* Priests press'd them to particular Confession, they never acknowledg'd any more than three, if they had been guilty, *Homicide, Adultery*, and *Theft*. To confess any more they could not be induc'd without great difficulty. The Offender is Absolv'd in very few words, together with some gentle stripes upon the Side with an Olive twigg, which is thought sufficient to deliver him from the Power of *Satan*. But as for them that have committed any of those great Crimes before named, they are not only chastis'd with severe Reprehension and bitter Language, but many times also severely Scourg'd, to the end they may not only hear, but be sensible of their Absolution. *Tellez* reports, That the Metropolitan sometimes hears Confessions himself, and that when he understands the heinousness of the Crime, he rises up, and after a sharp rebuke of the Penitent, he cryes out, *Hast thou done this? Dost thou not fear God? Go too, let him be Scourg'd*

thirty

thirty or forty times. Presently the Executioners are ready, who streight prepare their Scourges, and give the miserable Sinner six or seven cutting lashes; the rest being remitted at the Intercession of the Standers by. There was one who to avoid so sharp an Absolution of his Crime, requested of the Metropolitan sitting in his Seat of Judicature, that he might make his Confession in Private; to whom the Metropolitan, *How! Shall not thy Sin be made manifest at the last day, before all the World?* Tell therefore, *what it is!* The unfortunate Offender believing it his duty to obey, openly confess'd, it was the *stealing of Oxen.* By chance the Owner of the Oxen was there; who being glad that he had apprehended the Thief, presently accus'd him, so that the poor Fellow being Convicted of the Fact by his own Confession before so many Witnesses, was constrain'd to restore the Oxen, and undergo a severe Punishment beside.

But as the *Habessines* are generally of a soft and mild Disposition, for the most part, so soon as they have committed any notable Offence, they presently run to their Confessors, and confessing they have sinn'd, desire to receive the Communion for the quiet of their Consciences. But this they do not do, till they come to be at least Five and twenty years of Age. For till then they prolong their years of Indiscretion, pretending Childish Innocence. So that if a Young man die before he be Twenty years old, they bewail him in these words, *Oh! let my Soul be like the Soul of this Innocent.* So great a Confidence they have in the honest Inclinations of their Youth.

The whole Divine Service of the *Ethiopians* is compleated by the sole Administration of the Sacrament, and reading some few broken parcels of Chapters out of the New Testament: for they neither make use of Sacred Hymns nor of Preaching. Which when we seem'd to wonder at, *Gregory* ask'd me; *Whether we thought our Preachers could speak any thing better then what was written in the Sacred Scripture, or the Homilies of the Fathers of the Primitive Church? Whether we thought their Sayings more efficacious than the Word of God? Whether we did not fear, lest those Preachers should utter something which might be repugnant to our Faith and Salvation, which might prove of dangerous Consequence, especially among the Plebeian and rustic sort of People?* We answer'd, That the Worship of God requir'd it; and that the use and end of Preaching

Preaching was at large set forth in Scripture; to the end we might understand the benefit of them. But the *Habessines* to supply this defect, have Compos'd several Liturgies and Homilies, of which mention has been already made. To these they add several Portions of Scripture usually appointed to be read, which are fourfold, out of the Evangelists, the Acts, the Epistles of St. *Paul*, and the rest of the Canonical Epistles; to which they give the Titles of *Wangel*, the *Evangelist*, *Gheber*, the *Acts*, *Paulos*, and *Hawarys* the Apostle. But in the general Liturgy, which they call *Canon Kedase*, the *Canon of the Mass*, there are all their Ceremonies to be found, with all their Prayers accustom'd to be apply'd to the several Varieties of Duties to be perform'd; all their Instruments and Vessels being sanctify'd by certain Prayers and Ejaculations. For in the Sanctuary stands the *Holy Table*, which they call *Kedesat Terphez*, vulgarly *Menbar*. It differs from their Common Tables, for that you may go round about it, and place what you please upon it. Only it is cover'd with a Canopy, sustain'd with four Pillars at each Corner. Upon this they place the Sacred Vessels. First the *Tabot*, or *Chest*: A little Table so call'd; but the reason why, I never yet could find; for that it has no resemblance of a Chest; it being an Oblong Quadrangular Table, upon which the Dish and the Cup are set; and therefore I must repair to conjecture, which I shall willingly submit to the Judgment of the Learned.

The most ancient Christians, when for almost three Ages together, they could not have the Opportunity of Administring or receiving the Communion in Public, were constrain'd to take their Opportunities in Dens and Caves; but for the most part in the Church-yards, in the silence of the Night. To which purpose, they either carry'd the Bread, Wine, Cup, and other Utensils wrapp'd up in Linnen, or otherwise conceal'd to the place where the Congregation met. Whence it seems very probable to me, that they might make use of the Coffins themselves, or some Chest in the fashion of a Bier, to conveigh their Sacred Utensils, under the pretence of carrying forth their Dead. Which Chest being thus conveigh'd into the Church-yard or Cave where they met, serv'd also instead of a Table, about which the Communicants sate, and receiv'd in their Order. If they found any Bones of the Holy Martyrs scatter'd about,

they

they gather'd them up, and put them up in this Chest, which Custom in after Ages became a Law. If they were driven from their Habitations, or constrain'd for fear of Tyrannical fury to seek new abodes, this Chest was still carry'd from place to place, where the Bishop or Presbyter resided, who was to perform the Sacred Duty. And thus they came to be call'd either Chests by their proper Names, or Tables in reference to their Use, the Name of Altar growing out of Mind. For so *Minutius Felix*; *D'ye think*, says he, *that we conceal the Deity whom we serve, because we have not Temples and Altars*, properly so call'd? Afterwards they began in respect of the Oblations to be call'd Altars. But in process of Time, when the Sacrament came to be Administer'd without controul, there happen'd a great Change. For that some thought it not lawful to perform the Sacred Duty, otherwhere then at those wooden Chests, which long Custom had now made *Religious*. And therefore being brought forth of the Caves where they had been Consecrated, they were set apart for the Administration of the Eucharist; and it is not unlikely, that in regard they were to be plac'd upon low Tables, they were made the more plain, and the lesser, that they might be more fit for use; till at length they came to be made like the Tables themselves; so that now the form being chang'd, the name only appears among the *Ethiopians*. But after that, when Christians began to rear great and stately Fabricks those Arks or Chests together with the Tables, were plac'd in the Sanctuary; and in most Churches the Name of *Table* remain'd; but in Latin Church the Name of *Altar*, as the more worthy and decent Appellation prevail'd.

But this was an establish'd Custom among the Ancients, That the Basis upon which the Sacred Vessels were to be set, should be first consecrated. Whence it came to pass, that the *Tables* or *Altars* themselves were consecrated; and so the use of those Arks or Chests ceas'd. But where there were no Altars, or that the question was, whether they were consecrated or no, there the Greeks had their *Antimensa*, or little Crickets; the Latins, their *Portalia* or small Portative Tables, which they set upon those Altars that were not consecrated. But for the *Ethiopians*, they make use of their Chest and their Table both together; to the end the Service may be the more fully and absolutely perform'd, and nothing left undone. Now in regard theſe Cheſts were formerly made of Wood, it was not material what ſort of Wood. But after the Popes had commanded that the Altars ſhould be made of *Parget*, the little Portative Altar was alſo made of the ſame matter, for that reaſon call'd *Lapis Sacratus*, or the *Conſecrated Stone*. The little Cheſt which the *Ethiopians* uſe, is generally of Wood, though they do not Prohibit thoſe that are made of Stone, or caſt Metal. However the Fathers of the Society would not permit them to make uſe of any but of Stone; the reſt they either burnt or melted down.

Now the better to ſupport and give credit to Conjecture, and to ſhew that the Primitive Chriſtians had beſides their plain and fix'd Tables, real Cheſts, like Cheſts of Drawers, we ſhall produce a Marble Monument digg'd up in one of the Chriſtian Church-yards. Which, if you obſerve it, is like a Trunk or arched *Bier*, cover'd with a Linnen Cloth in folds, not a Half-Moon Table like a C, as *Ariaghus* imagin'd. Neither am I apt to believe that they who ſate about it were celebrating their *Love Feaſts*, but the Holy Communion. Which is plain from the Sacred Loaves that are there repreſented, ſign'd with a *Saltir Croſs*, which the *Ethiopians* ſtill uſe in the Holy Communion. *Thuanus*, it ſeems, ſaw one of thoſe ſort of Altars, when he came to *Aix* in the Province of *Armagnac*, and deſcribes them to be like certain Cheſts. *Here*, ſays he, *we view'd the Temple of St.* Orentius, *of moſt remote Antiquity, where we beheld ſeveral Altars plac'd up and down in the Temple, being the Coffins of the Martyrs, round about which the Chriſtians formerly held their Meetings, not plain and level like our Tables, but riſing with a kind of Gibboſity, in the manner of a Trunk lidd: which were marked with two Greek Letters,* (χ.ρ.) *repreſenting the Name of Chriſt.* With *Thuanus* agrees *Gabriel Biel*, who diſcourſing of Wooden Altars, *Nor is it contradictory*, ſays he, *to what has bin ſaid before, that there is a Wooden Altar in the Lateran Church, which Altar is preſerv'd out of a particular Reverence to the Prince of Apoſtles, and the preceding Holy Martyrs, who were ſaid to have Celebrated the Holy Communion upon that Altar. This Altar was fix'd by Biſhop* Silveſter, *to the end that no Perſon, unleſs the Pope himſelf ſhould preſume to make uſe of it, for the Celebration of Divine Service. But the rage of Perſecution continuing from the time that the Prince of the Apoſtles was Biſhop, till the Pontificate of* Silveſter, *there was no*

fix'd

A MARBLE COFFIN *digged up in a* Church Yard *nere the highway calld Priscillas*
** Salares Way Representing the Communion of ye Ancients in a Cave. Book 3d Chap 6 P. 196*

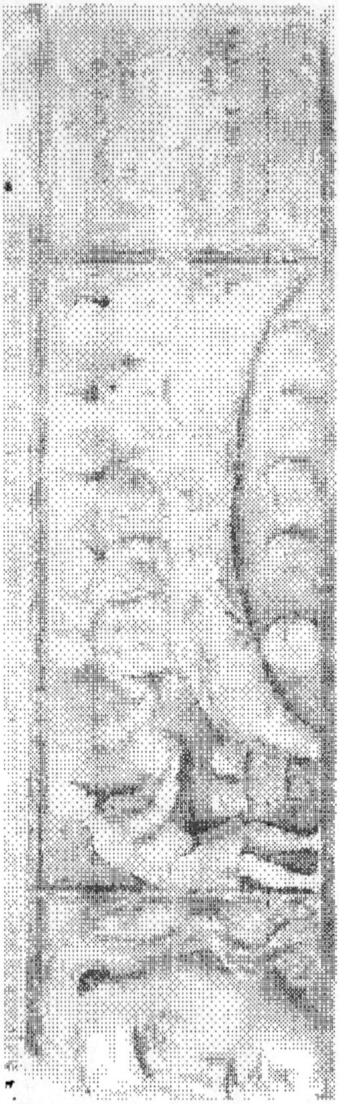

fix'd Episcopal See, *So that they were forc'd to perform holy Duties either in Caves or other private places upon a wooden Altar, in the form of a hollow Chest, which was carry'd about by the Priests, where-ever the* Roman *Bishop kept his secret Habitation.* Which is confirm'd by *Father Tellez*, who thus writes, where he Discourses concerning the *Chest* made use of by the *Ethiopians*.

Moreover 'tis well known, that in the Infancy of the Catholic Church, the Altars were of Wood, like little Chests, and there were no other Altars of Stone, till the time that Silvester *began to Consecrate Altars of kind. However he left remaining in the Cathedral of* St. Peters, *others say in* St. John Laterano, *a little wooden Chest, which for so many years had bin the Altar which so many Pious Popes had made use of, and upon which it is not lawful at this day for any Person but the Pope himself to Celebrate.*

Thus the Studious Reader may perceive frequent mention to have bin made of these *Chests*; and if that *little Chest* of which *Tellez* has given us a Relation, be still Extant at *Rome*, there can be no room left for any farther doubt concerning the Matter or the Form: and our Conjecture concerning their Original will stand good, till the Learned shall give us better Information. Now, that the *Martyrs* Bones were anciently put into these *Chests*, we gather from the *Council of Carthage*, which approves and confirms the Custom. For so runs the 14 Canon of the *Fifth* by Name, but *Third* in Order of Time. The Altars, *in which* (he doth not say *above*, nor *under*) *there are no Reliques of Martyrs, shall be remov'd.* Neither could those Bones be dispos'd of in Tables, nor in the Altars, so call'd, of the Ancients. And in this we have bin the more prolix, to the end the Original and Use of the *Ethiopic Chest*, appropriated to the Communion, might be the better understood.

The other holy Vessels are *Pabal*, the *Dish*, *Terwa*, the *Cup*, and Spoon for distribution of the Wine, call'd *Ertf Maskel*, the *Spoon of the Cross*, by reason that the handle ends in a little Cross. Besides these, they have their consecrated *Urns* and *Censors*, in regard they frequently fume with Frankincense, which Necessity constrain'd them to do while they were forc'd to make use of Caves and Subterraneal Places.

In the Administration of the Sacrament, they use a sort of leaven'd Bread (as was done in the Latin Church for many

Ages) Mark'd with a Cross +, imprinted into the Mass of the Loaf. This Bread they call *Korban*, and Bake it new every day, admiring at the Latins for keeping their Holy Bread till the Morrow. But upon the Fifth Holy-day of the great Week, in Memory of Christ's unleaven'd Loaves, they also use unleaven'd Bread; pieces of which the Priest distributes to the Communicants. For they all participate of one Loaf. The Wine is by the *Deacon* given out of the Cup in a Spoon indifferently to all, as well Layety, as Clergy. True it is, they want real Wine; the defect of which they supply by steeping the bruis'd Stones of *Raisins* in Water, and then squeezing and straining the Infusion, which makes a kind of *Raisin* Liquor. Yet not believing it thus made to be small enough, the *Subdeacon* pours a Spoonful or two of Water into the hollow of the Communicants hand, with which he first washes his mouth, and after that, sups it up. *Tellez* will not allow this Liquor to be other then meer Water; and for that reason laughs at the *Habyssines*, for believing they Communicate in both kinds, when they Communicate in neither; tho the Fathers of the Society, for want of Wine, were forc'd to use the same Liquor in the former Age. Which *Sandovall* calls a Holy and Provident Invention. Most certain it is that many Countreys, especially inhabited by barbarous People, and remote from the Sea, are destitute of Wine; as the *Copts* in *Egypt*, and the Christians of the Order of St. *Thomas* in *India*. Nay, some there were, who were put to harder shifts than all this: having no other way but to dip a linnen Cloth in Wine, when they could come at it, and dry it again. This Cloath they kept very charily, and when they had an occasion to Administer the Sacrament, they moisten'd a part of the Cloath in water, and wrung the moisture out again with their hands. Which water so relish'd and tinctur'd, they gave to the People.

These Shifts Pope *Julius* condemns, however in a case of Necessity, he permits the cluster it self to be squeez'd into the Cup, and the Liquor to be mix'd with water.

The time of receiving the Sacrament, is left to every man's liberty; some receive every Week, some every Month; but always within the Church. For they hold it a great Sin to carry the Holy Mysteries out of the Church into private Houses: Neither does the King, nor the Metropolitan assume to themselves that Priviledge. They never spit, that

that day they have receiv'd. They also receive Fasting, and toward the Evening too, if it be a fasting day.

But now to Administer the Sacrament in large and crowded Churches, and upon Solemn days, it requires four or five Men at least. *Bahan*, the *Priest*; or *Kasis*, the *Presbyter*. *Nesek Kasis*, the *Sub Presbyter*; *Daykan*, the *Deacon*; and *Nesek Daykan*, the *Sub-Deacon*. There are also present other Assistants, to hold the Candles, and to attend upon the Priests. These every one taking his particular part, perform the whole Duty, reading of several Prayers, as the variety of Action, and the use of distinct Vessels require. Lastly, they recommend both the *Living* and the *Dead* to God, which they call *receiving the Daptukon*, the *Diptych*, or *Church Register*; which among the Ancient Greeks, consisted of two Tables, wherein the Name of those were written, who were to be Pray'd for in the Register. There are some that bring their Offerings to the Holy Table, as Bread, Oyl, Tithes, first Fruits, and the like, which at the Conclusion of the Sacrament, are distributed to the Poor. Which I take to be understood of that ancient Custom mention'd by *Claudius*, in his *Confession of Faith*. *Vangaber Bat Mesab, that day*, meaning the Sabbath, we make a Charitable Feast. These Holydaies they keep two days every Week; that is to say, upon the Sabaoth and the Lord's-Day. That they call *Sanbat Eschude*, which they say they celebrate in commemoration of the professed Creation, and therefore they do not keep it so solemnly as the Lord's-Day. But upon the Lord's-Day, which they call *Sanbat Ehud*, or the Sabbath of the first Holyday, or *Ehude*, the *first Holyday*, singly, or *Sanbat Christejan*, the Christians Sabbath, they keep after the custom of the Catholic Church, and read over all the Offices and Services requir'd.

They have no Bells of Brass, or mix'd Metal like ours; instead of which, they only use a kind of hollow Vessels resembling Bells, made of Iron, Stone, or Wood, more for Noise, than delightful to the Ear. Neither is their Church Music any thing more pleasing. For besides that, the Voices of their Singing Priests, whom they call *Dabetra*, are very harsh and ungrateful; the Instruments they make use of after the *Egyptian* manner, such as Cimbals, Morrice Bells, and Kettle Drums, which the Grandees themselves think no dishonour to rattle upon those Solemnities, are no

way

way agreeable to the Harmony of *Europe*. With their Music they use Skipping and Dancing, in imitation of *David* Dancing before the Ark of the Covenant. At what time they make the Floor ring again after such a rude manner, that you would believe them rather at a Wedding, than at a Christian Solemnity. This they call *exulting*, *rejoycing*, and *clapping hands to the God of Jacob*, as they are commanded in the Psalms; and this they call Praising God upon the Harp and Organ, and with *Cymbals*, tho it cannot be said they are so sweet sounding as those in *David's* Time may be imagin'd to be. Which things tho they seem to us, not to correspond with the gravity of Christian Worship, yet will not they much admire, who well know, that in some places among the Latins, the Feast of the Body of God was solemniz'd with Dancing; which as it could not be done without Music, there were others that play'd in disguise before the Dancers upon Harps.

Fasting days are no where more exactly observ'd. Not that they abstain from some Meats, and gluttonize upon others. For that they look upon as a mockery of Fasting. For they keep themselves whole dayes without either Food or Drink, even till Sunset of the third Evening. Others there are that abstain the two Holydays of the Passion Week. The Monks put themselves upon greater Extremities than all this; by which means they not only mortifie but destroy. Besides all which they fast twice in seven days, upon the Fourth and Sixth Holyday, like the rest of the Eastern Churches. The reason of which was by *Tzagazaab* said to be, for that the Fourth day the Murther of Christ was concluded upon, and the Sixth it was executed; according to what many of the Ancients taught. But we believe that these two Fasting-days, as many other things, were admitted and observ'd in imitation of the *Jews* by the Primitive Christians, who were either *Jews*, or else had learn't from the *Jews*, that this Custom was introduc'd and us'd as a Duty both Pious and Necessary for those times. For the *Jews* fasted twice in a Week; which is that which the Pharisee boasted, *I fast twice upon the Sabbath*, that is within the two days in seven, viz. upon the Second and Fifth Holyday; which the Christians, because they would not fast upon the same day with the *Jews*, alter'd for the Fourth and Sixth. Afterwards *Innocent*, and *Gregory* the Seventh, abrogating the Fast of the Fourth Holyday, imposed

pos'd

pos'd Abstinence from Flesh upon *Sunday*, not minding the ancient Canon, *If any Clergy-man shall be known to Fast upon any Sabbath or Lord's-Day, one excepted, let him be suspended from his Office*.

That one Sabbath is *Easter Eve*. Otherwise to fast upon the Lord's-Day, the *Ethiopians* account it Criminal, like the ancient Christians; as *Tertullian* witnesses. Besides these, and other Fasts of the Eastern Church, they observe in the first place, the Forty days *Lent*, which they make up Fifty. For it begins Ten days before the Roman *Lent*; That is, upon the second Holyday after *Sexagesima Sunday*. And this as a Command of God, they observe both healthy and sick People, most exactly and religiously; only as we said before, upon *Sundays* they eat Flesh. After *Easter*, they supply the pinching hardship and sobriety of the past Weeks with the Jollity and Mirth of those that succeed. For during all the time of *Pentecost*, so formerly was the interval of the Fifty days call'd, (from the Feast of the Resurrection till the Feast of sending the Holy Ghost) they spend their time in all manner of Feasting and Jocundity, suitable to the Country. All that time, as of old with the Latins; so among the *Ethiopians*, being still observ'd as one continu'd Festival. *Gregory* considering these things, and admiring that the Protestants in *Germany* observ'd no other Fasts, but what were commanded by their Princes in case of Public Calamity, was answer'd out of St. *Ambrose*; *we do not Fast because the Lord abideth with us, not only these Fifty days, but all the year long, nay as long as we live*. Thus Christ answer'd them, who objected to his Disciples.

Can the Sons of the Bridegroom mourn while the Bridegroom is among them. But the time shall come, that the Bridegroom shall be taken from them, and then they shall fast.

Therefore the ancient Christians, when those days came that Christ had foretold, that is to say, the days of Persecution and Affliction, did well and truly in that they frequently fasted. But we, in regard our Bridegroom is return'd with his favour and his Grace, and has restor'd Peace and Tranquillity to his Church, have no need to observe set Fasts as necessary; but to say with St. *Ambrose*, *That true Fasting is an alienation from Incontinency of Language, Suppression of wrath and ill Desires, and Abstinence from Slander and Reproach*. And with St. *Austin*, *The Great and General Fasting is to abstain*

from

from Iniquity, and the unlawful Pleasures of the Age, which is perfect Fasting.

Besides the Sabbath and Lord's-Day, they observe all the chief and ancient Festivals of the Catholic Church; The *Annunciation, Nativity, Circumcision, Baptism, Passion, Resurrection, Ascension,* and the *Descension* of the Holy Ghost, call'd *Baqenah Arbgna*, or the Feast of Forty days; as also that most ancient Festival of the Primitive Church call'd *Rakeb*, in the Middle of the Pentecost, by the Latins call'd *Cantate*, at what time the Bishops are commanded to assemble a Synod, by the Canons commonly call'd *Apostolical*. As for the other Festivals, which were introduc'd by the *Kopts*, *Greeks* or *Latins*, after the Variances of the Council of *Chalcedon*, some they admit, some they receive, according as they think most agreeable to their Religion.

They begin in the year from the Calends of *September*, with the *Greeks*, *Armenians*, *Russians*, and other Oriental Christians. For they believe that the World was created at the time of the Autumnal Equinoctial. They farther also compute Five thousand and five hundred years to the *Nativity*, Eight years less than the Greeks, and they who follow the Translation of the *Seventy Interpreters*, from whence that Computation was made. The Supputation of the Christians is the same, which *Scaliger* says was therefore don, because the Christians believe the World to be less ancient by Eight years then the Greeks do, but he does not apply his reason home. We are apt to believe it came to pass through some erroneous Substraction of the years of the World. For that finding perhaps that the Greeks, to perfect the Calculation of the Years of Christ, had substracted 5508 years of the World; they also did the same, forgetting that those Eight years were already wanting; or else having settl'd the years of Christ, according to the Greek Computation, and coming afterwards to reform the Age of the World, they found these Eight years to be over and above. However it fall out, let any one year of Christ be granted by them, Eight years must be added to their Computation, if you desire to know the agreeing time of any certain Transaction.

Their year consists of Twelve Months, as among us; But each Month, as among the *Egyptians* having but Thirty days; therefore to supply the *Solar* Year, to every Three years they add Five days, to every Four years Six days; which by a word borrow'd from the Greek they call *Pegomen*. Hence it happens, that their Feasts go according to the *Julian* Accompt, and fall upon the same days; yet are otherwise number'd. For the Feast of the Nativity of Christ is celebrated the same day with us, which happens among the *Europeans* using the *Julian* Accompt, to be upon the 25 of *December*, but with them falls upon the 28 of *December*. Neither did the Catholic Church in any part of the World ever observe it upon any other days; So that it is to be admir'd that *Scaliger* should go about to Translate it into Autumn. It is farther observable, that to the space of Four years they give the Denomination of one of the Evangelists; it being the Custom to finish the reading of one Evangelist quite through in that time. Which is the reason that in some of their Chronological Computations, you shall find added, *in the days of* Mark, *in the days of* John *the Evangelist*, &c.

As to what concerns their Nuptial Rites, most certain it is, that *Polygamy* is not allow'd by the *Habessine* Church, however it be tolerated by the Civil Magistrate. For they that Marry more than one are not punish'd by the Magistrates; yet they are prohibited from the Holy Sacrament; as being of those sort of People, that do no injury to the Common-wealth, but only contradict the Rules of Christian Sanctity; as if it were not the Office or Duty of Kings and Princes, but of the Bishops of the Church to make Men Godly and Christianly vertuous. This *Alvarez* asserts upon his own Knowledge: Whose Host at *Dobarva* had Three Wives which had brought him Seven and thirty Children; for which there was no other notice taken of him, but only that he was not admitted to the Church, or to the Communion, until he at last put Two of them away. Here it may not be improper to inquire how the Metropolitan behaves himself toward their Kings, who have more Wives than one. For the *Habessinian* Kings, by vertue of an old Ill custom, besides several Wives lawfully Marry'd, are not asham'd to keep several Concubines; as if they did it in imitation of *Solomon*, from whom they boast their Descent. True it is, That the Fathers of the Society would not grant Absolution to *Susneus*, before he had dismiss'd all his Supernumerary Wives, retaining only the first. Indeed it is to me no small wonder, that the Laws of the Church, and the

Kingdom should no better agree; that the one should be so loose in point of Marriages, the other so strict, especially where the dispute arises, not so much as to the Matter, as to the Name. Thus we find the Marriages of Kindred forbidden, even to distant degrees; for that the *Ethiopians* wanting terms of distinction, call one another all by the Names of Brothers and Sisters. Thus a Church-man may not Marry his Brother's Wife, but a Lay Person may. However no Marriages but those that are approv'd by Divine Authority, are honour'd with Sacerdotal Benediction; nor those neither publickly in the Church, unless they be such Clergy-men, to whom the *Halleluiah* is Sung. Other People are Marry'd either at home, or before the Dores of the Church. However all Secular Persons have also this Priviledge, that they can throw off the Yoke when they please. For upon any slight Difference between a Man and his Wife, if they cannot be reconcil'd, the King's Judges presently dissolve the Marriage. But as for the Clergy, if it be their desire to put away their Wives, or to Marry another, the first being Deceas'd, they are oblig'd to renounce their Function. Whereby it happens, that their Marriages are much more peaceful, and more durable.

To conclude with their Burials, the Dead Bodies being well wash'd and fum'd with Incense, they wrap them up in proper Garments. If the Party deceas'd be of Noble Extraction, he is lay'd upon the Bier, cover'd with a Bulls Hide, which done, the Clergy carry him to the Grave, laden with Crosses, Censors, and Holy-water; and that with a pace so swift, that it is a difficult matter to follow them. The Body is for some time set down by the Grave, during the reading of a certain Paragraph out of St. *John's* Gospel; after which, the Body, being found and sprinkl'd with Holy Water, is not let down, but thrown into the Sepulcher.

King *Claudius* being desirous to Solemnize the Exequies of *Christopher Gomez*, upon the Anniversary Day, that he had lost his Life, for the Recovery of *Abassia*, summon'd together all the Priests, Canons, Monks, and all the Neighbouring Poor People; and to the first, being about Six hundred, he gave a Royal Funeral Supper; to the last, being about Six thousand, he distributed a large and noble Alms. They on the other side recited the whole Psalter quite thorough, and made the Sky ring with innumerable *Alleluiahs*, a Ceremony, that

serves

serves alike as well upon sad, as joyful Occasions. Thus when *Marcus*, the Eldest Son of *Susneus*, was Buried, they sounded forth,

> Marcus *is Dead, Hallelujah,*
> Marcus *is Dead, Hallelujah.*

And this they repeated so often and so loud, that the Fathers, but newly then arriv'd in *Ethiopia*, were astonish'd to hear such an unwonted cry; not being able to tell, whether the *Ethiopians* rejoyc'd, or lamented. So strangely are all Nations delighted with their own Customs.

CHAP. VII.

Of the Constitution and Form of Ecclesiastical Government in Ethiopia, *as also of the Priviledges of the Clergy.*

The Clergy enjoy no Immunity. Their Head or Abuna *created by the Metropolitan of* Alexandria. *His Place in Councils. The present State of the* Alexandrian *Church deplorable. The Clergy ignorant, the Patriarch illiterate. The* Habessine *Metropolitans ordain the Clergy only. No Bishops, nor Arch Bishops. The* Icegue *governs the Monks. They acknowledge but four Oecumenical Patriarchs. The Catalogue of Metropolitans uncertain. They do not reck'n those sent by the Pope. After* Mendez, *one call'd the* Coptite. *His Successors. The Orders of Deacon, Presbyter, and Sub-Presbyter. The Clergy Marry, but not twice.*

WE have already declar'd, That the Supream Power in Ecclesiastical Affairs, is invested in the King. Therefore all Ecclesiastical Causes, except only in very slight Matters, are all determin'd by the King's Judges. Neither do the *Clergy* or *Monks* enjoy any sort of Ecclesiastical Immunity, or Priviledge of Exemption. Nor does the Canon, *Siquis suadente diabolo, hujus Sacrilegii reatum incurrerit, quod in Clericum vel Monachum violentas manus injecerit,* &c. help them at all, but that upon offences committed they are punish'd, as Lay Persons, by the Secular Judges: And many times they are sensible of the rough and violent hands of wicked Men, without any fear of Excommunication.

munication. But as to what concerns the *Law of Order*, or the *Diedire Era*, those things are left to the Clergy. Their Chief Head is call'd *Papas*, or *Metropolitan*. Tho the Title or Sirname of *Abuna*, that is to say, *Our Father*, be more frequently given him. He by ancient Custom, at the King's desire, is Consecrated to that Dignity by the Patriarch of *Alexandria*, and sent out of *Egypt* into *Ethiopia*. For they do not think it fitting for the Patriarch to nominate any one out of their own Nation, tho never so skilful in their Language, Laws and Customs. It being provided by those *Nicene* Canons, extant in the Arabic Language, *That the* Ethiopians *shall not Elect or Create a Patriarch, but that their chief Chief Prelate shall be under the Jurisdiction of Him that resides at* Alexandria. And a little after, *That if the Council be held in* Greece, *and the Prelate of* Ethiopia *be present, he shall have the seventh place, next the Prelate of* Seleucia. For they are very obstinate in maintaining their old Customs, tho it happen to be one of their greatest Misfortunes. The State and Condition of the *Alexandrian* Church, being quite different now from what it was formerly; that is to say, altogether miserable and deplorable. For both the Patriarch and his Clergy, are a poor sort of contemptible and rustic People, and void of all common Endowments. They are as it were the Servants and Slaves of the *Turks*, whose continual vexations so terrifie them from undertaking Ecclesiastical Employment, that many times they receive their Ordination by constraint, and with Tears in their Eyes; which requires nothing more from them than to read *Arabic*.

For the *Coptic*, or ancient *Egyptian* Language, as it was spoken in the times of the *Grecian* Kings, and as *Athanasius Kircher* has given a view of it to the *Europeans*, is now almost buried in Oblivion. Their Churches are either all destroy'd, or very near to Ruin; the *Turks* not suffering them either to Rebuild or Repair. The Patriarch, if he can but only read and write, and understand the Scripture after an ordinary manner, is thought sufficiently worthy of St. *Mark's Chair*. Hence it may be easily conjectur'd, what sort of Persons are sent into *Ethiopia* for the Government of so many Churches. In the time of the Fathers of the Society, there was sent such a sad Tool into *Habeshinia*, to be the *Abuna*, that being rejected for his Simplicity, he was forc'd to Grind Corn for his living. To whom another Succeeding, not much better

gifted,

gifted, gave occasion to the Courtiers to jest, and cry, *We have a Miller still.* Now as these Patriarchs know very little, so they do as little, only in set forms of Words, they ordain Under-Clerks, just as wise and learned as themselves.

For this reason the Fathers of the Society, little regarded the Ordinations of the *Abuna*, but when any of the *Abessine* Priests came over to them, they ordain'd them again after the *Roman* manner, not without the great resentment and indignation of the rest.

In none of their Kingdoms or Provinces have they any *Bishops* or *Arch-Bishops*. So that unless the *Icegue*, with the assistance of his Monks, had taken some care of the Church, all thought of Religion had fallen to the ground long e're this.

This *Abuna* is by some, tho improperly call'd *Patriarch*, his truer Title being that of *Bik Papas*, or *Bik Papasse*, Prince or Master of the Metropolitans; of whom they acknowledge only Four to be of equal Power and Dignity among themselves. Among these they reckon the *Roman* Patriarch to be the First, and call him *Bik Papasse Zaromeja*, or the *Roman Patriarch*. For they have no higher Title to give to any one who may be thought Superior to a Patriarch.

The first Metropolitan of *Habessinia* was *Frumentius*, the Ethiopic Apostle. From him to *Simeon*, who dy'd with *Elius* in defence of the *Alexandrian* Religion, they reck'n in order Ninety five Metropolitans. We have not yet seen the Catalogue, but in the Ethiopic Register, they are Number'd up in this Order.

Abuna *Abba Matthew.*
Abba Salama.
Abba Jacob.
Abba Bartholomew.
Abba Michael.
Abba Isaac.
Abba John.
Abba Mark, who was Metropolitan in the Time of *David*,

Abba Joseph,

In the Reign of *Claudius* was receiv'd into the Kingdom with great Pomp; without any regard had to *John Bermudez*, whom

whom the Pope had sent into *Abessinia*, with the Titles of Patriarch of *Alexandria* and *Ethiopia*. As little respect did the *Habessines* give to *John Nonius Barret*, and *Andrew Oviedo*, Portugueses, dignify'd at *Rome* with the Titles of *Patriarch*, and sent into *Ethiopia* by the King of *Portugal*. About the beginning of this last Century, one *Peter*, upheld by the Factious Party, withstood *Za-Dengbel*, who favour'd the Romanists. In the Time of *Susneus*, *Simeon*, already mention'd, came into the Kingdom, who being Slain, and the Miller depos'd, *Alphonsus Mendez* was by the Pope at the Instance of the Fathers of the Society, preferr'd, and by the *Abessinians* admitted to be their Patriarch, tho not acknowledg'd under any other Title then that of *Abuna Zaromeja*, or the *Roman Abuna*. But he, together with his Companions being soon after expell'd, another call'd the *Cophtit* was sent, in whose Company *Peter Heyling* of *Lubeck* travelled to the *Habessine* Court. To him succeeded one *John*, and about the year 1651. another call'd *Mark*, who being depos'd for his vitious life, *Michael* succeeded him. Lastly, about the year 1662. one *Gabraxas* was order'd to supply his Decease.

As for the Cathedrals or Principal Churches, they have their chief *Overseers*, which they call *Komasat*. Such a *Komos* was *Peter* the *Ethiopian*, whose acquaintance was courted by *Paulus Jovius*. It is their Duty to take care of the Secular Matters of the Churches, and to compose the differences between the Clergy-men, so far as their Jurisdiction extends. Over the Churches that belong to the Camp, the *Debtera Gueta* Presides, as much as to say, the *Ruler of the Canons*.

The *Debterat*, or Canons, being those Persons who are particularly employ'd in those Offices that require the addition of Hymns and Sacred Melody. The *Nebrat* seems to be their *Dean*. Next to whom in Dignity are the *Kasis* or *Presbyter*, and the *Nephek Kasis*, or Sub-Presbyter; the *Dejakon* or Deacon, and *Nephek Dejakon*, or Sub-Deacon. As for those *Under-Ministers*, which in the Primitive Church were known by the Name of *Readers*, they are quite out of Use: as are also *Deaconesses*, of which however they have the greatest need, by reason of the frequent Baptizings of full-grown Women, to whom their assistance, while the Ceremony of their Baptism requires them to be naked, is most necessary.

All

All Ecclesiastical Persons, when they walk publickly abroad, carry a Cross in their hands, and offer it to all they meet to be Kiss'd, having hardly any other note of Distinction from the Layety. The same sort of Cross the *Seculars* also carry, who to the end they may be admitted into the Sanctuary, desire to be ordain'd Deacons; as also most young Children.

All the Clergy, except the Monks, are permitted to Marry. Neither will any man deny, but that it was Lawful for the Catholic Bishops of the Primitive Church, the Presbyters and Deacons to do the same; which was also upon the Perswasion and Arguments of *Paphnutius* a most Holy Man, allow'd of and approv'd by the Fathers of the *Nicene* Council, as both *Socrates* and *Sozomenus* testifie; whose Credit justify'd by all Antiquity, was never yet call'd in question; especially being confirm'd by the practice, and so many clear and undeniable Presidents of the Primitive Church, till *Siricius* and *Innocent* the First, took upon them to order it otherwise in the Latin Church.

Among the Eastern Churches, honest and lawful Matrimony was in much more high esteem, than faithless Batchelorship, obnoxious to perpetual concupiscence. Wherefore the *Grecians*, *Armenians*, *Russians*, but more especially our *Ethiopians* not only permitted their Presbyters to Marry, but soonest prefer the Husbands of Wives; insomuch that the nearest way to that Preferment is to Marry. For they take the words of the Apostle, *Let him be the Husband of one Wife*, *for a Precept*; yet understand it only so, as not to extend any farther, but to one single Marriage. And therefore their Clergy never offer to cover repeated Wedlocks; which even by the Seculars were not approv'd in the Eastern Churches. The *Novatians* detested a second Wedlock after Baptism, as equal to the Crime of Adultery. The Latin Fathers also gave it an Ignominious Character, reproaching it with the Scandalous Title of honest Adultery. But in after Ages, the Matter being more wisely consider'd, it was not thought material, whether the same Person Married one or more Wives, after Death had once made the Seperation, so that the Matrimony were lawful; since there appear'd no reason to the contrary. For which was alleadg'd the famous example of one Woman at *Rome*, that had surviv'd the Two and twentieth Wedlock. But the *Habessines* still observe

observe their ancient Laws: in regard that by the ancient Canons, they that Marry twice, are accompted unworthy of Holy Orders.

Chap. VIII.

Of the Separation of the Habessines *from the* Greek *Church, in the Time of the Council of* Chalcedon.

The Council of Chalcedon. Dioscorus *Condemn'd. From thence the* Melchites, *and* Jacobites. *The great Damage to the Church by that Schism.* *The* Ethiopians *defend* Dioscorus. *The* Ethiopians *Condemn the Council of* Chalcedon; *and call* Timotheus *and* Eutyches *Hereticks. They acknowledge two Natures in Christ. The words* Essence, Substance, Person *and* Nature, *ambiguous to the* Abessines. *A doubt concerning the Disputations of the Fathers with the* Abessines *about the two Natures. How they are to be Dispensed with. The* Jacobites *abstain from the* Arabic *word for* Nature, *which the* Eutychians *use. The Dissention deplor'd.*

THE *Alexandrian* Church remain'd in Unity with it self, and with the *Greek* Church, till the *Council of* Chalcedon, by us call'd the *Fourth Universal Council*, which *Marcian* the Emperor Summon'd, to appease the Discords and Dissentions that were risen among the Bishops and Divines, by reason of the Doctrine of *Eutyches*. This *Eutyches*, a Constantinopolitan Abbot asserted, *That both the Natures of Christ, the Divine and Human, upon his Incarnation, immediately became one and the same; and that therefore there was but one Nature, and one Will in Christ.* For which reason, they that held this Opinion were call'd *Monothelites*. Thereupon it was Decreed in this Council, *That Christ was of the same Substance with the Father, according to his Deity, but Sin excepted; of the same Substance, and like to us in all things, according to his Humanity. One and the same in two Natures united, yet without mixture, mutation, division or distance, both Natures acting that which was proper to it, by Communion with each other.* Dioscorus also, the Patriarch of *Alexandria*, was condemn'd as a Heretic, & Defender of *Eutyches*; and not only so, but being publickly whipp'd, he was sent into Exile, and another put up in his room, who because he follow'd the Emperors or the Royal Religion, was therefore call'd a *Melchit*, or Royalists according to the *Arabic* word. The Contradicters of this Opinion were call'd *Eutychians*, afterwards *Jacobites* from one *Jacob*, a Syrian, who stoutly defended the Doctrine of *Eutyches*. Hence arose a most fierce and outragious Schism in the Church of *Alexandria*, defil'd with Blood and Slaughter, which was the reason that not only the greatest part of the *Alexandrian* Church was rent and torn from the rest of the Catholic Church; but that *Egypt* also, weaken'd with it's own civil Dissentions, became a Prey to the *Saracens*, who taking advantage of the Discords of the Christians among themselves, overcame and subjugated the upholders of both Opinions: so that now there is little or nothing remaining of Christianity in *Egypt*. Thus our Ecclesiastical Writers.

But the *Ethiopians* relate, that *Dioscorus*, his Successors, and their Followers, heavily complain'd of the Injury done them: for that he never follow'd *Eutyches*, nor ever deny'd nor confus'd the Divinity and Humanity really existing in Christ; only he would not acknowledge the word *Nature* to be common to the Divinity and Humanity of Christ: and that he only endeavour'd to prevent the Asserting of two Persons in Christ, contrary to the Opinion of the Catholic Church, and the Decrees of the Council of *Ephesus*; believing that absurdity would follow, should we admit two Wills and Natures in Christ. Lastly, That the word *Nature*, signifying something Born or Created, did no way quadrate with Divinity, neither could two Wills in two Natures, united without Division, Separation, or Distance be conceiv'd by the understanding of Man: That it was not to be thought that Human Nature exalted to a State of Glory, would desire, act, or suffer, what is suffer'd, acted, or desired in the State of Mortality; or that Humanity in a present State of Glory, should desire or be sensible of that which Divinity was not sensible of or desir'd. Which Opinion of his being heard and understood, it seem'd an idle Question, a meer brangling Dispute, that little deserv'd to be the occasion of so much Enmity among the Christians, as being become rather a Quarrel to be decided by the Sword, and not by Argument. And therefore these things consider'd, it was evident that *Dioscurus*, was neither sufficiently heard nor rightly understood, but in his absence condemn'd as an obstinate Heretick, rather out of Hatred and Envy then by

Law. These and such like things when I heard *Gregory* discoursing, I began to apply my mind more particularly to this Affair, as being willing to know whether he only expressed his own Thoughts, or according to the Opinions and Writings of his own Country Doctors.

In the first place therefore I found it beyond all doubt, that the *Habessines* do reject the Council of *Calcedon*, tho they understand not what was done therein, as having never receiv'd or thought worthy of their Transcription the *Canons* there made. Nevertheless they inveigh most bitterly against the Council, and the Fathers there assembled, and load them with most injurious reproaches, calling them *Mabebar Abdan*, a *Convention of Fools*, & *Qualqedanawejan*, reck'ning the *Chalcedonians* among the worst of Heretics and Malefactors. In the second place, I observ'd them fix'd in this Error, as believing the Fathers of the Council of *Chalcedon* went about to divide the Substance of Christ, and contrary to the preceding Council of *Ephesus*, to make two Persons of one, which they also attribute to the Latins. For this reason they condemn Pope *Leo*, and extol *Dioscurus* to the Skies, as the Champion of the Orthodox Faith, as being the Person, that out of a just and zealous Indignation, tore *Leo's Diploma*, as soon as it was deliver'd to him, and reck'n him among the Number of Martyrs, for suffering himself to be scourg'd, his Teeth struck out, and his Beard pull'd off, for standing to the Truth.

Peace to Dioscurus, *that still reproach'd*
The vain Opinions that the Melkites *broach'd,*
United God dividing into Two:
Then to confirm his Own *in what was true,*
His broken Teeth and Beard torn from his Chin,
Sends round the World t' expose Chalcedon's *spleen.*

They also ascertain themselves of a great reward laid up for Him in Heaven, in recompence of his so rigid Sufferings.

In the third place, I found that they expresly condemn *Eutyches* as a Heretic, but on the other side applaud *Timotheus*, the Patriarch of *Alexandria*, (whom our Writers affirm to have bin condemn'd in the Sixth general Council) by whose Doctrine, the followers of *Eutyches* were convicted; for so the same Poet, tho otherwise a cruel Enemy of the *Chalcedonian* Fathers writes of him.

They

They that believ'd the Heretical Doctrine of Eutyches, *were burnt by the Flames of his Expressions.*

Tho *Gregory* being demanded what he knew concerning him, made answer,

That there were in Ethiopia, *as well they who believ'd that* Eutyches *had made a confusion of the two Natures of Christ, as they who believ'd he had not done it.*

Whence it appears that *Eutyches*, not his Errors, is defended by some of the *Ethiopians*.

Fourthly, it is apparent, That they acknowledge both *Mahyat* and *Tebat* the Divinity and Humanity to be both Abstractively and Conjunctively in Christ. Which is as much as to allow two Natures together in Christ.

Fifthly, *Tellez* attests from the Relation of the Fathers of the Society, that both Natures are to be found in their Books, and imputes it to their Contumacy, that they will not acknowledge in words what they believe concerning the Catholic Truth, when they teach the same thing in their Writings, *That the Catholic* Habessines *suffering Persecution from the Hereticks, cry'd out,* God and Man, *whereby they both asserted the Catholic Faith, and the two Natures in Christ.* But more then this, we have the Testimony of *Susneus*, in one of whose Orations to his Soldiers, we find that all the *Habessines* confess, *That Christ is the true God, and true Man*; and consequently, we must allow what the *Fathers* of the Society relate, that they acknowledge two Natures in Christ.

Sixthly, we are to take notice, That the words which the Greeks use, and which the Latines have made use of in these difficult questions of Faith, as *Essence*, *Substance* or *Subsistance*, *Person*, *Nature*, among the *Ethiopians* are interpreted by words Equivocal, from whence it is no wonder there should be such a spring of Errors. For *Helave*, sometimes signifies *Essence*, sometimes *Hypostasis* or *Subsistance*. *Gregory* also affirm'd, That there were some who assert *Qalet Helawjet*, two Essences, that is the Divinity and Humanity in Christ, and that each Nature retains its proper Essence. Others for fear of falling into the *Nestorian* Error, rather chose to make use of the word *Bahreye*, which properly signifies a *Pearl*, affirming there are in Christ *Qalit Bahreyat*, two precious Substances; in imitation of the *Arabians*, who use their own word, which signifies a *Pearl*, by which to express the Divine *Subsistance*. Which others again dislike, as being a word

word no leſs Equivocal, becauſe it may be taken either for *Subſiſtance* or *Perſon*; as when they of the Son, *Zatowalda emhaba rejm Buub, who was born of the Subſtance of the Father.* Thus the Author of a certain Manuſcript call'd, *The Eccleſiaſtical Computation* concludes,

Who were witneſs of one Perſon of Chriſt, Synodius *Patriarch of* Alexandria, *&c.*

From whence we gather, that when we from the Council of *Chalcedon* diſpute of the *Nature*, they mean the *Perſon*. Now adays, when they ſpeak of the *Perſon*, they make uſe for the moſt part of the word *Akal*, as being leſs Equivocal; tho' ſometime we ſhall meet with the word *Gaz* to ſignifie *Perſon*, ill render'd when taken for the *Countenance* or *Face*. Which Circumſtances, when I read and conſider, I find all things to be perplex'd and obſcure; no certain State of the Queſtion, and the words themſelves without limitation Equivocal. Perhaps *Eutyches* himſelf could not explain what ſort of *Nature* was meant, how it was made out of the *two*? How it was call'd? or what the Qualities of it were? But that he was ſo egregiouſly ſtupid, as to think the two Natures ſo mix'd in Chriſt, as *Water with Wine*, and that he had ſo many Wiſe and Learned Men to follow him in that Opinion, is almoſt incredible. As for the *Ethiopians*, they are moſt certainly not guilty of ſo ſottiſh a Hereſie. For which reaſon I confeſs, I cannot apprehend what theſe frequent Diſputations were, which the Fathers of the Society had with the *Habeſſines*, wherein, they ſay, the *Ethiopians* were always forc'd to ſubmit, as being convicted out of their own Books. Which is the more eaſie to believ'd, in regard they ſo willingly acknowledge the Divinity and Humanity of Chriſt. But that they ſhould out of Contumacy and Heretical Pravity contradict the Fathers, and chooſe to ſuffer Exilements, and other Puniſhments, or run the hazard of Civil Diſſentions, rather than forego their Opinion, is hardly to be credited. To me it ſeems therefore more probable, that they could not agree about the words. For if a man ſhould firſt explain his meaning, and tell them, that by the two Natures in Chriſt, we underſtand as well his Divinity as his Humanity, and then upon this Explanation ask them, *Which Nature was wanting in Chriſt, ſeeing they acknowledge but one?* Certainly they

they would answer, *That neither his Divinity nor his Humanity were wanting, but that both continue and endure for ever.* And thus it will appear, that they understand the word *Nature* far otherwise than we do, and that the true state of the Question among the *Habessines* consists in this, *Whether by any, or by what name both the Abstract Natures* (which undoubtedly they admit) *are to be call'd!* Now therefore because *Tellez* does not say in what Language they Disputed (for the *Habessines* understand neither *Latin* nor *Portuguese*) how they express'd themselves when they mention'd the words *Essence, Person,* and *Nature,* how they explain'd Equivocal words, or how the Interpreters render'd them, whether they could not agree upon the common *word*, or whether the word *Substance* displeas'd, as fearing that to grant two *Substances*, would be to grant two Persons, I leave to farther enquiry. Nor can I find out in so much Variety and Ambiguity of words, what word is most proper to be us'd in our sense for the word Nature. For the *Jacobites* when they make use of the Arabic *Tabia*, or the Ethiopic *Tabaye*, which answers to the Greek word *Physis*, and by the *Copts* is call'd *D Physis*, apply it only to things created, more especially to the Elements, but never to the *Godhead* which the *Melkites* and *Greeks* being destitute of any other, make no scruple to do. Hence the Contention. For thus saith *Eutychius*, Patriarch of *Alexandria*, a *Melkite*; In Christ there are,

> *Two Substances, a Substance of Divinity, and a Substance of Humanity; but one Person. To every Substance there belongs a Nature; and so two Substances, two Natures, but one Person.*

For this reason, in *Egypt*, where this unhappy difference still remains, when the *Copts* cry out in Arabic *Mashiah Wahid, Tabiah Wahid, One Will, one Nature*; the Melkites answer, *Mashiatan tabiahtan, Two Wills, two Natures.*

In the year 1634. an *European* of great Quality residing in *Egypt*, and having view'd and read the Books of the *Copts*, deliver'd his Opinion afterwards, *That the difference and quarrel of the Parties proceeded more from a fear of the Consequence, than from the Thing it self. For the* Greeks *are for the Destruction of those Hereticks that confuse and mix the Divinity and*

and Humanity of Christ. The Cophtices oppugn those that assert two Persons in Christ.

Which if it be so, that the Contention and Debate, either formerly, or now, is only about the sence of words, What Tears and Lamentations can suffice to bewail the sad Effects of such an Unfortunate Pedantic Brabble? What breast that lodges a heart so hard, that can refrain from bemoaning the sad and calamitous Contentions of those, to whom Christ has so earnestly recommended the most strict Bonds of Charity by his own Example? Humanity one would think, should not be so inhuman, for the sake of one word *Nature* misunderstood, to tear up the foundations of Concord between those, whose Nature the Eternal Word has assum'd into his most Holy Subsistence. But as it is the Infirmity of our most corrupted Nature, where Ambition, from Ambition Emulation, from Emulation Envy, from Envy Hatred have taken root, that the Mind possess'd with various Passions and Affections, seeks no farther after Truth, hence it is that Men with Ears obstructed, and blinded Eyes, pursue disputes to satisfie their private Ends; not considering the true end of Arguing and Dispute.

CHAP.

Chap. IX.

Of the Differences which happen'd between the Habessines *and the Church of* Rome, *more especially the Fathers of the Society to the beginning of this Century.*

The Patriarch of the Melkites *and* Jacobites, *which the* Habessines *following, dissunited themselves from the* Greeks *and* Romans. *They had knowledge of the Pope.* Alexander *the Third writes to the King of* Ethiopia. *An Embassie to* Eugenius *the Fourth, and* Clement *the 7th.* John Bermudes *confirm'd by* Paul *the Third. Whence Hopes of subjecting the* Habessines *to the See of* Rome. Barret *and* Oviedo *made Patriarchs. They send before to sound the King. They Dispute with the King concerning Religion. The* Portugueses *suspected.* Barret *stays in* India, Oviedo *kindly receiv'd.* Claudius *acts moderately. Grants Liberty to the* Latins. Oviedo *desires more. The King delays. Mov'd with* Oviedo's *Epistle.* Oviedo *Attempts Severity but in vain. To* Claudius *his Brother Succeeds. The* Latins *Liberty revok'd.* Oviedo *threaten'd.* Melech Saghed *milder to the* Portugueses. *All their Priests Die.*

THE Horrid flames of Discord being thus broken forth, all those Nations that were Subject to the Alexandrian *See*, separated themselves into Parties almost equal in Strength. And every Faction chose its particular Faction. The *Grecian* Christians, who were in Subjection to the *Constantinopolitan* Emperor, adher'd to the Patriarch of the *Melkites*; The rest who inhabited the innermost Parts of *Africa*, and among them the *Axumites*, follow'd the Patriarch of the *Jacobites*; and thus being rent not only from the *Greek*, but *Roman* Church, they had little or no knowledge of either. After this, the Power of the *Saracens* increasing, and all *Egypt* being by them subdu'd, all Correspondence and Communication of Arts and Knowledge ceas'd between *Them*, and the *Christians* of our part of the World. Nevertheless some glimpses they had of the *Roman Pontiffs*, from the *Acts* of the Ancient Councils, and reverenc'd them as Chief among the Oecunomical Patriarchs. On the other side the Pope laying hold of the occasion, endeavour'd to Re-establish the former Correspondence and Amity, not taking any notice of their being *Monothelites*;

or

or Favourers of the condemn'd *Dioscurus*. To this purpose *Baronius* has set forth an Epistle taken out of *Roger*'s *English Annals*, written by *Alexander* the Third, with this Superscription. *To our most dear Son in Christ, the Illustrious and Magnificent King of the* Indians, *the most Holy of Priests*. Which Epistle he erroneously believes to have bin written to *Prester John*, whose Dominions were then very large in *Ethiopia*. For that when *Baronius* wrote, the King of the *Habessines* was reputed and commonly taken for *Prester John*. But when *Alexander* the Third liv'd, the real *Prester John* was then reigning in *Asia*. Neither is any thing to be gather'd out of that whole Epistle, that has any Relation to *Africa*, or *Ethiopia*, or the King of the *Habessines*; nor are the Consequences of that Letter known to *Baronius*. Only upon that occasion, he conjectures that the Church of St. *Stephen*, with the Buildings behind St. *Peter*'s Cathedral, were thereupon assign'd to the *Habessinians*; though he is not certain by whom that Assignation was made, whether by *Alexander* or any other Succeeding Pope. Therefore, if the Epistle were real, we rather think it was written to the Asiatic *Prester John*, then to the King of the *Ethiopians*. Others there are, that believe there was an *Abessinian* Embassy to *Clement* the Fifth, residing at *Avignon*. Nor is there any doubt made of the Embassy which *Zera-Jacob* sent to *Eugenius* the Fourth, in the year 1439. toward the Conclusion of the Council of *Florence*. *Gregory* had known nothing of it, had he not seen the Embassador and his Retinue painted at *Rome*, and known his own Countrymen by their Habit.

In the former Century, *Francis Alvarez*, Priest to the *Portugal* Ambassadors sent into *Ethiopia*, brought Letters from *David* to *Clement* the Seventh, which he delivered to the Pope in a public Assembly of the Cardinals, *Charles* the Fifth being there also present, promising Reverence and Obedience withal to the Holy See, in the Name of the King of *Ethiopia*. It was a thing very grateful to the Pope, that at a time when so many Northern Nations had revolted from the *Roman* See, so many Kingdoms of the East and South, should voluntarily submit to his Jurisdiction. For which reason, neither *Alvarez*'s Credentials, nor the words of the Epistle were over-nicely examin'd, nor any extraordinary Scrutiny made to what Church or what sort of Religion the King himself was enclin'd, to the end that had it been needful, he might

have

have him absolv'd from the guilt of Heresie, before his Admission into the Bosom of the Church. For as we shall afterwards declare, the *Habessines* made quite another Interpretation of their King's Intention. In the mean time a certain form of Friendship long remain'd. For when *John Bermudes* came to *Rome* to crave Assistance from the *Europeans* in the behalf of *David*, so often vanquish'd by the *Adelans*; *Paul* the Third, hearing that the said *Bermudes* was by *Mark* the Metropolitan, nominated his Successor, and invested with Holy Orders, made no scruple to confirm him, and to ratifie the Ordination of a Schismatical Prelate. There were then residing certain *Habessines*, very good Men, who Printed the New Testament with their Liturgies in the Ethiopic Language, whom the Pope did not only tolerate, but assisted at his own Expences. In recompence of which Kindnesses, they extoll'd and applauded the Benevolence of the *Romans*, the Munificence of the Chief Pontiff, and his Spiritual Daughter *Hyeronyma Farnesia*, and acknowledg'd the Pope as the Head and Supream over all the Orthodox Christians. *Pius* the Fifth also in his Letters to *Menas*, tho a professed Enemy to the *Romans*, call'd him his *most dear Son*; whether he were ignorant of his hatred to the *Latins*, which was a wonder; or whether he had hopes to reclaim him by flattering Titles, which *Gadignus* rather conjectures to be the Pope's true Intention. For this reason, some there were who believ'd the *Habessines* to be Catholicks in the highest perfection, and subject to the See of *Rome*, tho *Tellez* deservedly taxes and derides their Credulity. Nevertheless a vain hope had possessed the Minds of many of the more Zealous sort, that that vast Kingdom, then look'd upon to be four times as big as really it was, might in a short time, with little difficulty, be annexed to the Pontifical Jurisdiction. Among the rest, the Founder of the Society of *Jesus*, *Ignatius Loyola*, bent all his Study to bring it to pass, and to that end he shew'd a most Ardent desire to go himself, and win the honour of Converting *Ethiopia*. Which tho *Julius* the Third would not grant him the liberty to do, nevertheless he so far prevail'd with him, that by the connivance of *John* the Third King of *Portugal*, the Patriarchal Dignity was confer'd upon *John Nonius Barret*, one of his Companions, contrary to the Institutions of his Society, tho *Bermudes* were then in *Ethiopia* already dignify'd with the same Title. With him was joyn'd *Andrew Oviedo*, a Bishop, that if *Barret* through Mortality should miscarry, he might not want an immediate Successor. They, Embarking in several Ships, sayl'd into *India*. In the mean time *Claudius* was become Successor to *David* his Father, whose affection they thought it first expedient to sound, before the Patriarch should expose himself to Casualties and Indignities. *Jacobus Dias* was therefore sent before, together with *Gonsales Rodriguez*, and *Fulgentio Freyre*, Jesuites; who toward the beginning of *February* setting Sail from *Goa*, and a Month after arriving at the Port of *Arkiko*, were there curteously receiv'd by the President of the Maritime Province, and within the space of two Months brought to the King. Who understanding that the King of *Portugal* was about to send Priests, and other Ecclesiastical Persons to teach him and his People a new Religion, was very much perplex'd in his Mind, and long in Suspence what answer to return; for he neither thought it convenient to admit them, neither was he willing to offend the King of *Portugal*. However he ventur'd upon several Colloquies with the Envoys, the sum of which, manag'd for the most part by *Gonsalez*, tended to this, *That the Pope of* Rome *was Christ's Vicar upon Earth, and the Supream Head of all Christianity, and therefore if the* Habessines *were desirous of Eternal Happiness, they should once more return and joyn themselves to their Lawful Head; for that Christ himself had from his own lips afferted, that his Church was but one Fold, and over that but one Shepheard*, &c. On the other side, the *Habessines* made answer, *That an Affair of so great Consequence was to be consider'd and consulted upon with the other Patriarchs; for to abandon their ancient Rites and Ceremonies upon private admonition, and receive new ones, was a thing full of danger and offence.* At length the King told them, *That if those Persons whom the King of* Portugal *should send, would take the pains to come to* Matzua, *he would order some Person to be there, both to give them a befitting Reception, and Conduct them to his Court.* Besides all this, the King was no less fearful, least the *Portugals*, as it had befallen several other Kings in *India*, should make him their Tributary, and under the pretence of Religion, powre into his Country a great force of Soldiers, Arm'd and furnish'd with Fire-Arms; Especially remembring what great Exploits a small Number of *Portugals* had perform'd in his Kingdom but a few years before. A Jealousie that not long after increas'd to

that

that height, that when King *David* had seriously negotiated with *Rodergo Limez*, the *Portugal* Embassador, about the Recovery and Fortification of *Mazua*, and *Suaquena*, and had also offer'd assistance of Forces, Provision and Money, afterwards the Business was not only no farther mention'd, but also the *Portuguese* Aid, so necessary, and so much desir'd was utterly refus'd; so that he chose rather to leave the Port of *Arkiko*, with the Island adjoyning, in the hands of the *Turk*, then to give Admission to the *Portugals*. *So prevalent is the fear of Foreign Domination.*

But now *Claudius*'s answer being return'd into *India*, strangely surpriz'd the Patriarch *Barret*, and his Associates, who imagin'd that all things would have bin smooth and easie according to their wishes. Thereupon after long deliberation, they came to this result, *Lest the Patriarchal Dignity should be hazarded with a Prince ill affected, which would be to the Detriment of the Pontifical Authority, and a contempt of the King of* Portugal, *by whose recommendation and favour they were sent, that the Patriarch should remain in* India *with* Melchior Caymero *Bishop of* Nice, *and that* Oviedo *should go alone, to the end he might take his measures by the Event of* Oviedo's *Success.* *Oviedo* being thus dispatch'd away with Five more Associates, was kindly receiv'd by *Isaac* at that time *Bahrnagash*, or Governor of the Sea-Ports. The Common People ignorant of their Errand, nor altogether averse to the *Romish* Ceremonies, receiv'd the Bishop and his Associates with great testimonies of Kindness, even to the kissing their hands. The Romanists laying hold upon the occasion, resolv'd upon a *Procession* from their own to the *Habessine* Church, and were by them beheld with mutual Charity, without the least upbrading or reproach of the Novelty. The King also entertain'd them with great kindness; only he took it ill that they should talk to him of yielding obedience to the *Roman Pontiff*. Nevertheless as he was a most Prudent Person, and worthy the high Dignity he enjoy'd, he always carry'd himself with so great Moderation toward the Bishop, that he still left him with some hopes of Success. In the mean time the *Roman* Religion was every where freely exercis'd, and no man forbid who desir'd to embrace it. But the Bishop not content with so much favour, began to press the King more urgently, *That at length without more delay, he would submit himself to the* Roman *Pontiff*. He reply'd, *That his Ancestors cessors had in sacred things given their Obedience to none but the Successors of* St. Mark; *nor did he see any cause why he should desire Innovation, and disturb his People well contented with their* Abuna: But the Bishop still continuing his Importunity, The King told him, *That since he was come to him from a Region so far distant upon so honest a Negotiation, he would consult with his Friends and his Learned Men upon a Matter of so great Importance.* *Ovedo* understanding that the King did nothing but spin out delays; and hearing withal, that the King's Mother, and all the Blood Royal, together with the Nobility and greatest Doctors of the Nation were utterly averse to any Alterations, wrote an Epistle to the King, wherein he put him in Mind, *That his Father had acknowledg'd the Pope of* Rome *for the Vicar of Christ; that several of his Learned men had besought him; that* Claudius *had wrote to the King of* Portugal; *and that his Father had Commanded, that they should not desire an* Abuna *from any other place then from* Rome: *and that He himself had publickly promis'd Obedience to the See of* Rome. *That if any doubt remain'd concerning any Articles of Faith, he should bring those things to a Publick Dispute, and hear the Arguments on both sides: it being but just, that the Party that was foil'd, should acknowledge and follow what the other had maintain'd for Truth: and that the King should well consider whose advice he took, or what Persons he consulted in so important an Affair. That the Ends and Interest of Parents or Kindred were not to be regarded: That the love of Christ was to be preferr'd before the love of Relations, who being busied in Teaching his own Doctrine in the Temple of* Jerusalem, *would not make use of his most Holy Mothers advice; by which he shew'd, that in the Cause of God no Man is bound to Communicate his Intentions to his nearest Friends.* Whether the King made any Answer, or what it was, is not known. But *Gregory* told me, That the sence of the King's Commands and Letters, was quite different from the Expositions of *Alvarez*, *Bermudes* and others addicted to the *Roman* Religion made of them at *Rome*: and that it could not be otherwise, in regard that before the Reign of *Susneus*, the *Habessines* had never known what that Obedience meant. Hower the King, that he might not seem to distrust the strength of his own Cause, and the learning of his own Subjects, permitted frequent Disputes, not yet made Publick by the Fathers of the Society. From this *Tellez* reports, That *the* Habessine *Doctors appear'd very ignorant and illiterate in all*

their

their *Disputes*; *as never having Study'd Logic, Syllogisms, nor Enthymemes, nor having any knowledge of the Subtleties of Scholastic Divinity.* From whence the Reader may readily Judge of the Progress and Events of such Disputes. *Telles* goes on, and says, *That* Claudius *weary of the illiterateness of his own People, for the most part undertook the Discourse himself, and gave* Oviedo *not a little Trouble.* Moreover he complains, *That the* Habessines, *when they were worsted, would never acknowledge it, but always boasted of the Victory, and so all those Disputes came to nothing.* It was therefore thought more convenient to betake themselves to *writing*. Nor did the King decline the Combat, but answer'd them with other Writings, tho they have not as yet bin permitted to visit the *European* Regions. *Oviedo* impatient of his ill Success, and finding he could not bring the *Ethiopic* Prince to do as he would have had him, resolv'd to a more severe but unseasonable course. And therefore, to testifie his Indignation, he left the Court, and publish'd a Writing, *Wherein he branded the* Habessines *with several Heresies, and exhorted his* Portugueses *to have a care of them.* Which did not a little offend *Claudius*. For a mind free, and subject to none, when once it refuses the persuasion of Argument, is the more exasperated by affront and reviling. Nor can it be thought that any Prince will suffer himself and his Subjects to be traduc'd for Heretics within his own Dominions.

Not long after *Claudius* was slain in a Battel against the *Adelans*; to whom, in regard he dy'd without Issue, his Brother *Adamas-Saghed* Succeeded, a Person quite of another disposition, as one that retain'd nothing of his Moderation or Clemency. For whatever Indulgencies *Claudius* had granted to *Oviedo*, and the Embracers of his Doctrine, he recall'd them all; nor would he so much as permit that the *Habessine* Women, who were Marry'd to the *Portugueses*, should exercise the Religion of their Husbands; to which he added many other severe Edicts, declaring openly, *That his Brother was therefore punish'd by God, because he did not persecute the Religion of the* Franks; as it is frequent to attribute Adversity or Prosperity to neglected or protected Religion. Nay, he proceeded so far, that having sent for *Oviedo*, he threaten'd him with Death, if he continu'd divulging and sowing *Roman* Paradoxes in his Dominions. Which when the Bishop refus'd to consent to, saying, *That God was to be*

obey'd

obey'd, rather then Man, he drew his Seymiter in a rage, and unless the Queen, and some of the chief Nobility had prevented him, had undoubtedly dispatch'd the Bishop to the other World. The Bishop therefore, in this desperate Condition of Affairs retires to *Fremona*, where he lay conceal'd, thirty whole years together, and assuming to himself, after the Death of *Barret*, the Title of Patriarch, officiated among his own *Portugueses*, without any further molestation: in regard that *Melec-Saghed* after his Father's violent Death, shew'd himself more mild, and temperate to the *Portugueses*, who behaving themselves more modestly, gave him no cause of Provocation. But at length all the Avenues into *Habessinia* being shut up by the *Turk*, and the Fathers that were sent thither being all taken and slain, the State of Religion among the *Portugueses* was reduc'd to that extremity, that all the Fathers being deceas'd, there was none remain'd alive to officiate Divine Service. At length *Melchior Silvanus* an Indian, Vicar of the Church of St. *Anne* in *Goa*, and for that reason disguis'd both by his Language and Colour, ventur'd into *Ethiopia*, and there officiated till the Arrival of *Peter Pays*, after which he return'd into *India*, leaving the said *Peter*, as he had bin before, all alone in his office of Priesthood.

CHAP.

CHAP. X.

Of the New Mission, and its Success, till the Coming of the Roman *Patriarch.*

The Religion of the Portugueses *very low in* Habessinia. *New Hopes upon the arrival of* Peter Pays. *Who Taught School at* Fremona *with the admiration of all. The King sends for him. Curteously receives him. And promises Obedience to the Pope. He abrogates the Observation of the Sabbath. He obtains the King's Friendship by the Pope's, and K. of* Portugal's *Letters. The King therefore hated, and slain.* Susneus *Succeeds. He perceives the Ignorance of his own Doctors, and applys to the Fathers. Several Disputes. The King's Brother Embraces the* Roman *Faith.* Susneus *promises Obedience to the Pope. He causes a publick dispute concerning the two Natures in Christ. The* Habessines *agitated. The King's Edict. A disobedient Monk punish'd. The Metropolitan complains. The Event. The Edict renew'd. The* Alexandrians *provok'd. They Excommunicate the* Romans. *The King resists.* Simeon *replies. Thence a Rebellion. The Metropolitan's* Anathema. Elius *the Head of the Conspirators slain. So is* Simeon. *The Sabbath abrogated. The Effects.* Jonael *the Viceroy Revolts. The King defends the Abrogation.* Jonael *hides himself. Slain by the* Gallans. *The People of* Damota *Rebel. Vanquish'd. The King publickly Embraces the* Roman *Faith. New Commotions by his Son* Gabriel. *He is slain.*

THE Arch-Bishop of *Goa*, and the Fathers of the Society were not ignorant of the afflicted Condition of the *Roman* Worship in *Habessinia*. And therefore, whereas before they had conceiv'd vast hope of Total Conversion of *Ethiopia*, now the case was so far alter'd, that they found themselves put to a Necessity of providing for their own few Countrymen, least they should be utterly destitute of Provision for the Salvation of their own Souls, as not having any Priests to perform Religious Duties among them. Mov'd therefore by the Instigation of Conscience, they took it into serious Consideration, least while they were busyed about Subjecting *Abassia* to the See of *Rome*, that nothing belong'd to it, they should loose their own Countrymen, Professors of their own Religion, who had reason enough to forsake those that forsook them. And therefore they made it their whole study how to supply them with Priests, to govern their Ecclesiastical Affairs. And indeed many had attemped the Journey, but in vain.

Till

Till at length with the dawn of the new Century, new hopes began to shine forth. For *Peter Pays*, after his first unfortunate Attempt, which had expos'd him to various Hazards, and a Captivity in *Arabia*, undertook a second Journey into *Ethiopia*, wherein he prosperously Succeeded; being well skill'd both in the Countries, Customs and Foreign Languages, and able to endure the temperature of those Climates. *John Gabriel* a famous *Portuguese* Collonel, had given King *Jacob* then reigning, notice of his coming, and had so possess'd the young Prince with the worth of the Person, by the high Commendations which he gave him, that so soon as the Winter was over, the King sent for him. But he being soon after depos'd, *Zadenghel* was advanc'd in his Room. Thereupon *Peter Pays* kept himself still at *Fremona*; where, not believing his time could be better spent than in instructing the *Portuguese* Children, he chose out some of the riper Ingenuities, and in a short time so manur'd them, that they were able to answer to any Question propounded to them concerning the Christian Faith. A thing both unwonted and wonderful to the *Habessines*, to hear from Children what they could hardly expect from Persons of years and Experience. But considering the Person, he was not so much wonderful neither; for he was a Man of a quick and ready Wit, that could fit himself to all Humours, of an affable and complaisant Temper, and well skill'd not only in the Liberal Sciences, but Mechanic Arts. The fame of so acute and laborious a Person, and so happy in his Instruction, being spread over the Neighbouring Regions, in a short time reach'd the young King's Ears; who being covetous to see such a Master and such Scholars, by his Letters invited him to Court. Thereupon in the Month of *April*, 1604. accompany'd with two *Portuguese* Youths arriving at Court, he was honourably receiv'd by the King, as if he had bin one of the Nobles of his Kingdom, not without great distast taken by the Monks, whose Sloth compar'd to *Peter's* Diligence and Industry, render'd them contemptible to most. The next day several Disputes began about Controversies in Religion, which the King was pleas'd both favourably and patiently to hear; Mass was also said after the *Roman* manner, and a Sermon Preach'd; with which *Zadenghel* was so taken, that having Communicated his Intentions to some of his intimate Friends, he resolv'd to submit himself to the Pope.

But

But in regard he durst not adventure to do it publickly, he first conjur'd *Peter* not to reveal the Secret, and then told him, *That he was Convinc'd by his Arguments, that there was no other Universal Pastor and Vicar of Christ upon Earth beside the Pope of* Rome. *That to deny it to him, was to deny it to Christ; that whoever did not follow his Example, was not of the true Church; and that therefore he had Decreed to request a Patriarch and Fathers from* Rome *to instruct his People.*

Altho so sudden and so unexpected a Declaration of a King could not choose but infuse a joy unspeakable into the heart of *Peter*, yet he contain'd himself; only what his duty bound him to, he could not but highly extol the Pious Intentions of the King. Nor did the King delay: The Secret with which he had trusted *Peter* under Oath, he himself made Publick, and presently set forth an Edict, *That no Person should any longer observe the Sabbath as a Holy day.* And indeed he was so forward, that *Peter* was fain to check his Celerity, and put a stop to his Career. However Letters were written to *Clement* the VIII. and *Philip* the Third, King of *Spain* and *Portugal*, and deliver'd to *Peter's* care, for their safe and honourable conveyance. In these Letters *he offer'd his Friendship, his Soldiers, and his Workmen; and withal requested some of the Fathers of the Society of Jesus to instruct his Subjects.* These things were not so privately carry'd, but that they were discover'd by some of the chief Nobility of the Kingdom, who were no way satisfy'd at these underminings of their antient Religion: wherefore they conspir'd against their Prince, and slew him in Battel. *Zadenghel* being slain, all *Peter's* great Hopes vanish'd of a sudden, not only through *Zadenghel's* fall, but by reason of the Civil Wars that ensu'd between *Jacob* and *Susneus*, contending for the Royal Diadem. And so all Promotion of the *Roman* Religion surceas'd, till *Jacob* being vanquish'd and kill'd in the Field, *Susneus* became Lord of *Habessinia*. Who again kindly receiv'd and entertain'd *Peter* together with his Companions, and to all his Requests lent a most gracious Ear.

The Ecclesiastical Affairs of *Habessinia*, were then but in a Low Condition, there not having bin any Peace in the Country for about Fourscore years: so that perpetual Wars had almost extinguish'd the Studies of peaceful Arts; nor were there enough to perform Religious Duties in their Churches, but less to obviate the Encroachment of insinuating

Errors and Abuses in Religion. The Metropolitans, Persons for the most part the most ignorant that could be imagin'd, took no more Cognizance of the Churches which they were appointed to govern, then if they had bin under Foreign Jurisdiction, only they took up their time in the Ordination of all sorts without any due Examination. Therefore the King and his Nobility observing the Diligence of the *Fathers* in instructing the *Habessine* Youth; their Zeal in the Conversion of the People; their Eloquence in Preaching unheard of before; their Sanctity of living, so necessary among *Neophytes* and *Proselytes*, were possess'd with so much Admiration and Affection toward them, that they could promise to themselves no other way for restoring their decay'd Ecclesiastical Worship, but by their means. Therefore Letters were sent to the *Pope* and the *King of Spain*, to request their Friendship, and the Assistance of the *Portuguezes*. *Peter Pays* enlarg'd upon the same Subject, and added much more concerning the King's Affection to the *Roman* Religion. Frequent Disputations also were appointed, of which the chief Theme was concerning the *two Natures in Christ*, which, being easily demonstrable out of the Writings of the *Abessines* themselves, gave the *Fathers* great Advantage over the *Ethiopian* Doctors.

The Chiefest of all the Nobility, *Ras-Sela-Christos* the Kings Brother by the Mother's side, publickly professed the *Roman* Religion, and receiv'd the Eucharist openly, according to the *Roman* Manner, whose example many of the Great Commanders in the Army, both Collonels and Captains follow'd, especially seeing the King's favour so constant toward the *Fathers of the Society*. At length the King himself, having receiv'd the Answer of *Paul* the V. in a Letter dated the 31 of *January*, 1623. *Promis'd to yield him Obedience as Universal Pastor of the Church, and that he would admit a Patriarch sent from* Rome, *so that necessary Succours were sent him withal, without which, it was impossible to accomplish a business of so much Difficulty and Importance.* He also signified his Intentions to send an Embassador with Father *Antonio Fernandez*, after another manner, and in another Equipage, then had yet bin usual. To say truth, the King publickly favour'd the *Roman* Religion, without any opposition; in regard that the Sword had cut off the greatest part of the stiffest and most obstinate Defenders of the *Alexandrian* Worship. Only the *Monks* remain'd behind,

who

who were baffled still in all their Attempts of Dispute. Therefore the King, to the end he might make it manifest to his whole Kingdom, that he had not rashly, but upon Mature Deliberation, and as it were overcome by the force of Truth, given way to a new Religion; appointed a Solemn Dispute, where he enjoyn'd most of the Nobility of his Kingdom to be present. The Subject of the Disputation was again the repeated Question concerning the two Natures in Christ; as if that had bin the utmost limit of all their Controversies. And no question it might be true what *Tellez* has written, that the *Habessines* were vanquish'd upon the first onset. For the reality of the thing supported by so many Authorities and Reasons afforded an easie Victory. Nevertheless there was another Dispute appointed some few days after, which prov'd no less successful than the former. Wherefore the King, as if the War had now bin at an end, and that now Truth had merited her Triumph, put forth an Edict, that all Persons for the future should believe and hold, *That there were two Natures in Christ, between themselves really distinct, but united in one Divine Person.* This Edict was little regarded by one particular *Monk*, more wilful and stubborn than truly zealous, who being for his Contumacy brought before the King, and speaking in his presence more irreverently than became him, was severely Scourg'd for his sawciness. Of the Pain and Anguish of which Chastisement, tho the Monk was only sensible, yet the fear of it kept others in awe, who not understanding that he was punish'd for his malapertness, thought he had bin so severely dealt with for denying the *two Natures*.

These things being spread abroad, *Simeon* the Metropolitan, at that time absent, hastens to the King with his Complaints, *That unusual things had bin done without his knowledge, and that Disputes about Religion had bin appointed in his absence.* The King well understanding how unable he was to grapple with the Fathers in Dispute, made him answer, *That since he was come, he would appoint the same Disputations to be heard over again.* To which *Simeon* had not a word to say. And thus a second Victory being won from the Primate of *Ethiopia* himself, a more severe Edict concerning the *two Natures* was publish'd by the *Cryer*, making it Death for any Person to deny the contrary.

By this so sharp a Decree, as if it had bin the loud signal to Battel, it is incredible to think how the minds of the People were incens'd. As for the Controversie it self, they did not think it of so high a Concernment, as to engage divided Parties in Blood and Massacre about it. *In regard that all acknowledg'd both Divinity and Humanity in Christ; so that the Question was only about a word. But let the Question be what it would, such a severe way of proceeding was never heard of before in* Ethiopia, *as being altogether contradictory to the mildness of Christ and his Apostles, and the Lenity of the Primitive times. So then if Men were to be scourg'd and whipp'd, because they could not apprehend two Natures in Christ, what must they expect if other Questions should be started about Innovations of greater difficulty in the Doctrine and Ceremonies of the Fathers?*

Exasperated with these fair pretences, *Simeon* the Metropolitan, together with several of the Nobility; and among the rest *Jamanaxus*, alias *Emana Christos*, another of the King's Brothers by the Mothers side; and lastly, almost all the interested Clergy and Monks met, and held Consultations together to prevent the threatning Mischiefs; and lastly, combin'd *to live and dye for the Defence of their ancient and setled Religion.* To this end *Simeon*, under pretence of incumbent Duty, which was to be watchful over the Preservation of the *Constantinopolitan* Religion, fix'd an *Excommunication* Publickly upon the Dores of the great Church belonging to the Camp, against all that embrac'd the Religion of the *Franks*, or ventur'd to Dispute concerning it. The King, tho highly offended with this unexpected boldness of the Metropolitan, durst not adventure to revenge himself; However he Publish'd another Edict, *whereby Liberty was granted to every Person that so pleas'd, to embrace and exercise the Fathers Religion already establish'd by fair Disputes and Arguments on their side.* Which so little terrify'd the undaunted Metropolitan, that he thunder'd out his Anathema's against all that maintain'd *two Natures in Christ.*

The Moderate Party bewail'd these Paper Skirmishes, which they foresaw would break forth, *and end in Slaughter and Misery, and that the King's Decrees would never be establish'd without the effusion of much Blood.* Sensible of these Fears, several of the great Personages of the Kingdom, together with the King's Mother, *Ite Hamelmala*, most earnestly besought the King, to desist from what he had begun, and not to raise up implacable Seditions to the Ruin of himself and his Kingdom. After which the Metropolitan, with many Monks and Nuns came to the Camp, and implor'd the King, not to innovate any thing in Religion, otherwise that they were prepar'd to lay down their lives for the Religion of their Ancestors. At last the King referr'd the whole Business to another Colloquie, which continu'd for six days one after another, but without any Success: A clear Testimony that Controversies in Religion are not to be decided by Disputes. After that, all the Clergy threw themselves at the King's Feet, and with Sighs and Tears beseech him, *Not to change a Religion so quietly Establish'd in* Ethiopia *for so many Ages, by so many of their Emperors.* But nothing would prevail; the King remain'd inexorable and immoveable, so that the Petitioners departed full freighted with Exasperation and Rebellion. Immediately, all hopes of Concord and Agreement being lay'd aside, the Sword was next unsheath'd, whence follow'd those terrible Commotions and Bloody Wars that have almost ruin'd the most flourishing part of *Ethiopia*.

The Chief of the Conspirators were *Jonaelus*, *Ælius* the King's Son in Law, Viceroy of *Tigra*, the Eunuch *Caflo*, and several others. But to give the better Colour to their Rebellion, and Design of Killing the King, the Metropolitan, caus'd a new and more severe Excommunication to be fix'd upon the Chief Church in the Camp, by which all the partakers of the Latin Religion were Anathematiz'd. In the mean time the Fathers of the Society relying upon the King's Favour, hasten'd to get all things ready that might be of advantage to Establish their Doctrine. To that end they translated *Maldonatus* upon the Four Evangelists, *Toletus* upon St. *Paul's* Epistle to the *Romans*, *Ribera* upon the *Hebrews*, and some others, into the *Ethiopic* Language, which some esteem'd, others by reason of the intermixture of *Amharic* words, contemn'd, as full of Barbarisms and Solœcisms. But as for the Lord's Prayer, and the Salutation of *Mary*, being nothing but the Latin written in *Ethiopic* Characters, they abhorr'd 'em, as looking upon them to be nothing but Magic Spells. On the other side, the *Alexandrians* fell upon the Fathers with all the bitterest Invectives that might be, those Paper Skirmishes being generally the fore-runners of more Bloody disputes. In pursuance of which, *Ælius* by an

Edict

Edict, Commands all the *Franks* to depart out of *Tigra*, and the *Alexandrians* to follow him: by which means, having muster'd up a compleat Army, he openly Rebels. *Simon* Curses the *Franks*, but loads *Ælius* with his Blessings; upon which he no doubt relying, resolv'd to fight his Father in Law, then upon his March against him with a strong Force, notwithstanding all the Perswasions of his Wife to the contrary. Fierce therefore, and in the heat of his young Blood, and over confident of his own Faction, not staying so much as to take his Breakfast, but as it were Drunk with Fury and Rage, only with a small Troop about him, he leaps his Horse into his Father's Camp, asking, *Where the King was*; and so what between the astonishment of some, and the wonder of others what the Matter should be, he rode up without any hurt to the King's Pavilion; where at length the Alarum being taken, he was soon surrounded, Scorn'd and Stabb'd to Death, and so dearly paid for his rashness. The Captain thus Slain, the Soldiers betake themselves to their heels; *Simon*, between the Fugitives and the Pursuers, stood alone by himself, like a man stupifyed, whether not at first observ'd, or neglected as a Clergy-man, but at length being known, he was Slain among the Crowd. Both their Heads were sent about the Kingdom, and expos'd as a Public Spectacle. The Eunuch *Cafo* had his Head struck off: *Jamanaxo* was pardon'd. Thus the Kindred of Kings for the most part escape the Punishment of those Rebellions to which they themselves have given Life and Encouragement.

The King who was never fearful, now more emboldened by his Victory, now questions other Heads of Religion; and soon after by Public Edict prohibits the Observation of the Sabbath, as *Judaical*, and Repugnant to Christianity. In answer to this Edict, some Person without a Name, had written contemptuously of the *Roman* Religion, reflecting severely upon the Fathers of the Society, whom he call'd *the Kindred of* Pilate, as being a *Roman*, and withal sharply menacing the King himself. *Tellez* reports, That it was stuff't with places of Scripture, but nothing to the purpose. The King more incens'd by this Writing, renew'd the Edict about the Sabbath, and commanded the Husbandmen to Plough and Sow upon that Day, adding as a Penalty upon the Offenders, for the first Fault the Forfeiture of a weav'd

Vestment

Vestment to the value of a *Portugal* Patack; for the second, Confiscation of Goods, and that the said Offence should not be prescribed to Seven years; a certain form usually inserted in their more severe Decrees.

Certainly it must of necessity be true what *Tellez* reports of the Natural Piety of the *Habessines*, since they were thus to be compell'd to the Neglect of the Sabbath by such Severe Laws, when we can hardly be induc'd by stricter Penalties to observe the Lord's-Day. Among the rest, one *Bucna* a stout and famous Soldier, felt the utmost rigour of this Decree, for being accus'd to have observ'd the Sabbath, he was made a most severe Example, that others of less consequence might not think to expect any Mercy.

From thence *Jmael* Viceroy of *Bagemder* took an occasion to Revolt, alluring all to his Party who were displeased with the Edicts. Upon which News, many of the chiefest of the Court, both Men and Women, of which several were near allyed to the King, with Tears in their Eyes besought him once more, not to expose himself and the Kingdom to Calamity, but to take Pity upon so many poor afflicted People, offending out of meer Simplicity and Ignorance, and not to disturb the Minds of his People with such unseasonable Changes.

The King far from being mov'd with their Tears; but rather the more displeas'd to see so many all of one Mind, that at once he might answer all, confirm the wavering, and terrifie the Headstrong, having summon'd together the Chief Nobles and Commanders of his Army that attended the Court, in a short, but grave Oration, put them in mind of past Transactions, upbraiding them among the rest, *For that they had depriv'd* Zadenghel *both of his Life and Kingdom, because he had forsaken the* Alexandrian *Religion to embrace the* Roman *Faith. That for his part, after his Victory obtain'd against* Jacob, *he had been severe to none; but rather had pardon'd all; nevertheless he was disturb'd with daily Seditions and Rebellions, under pretence of changing his Religion, when he only reform'd it. For that he acknowledg'd as much and the same that others did,* That Christ was true God, and true Man: *but because he could not be* Perfect God, *unless he had the* Perfect Divine Nature, *nor perfect Man without perfect Humane Nature, it follow'd, that there were two Natures in Christ, united in one Substance of the Eternal Word. Which was not to abandon but explain his Religion. In the next place he had abrogated the Observation of the Sabbath Day, because it became not Christians to observe the* Jews *Sabbath. These things he did not believe in favour of the* Portugueses*, but because it was the Truth it self determin'd in the Council of* Chalcedon*, founded upon Scripture, and ever since the time of the Apostles deliver'd as it were from hand to hand; and if there were occasion, he would lay down his life in defence of this Doctrine; but they who deny'd it should first examine the Truth of it.*

Having finished his Oration, a Letter was brought him from *Jonael*, containing many haughty Demands, and among the rest the Expulsion of the Jesuits. The King believing there would be no better way than to answer him in the Field, Commanded the nimblest of his Armed Bands to March: of which the Rebel having Intelligence, and not willing to abide his Fury fled for shelter among those inaccessible Rocks, whither it was in vain to pursue him. Thereupon *Susneus*, well-knowing that the Revolters would not be able long to endure the Inconveniencies, and Famine that lodg'd among those inaccessible places, blockt him up at a Distance. So that *Jonael* at length, weaken'd by daily desertions, fled to the *Gallans*, who being at variance among themselves, kept their promis'd Faith but a short time; for being underhand tempted with Rewards by the King; they at length turn'd their Protection into Treachery, and slew the Unfortunate Implorer of their Security.

This Bad Success however did not terrifie the Inhabitants of *Damota*, inhabiting the Southern parts of *Gojam*, who upon the News of the *Prophanation of the Sabbath*, as they called it, with their Hermites that skulk'd in the Deserts of that Province, ran to their Arms. *Ras-Sealax*, otherwise their Lord and Patron in vain Exhorting them to continue their Obedience, whose kind Messages of Peace and Pardon they refus'd, *unless he would burn the Books Translated out of* Latin *into the* Habessine *Language by the Fathers, and deliver up the* Fathers *themselves to be Hang'd upon the highest Trees they could find*. Thus despairing of Peace, *Ras-Sealax* set forward, tho deserted by the greatest part of his Forces, who favoured the Cause of their Countrymen; so that he had hardly Seven Thousand Men that stook close to him, while the Enemies Body daily encreas'd. However he resolv'd to Fight them, knowing his Soldiers to be more Experienc'd,

and

and better Arm'd, besides that he had about Forty *Portuguese* Musquetiers in his Camp. When they came to blows, the Victory fell to the King's Party, tho it cost dear; in regard that about Four hundred Monks, that had as it were devoted themselves to die for their Religion, fought most desperately: of which a Hundred and fourscore were Slain.

Hitherto the King had not made Publick Profession of the *Roman* Religion, partly out of fear of stirring up Popular Tumults against him, partly being loath to dismiss his Supernumerary Wives, and Concubines; but at length encourag'd by so many Victories he lay'd all fear aside, and publickly renounc'd the *Alexandrian* Worship, and confessing his Sins after the *Roman* manner to *Peter Pays*, dismiss'd all his Wives and Concubines, only the first of those to which he had bin lawfully Marry'd. His Example convinc'd many others, who were not asham'd to keep many Mistresses, but Adulteresses also. Not long after, the King signify'd his Conversion to the *Roman* Religion to his whole Empire, by a Publick Instrument, not without the Severe reproof of the *Alexandrian* Patriarch. The sum of his *Manifesto* was, *That having deserted the* Alexandrinian, *he now reverenced only the* Roman *See, and had yielded his Obedience to the* Roman *Pope, as the Successor of* Peter, *the Prince of the Apostles; for that that See could never err either in Faith or good Manners*, and then he exhorted his Subjects to do as he had done. He also discoursed at large concerning the two Natures in Christ, and tax'd the *Ethiopian* Primates as guilty of many Errors. But neither the King's Example, nor his Exhortation wrought upon many. For at the same time his Son *Gabriel* began to study new Contrivances, tho with no better Success than they who had taught him the way. For when he had intelligence that *Ras-Sela* was marching against him, finding himself Inferior in Force, he betook himself to the inaccessible Rocks of *Shewa*; from whence at last by the Craft of a certain well-brib'd *Gallan*, he was allur'd to come forth; who feigning himself to be highly offended with *Ras-Sela*, came to the unwary young Prince, and promis'd him the Assistance of all his Friends; which while he was inveagled out to expect, in a neighbouring Wood, he was there surrounded by a select Party of the Enemy, and pay'd for his rash belief with the loss of his Life.

Chap. XI.

Of the Coming of the Roman *Patriarch into* Habessinia, *and how he Managed his Affairs there.*

Alphonsus Mendez *made Patriarch of* Ethiopia. *His Inauguration and Journey to* Goa, &c. *Their miserable Reception at first. His difficult Passage by Land. Met by the Jesuits. He comes to* Fremona, *thence to the King. The King swears Obedience to the Pope. So does the Court.* Ras-Sela[illegible] *behaviour blam'd. The Solemnity concluded with an Anathema. New Edicts in favour of the Romish Worship. The Women Commanded to swear. The Patriarchal* [illegible]. *New Disturbances occasion'd by the new Computation. Baptism and Ordination reiterated; Sermons, Confession and Confirmation. A Countryman's Jest. A Seminary.* Tecla-George *Revolts, Suppress'd and Hang'd. The Confessor of the Church excommunicated upon a slight Occasion by the Patriarch; but Pardon'd at the King's intercession. Three Courtiers offended. Their Indignation increases, and why. A Witch imprison'd by Command of the Patriarch; Which alienates the King's Affection from him. His Authority decreases, through private Grudges, and an ill of* Ras Sela. *The* Agawi *Revolt. The King's ill Success.* Ras Sela *more Prosperous against* Lasta [illegible], [illegible] *and* [illegible]. *These Mishaps attributed to the Romans.* [illegible] *takes upon him the Regal Power.* Ras Sela *accus'd; His Goods confiscated. The Fathers render'd odious to the King. Their Indulgences laugh'd at.* Serzax's *unhappy Revolt. A New Expedition against the* Lasta. *Prosperous at first, at last Unfortunate. The Fathers tax'd. The King indulges the Old Ceremonies. The Patriarch offended. Another more* [illegible] *Edict; but too late.*

Of These prosperous Successes, the Fathers wrote presently to *Rome*, and into *Portugal*. But very prudently, there was nothing rashly decreed at first, lest the Design of another Patriarch, like that of *Nonius Barret* should come to nothing. But when King *Susneus* himself, had by his own Letters requested a Patriarch, and had made publick Profession of the *Romish* Religion, the Conclave then thought it not expedient to make any longer delays. And therefore, as if they had bin to send into some *Portuguese* Province, upon the Nomination of *Philip* the Fourth, then King of *Portugal*, as well as *Spain*, *Alphonsus Mendez*, a Person of great Eminency, by Nativity a *Portuguese*, a Doctor in Theology, and of the Society of *Jesus*, which claim'd *Ethiopia* peculiarly to it self, as a Province by them wholly converted to the Faith, was created Patriarch,

Besides, that it might have occasion'd great Emulation, had a Person bin chosen out of any other Nation or Society. Being inaugurated with the usual Ceremonies at *Lisbon*, in the Month of *May* 1624, he set Sail, and arriv'd at *Goa*, where understanding that all things succeeded to the wishes of the *Fathers*, he prepar'd for his farther Journey. In *November* of the same year he arriv'd at *Diu*, hoping there to find some of the *Bannian* Vessels, to carry him into the *Red-Sea*: But they being the year before over-burthen'd by the covetous Exactions of the *Turks*, and fearing the *Arabian* Pirates had left off Trading into those Parts. While he stay'd at *Diu*, he was seasonably forewarn'd by the King's Letters, by no means to come near *Suaquem* or *Mazua*, but to make to rights for *Baylur* a Port of *Dancali*. There he arriv'd the Third of *April* following with six Companions, four *Fathers*, and two Friers.

The Fathers were,

1. *John Velasco Castellano.*
2. *Hierome Lobo*, or *Wolph*. Which Name, lest the *Ethiopians* should take an occasion to turn to an ill Omen, they made a shift to change for another.
3. *Bruno de Santa Cruce.*
4. *Francesco Marquese.*

The Friers were,

Emanuel Luis, Steward.
John Martin.

Attendants he had Thirteen.

One Servant.
Five Musicians.
Three Habessines.
Two Bricklayers, and their Apprentices; for the Building of Churches and Houses, which the Ethiopic Fathers had desir'd him to bring with him.

The King had recommended him to the care of the Viceroy of *Dancala*, a Mahometan, but in Friendship with the *Habessines*. But the recommendation was so early, and he came so late, that the Viceroy had forgot it. So that his Reception there was very lamentable, there being little or no Provision, so much as of Necessaries made for him. And their Hosts where they Lodg'd, were so poor and covetous, that instead of receiving any Kindnesses from them, they were forc'd to purchase their sorry Convenience with the continual Supplies of their Avarice. They could not get Mules or Horses anow to carry themselves and their Luggage; so that most of them were forc'd to travel over the rugged and parch'd Earth in continual conflict with hunger, thirst, and intolerable heat.

Neither were they much better entertain'd for Sixteen days in the Court of the Viceroy himself, all their Presents not sufficing to gratifie the impatient Appetite of his Avarice. Parting from thence, at the Mercy of those wicked and covetous Varlets that were their Guides and Owners of their Carriage-Horses, they travel'd as they were led, in daily fear of the *Gallans*, over places where Battels had bin fought, as it were Pav'd with the Skulls and Bones of the Slain, till at last all these Difficulties and Dangers overcome, they were met by *Emanuel Barradas*, with some other *Portugueses* and *Habessines* upon the Confines of *Tigra*, who furnish'd them with Provisions, Carriages, and all other things necessary. Upon the strength of which Refreshments, they began to ascend the towring Mountains of *Abassia*, and the Fifth day after, through more gladsom and verdant Fields, and more grateful opportunities of resting themselves, they arriv'd at *Fremona*; where they stay'd not only all the Winter, but all *October* and *November*, being both unhealthy Months. In *December* they arriv'd at *Gorgora*, where upon a day appointed, with a Noble Attendance, and great Applause, the Patriarch enter'd the Camp, and after Mass said, was conducted into the King's Pavillion, and there by the King Commanded to sit down by him in a little Chair equal to his own. In which great Pomp and State, at length the Patriarch came to the point, and agreed with the King, that upon the XI day of *February*, 1626. he should publickly swear Obedience to the Pope.

Upon which day, together with the King and his Eldest Son *Basilides*, appear'd the King's Brothers, the Viceroys and Governors of Provinces, and all others that were conspicuous for their Dignity and Quality. In the Room were two

little

little Chairs, but very rich, set one by the other, upon which the King sate down on the right hand, and the Patriarch in his Pontifical habit upon the left. Being so sate, the Patriarch made a most lofty Panegyric in Praise of the Pope, not without some Reflections upon the Blindness of former Ages: then he fell to commemorate what had been done of later Times, How, *That the Emperors of* Habessinia *had sent their Embassadors formerly to* Rome, *and that lately one of them had requested thence a Pastor, and Evangelical Preachers: that therefore now the Time was come, wherein his Majesty was bound to satisfie the desire of his Ancestors, and to submit himself and his Subjects to the See of* Rome. The King Commanded the Grand Chamberlain of his Houshold *Melca Christos*, Prince of *Samena* to return an Answer; who after he had extoll'd the Merits of the *Portugueses*, *It is now the King's Intention*, said he, *to fulfil the Promises of his Ancestors; by yielding Obedience to the* Roman *Pope*; But as he was going on, the King interrupted him, saying, *That this was not the first day of his Intention to surrender his submission to the* Roman *Pope, as having long before promis'd it to the Superior Father of the Society of* Jesus. Presently the Patriarch after a short answer, unfolded a Book containing the four Evangelists; and then the King falling upon his Knees, took his Oath after this manner:

We Sultan-Saghed *King of the Kings of* Ethiopia, *believe and confess, That* St. Peter, *Prince of the Apostles was by Christ our Lord, Constituted Head of the whole Christian Church, and that Principality and Power over the whole World was given to him when he said,* Thou art Peter, and upon this Rock will I build my Church, and I will give to thee the Keys of Heav'n; *and at another Time when he said to Him,* Feed my Sheep. *In like manner we believe, That the Pope of* Rome *lawfully Elected, is the true Successor of* St. Peter *the Apostle, in his Government, and that he has the same Power, Dignity, and Primacy of the whole Church of Christ. Therefore we Promise, Offer, and Swear true Obedience, and humbly submit our Person and our Empire, at the feet of our Holy Father* Urban *the* VIII. *of that Name, by the Grace of God Pope, and our Lord, and to his Successors in the Administration of the Church. So God help us, and these Holy Evangels.*

After

After the King had done, his Son *Basilides*, the King's Brothers, all the Viceroys and Peers; as also all the Clergy and Monks then present took the same Oath.

After this, *Ras Seelax*, hastily Drawing forth his Scimiter, brake forth into these passionate Expressions: *What is done, let it be done*; that is to say, Let past things be forgotten; *But whoever for the future shall not do it, since it becomes every one so to do, shall feel the weight of this.* An Act, which to most that were present, seem'd very severe, especially to those who had taken part with *Gabriel*, at whom those words were constru'd to be principally levell'd. Moreover, he added an unusual Clause to his own Oath; *That he also swore Allegiance to* Basilides *as Heir and Successor to his Father; and that he would also be his faithful Vassal, so that he would promise to Protect and Defend the Holy Catholic Faith; otherwise that he would be the first and most profess'd of his Enemies.* As if it had bin lawful for a Subject to impose new Conditions of his Subjection upon a most Absolute Prince and Monarch, not bound by any Laws of Man, such as is the King of *Habessinia*. However the King said nothing, nor durst *Basilides*, as being under the Tuition of his Father, take notice of it. Nor indeed was this Condition added to his Oath, any advantage to the *Roman* Church, but rather serv'd to hasten the Ruin of *Ras-Seelax*. This Solemnity concluded with an Anathema, after the *Ethiopian* manner, upon all those that for the future should forget or break this Oath. Immediately after, several Edicts were Publish'd, *That none for the future should say Mass, or Exercise the Priestly Office, except such as were licens'd by the Patriarch.* Thereupon, the Ordinations of the *Alexandrian* Metropolitan not being accompted lawful, most of the Priests were constrain'd to receive new Ordinations from the new Patriarch, upon this Condition, *That they should all observe the* Roman *Forms of Worship, and not give any succour or harbour to Rebels; who offended in that Nature was to be severely punish'd.* It was also farther enjoyn'd that in the Celebration of *Easter*, and Observation of *Lent*, the Canons of the Church of *Rome* should be faithfully follow'd. There was also one thing more than usual exacted by the Patriarch, who having a great mistrust of the Ladies of the Royal Blood, caus'd a

It is still a Proverb among the Ethiopians, Zagon Qomino, *What is done, let it be done.*

Decree

Decree to be made, that they also upon a prefix'd day, as being more zealous for the *Alexandrian* Opinions than the Men, should take the Sacred Oath of Supremacy to the Pope, as if they had bin a distinct Body Politic from the Men. But whether it were put in Execution, or how done I do not find.

In the next place, great care was taken for Building a Patriarchal Seat, and for setling an Annual Revenue for support of the Dignity of the new Primate; to which purpose a place was chosen out in the Confines of *Begemdra*, and *Dembea*, call'd *Debsan*; as also another in the Imperial Camp near *Dancaz*. *Residencies* also for the Fathers were built in several Provinces of the Empire to stock it with Jesuits.

Maiguagua or *Fremona* in *Tigra*.
Ganeta Jesus, with a fair Church.
Gorgora in *Dembea*.
Azazo.
Enabesse, vulgarly *Nebesse*.
Hulash, by the Portugals *Alaxa*.
Kolala.
Leda-Negus.
Serca.
Tembhua.
Atbana in *Begemdra*.

The same year also *Lent* was kept after the *Roman* manner, with all the Solemnities of the Passion Week, as also *Easter* according to the *Roman* Calendar. Which occasion'd most violent Commotions over all the Empire, and more especially among the Clergy and Monks. Who being ignorant of the Computation and the Cause, thought it a high breach of the Canons of the *Nicene Council*, and the *Paschal Cycle* therein prescrib'd. Neither could the Edict be equally dispers'd over so many far distant Regions for want of Printing.

In the mean time they were very busie in Baptizing the Converted, and ordaining of Ecclesiastical Persons, many of which had bin already Baptiz'd and Ordain'd. Sermons were also Preach'd in several places after the manner of *Europe*, wherein it was necessary for the Fathers to Cite many places of Scripture, if they desir'd to be accompted Learned.

This

Thus the Fathers of the Society made a daily and very great Progress, insomuch that the Number of Baptiz'd and Converted to the *Roman* Religion amounted to many Thousands.

About two years after, the Patriarch made a Visitation assisted by some of the Sodality, in which vast Numbers of People were some of them Rebaptiz'd, others Confirm'd, to the great good-liking and applause of the King and his Peers, who had never seen such things perform'd by any of their Metropolitans before. Others look'd asquint upon these prosperous beginnings, seeking all Occasions of new Disturbances. Some there were that openly resisted, and would not permit any Priest under *Roman* Ordination to officiate in their Churches, nay some of them they kill'd out-right. As for the Countrey People, tho they were passively Obedient to the King's Commands, yet they lik'd their own old way best. Among the rest there was one, who having receiv'd the Cuff of Confirmation, as their manner is, and being ask'd by his Neighbour how he did: *Never worse,* said He, *than I have bin since I receiv'd the Patriarch's Box o'th' ear.*

More than all this, there was a *Seminary* set up, for the Education as well of the *Habessine* as *Portuguese* Children: for the Encouragement of whom, and to invite others, they caus'd some of the young Lads to Act a Comedy after the *European* manner. But when they brought in Devils upon the Stage, as the Scene requir'd, some of the ignorant People, believing them real Hobgoblins, were so terrify'd, that they flung out of the School, crying out, *Wajelan, Wajelan, Sajtanat anetzu: O Dear! O Dear! they have brought us Devils.*

But the ensuing Tragedies more terrify'd the wiser sort. For *Tecla-George*, another of the King's Sons in Law, for his Wives sake, at difference with his Father, having drawn into the same Conspiracy with him two Noblemen, *Gebra-Marjam*, and *John Acayo*, revolted openly, and by a Cryer solemnly proclaim'd, *That he renounc'd the* Roman *Worship, and would Protect the* Alexandrian *by force of Arms.* And that the world might believe he was in Earnest, he caus'd all the Crucifixes, Rosaries, and other Ornaments of Popish Superstition to be burnt in a publick fire; and to the end there might be no hopes of Reconciliation left for the Expectation

of

of Confederates, he took his Chaplain *Abba Jacob*, who officiated after the *Roman* manner, and after he had dispoyl'd him of his Stole and Hood, put him to Death.

The King could not brook so great an Indignity, and therefore sent *Kebax*, Viceroy of *Tigra*, with an Army against him, who us'd such extraordinary Diligence, that he soon surpriz'd the secure and unprovided Rebel, overthrew his Army, and took him and his Sister *Adera* Prisoners: who, because they had so furiously and contemptuously acted against the *Roman* Religion, were both hang'd upon a high Tree. Nor could all the Intercessions of the Queen, nor of all the Noble Ladies could prevail, tho they pleaded hard the disgrace done to their Sex, and that it was never before known in *Ethiopia*, that a Noblewoman was Hang'd: especially being call'd by the King to behold so sad and infamous a Spectacle. For they did not pity her because they thought her Innocent, but for the Ignominy of her Punishment.

After this follow'd several other Accidents, which as they brought a very great Odium upon the Patriarch and the Fathers, so were they reckn'd to be the Causes of the general averseness of the People to the *Roman* Religion. The Patriarch, that he might exercise all his Authority in one single Act, and shew the full extent of his Power, having taken a pett against the Captain of the King's Guards, for some frivolous Business that nothing belong'd to his Jurisdiction, publickly in the Church, in the presence of the whole Court, thunders out an Anathema against him, and sent him Post to the Devil. It seems he had taken Possession of certain Farms, which the Monks lay'd claim to, and refus'd to restore them, notwithstanding all the Admonitions of the Patriarch. The Nobleman, tho a Soldier, hearing such a most Dreadful Excommunication, by vertue whereof he was sent packing to Hell, laden with all the Curses of *Dathan* and *Abiram*, like one Thunder-strook, fell into a Sound, and lay for Dead. But the Storm did not continue long: For presently the King stept in to his relief, by whose interposition, and the Mediation of several of the Nobility, he was readmitted into the state of Grace. However it was an Act which the Nobility took most heinously to heart; among whom there were some that frown'd and chaf'd out of meer Indignation, to see that their Church should be brought to such a degree of Servitude, that a Foreign Priest should take upon him with so much Arrogance to Excommunicate and Bequeath to Eternal Damnation, one of the Chief Counsellors of their Kingdom, an Ancient and Famous Personage, for the sake of a Litigious Farm, which the King might take when he pleas'd from the Monks themselves, if they were the Owners.

This Flame was fed by the addition of more fuel; For the *Iegue* or Chief Abbot of the Monks being at that time lately Deceas'd, who as we have already said, is the next in Dignity and Authority to the *Abuna*, he was Buried in a certain Church, consecrated after the *Roman* manner, tho he had bin an obstinate Zealot for the *Alexandrian* Religion. Thereupon the Patriarch, after he had soundly reprov'd the Rector of the Church, *Pronounc'd the Church profan'd by the Burial of a Heretic; and therefore that Mass could not be said in it.* The Rector dreading the fatal stroak of the same dismal *Dathan* and *Abiram* Thunderbolt, that lay'd the Great Commander sprawling, without expecting any new Command, causes the Carkass to be digg'd up again, and thrown by. This the *Habessines* heavily exclaim'd against, crying out, *That the* Franks *exercis'd more cruel Severities upon them, then their most exasperated Enemies ever practis'd among them, to deprive their Dead of decent Burial: now they might all see what the Living were to expect.* *Tellez* adds, That a certain old Woman was cast into Prison, upon Suspicion of being a Witch, but was presently set at liberty, because it gave distaste. For that the most Learned of the *Habessines* are of Opinion, *That there are now no more Magicians or Witches in the World, and therefore that the Woman was unjustly wrong'd, who was thrown into Prison by the Command of the Patriarch.*

Thus the Minds of the People being generally incens'd, the King himself began to look upon these acts of separate Jurisdiction in the Patriarch, as Diminutions of his Prerogative (the ancient Metropolitans never daring to attempt such things), and consequently to alienate his Affections both from him and from the *Fathers*, so that at length he gave ear to their Adversaries. Who to bring down and curb the Excessive Power of the Patriarch, which seem'd so intolerable to them, more especially because they found him still inexorable in Matrimonial Causes, prohibited by Divine and Canon-Law, but chiefly in cases of Polygamy and Divorce; they began their Addresses to him for those things, which

they

they knew he could not deny without bringing great mischief upon himself. Fifth, *That they might have liberty to say Mass after the ancient* Ethiopian *manner; for that the Patriarch might mend the ancient forms, where Necessity requir'd, without abrogating the whole. That the People having their ancient Services, would be the more quiet, in regard they would not so much mind the difference between the New and the Ancient form of Worship.* The Patriarch gave way to their desires, only mending the Ethiopic Mass, but with apparent Detriment to his Authority. For now the ancient Liturgies were every day read again without Contradiction: the Report running abroad that the Emperor was return'd to the Old Religion. The Patriarch's Power thus shaken, the Courtiers still whisper'd in the King's Ears, *That the* Roman *Religion was become odious to all the People, and that his Person would be in great Danger, unless he also forsook it himself.*

These Insinuations were back't by an Accident, which tho ridiculous in it self, gave a *being* to several Rumours and Reports. For one day an Enthusiast came into the Palace, and cry'd out, That he was *sent* from God and the most Holy Virgin, to declare in their own words to the *King*, *that unless he forthwith return'd to the ancient Religion, he should within a Fortnight undergo most severe Chastisements.* The King made answer, *That he would live and die in the* Roman *Religion*: and that the Messenger might the more speedily return his answer, *Commanded him to be Hang'd.* But at the Intercession of several who assured the poor Fellow to be Frantick, he only receiv'd a severe drubbing, for the reward of his sawcy Prophesie. However tho he were laugh'd at by the Courtiers, yet he so strangely stirr'd the minds of the Vulgar, that they publickly reported, *That an Angel had him sent from Heaven, and that he had admonish'd the King to return to the ancient* Alexandrian *Faith.* In the mean while the inbred hatred against the Fathers daily increasing, was greatly augmented by the envy of the Courtiers. For they incens'd the King and his Eldest Son against *Ras-Sela Christos*, the Fathers chief Friend, and Patron of the *Portugueses*, under pretence of their great care, admonishing the two Princes, *To take heed that he did not abuse the Renown he had won in War, and the favour of the* Portugueses, *to invade the Royal Dignity.* That which more heighten'd these growing Jealousies, was a misinterpreted act of *Ras Sela Christos*, who having order'd one *Lecanax* to be ap-

 prehended

prehended for Calumnies and Scandalous Reports thrown upon himself, caus'd him afterwards to be put to Death, tho he had appeal'd to the King. This they said was done by *Seelax*, not that the Person was guilty of the Crimes which were lay'd to his Charge, but to remove out of the way one that was Privy to the Treasons and Conspiracies of *Seelax*. Whereupon the King depriv'd him instantly of great part of his Lands, remov'd him out of *Gojam*, and took from him his Military Commands.

In the mean time, tho *Tecla-George* had suffer'd, and that the Heads of the Rebellion were taken off, yet the Rebellion it self continu'd, and the strength of it daily increas'd in such manner, that it became the Original of Dismal and Diuturnal Commotions. For the *Agawi*, that inhabit the Mountains of *Begemdra*, had not yet lay'd down their Arms; but being, as they pretended, more and more provok'd by the King, kept them in their hands to revenge their Injuries. And the better to defend themselves, they call'd to their Aid, one *Melcax*, a young Man of the Royal Blood, who had bin bred among the *Gallans*, and created him their Leader. To him therefore, as to a Sanctuary, flock'd all those that bare any disaffection to the King, all that hated the *Roman* Religion especially the Monks; and lastly, several of the Villagers and Country People. All these thus embody'd, were call'd *Lasteuers*, from *Lasta*, a most invincible Rock, and the chief Seat of the Rebellion. And indeed it seem'd a vast Torrent of War, ready to break forth to the utter Extirpation of the Fathers, and all those of the *Roman* Religion, if it prov'd so kind to spare the Royal Family it self. Against these therefore the King, having rais'd an Army of Seven and twenty Thousand Men, marches himself in Person, but with ill success at first. For the Country People, defended by the Security of the place, as the Royalists came on, still beat them off, by rolling down whole Quarries at a time of ponderous Stones upon their heads, which having put the Royalists into great disorder, they came down, and surrounded all the King's Left Wing, so that had not *Kebax* come to their relief with 300 fresh Men, they had bin all cut to pieces. The Soldiers being discourag'd by this overthrow, the King who for that reason durst not adventure any further for that time, left part of his Army to defend the Borders, and hast'ning home, was forc'd to recall *Seelax*, lurking

lurking like an Exile in *Gojam*. In the mean time the Tutelar Bands, whether for fear, or finding themselves too weak, forsook their Posts, so that the *Lastaneers* ravag'd all the Country as they pleas'd, without Opposition, till *Seelax* being got within their reach, drave them back into their former Holes.

While this Rebellion rag'd in *Begemdra*, another broke out in *Ambara*; being headed by *Luca-Marjam*, near in Blood to the Royal Family; but he being prevented and surpriz'd by the swift March of *Ras-Seelax*, ended his Days and his Design together, by falling from the Precipice of a Rock.

But the same good Fortune did not attend *Kebax*, who impatient of delay, and observing the Avenues more negligently guarded than they us'd to be, the bait that betray'd him, conceiv'd no less than that *Opportunity* it self had now proffer'd him the Victory. So in he marches, finding all clear before him for the present; but no sooner was he in, when those Mountaneers accustom'd to clamber their own Rocks, and us'd to the By-ways and conceal'd Passages of that Rock, were all on a sudden before and behind him; so that after a great Slaughter of his Men, deserted by the rest, he was himself after a matchless defence, oppress'd by Multitudes, and Slain.

His, and the Fall of *Tegre-Egzi*, which soon after follow'd, gave the Fathers no cause of Thanksgivings, but afforded their Enemies great Opportunities, and great Arguments to press the King to withdraw his Favours from them. For observing their time, when they perceiv'd him sad, and perplex'd at so much ill Success, and so many Revolts, *Oh Sir*, said they, *What will be the Issue of all these Combats and pernicious Wars? Those illiterate Swains understand not the Mysteries of the* Roman *Worship, nor any other* Service *of God then what they have bin bred and brought up to. They call us* Turks *and* Mahumetans, *because we have abandon'd our ancient Liturgies; for this reason they have taken Arms, and chosen to themselves a King.*

For *Melcax*, puff't up with the Success of his Affairs, was arriv'd at that height of boldness, that nothing now would serve him but the assum'd Title of a King. He had distributed his Court-Employments after the manner of the Kings of *Ethiopia* among his Friends; and daily increas'd in Num-

ber.

ber. For all that abominated the *Fathers*, chiefly the Nobility of *Tigra*, privately gave him Encouragements, and exhorted him, *not to desist from what he had so prosperously begun; and that then, neither the Affections of the People, nor the Assistance of his Friends would be wanting.* Elated with these golden Promises, his Temerity carry'd him so far, as to send, as if he had now bin the undoubted King of *Ethiopia*, a Viceroy into *Tigra*. To this Viceroy he allow'd a Select Band of Soldiers for his Convoy; but they, neglectful and careless of their Military Duties, took their Pleasure so much, that at length surpriz'd in the midst of their Jollity by the Royalists, they were forc'd to leave Four thousand of their Party behind them, Slain upon the Spot; while the shatter'd Remainders speeded back, to lay the blame of their ill Success upon the unwary Conduct of their Leaders. But the *Lastaners*, intent upon revenge, had at length the same advantage against the Royalists, who were stragling to destroy the approaching Harvest, and pay'd them home with equal Slaughter for Slaughter. Thus Fortune ballancing both sides, the Author of these Miscarriages was enquir'd after, and as soon found by those that watched their Opportunities. For presently *Ras-Seelax* was accus'd, as if he had bin negligent in Executing the King's Orders, and had not sent timely Succors to the over-power'd Combatants. And his Enemies so far prevail'd, that Articles were fram'd against him, to which he was compell'd to answer: which he did, and justify'd himself so well, that in words indeed he was acquitted, but in Fact condemn'd. For he was again degraded, and all his feudary Possessions and Military Employments granted away to *Basilides*.

Thus *Ras-Seelax* being once more lay'd by, it was no difficult matter to undermine the Patriarch and the Fathers. For against them the general Complaint was made, *That they had no other Design, but as they had subjected the Empire in Ecclesiastical Affairs to the* Roman *Pope, so to bring it under the Dominion of the King of* Portugal *in Seculars. To this end under the pretence of Temples and Residencies they rear'd up Castles and Walls, from whence they could never be expell'd with Spears and Arrows.* Many other things of the same Nature, they suggested, which if the King now through Age more jealous, did not absolutely believe, yet he hearken'd to them with a more easie Attention. However outwardly and publick he shew'd

the

the same Kindness and Affability to the Fathers as before, and kindly receiv'd the Bishop sent from *Rome* to be a Coadjutor to the Patriarch. But when he brought the *Diploma's* of the Jubilee open'd at *Rome* in the year 1625. and then granted to *Ethiopia*, he was derided by most Men, who could not comprehend those great Vertues of Indulgencies which the Bishop boasted of. For some began to Discourse among themselves like the Pharisees, *Who is this who also forgives Sins? Who can forgive Sins but only God?* To which the King made answer with a severe Countenance, *That the Keys of the Kingdom of Heaven were given to* Peter, *and that the use of those Keys belong'd to the Pope, for the Granting Indulgencies.*

However the *Habessines*, as if those Indulgencies had afforded Materials for Sin, bent themselves still more and more to Sedition and Tumult. For the Revolt of the *Lastaneers* so well succeeding, *Sertzegaae*, newly made Viceroy of *Gojam*, so ill repay'd the King for his new favours, that he not only revolted from him himself; but which was more detestable to think, he would have drawn in the young *Basilides* to have conspir'd with him against his own Father. And when he could not prevail upon the young Prince, he endeavour'd to have advanc'd another young Noble Gentleman of the Blood Royal, to the end he might have reign'd himself under his Name. But being overthrown and taken, he was drubb'd to Death. Seven of his Accomplices lost their Heads. One of his chief Agents, because he had vented horrid Blasphemies against the See of *Rome*, and opprobrious words against the King, was hung up upon an Iron Hook driven into a high Stake; upon which, after he had hung a whole Day, because he repeated the same Provocations in the midst of his Torment, he was at length run thorough the Body with several Spears; and so ended his miserable Life. So many, and such lamentable Accidents as these pierc'd the very hearts of most People, and the *Lastaneers*, dispairing of Pardon, hearing of such horrid Executions, were the more resolute in their Rebellion.

Thereupon the King undertook a new Expedition with all his Forces against them, and had taken the very Head and Ring-leader of all the Rebels, had he not with a small Retinue made a shift to Escape; yet he left behind him great ſtore of rich Plunder. But he could not be utterly Subdu'd, in regard that ſo many Sculking Holes, ſo many wide and ſpacious Rocks, where thoſe Savages liv'd and hid themſelves, like ſo many wild Beaſts, could neither be aſſail'd nor taken. It happen'd therefore, that Fortune wheeling about, the Rebels overthrew a Select Party of the King's Forces: and by and by with all their force lay hovering about the King's Army, which they foreſaw would in a ſhort time want Proviſion. The King therefore fearing to be cloo'd up in thoſe narrow Streights, retir'd into *Dembea*, before the War was at an end. Which he did with ſo much haſt more then it was thought he needed to have done, that as it diminiſh'd his own fame, ſo it gave Courage to the Rebels.

And now the Fathers great Enemies beholding the King's Melancholly, redoubled their Complaints. *That there would never be peaceful Days in* Ethiopia, *ſo long as the* Roman *Religion bare ſo much ſway. That it was a very good Religion, but above the Capacity of the People, who would ſtill prefer the Worſhip of their Anceſtors, to which they had bin bred from their Infancy, before forreign Innovations, which they underſtood not. For who ſhould perſwade them,* That Circumciſion was evil, That the Holydaies of the Sabbath are not pleaſing to God; that the ancient Liturgy cannot be prov'd; That the *Roman* Calendar is better then the *Ethiopic*; That the Faſts of the Fourth Holyday are leſs acceptable to God, then the Faſts of the Seventh? *How much more expedient and profitable were it, to retain the ancient Ceremonies in ſuch things as do not contradict the Subſtance of Faith! But as for* Ras-Sela, *and others that endeavour the Contrary, it was apparent they did it meerly to advance their own Deſigns againſt the King and Kingdom.*

With theſe and ſuch like Expoſtulations, the King being overcome, eſpecially finding no other way of appeaſing and quieting the *Laſtarers*, and that *Begemdra* was almoſt all in the Hands of the Enemy, and at the ſame time all his Friends, eſpecially the Ladies of Quality laying before him the Danger he would be in, ſhould he be deſerted by his Soldiers, he at length preſs'd the Patriarch, to remit whatever poſſibly might be remitted. He foreſeeing a terrible Storm, tho ſore againſt his Will, thought 'twas high time to lower his Sails, for fear of Loſing all, while he hazarded the Saving of all. Whereupon he ſubmitted to the King's requeſt; nevertheleſs

theless upon Condition, *That nothing Decreed should be remitted by Publick Acts, but only by a Tacit Connivance, and that in the mean time there should be a Cessation of all Penalties, and Mulcts.*

Upon this the King intending a Third Expedition against the *Lasteners*, to make his Soldiers the more stedfast and obedient, he put forth an Edict; by which, in general words an Indulgence was granted for the Exercise of all ancient Ceremonies, not repugnant to Faith. Thus every Person being left to his particular Liberty, the *Alexandrian* Worship was again, to the great Satisfaction of the People, freely exercis'd; but to the great grief of the *Portuguezes*, especially the Patriarch, who presently wrote to the King, complaining, *That contrary to his advice, a Lay Prince should publish an Edict of that Nature in reference to spiritual Affairs*; for that it belong'd to him to set forth such Decrees; putting him in mind of the words of *Azariah* the High-Priest to King *Uzziah*, and of the Punishment that follow'd, and admonishing him to amend that Fault, by publishing some other Edict, which should be propos'd by the assistance of some one of the Fathers of the Society. The King obey'd and propounded an Edict, which contain'd Three Articles.

1. *That the Antient Liturgy, but Corrected, should be read in the Mass.*

2. *That the Festivals should be observ'd according to the antient Computation of Time, except* Easter, *and those other Festivals that depended upon it.*

3. *That whosoever pleas'd, instead of the Sabbath, might fast upon the fourth Holyday.* And then as for answer to the Patriarchs Complaints, he made this reply, *That the* Roman *Religion was not introduc'd into his Dominions by the Preaching or Miracles of the Fathers, but meerly by his Edicts and Commands, not by the assent of his People, but of his own free will, because he thought it better then the* Alexandrian. *Therefore the Patriarch had no reason to Complain.* But these Concessions not being sufficient, and coming too late, prov'd altogether ineffectual; not serving in the least to pacifie the *Lasteners*, or any other of the Discontented Parties.

Chap. XII.

Of the Decrease of the Roman *Religion, and the Restoration of the* Alexandrinian.

The Fathers ill Success. The King prepares to restore the Alexandrian Religion. Over-perswaded by the Queen and his Son. The Decree refute'd in Council. The Patriarch makes a grave Speech to the contrary. Upbraids him with his Victories and threatens him. At length he Supplicates, but in vain. The Edict passes. Signify'd to the Patriarch, who proposes a Medium. The Edict publish'd to the great Satisfaction of the People. The Ancient Ceremonies us'd. An Invective Satyr against the Fathers. The sudden Change censur'd.

WEE have hitherto seen the great Progress of the *Roman* Religion in *Ethiopia*; the Authority of the Patriarch advanc'd to the utmost extent, the King and his Brothers, together with a great many of the Nobility, some sincerely, some feignedly favouring the Jesuits. For the Latin Worship was with great diligence impos'd and exercis'd all over several Provinces of the Kingdom. Many of the *Habessine* Priests were Ordain'd by the Patriarch; and great diligence was us'd for the building of Churches and Colleges. Already besides the Patriarch they had increas'd their Number to One and twenty Companions, that is to say, Nineteen Fathers, and Two Brothers of the Society, distributed into Thirteen Residencies. Nor could the Fathers but be well pleas'd with so many Thousands of Baptized and Converted People; for certainly the gaining of so many lost Souls by Baptism was not to be despised. When on a suddain behold a suddain Change, upon which the Banishment of the Fathers, and the Subversion of the *Roman* Religion ensu'd.

For the Fathers believing that the opportunity of the time was not to be neglected, made it their Business to abrogate all the *Alexandrian* Rites, even those which were formerly tolerated under the *Roman* Bishops: on the other side, the Common People Wedded to their Old Customs; but more especially the Monks and Clergy, the chief Supporters of the old Religion, most stoutly oppos'd their Proceedings. Besides them, several of the Nobility, either out of Hatred of the *Romans*, or out of Ambition, frequently revolted, and through the strength of their unaccessible Rocks easily eluded the King's more mighty Power. A most remarkable Lesson to teach us, *That that sort of Worship to which the People are averse, is not easily to be introduc'd by the Prince; and that it is no piece of Prudence or Policy to attempt the Liberty of those who are well defended by the Situation of their Country.*

Therefore the King, tho otherwise most addicted to the Fathers, wearied with so many Exclamations of his own People, growing in years, utterly disliking the present posture of Affairs, and fearful of what might ensue, tormented with the continual importunities of his Friends; his Jealousie of his Brother, the Contumacy of the *Lasteners*, the Diminution of his Prerogative, and the dread of losing his Kingdom, at length began to think of abrogating the *Roman*, and restoring the ancient *Alexandrian* Worship. And which was more to be admir'd, a prosperous Fight with the *Lasteners*, was that which setled his wavering Thoughts. For making a fourth Expedition against them, he came upon them so unlook'd for, that he gave them a Total rout, Killing eight Thousand upon the place, with several of the Leaders of the Faction, and chief Deserters of their King and Country. The *Portuguese* rejoyc'd at the News, believing the Rebellion quieted by this Victory; and that for the future nothing would presume so much as to hiss against the *Roman* Religion. But it fell out quite otherwise. For they who favour'd the the *Alexandrian* Religion, the next day carry'd the King to view the Field of the Battel, and shewing him the multitude of the Slain, thus bespake him. *Neither* Ethnics *nor* Mahumetans *were these, in whose Slaughter we might have some reason to rejoyce. No, Sir, they were Christians, once your Subjects, and our dear Countrymen, and partly to your self, partly to us related in Blood. How much more laudable would it have bin for these couragious Breasts to have bin oppos'd against the most deadly of your Enemies? This is no Victory, because obtain'd against your own Subjects. With the same Sword wherewith you Slaughter them, you Stab your own Bowels: Certainly they have no hatred to us, whom we make War upon so cruelly. Only they are averse to that Worship to which you would compel them. How many have we already kill'd upon this Change of Ceremonies? How many remain behind reserv'd for the same Slaughter? When will these Bloody Conflicts end? Forbear, we beseech your Majesty, to constrain them to Novelties, and Innovations, lest they renounce their Allegiance; otherwise we shall never behold the Face of Peace again. We are hated even by the* Gallans *and* Ethnicks *for abandoning our antient Ceremonies, and are therefore by them call'd Apostates.* For it seems that the King of *Adel*, having apprehended and put to Death two of the *Fathers* travelling into *Habessinia* thorow his Country, in the accompt which he gave to *Susneus* of what he had done, haughtily call'd him Apostate. Nor is it to be question'd but that the *Mahometans* and Neighbouring Nations were much Scandaliz'd at the Alteration of the *Habessinians* into the *Roman* Religion; not out of any love to the one, or hatred to the other; but for fear the *Portugueses*, strengthen'd by the *Habessines* should become their Masters. The *Turks* also were mad that the Metropolitan of *Ethiopia* was no more to be sent for out of *Egypt*; for by that same Tye they held the *Habessines* fast, and lyable to what Conditions they pleas'd.

To these incessant Importunities, the Queen joyn'd the pow'rful Charms of her own Supplication, conjuring him by all the Obligations of Sacred Wedlock, and common Pledges of their undoubted Offspring, *To be well advised what he did; and not to ruin his Kingdom, Himself, his Fortune, and his whole Family.* With the same importunity his Eldest Son *Basilides*, and his Brother by the Mothers side *Jamanax*, hourly sollicited his disturb'd mind: and the better to accomplish their ends, they underhand procur'd the *Gallans* that serv'd the King, to desire a dismission, as being unwilling to fight any longer against the *Habessines* in a quarrel about a new Religion. Thus the King's rigor mollify'd at length, *Basilides*, after he had summon'd the Nobility and chiefest of his Father's Counsellors together, held a Council, wherein it was concluded, That there was no other remedy to allay the Disorders of the Kingdom, but by restoring the *Alexandrian* Religion. And the better to perswade those that were of the Contrary Opinion, they gave it out that the *Romanists* and *Alexandrians* were of the same Opinion in points of Faith; That both affirm'd that God was true Christ, and true Man. And as for the asserting One or Two Natures, they were only words of little Moment, and not worth the Ruin of a Mighty Empire. So that the King induc'd by these reasons, gave liberty to every one that pleas'd to return to the *Alexandrian* Forms.

The

The Patriarch was not ignorant of these Transactions. Whereupon being accompanied with his Coadjutor, & the chief of the Fathers, he desir'd Audience of the King. Which being granted, after a short Pause, Sir, said He, *I had thought that we had lately bin the Victors, but now I see we are Vanquish'd: On the other side the* Lasteneers, *being overthrown and put to flight, have obtain'd their desires. Before the Battel was fought 'twas then a time to Vow and Promise, but now to fulfil. The Victory was gain'd by the Catholic and* Portuguese *Soldiers, the God of Hosts favouring the Catholic Religion. These are therefore but ill returns to his Divinity; For I understand, here has bin a Decree made, giving free toleration again of the* Alexandrian *Religion. But this is not a place I see to advise with Bishops and Religious Persons; the illiterate Vulgar, the* Gallans *and* Mahumetans, *Women here give their Judgments in Matters of Religion. Consider how many Victories you have gain'd from the Rebels, since you have embrac'd the* Roman *Religion: Remember, that you embrac'd it, not compell'd by force or fear, but of your own free choice, as believing it the Truer. Neither did we come hither as Intruders; we were sent hither, by the Pope and the King of* Portugal *at your request. Neither did they ever design any other thing in their thoughts, but only to unite your Empire to the Church of* Rome. *And therefore beware of exciting their just Indignation. They are 'tis true far distant hence; but God is at hand, and will require the Satisfaction which is due to them. You will throw an indelible blemish upon the Lion of the Tribe of* Juda, *which you bear for your Atchievement; You will blur your own renown, and the Glory of your Nation: Lastly, you will be the undoubted occasion of innumerable Sins by your Apostacy; which that I may not see, nor feel the threatning revenge of the Almighty, Command this Head of mine to be immediately struck'n off.* This said, with tears in their Eyes, the Patriarch and his Companions fell Prostrate at the King's feet, in expectation of his Answer. The King not any way concern'd, reply'd in few words, *That he had done as much as he could, but could do no more, neither was a total alteration of Religion intended, but only a Concession of some Ceremonies.* To which the Patriarch answer'd, *That he had already tolerated some, and was ready to indulge more, which did not concern the Substance of Faith: So that he would put forth another Edict, that all things might remain as they were.* To which he receiv'd no other reply, but *That the King would send certain Commissioners to Treat and Discourse with the Fathers.* Nor had they a better answer from the Prince, who being an Artist at Dissimulation, sent them away unsatisfy'd, with ambiguous words.

Upon the 24*th* of *June*, The favourers of the *Alexandrian* Religion, to the end they might get the Decree already mention'd put in Execution, Address themselves to the Emperor, and choosing *Abba-Athanasius* for their Prolocutor, beseech him, *That he would by a Publick Edict be pleas'd to give his Subjects Liberty to return to the Religion of their Ancestors; that otherwise the Kingdom would be utterly ruin'd.* The King assented, and order'd certain Commissioners to signifie his Pleasure to the Patriarch. They presently fell sharply to work with him, and upbraided him, *with the frequent Rebellions of the People;* Ælius, Cabraei, Tecla-George, *and* Sertzac, *and with the Slaughter of so many Thousands as fell with them. That the* Lasteneers *were still in Arms for their ancient Religion; that all ran to them, and deserted the King, because all the* Habessines *pin'd after their ancient Religion. However, that for the future it should be free for every one to be at his own choice which to follow: for so from the Time of* Claudius *till lately, there had bin Peace and Quietness between different Opinions, while the* Portugueses *exercis'd theirs, the* Habessines *their own Religion.*

After a short time of Deliberation, an Answer was carry'd back to the King by Father *Emanuel D' Almeyda; That the Patriarch understood that the Exercise of both Religions would be free in his Kingdom. That for his part he had an equal love for* Ethiopia, *as for his own Native Country; and therefore for his part he was ready to grant whatsoever might be done, with safety to the Purity of sound Doctrine. But that there was still a difference to be made between those who had not yet embrac'd the* Roman *Religion, as the* Lasteneers, *for that they might be conniv'd at; but they who had positively embrac'd the* Roman *Faith, and had bin admitted to Confession and the Sacraments, no indulgence could be granted to them, without committing a great Sin, to return to the* Alexandrian *Schism.*

By this Temperament the Patriarch design'd to have put a Bar upon the King and all the Court, which had already publickly made Profession of the *Romish* Ceremonies. But the King, almost spent with Vexation and Grief, made no other answer than this: *How can this be done? I am now no more Lord of my own Kingdom.* So they were forc'd to depart as they came. Presently the Drums beat, the Trumpets sounded, and Proclamation was made by the Voice of the Cryer. *Oyez, Oyez; In the first place we propounded to ye, the* Roman *Religion, esteeming it the best. But an innumerable multitude of Men, have perish'd through dislike of it with* Ælius, Cabriel, Tecla-George, Sertzac, *and lastly, with the Rustick* Lastaneets. *And therefore we grant you the free Exercise of the Religion of your Ancestors. It shall be lawful for you henceforward to frequent your own Churches, make use of your own Eucharistic Arks, and to read the Liturgies after the old Custom. So farewell and Rejoyce.*

It is a thing almost impossible to be believ'd with what an Universal Joy this Edict was receiv'd among the People. The whole Camp, as if they had had some great Deliverance from the Enemy, rang with Shouts and Acclamations. The Monks and Clergy, who had felt the greatest weight of the Fathers Hatred lifted up their Thankful voices to Heaven. The promiscuous Multitude of Men and Women danc'd and caper'd, The Soldiers wish'd all happiness to their Commanders: They brake to pieces their own and the Rosaries of all they met, and some they burnt. Crying out, that it was sufficient for them to believe, That Christ was true God and true Man, without the unnecessary Disputes concerning the two Natures. From thenceforward the old Ceremonies were made use of in the Communion; Grapestone Liquor instead of Wine. And the Holy Name of Jesus forbidden to be so frequent in their Mouths, after the *Roman* manner; and some that did not observe this Caution, they ran through with their Lances. Some few days after, a general Circumcision was appointed, not minding the pain of such a piece of Vanity, so they might not be thought to have neglected any thing of their ancient Rites in favour of the Fathers. Some there were also that us'd the ancient manner of washing themselves upon the Festival of the Epiphany, believing themselves thereby purify'd from the guilt of having admitted the *Roman* Religion.

Others ran about Singing for joy that *Ethiopia* was deliver'd from the *Western Lyons*, Chanting forth the following Lines.

At length the Sheep of Ethiopia *free'd*
From the Bold Lyons of the West,
Securely in their Pastures feed.

St. Mark *and* Cyril'*s Doctrine have o'ercome*
The Folly's of the Church of Rome.
Rejoyce, rejoyce, Sing Hallelujahs *all*,
No more the Western Wolves
Our Ethiopia *shall enthrall.*

And thus fell the whole Fabrick of the *Roman* Religion, that had bin so long rearing with so much Labour and Expence, and which had cost the Effusion of so much Blood to pull it down. So vast and haughty Tow'rs that have bin long time Built, if once you undermine the Foundation, tumble in a moment. Some there were who accus'd the Fathers of the Society, as if they had ruin'd the fair Progress they had made by double Diligence, and over-hasty Zeal. For most of the *Portuguests*, and many of the *Habessines* themselves that were well affected to the *Roman* Religion took it ill, that things should be so suddainly chang'd, which might have bin longer let alone, without the least injury done to fundamental Faith. For as tall Trees, that have taken deep root, are not easily Eradicated, so Inveterated Opinions, which we have as it were suck't in with our Mother's Milk are not to be overcome but by length of time, great Lenity, and much Patience. For Humane understanding, if compell'd, puts on Obstinacy as it were in revenge of injur'd Liberty. Nor did some that were the Fathers great Friends make any Question, that had they left some things indifferent, which the *Pope* himself many times freely tolerates, so it be acknowledg'd as the Act of his Benignity and Dispensation, as the Computations of the holy Times, the Communion under both Kinds, and some other things which the Primitive Church without any Scandal tolerated and permitted, as the Marriage of Priests, the Fast of the fourth Holyday, the Observation of the Sabbath, and some other things which depended meerly upon Custom, and not upon Divine Precept, and had only minded in the mean time the Business of Conversion and Preaching, they had gain'd not only the *Habessines*, but the Pagans themselves, and working by degrees, had brought their design at length to perfection. But they relying wholly upon the Favour and Successes of the King were presently for compelling the *Habessines* to conform of a suddain in all things to a strange and uncouth Innovation. The Latin Tongue must be us'd in

their

their Publick Sacred Worship, and their daily Prayers, the Angelical Salutation, the Lord's Prayer and the Apostolic Creed must be said in Latin, written in the Ethiopic Characters, in which *Eve Maria gratia Plena*, &c. sounded strangely and odly to the *Habessinian* Pronunciation. Which by degrees so alienated the Affections of the *Habessinians* from such a sort of aukward Devotion, so that at length all the Wars, Seditions, Pests of Locusts, Famine, and all the Calamities that follow'd, and the severe Penalties that were inflicted upon the *Alexandrians* were lay'd upon the *Fathers*; which begat them Hatred instead of Reverence, and Banishment in the room of Favour and Affection.

From what has bin said, Men of Prudence will easily find the causes of so great a Mutation. Nevertheless it will not be improper to add those other which *Tellez* has assign'd.

First he says, That the strict Tyes and Laws of Matrimony according to the Catholic Faith, were not so well brook'd by the *Habessinians*, being allow'd by the *Alexandrian* Religion, to Marry one or more, and to Divorce, as they saw good.

Secondly, That besides Incontinency, Avarice, Ambition, Envy, Hatred had got a head among them, especially against *Ras-Sela* *Christos*, whose Power they could find no better way to pull down, than by Persecuting the *Fathers*; for whom he had so indear'd a Kindness.

Thirdly, That many were possess'd of the Church Lands, of which they were unwilling to make restitution.

Fourthly, That the Secular Judges complain'd that the Patriarch summon'd all Matrimonial Causes to his Tribunal.

Fifthly, That others were enrag'd to see Churches built with Lime and Stone; for they call'd them Castles, not Churches, built by *Ras-Seelax*, to the end he might make himself Master of *Ethiopia*.

Sixthly, That the Monks were incens'd, to see the Fathers only in Esteem, and themselves formerly so highly reverenc'd, afterwards contemn'd and slighted; so that as the other grew great, they should become nothing at all.

Seventhly, That the *Habessines* always appeal'd to the Manners and Rites of their Ancestors, not believing it to be just, to condemn them of Error, who had bin accompted Holy Men for so many Ages; or to hear and follow Innovations, neglecting the Laws and Customs of their Forefathers. For through the vitiousness of Humane Malignity, saith *Quintilian*, Old things are always applauded, Novelties held to be loathsome. So that although you overcome the reason by Argument, you can never subdue the Will.

Eighthly, That the Devil had put it into the Heads of several Catholicks to make a corresponding Agreement between the Catholick and the *Alexandrinian* Religion; affirming all to be Christians, as well *Alexandrians* as *Romans*. That all believe in Christ; That Christ saves all; That there is little Difference between both Religions; That both have Conveniencies and Inconveniencies, their Truths and their Errors, but that the Wheat was to be separated from the Cockle.

Ninthly, That the Ecclesiastical Censures seem'd very heavy to the *Habessines*; especially when they heard the Patriarch name *Dathan* and *Abiram* in the Excommunication.

CHAP.

Chap. XIII.

Of the Expulsion of the Patriarch, and the Exilement of the Fathers of the Society.

The Alexandrians *quarrel with the Fathers; who are accus'd. Their Churches taken from them.* Susneus *Dyes.* Ras-Seelax *renouncing the* Alexandrian *Religion is Overthrown and Banish'd. Others put to Death. The Fathers Dispossessed of their Goods. Sent to* Fremona. *The Patriarch by Letters Demands of the King the Causes of his Banishment, and a New Dispute. The King's Answer. The Fathers depart for* Fremona; *Afterwards quite thrown out of the Kingdom.*

After the Publication of the King's Edict, the *Alexandrians* being now absolute Victors, endeavour'd with all their industry to be quit with the Fathers, and expel them quite out of *Habessinia.* To which purpose they omitted no occasion of daily quarrel and contention: First accusing the Patriarch for endeavouring by Seditious Sermons to stir up the People to Sedition, and to turn them from the *Alexandrian* Religion; for that he had openly exhorted his Hearers to *Constancy.* But understanding that *Basilides* was displeas'd, and gave out threatning words, they thought it requisite to act more moderately. Soon after the *Fathers* Churches were taken from them, believing that would be a means to put a stop to the *Roman* Worship. And first they were constrain'd to quit their Cathedral at *Gorgora*, a stately Structure after the *European* manner. At their departure they carry'd with them all their Sacred Furniture, brake all the Sculpture, and spoil'd the Pictures, that they might not leave them to be the sport of their Adversaries: doing that themselves, which they thought the *Habessines* would do. And this Example they follow'd in all other places from whence they were expell'd. In the mid'st of these Transactions, *Susneus's* Distemper increasing, and more and more augmented by his continual anguish of Mind, he ended this Life the 16th day of *Decemb.* 1632.

The King being Dead, the Fathers Adversaries set upon *Ras-Selax* in the first place, as the Principal Favourer and Protector of the *Roman* Religion: and first of all they promise him all his former Dignities, all his Possessions and Goods, upon Condition he would return to the *Alexandrian* Religion. Upon his refusal, they bring him bound in Chains before the King, and pronounce him guilty of Death. But the King declaring that he would not pollute his hands with the Blood of his Uncle, commanded him to be carry'd to a certain remote Place, near to *Samenar*, and sequester'd his Goods. And as he was great, so was he attended in his fall by several others, as *Akga-Tino*, Secretary of State, and the King's Historiographer, *Walata Georgissa*, the Queens Cousin. In short, whoever had favour'd the Fathers, were all sent into Exile, and some put to Death, perhaps because they had bin more bitter in their Expressions than others against the *Alexandrian* Religion. For some had call'd it, *a Religion for Dogs*. After all this the Enemies of the Fathers still insisted, *That nothing was yet done, so long as the Patriarch and the Fathers were suffer'd to abide within the Confines of the Kingdom: Neither would the* Lasitaneers *be quiet till they heard the Fathers were all thrown out of* Ethiopia, *but would look upon all things transacted for the re-establishment of the* Alexandrian *Religion as fictitious Stories.*

There needed not many words to press him that was already willing. First of all therefore, their Goods and Possessions were taken from them; then all their Arms, especially their Musquets and Fire-Arms. But before that, they were sent to *Fremona*, where, as we have already declar'd, *Oviedo* the Patriarch resided for some time. But before their Departure, the Patriarch wrote a certain Letter to the King, to this Effect:

I did not adventure to come into Habessinia *with my Companions, of my own accord, but by the Command of the* Roman *Pontiff, and the King of* Portugal, *at the request of your Father, where having taken the King's Oath of Obedience, I officiated the Office of Patriarch in the Name of the* Roman *Pontiff, and the King of* Portugal. *Now because you Command*

mand me to depart, my humble request is, that your Majesty would set down the Causes of my Excitement in Writing, subscrib'd with your own, and the hands of some of your Counsellors and Peers, that all the World may know whether I am compell'd to suffer for my Life and Conversation, or for the sake of my Doctrine. I granted the Ceremonies desired by your Father, except the Communion under both Kinds, which only the Pope himself can dispense with. The same also I again offer, so that you and your Subjects will yield Obedience to the Church of Rome *as the head of all other Churches. My last request is, That as the Matter was Debated at first, so it may be referr'd to another Dispute, by which means the Truth of the whole affair will more manifestly appear.*

To this Writing the King thus reply'd, *Whatever was done by me before, was done by the Command of my Father, whom I was in Duty bound to Obey; so that I was forc'd to wage War under his Conduct, both with Kindred and Subjects. But after the last Battel of* Wainadega *the Learned and Unlearned Clergy and Layety, Civil and Military, young and old, all sorts of Persons made their Addresses to my Father, Crying out,* How long shall we be perplexed and wearied with unprofitable things? How long shall we encounter Brethren and Kindred, cutting off the right hand with the left? How long shall we thrust our Swords into our own Bowels? Especially since we learn nothing from the *Roman* Religion but what we knew before. For what the *Romans* call the two Natures in Christ, his Divinity and his Humanity, that we knew from the beginning to this time. For we all believe that our Lord Christ is perfect God and perfect Man; perfect God in his Divinity, and perfect Man in his Humanity. But in regard those Natures are not separated nor divided; for neither of them subsist of its self, but both of them conjoyn'd the one with the other; therefore we do not say that they are two things. For one is made two, yet so as the Natures are not mix'd in their Subsistence. *This Controversie therefore among us is of little moment; neither was it for this that there has bin so much Bloodshed among us, but chiefly because the Blood was deny'd to the Layety, whereas Christ has said in his Gospel,* Unless ye eat the flesh of the Son of Man, and drink his blood,

ye

ye ſhall not have life everlaſting; *and when he inſtituted the Holy Supper, he did not ſay, The Blood is in my Body, which I have given to you alone; but take and drink, and partake all. From that time the Diſciples did as they were commanded. The Intermiſſion of the Faſt of the fourth Holyday, which is nevertheleſs enjoyn'd by the Canons of the Holy Apoſtles: as alſo a various manner of Faſting in the Time of* Lent. *Beſides by altering the Order of the whole Eccleſiaſtical Computation in reference to the Annual Feſtivals, and the Permiſſion of all Perſons to enter into the Church, without any diſtinction of clean or unclean; theſe are the things that gave offence to our People. But they deteſted nothing more, than the reiteration of Baptiſm, as if we had bin Heathens, before we had bin Baptiz'd by the Fathers. They reordain'd our Prieſts and Deacons, they burnt the wooden Cheſts of our Altars, and Conſecrated ſome Altars of their own, as if ours had not bin Conſecrated before. The Monks alſo complain'd, that their Inſtitutions were abrogated. Theſe and others of the ſame Nature were the true Cauſes, that we abandon'd the* Roman *Faith, tho it was not we who gave it Protection but our Father. And therefore, becauſe the* Alexandrian Abuna *is now upon his Journey hither, and hath ſent us word, that he cannot live or joyntly act in the ſame Kingdom with the* Roman *Patriarch, and the Fathers, we command you to haſten to* Fremona. *Theſe things are offer'd now too late, which might have bin eaſily at firſt allow'd: For now there is no returning to that, which all the whole Nation abhors and deteſts: for which reaſon, all farther Colloquies and Diſputes will be in vain.*

The Patriarch relates in his Epiſtle to the King of *Spain,* That that ſame Metropolitan, of whom the King makes mention, came ſome years before into *Ethiopia,* but lay privately conceal'd in *Baarva,* where hearing of the diſowning and caſting off the Patriarch, he brake out into this farther Expreſſion, to the King, *That he could not officiate in his Office, unleſs the Patriarch and the Fathers were either put to Death, or Baniſh'd in perpetuity.* So that the Patriarch and the Fathers were forc'd to obey the King's Command, not without a long Diſpute about their Guns, which they would willingly have kept for their own Preſervation; but they were forc'd to deliver them up, that they might be of no uſe to the *Portugals,* who were coming, as it was fear'd and reported, to their aſſiſtance. Thus the Patriarch with all the Fathers that were then in the Country, were conſtrain'd to leave

their

their warm Seats after an Enjoyment of Eight years standing. In their return they met with various Misfortunes, and were frequently infested with Thieves, before they could get to *Fremona*. But because they foresaw, that would be no abiding place for 'em of any long continuance, they privately resolv'd to send away some of the Fathers before into *India*, to give the Vice-Roy an accompt of the state of their affairs, and to desire some remedy, that is to say, a good sufficient strength of *Portugueses*. But before they could obtain that, they receiv'd fresh Commands from the King (who 'tis very probable smelt their Design) to remove from *Fremona* and be gon. But they stay'd loath to depart a great while, and to spin out time, privately retir'd to one *John Akay*, formerly an Enemy to the King, who not being able to defend them, they were pull'd out thence by the Ears, and in *May* 1634. deliver'd to the *Turks*, and first carry'd to *Arkiko* and *Mazzua*, after that to *Suaquena*, and brought before the *Turkish Bassa*. And indeed there was nothing more that provok'd the *Habessines*, as *Gregory* told me, then that they should require aid of the Military Power from *India* to establish their Religion: *They might*, said he, *have shaken the dust from their feet at their departure, as the Apostles were commanded; but they were for settling Religion with Swords and Guns*. Which was not done so secretly but it came to the Ears of the *Habessines*; for it seems that some of their Train, vext at some Misfortune or other, had impudently threaten'd it. Which was one reason among others that their Churches built of Stone and Morter, and their Guns were taken from them.

Chap. XIV.

Of what happen'd after the Departure of the Patriarch and the Fathers out of Ethiopia.

The Condition of the Bishop and his Associates privately left behind. The Patriarch's misery among the Turks. Peter Heyling *a German Disputes with him.* Peter *entertain'd by the King of* Habessinia. *Various reports concerning his Death. The Patriarch redeems himself. He sends* Hirom Dibo *for Assistance, who cannot speed. The persecuters of the Fathers put to Death in* Ethiopia. *New admitted into* Habessinia. *Six Capuchins sent again; their ill success. Three more sent after them; their sad Misfortune.* Nogueira *Hang'd.* Mendez *dyes in* India. *After that no News from* Habessinia.

NOtwithstanding the King's Commands to all in general, the Patriarch left behind privately in several places *Apollinaris Almeyda*, *Hiacynthus Francisco*, *Ludowigo Cordeyra*, *Bruno Bruni* and some others, who after they had liv'd miserably for some time, lurking up and down, at last were most of them Hang'd. In the mean time he himself spent almost a whole year in great Vexation, and full of sorrow among the Barbarous *Turks* in *Suaquena*, almost melted by the Sun. But nothing more increas'd the anguish of his Mind, than the News of the New Metropolitan's arrival out of *Egypt*, and that it should be his misfortune to be constrain'd to behold him as he pass'd by. He had in his Train a certain *German*, whose Name was *Peter Heyling*, a Native of *Lubeck*, a young Gentleman eminent for Probity and Learning, a Professor of the *Augustan*, or *Lutheran* Religion, and generally call'd by the Title of *Muallim*, that is in Arabic, *Doctor Peter*. He being desirous to see the world, and learn the Arabic Language, was arriv'd about that time in *Egypt*, and was very much esteem'd for his Piety and Modesty by the *Cophtites*, and hearing that the Metropolitan was going for *Ethiopia*, he obtain'd leave to go in his Train, and by that means met the Patriarch *Alphonsus* at *Suaquen*. Presently he undertook to encounter him, opposing several Opinions and Tenents of the *Roman* Church, and expounding in Arabic to the standers by, whatever was said on both sides. The Patriarch in a heat desir'd desir'd him to forbear that Explanation, because he did not understand the Arabic. To which the other answer'd, That he Disputed, for others to hear as well as himself. The Disputation being ended, The Patriarch, turning to his Companions, sighing, told them, *That if that Doctor went into Habessinia, he would precipitate the whole Country into Heresie.* He was no sooner arriv'd there, but he became very acceptable to the King, who gave him a Tent, and all things necessary. Concerning his Death, various Reports were spread abroad. For some said, That being most graciously and kindly entertain'd by the King, he dy'd in *Habessinia*: Others, that being honourably dismiss'd by the King, he was murder'd by certain Arabian Thieves.

As for the Patriarch, after a long Captivity and very bad Usage from the *Turks*, he was at length set at Liberty, after he had pay'd for himself and his Companions a Ransom of 4000 *German* Dolars, and so at length got safe to *Goa*. Where, tho he were advis'd to go himself into *Portugal*, and give an accompt of the afflicted State of *Ethiopia*, he thought it the better way to send *Jeronymus Lobo*, with order to desire the Aid of a sufficient Military Power, to restore him to his lost See. Thereupon the diligent Jesuit, not only went into *Portugal*, but also to *Mantua* to *Philip* the Fourth, and from thence to *Rome*. But all his Negotiations prov'd ineffectual, whether it were that they did not think it at that instant so Apostolical a way to propagate the Gospel by Force of Arms, or whether it were that they did not like the Charge of an Expedition, from whence they could hope for little good, there being no considerable Party in the Kingdom to give them footing, and the encouragement of Assistance. For the King watchful over all casualties, put all to Death that favour'd the *Roman Fathers*. Which occasion'd the Ruin of many of the Nobility; among the rest *Tecla-Salus*; and several Priests that had taken *Roman* Orders; and all the Fathers, except *Bernard Noguera*, whom the Patriarch had created his Vicar. For tho the Patriarch attempted afterwards to send several other Fathers, yet all their Endeavours were in vain; so that for a long time he could learn no News concerning the State of Ecclesiastical Affairs in *Habessinia*. For the King fearing lest the *Portuguese* should invade his Dominions in revenge of the Fathers, had brib'd the *Turkish* Basha's of

Suaquem and *Mazua*, willing enough to that of themselves, not to admit entrance to any of the *Franks*.

The News of which coming to *Rome*, the Minds of men were variously affected. The greatest part were sorry that all their fair hopes of retaining *Ethiopia* in Pontifical Obedience were quite cut off. Others blam'd the Fathers of the Society, that through their Arrogance and Imprudence in managing the Temper and Disposition of the *Habessines*, they had ruin'd both themselves and the *Roman* Religion; whereas they ought to have made it their Business to have acted chiefly and in the first place for the Majesty, and Authority of the Pope over the Universal Church, and willingly to have suffer'd all Miseries, and Martyrdoms, rather than have quitted their Station. *Tellez* involves these particulars in a general Relation, saying, That several Malevolent Reports were spread about in *Rome*; and some there were who gave out, That the *Fathers*, out of meer detestation of their Persons, and hatred of the whole Nation of *Portugal* were ejected out of *Habessinia*: and that if other Preachers were sent, the *Habessines* would willingly embrace both them and their Doctrine. Which was a thing to be done with much less Expence, and more probable to come to effect than *Lobo*'s Project of sending an Army.

Therefore the *Congregation for propagating the Faith*, took another Course, and sent Six *Capuchin* Fryers, all *Frenchmen*, with Letters of Recommendation and safe Conduct from the Emperor of the *Turks* himself, with Orders to try what they could do in *Habessinia*. Two of these going by Sea, landed at *Magadoxa*, seated upon the Eastern Coast of *Africa*; but before they could get many Leagues up into the Countrey, they were knock't o'the head by the Cafers. Two of them got as far as the Confines of *Habessinia*; but being discover'd, they were presently Commanded either to return back, or make Profession of the *Alexandrian* Religion; and upon their refusal to do either, were presently ston'd to Death. Of which, when the other two that stay'd at *Mazua* had notice, they rather chose to return home again than suffer Martyrdom to no purpose.

Nevertheless Three other *Capuchins*, in hopes of better Fortune, resolv'd to make one tryal more, who when they arriv'd at *Suaquem*, I know not by what advice, wrote Letters to the *Abyssine* King as it were to Congratulate him upon

their

...nd of Basilides King of the Habessinas

their arrival. But the King to retaliate their Kindness, wrote back not to them, but to the Basha of Suaquem, to send him only their Heads; which the Basha in hopes of a Reward, very readily did, with a more than ordinary Ceremony. For after he had caus'd their Heads to be strucken off, he order'd the Skins to be flea'd off, and so sent them to the King, that by their Colour he might know them to be *Franks*, and by their Shaving to be *Priests*.

At length also *Bernard Noguera* was apprehended, the last of all the Fathers, and fairly Hang'd. As for the Patriarch *Mendez*, he liv'd in *India* till the year 1656. Where in the 22d of his Exile, and the 77th of his Age he dy'd upon the 19 day of *January*. He was endu'd with most accomplish'd gifts both of Body and Mind, very Tall, and of a firm Constitution of Body, well read both in the Greek and Latin, and every way fitted for his Employment. Neither had he wanted Prudence, had not the King's Favour and Success which oftentimes intoxicate the Wisest of Men, transported him out of the way to act with that violence and severity where gentleness and caution were so requisite. By which means, instead of gaining, he was forc'd to suffer the shameful detriment of that Authority, which he had too far extended. Others, as *Gregory* told me, excus'd him, for that upon his arrival he found things so far driven on by the Missionaries, that he could not with Honour recede from what they had done. Since the Death of the Patriarch we have had no certain Relations out of *Habessinia*. In the year 1652. a new Metropolitan was sent into *Ethiopia*, who had bin seen by many *Europeans* in *Egypt*, and was succeeded afterwards by several others, as we have gather'd from certain Relations. From whence we may infer, That the report of *Tellez* was a thing fram'd out of Envy; as if the King of the *Habessines* had sent his Ambassadors into *Arabia*, to desire thence Mahometan Doctors, with an intention to embrace Turcism, which no man can think probable, from what has bin already related. For how is it likely that he who could not Protect the splendid Religion of the *Romish* Church, and the specious Doctrines of the Fathers, because they were thought by the *Habessines* to be repugnant to Scripture, and the Decrees of the Primitive Church, should be able to admit of the Vanity and Absurdity of Mahumetism; the Original and Progress of which is so well known to the *Habessines* already.

OF THE

Private Affairs

OF THE

HABESSINIANS:

More particularly of their

OECONOMIES.

BOOK. IV.

CHAP. I.

Of the Letters used by the Ethiopians.

They obtain'd the use of Letters with their Divine Worship. The Original of the Greek and Latine Letters. The Ethiopic *more agreeable with the* Samaritan *then* Hebrew *Characters. The Inventor of them, ignorant both of the* Hebrew *and* Greek: *The Letters ancient, but not all invented at the same time. The* Amharic *Characters. The story of the* Chaldaic *and Holy Character refuted.*

THat Learning and Divine Worship generally go together, we have hinted already. For we see it has so happen'd among most Nations of *Europe*; which when they gave the name to the Latine Church, entertain'd also its Letters, and most of its words. Sometimes also New Letters have abolish'd the use of Old ones, as we find by the Example of the (*a*) *Runic* Letters of the Ancient

(*a*) *They are call'd* Runer *in the North, and are to be seen engrav'd upon Stones in several places. See* Wormius's Runic Literature *and the* Runic Lexicon *Printed at* Copenhagen.

Goths, in the time of Christianity. Thus the *Russians* receiv'd their Letters, together with their Divine Worship from the *Greek* Church. Over all the *East*, and the greatest part of *Africa*, the *Arabic* Literature and Language crept in, together with *Islamism*, the Ancient *Persian* being thrown out, and all other Nations, if there were any that us'd the *Arabic* Letters before. And as for our own Native Characters, as we express them in Writing, though they seem to differ very much from the *Latine* and *Greek*, especially while the Letters are so vary'd and transform'd with the strokes and dashes of various hands as fancy and swiftness of Writing guides the Pen, yet if we more accurately consider the old Characters, and those the same as they appear in Printing, we shall find it no great difficulty to derive them from the Ancient *Latine*.

It is the Ancient Opinion of the Learned, That *Cadmus* recommended the *Phenician Letters* to the *Greeks*; and the *Greeks* to the *Latines*; and they to all the rest of *Europe*; first by means of their Conquests, then of their Religion, though there be every where a great difference in the shape of the Letters: among those Nations also that use the *Arabic* Letters, there is a vast variety of Writing. Not to speak of the *Persians* and *Turks*, but of the *Moors*, and *Western People* of *Africa*, whose Letters, though Originally *Arabic*, you shall hardly understand.

But as to what concerns our *Ethiopic Letters*, some of them indeed may correspond in Name, but in shape there is not the least appearance of similitude: so that if an Argument were to be drawn from the Letters, we might say, that the *Ethiopians* receiv'd neither their Divine nor Civil Worship from the *Israelites*. Nevertheless they seem to have some correspondence with the *Samaraean* Characters, which many most Judicious Men acknowledge for the Original and Genuine Letters of the Ancient *Hebrews*: and yet neither will those without a great deal of Labour, be brought to any Assimulation. We shall give you a view of the two *Alphabets* both together.

Samar.

Samar.		Ethiop.		Samar.		Ethiop.	
Aleph	ࠀ	አ	Alf.	Lamed	ࠋ	ለ	Lawi.
Beth	ࠁ	በ	Bet.	Mem	ࠌ	መ	Mai.
Gimel	ࠂ	ገ	Geml.	Nun	ࠍ	ነ	Nahas.
Daleth	ࠃ	ደ	Dent.	Samech	ࠎ	ሠ	Saat.
He	ࠄ	ሀ	Haut.	Ain	ࠏ	ዐ	Ain.
Waw	ࠅ	ወ	Waw.	Pe	ࠐ	ፈ	Af.
Zain	ࠆ	ዘ	Zai.	Tzade	ࠑ	ጸ	Tzadai.
Cheth	ࠇ	ሐ	Harm.	Kof	ࠒ	ቀ	Kof.
Teth	ࠈ	ጠ	Tait.	Resh	ࠓ	ረ	Rees.
Jod	ࠉ	የ	Jaman.	Shin	ࠔ	ሰ	Saut.
Caf	ࠊ	ከ	Caf.	Taw	ࠕ	ተ	Tawi.

In this Scheme, we have not follow'd any *Samaritan* Alphabet, but selected them out of the several Figures, which the most Famous *Walton* has produc'd in his preparation for the *Polyglotton*, which seem'd more like our *Ethiopians*. For my part I am not apt to believe, that the Inventor of the *Ethiopic* Letters who is yet to me unknown, had any knowledge either of the Ancient *Greek*, or these *Samaritan* Letters; or that he receiv'd them from any other for the certain use of Religion, but that they were found and ordered by particular fancy, for the use of the *Ethiopic* Pronunciation, which is manifest from the different disposition of the Letters, the different Order of the Points, and manner of Reading, contrary to the Custom of all the *Eastern* People, who begin from the Left to the Right; and lastly from the *Greek* Numerical Characters. But that they are very old, is apparent from hence, for that several Characters carry the same Pronunciation, and are therefore by the *Abessines* promiscuously us'd in their Writing. Formerly I am of Opinion, they had a different sound; for it seems not probable that the first Inventor would accommodate two or three Letters various in shape, to one pronunciation. Then again they were not invented together, nor at the same time; for the *Greek* π or the *P* of the *Latines* was wanting of old among the *Ethiopians*, and the other *Oriental Languages* that were of the same Pedegree; instead of which, they us'd either their Forrain *Pait*, in pronouncing *Peter* and *Paul*, or else the Letter *Bet* B. after the manner of the *Arabians*, who

(a) *Many Learned men make use of* Dagesh *lene, instead of the invented Masoretick one; otherwise the Seventy Interpreters, who themselves were* Jews, *had expressed the Initial Letter* פ *which we now pronounce* Pe, *by a* π *and not* φ *in the words* [illegible] *which the* Jews *at this day utter* Peleg, Pareoh.

ſay and write *Beter*, *Baul*, *Braxis*, or the Acts of the Apoſtles from the Greek Word Πρᾶξις.

The Ancient *Germans* alſo wanted the Letter *P*, and therefore in *Pforain*, they put forth the Letter *F* with a kind of ſtraining.

Pfaff Papa. *Pfuel* A Lake. *Pfau* A Peacock.

Pfeben A Melon. *Pfund* A Pound. *Pfrund* A Prebendary.

Or elſe they uſed *B*, for *P*, as *Babenburgh*, now *Bamburgh* for *Papenburgh*, *Paper-Town*. *Bapſt* from the *Greek* Word *Pappas*. At length the *Habeſſians* alſo receiv'd the Letter *Pa*, and plac'd it laſt in their *Alphabet*. But after the *Amharic* Dialect took place of the Native Language, ſeven new Characters were to be added, that ſo the caſual Words of this Dialect might be expreſſed: beſides theſe, they have no other Letters either in Sacred or Prophane Books. The Book of *Councils* written Two hundred and forty Years ago, extant at *Rome*, has no other Characters; ſo that I am conſtrain'd to admire, what thoſe good honeſt *Habeſſinian Prieſts*, living then at *Rome*, otherwiſe very ignorant, meant, by talking to *Athanaſius Kircher*, concerning a double Character; telling him, *That the Prieſts and more Learned ſort made uſe of the Ancient* Surian *and* Holy Character; *but that now all the* Habeſſine *promiſcuouſly ſpoke the Vulgar and Common* Habeſſine. For where are any ſuch *Ethiopic* Books extant, written in the *Surian* or *Chaldaic* Characters? When, and where the *Sacred* Books began to be Written in the Vulgar Character? There never was any ſuch thing either written or ſaid by any Perſon of Credit.

CHAP. II.

Of the Books and Learning of the Ethiopians.

Books not holy reckon'd Ethiopic. *Their Studies what? No written Laws. Lamentable Physicians. Nor better Philosophers. Of the mixture of the Elements in Humane Bodies. They hold two Souls. In Mathematicks not absurd. They love Poetry, but only Divine; all in Rhime, various sorts. Riddles and Proverbs. Desirous of the Latine; The Fathers would not teach them.* Arabic *frequent. Their Epistolary Style.*

BEsides *Sacred Books*, the *Habessines* have but very few others. For the Story of (f) *Barratt*, who chatters of a Library containing Ten Thousand Volumes, 'tis altogether vain and frivolous. Some few we had an Account of. One call'd the *Glory of Kings* already mention'd. I know not whether it be that of which *Tellez* Writes, because it is of high Authority among the *Habessines*; and as it were a Second Gospel, and preserv'd in the Pallace of *Axuma*. In that is Recorded the History of the *Queen of Sheba* and others, to which the *Habessines* give great Credit. A *Chronicle*, cited by King *Claudius* in his Confession of Faith.

The *Book of Philosophy*, much esteem'd in *Ethiopia*.

The *Ladder*, a *Vocabulary*; in that the most difficult words are Expounded in *Amharic*, and *Arabic*, but very unfortunately and perversly: As the following Example about *Gemms* will Testifie: It was sent me by *Gregory*.

The *Jasper* in the *Pentateuch*, and *Apocalyps*, in the *Arabic*: the Colour of it is White and Red.

The *Saphyr* in the *Pentateuch* and *Apocalyps* in *Arabic*.----The Colour of it, is like a burning Cole: he meant the *Carbuncle*, now call'd the *Ruby*.

They meddle with no Studies, but those of their own Learned Language, and Sacred Matters. Most believe, they

---

(f) *Urreta did not think worth while to tell so modest an untruth; The most celebrated Libraries, saith he, that ever had Renown, were nothing in respect of* Presbyter John's; *the Books are without Number, richly and artificially Bound; Many to which* Solomon's, *and the* Patriarchs *Names are affixt.* Godignus *explodes him*, l. 1. c. 17. *The* Gallesius, *in his late Discourse concerning* Libraries *avers the same; and adds, That Chancellor* Seguier's *Library contains more Books than any* Ethiopic *Library.*

have enough, if they can but Read and Write: and that either the Parents teach their Children to do, or else certain of their *Monks* for a small stipend. They have no written Laws, Justice and Right is determined by Custom, and the Examples of their Ancestors: and most differences are ended by the Will of the Judge.

Their manner of Administring *Physick* is most Deplorable, They Cure Men by cutting and burning, as they do Horses. They cure the *Yellow Jaundies*, by applying a hot burning Iron in manner of a Semicircle, toward the upper end of the Arm, laying a little Cotton upon the Wound, that the Humour may issue forth, so long as the Disease remains. In most Distempers, every Person is his own Physitian, and uses such Herbs as he learnt were useful from his Parents. Some are of Opinion, that it is not a Pin matter, whether they make use of *Physitians* or Apothecaries or no, not believing it worth their while to be recover'd at so great Expences. If the King be sick, they come to him, ask him, as if it were out of pity, *What he ayles, and what is his Distemper?* And if any one have been ill of the same Distemper, he tells, what did him good, deeming the same Remedies applicable to all Constitutions. If a Pestilence chance to break out, they leave their Houses and Villages, and retire with their Heards into the Mountains, putting all *their Security* in flying from the Contagion. *Tertian Agues* they Cure, by applying the *Cramp-fish* to the Patient, which is an unspeakable Torture. *Wounds* they Cure by the help of *Myrrhe*, which is very plentiful among them.

I have not as yet ever seen the Treatise of *Philosophy*, which I mention'd at the beginning of the Chapter; but it appears by the Theological Disputations of their Divines, that they are none of the Acutest Logicians; nor have they any knowledge of Natural Philosophy, as is apparent to any one that reads their Books, concerning the mixture of the Four Elements in the Creation of Man; as also, concerning the Soul, the Author of the *Organum* gives this account.

God made a Miracle when he Created our Father Adam, *and Formed him of the Four Elements: he mixed the Elements, yet so that they should not disagree among themselves; the First with the Second, and the Third with the Fourth: he mix'd the dry with the Moist, and the Hot with the Cold; the Visible with the Invisible, the Palpable with the Impalpable: He made Two out of the Pal-*

pable

pable and Two out of the Impalpable: He made Three of the Dry, and One of the Moist: He made Three out of the Visible, and One out of the Invisible. The great Architect knew where the Inner Chamber was to be Seated, and plac'd the Corners of the House in the Four Elements*, and understanding that a vessel of Clay could not move nor speak, without the mixture of a Spirit that must come from Himself, therefore he Breath'd upon his Face and made him Rational and Self-moving; as saith the most Holy Law.* He Breath'd into the Face of *Adam*, the breathing place of Life; and he became Man by the Breath of Life. *Therefore the Soul dies not with the Body; for that proceeding out of the Mouth of the Lord, it was mixt with the Body: as saith our Lord in the Gospel,* Fear not those who kill the Body, but cannot kill the Soul. *Now as to what he said,* Thou shalt not kill the Soul; *he spoke concerning the sensitive Soul; because there are two Souls in Man; one the* Spirit of Life, *which proceeded out of the Mouth of God, not reckon'd among the* Elements, *and which never dyes. The other is, the* Blood of the Body; *that is to say,* the Sensitive Soul, *which has its Original from the* Elements, *and that is Mortal. Wherefore God said,* Thou shalt not eat the Flesh with the Blood; *because the Blood is the Sensitive Soul. But the Pillar of the House of God, is the* Spirit of Life. *Now after the* Spirit of Life *is departed, the Body becomes a Carcass; therefore the Law pronounc'd the Carcass Unclean, because the* Spirit of Life *is departed from it. But among us, we reckon the Dead Body of a* Christian *to be clean, because the Human Body was mix'd with the Blood of Divinity: besides that the Grace of* Baptism *departs not from it: and concerning the Carcass of the* Son of the Virgin, David *said,* They cast away their Brother as an unclean Carcass. *That is, they did not understand it to be holy; because the* Jews *were his Brethren in respect of his Mother: and by their Law the Carcass was reputed unclean.*

It is to be wondred, that the *Habessines*, who cannot understand two Natures in Christ united in one Existence, should find out two Souls in the body of Man. And yet it is no wonder when we consider, that there are some, who imagine Three Souls in Man; whereas they might feign a great many more, should they but take every Animal Faculty for a Soul.

But these, and such like Conceptions admit of Excuse and Interpretation, though what the vulgar believe concerning the *Fabrick of the World*, are altogether absurd, and not worth

relating,

relating, *viz.* That the Earth is a round Globe and pendent in the middle of the Air; this they look upon as a meer Fable. What think ye, they would say, should any one teach them, that the Planets are Animals, and instead of the Sun, that stands still, always walking the rounds of the Heavens? Or assert the *Antipodes* to them, with their Feet upwards, and their Heads downwards, and yet keeping a steady Motion? certainly they would think, that such people would necessarily drop into Heaven; though as to this we are not to deride their Ignorance, in regard several Holy and Grave Men have deny'd the *Antipodes*: nevertheless, they most idly dream that when the Sun rises and sets, he goes and comes again through a certain kind of Window; but which way he gets under the Earth, they are not very sollicitous about: and yet in this, they seem much wiser than *Mahomet* the great Prophet of the *Musselmen*, who fancy'd, That the Sun went to sleep in a Well; *Gregory* was taken for a very great *Philosopher* in his Country, for that he had made a certain Convex Model of Pastboard, like the Arch of Heaven, to the inside of which, he fastned several graines of Wheat, to represent the Stars of the First Magnitude, and then turn'd the Concavity uppermost, to shew how the Heavens mov'd about the Earth, encompas'd about by the Air.

As to the Liberal Arts they love *Poesie* above all the rest, but only that which is Divine: for Prophane Verses they hate, which made *Gregory* extreamly wonder, that after the Worship of the *Heathen Gods* was quite taken away, and the Temples of their Gods were wholly destroyed, that the Books and Verses which Treated or were Dedicated to them, were not as utterly Abolish'd. For that it was not fitting for Christians to read the Rude and Obscene Fables of their feigned Divinities, much less to imitate them, and fetch from thence the chief Ornaments of their Poems, seeing that the very Footsteps of Idolatry ought to be an abomination to Christianity. These Verses of the *Ethiopians* consist in meer Rithmes, if we may Assert Consonants of the same Order differing in the Vowels, to be Rithmes. For beside those, there is no other Matter to be observ'd: Of these they have several sorts, as we shall teach in another Place. They are also very much delighted with abstruse Sayings and Proverbs; as for Example, *The Mountains of* Kobal *as with a burning-Glass and so the prefix'd time of Man, is consum'd by the passing of his days.*

They

They are extreamly Covetous of Learning, and were extreamly importunate with the *Jesuits* to teach their Children the Latine Language. But they were more eager in promoting the *Latine Religion*, then the *Language*; pretending the difficulty of the Undertaking, and the vast difference between the *Latine* and *Amharick* Pronounciation. Indeed, it cannot be deny'd but that it is a most difficult thing to teach a Person who never heard of *Grammar*, as I found by the tryal of *Gregory*. For the *Habessines* learn Languages only by Converse, more especially the *Arabic*, which is frequently spoken by the neighbouring Merchants, the *Mahometans* who are subject to the King, and the Courtiers themselves; and in this Language the King Writes his Letters to Forrain Princes. On the other side the *Arabians* themselves, as they are very much inclin'd to propagate their Fables among the Christians, write them in the *Arabick* Language, but make use of the *Ethiopic* Letters, that thereby they may the more easily impose upon the simple people. Private persons seldom write Letters, nor do they know the method of sending them. But if any one has a desire to write, he goes to the Scribe of the *Province*, who is call'd, *Pahafe Hagare*, and for a small Sum of Money causes him to Compose them an *Epistle*: and you must know that the Exordiums of their Epistles are various in their Forms, for that in the Elegancy of their first Addresses, they place the chiefest ornament of their Complements.

CHAP. III.

Of the Names of Men among the Habessinians.

Their proper Names are signification not to be expounded Appellations, taken most commonly from the Sacred names of the Trinity, Christ, Mary, *&c. The Heathenish Names affected. The Names of their Women, common with the* Arabian *Appellations; some peculiar.*

THE Native Names of the *Habessinians*, as well Men, as Women, which were not first introduc'd with their Divine Worship from the *Hebrew* or *Greek* Languages, or were not deriv'd to them from the *Copts* or *Arabians*, as *David*, *Jacob*, *Andrew*, *Theodore*, *Gregory*, are all Sig-

 nificative.

nificative. And therefore they that take them for *Appellatives* may thereby strangely disturb and confound the sense and meaning of them: and therefore we thought it worth our while to expound some of them, to the end that by that means the rest may be the more easily understood. Those which have the Article *Za* affix'd before them as a mark of the *Genitive* Case, denote either some Devotion or Subjection: as for Example,

Zaslasse, That is, a Subject or Votary to the Holy Trinity.

Zachristos: that is, devoted to Christ.

Zawalda Marjam,	Of the Son of *Marie*.	Servant or Subject.
Za Marjam,	Of *Mary*.	
Zadenghel,	Of the *Virgin*.	
Za Michael,	Of *Michael*.	

Tecla Slasse, The Plant of the *Trinity*.

Many are compounded with the Name of *Christ*; as,

Gabra Christos The Servant of Christ.
Seala Christos, The Image of Christ.
Tzaga Christos, The Grace of Christ.
Acala Christos, The Substance of Christ.
Tensa Christos, Christ arose.

Which in speech are Contractedly pronounced thus, *Gabraxos, Seelaxos, Tzagaxos, Acalaxos, Tensaxos*.

Otherwise they are Compounded with the name of *Mary* or the *Virgin*; as,

Habta Marjam,	The Gift	Of *Mary* or the *Virgin*.
Tecla Marjam,	The Plant	
Mahtzentza Marjam,	The Gage	
Laica Marjam,	The Servant	
Atzsa Marjam,	The Mantle	
Serza Denghel,	The Blossom	

Other Names are fram'd out of other Divine and Sacred Words; as,

Tzaga-zaab,	The Grace of the Father.
Fekur-Egzi-e	The Beloved of God.
Jesus Moa,	Christ hath overcome.
Kefla-Wahed,	The Portion of the only Son of God.
Amda-Tzeion,	The Pillar of *Sion*.
Tesfa-Tzeion,	The hope of *Sion*.
Zer-a-Jacob	The Seed of *Jacob*.
Zer-a-Johans	The Seed of *John*.

Bahaila

Babaila Selus,	By the Vertue of the *Trinity.*
Babaila Michael	By the Vertue of *Michael.*

For they think it not becoming Christians to give their Children Heathenish Names; believing that their Children, by those Names which they bear, which were formerly those of Famous and Pious Men, are to be put in mind of their duties in matters of Religion and ordinary Converse: However the name of *Homodei*, so well known in *Italie* is found among these People, by the Name of *Seb-Waamla* which signifies *Man* and *God.*

The usual Names among the Women are,

Malacotawit,	Or Divine.
Wangelawit,	Or Evangelical.
Amataxos,	The Handmaid of Christ.
Romana Work,	The Golden Pomgranat.

The Men have also several Names which are common with the *Arabians* and *Copts*: as,

Bazen.
Abreha.
Atzbeha.

They have also some other Names which are peculiar among themselves, as *Susneyos*, or *Susneus* which are wonderfully corrupted and mistaken by our *European* Authors; as when they write *Sacinus*, and *Socinus*, instead of *Susneus.*

Chap. IV.

Of the Domestick Oeconomie of the Habessines: *Their Marriages, Dyet, Cloathing, Habitations and Burials.*

Their Marriages Christian. Polygamy Justified by the Civil Laws, not by the Ecclesiastical. Divorces. Nuptial Ceremonies. Benediction Sacerdotal. Their Dyet raw Beef, or half boyl'd; and Flesh half concocted by the Cattle. What Bread. Their way of making Butter. Their washing their Cloathes. Their Drink. Hydromel, Ale. Their Cloathing thin. Very Parsimonious, accustom'd to go Naked. They Curl and anoint their Hair with Butter. Mean Habitations. The Kings Palaces. Their manner of bewailing the Dead. The Funeral Pomp of their Kings.

THe *Habessines* Marry with every one of their Wives after the Christian manner: neither are they hindred by any Law of the Land from Marrying several, though they are Prohibited by their *Ecclesiastical* Penalties, as being contrary to the Sacred Canons and Institutions of the Christians: and therefore they that Exercise *Polygamie* are not admitted to the Communion, as we have already said: For they are of that Opinion, That whatever is not prejudicial to the Publick, or to the security and Tranquility of private Persons is not to be Prosecuted with secular Punishment; Neither are they scrupulous in suing out Divorces; assuming the same liberty to put away as to marry their Wives.

As for the particulars of their Nuptial Ceremonies, they are not of that importance as to Merit a Relation; nor are they the same in all Countries. Those which *Alvares* recounts, of the Nuptial Bed being brought forth and plac'd before the Door of the House by Three of the *Presbyters*, and then walking round it singing *Hallelujas*; or the cutting off the Locks of the Couple to be Wedded, for each to make an exchange, they were altogether unknown to *Gregory*; and that if it were the Custom any where so to do, it was only as he said, in some parts of *Tygra*: but that the *Sacerdotal Benediction* was necessary to all Weddings he absolutely granted.

Their Diet is not only very homely, but also far diffe-

rent

rent from ours; for they feed either upon raw Flesh, or half boyl'd. *Alvarez* gives you an Example of the Governour of *Hangot*, (*Angot-Rat*) who entertain'd *Roderic Limez* at his Table with no other sort of Junkets then such mean Fare, very loathsom to the *Portuguess* Embassadour; for instead of Sauce they bring the Gall, which pleases their vitiated Palates far better then Honey: but what is worse than all this, they covet as a daintie, the half Concocted Grass and green Herbs which they find in the Maws of the Beasts which they kill, and greedily devour those morsels, having first season'd them with Pepper and Salt, as if the Beasts better understood what Herbs were most wholsom then themselves: a sort of Oyer which none of our *Europeans* will envy them. Their Bread they bake upon the Embers, made in the fashion of thin Pancakes, which they call *Apas*.

We have already declared, That in some of the *Ethiopian* Territories the People live all upon Grazing; their Flocks and Herds are their only Riches, they eat their Flesh, and drink their Milk. Thus that *King and no King Jacob*, lurking in the recesses of the Rocks and Mountains, always carry'd his living Kitchen and Cellar with him, which were only three or four Goats at a time. Where the Air is temperate, they make excellent Butter and Cheese; but in the violent hot Countries they want that Food, by reason that the Excessive Heats hinder the Milk as well from thickning as turning. Also their manner of Grinding is both very difficult and very laborious, for they put the Grain into a dish, and rub it round about with a wooden Pestel till it be all bruis'd, afterwards they sift it, and make Bread of the Flower: this is properly the Maids and the Womens work, so that you cannot compel the Servants to this sort of Labour: but the Men wash their leathern, or woollen Clothes if they have any themselves, for Linnen is very scarce; and indeed the general Coverings of their Nakedness are the Skins of their own Beasts.

Their Drink is somewhat more dainty, and is the Glory and Consummation of all their Feasts; for so far they still retain the Custom of many of the Ancients, that as soon as the Table is clear'd they fall to drinking; having always this Proverb in their mouths, *That it is the usual way to Plant first, and then to Water*: they drink themselves up to a merry Pitch, and till their Tongues run before their Wit, and never give off till the Drink be all out. They make excellent *Hydromel*, and by reason of their plenty of Honey, which inebriates like Wine, they call it *Tzed*; they make it smaller for their Families, mixing six parts of Wine, with one of Water. Another sort of Liquor they have of their Fruits; whether an Invention of their own, or that they learnt it from the *Ægyptians*, they call it *Tzal*; and it may be said to be a kind of Ale rather than Beer; as being boyl'd without Hopps, and therefore it will not keep: it is white, and sweet, insomuch that our Ale was much more bitter to *Gregories* taste.

Their Apparel is no less mean and poor, only the Princes wear Silk; the Clergy and richer sort make use of Cotton: the poorer sort half-naked, cover themselves with Skins, that hardly hide their privy Parts; which is also common among some of the Nobility and Priesthood: which by the *Europeans* would be look t upon as a great Scandal, to appear in the Church or the Chancel without Breeches. However the more noble sort wear a kind of Breeches, or rather Trouses down to their heels, yet with such a frugality, that the King is not asham'd of; for from the Waste to the Knees, so far as the cloak covers them, they are only Linnen or else of some courser stuff, and only that which appears below is of Silk: nor are they concern'd though the other be seen as they sit, or Mount their Horses. The Boys and Girls go stark Naked, which the heat of the Country may excuse, yet Poverty is the main occasion; till riper Years calls upon them to hide their Shame; yet then having been so accustomed to go Naked, they the less regard it. But what they want in decent Habit, they endeavour to supply in the Ornament of their Hair, for you may safely say, it is a full year before they Trim and Comb themselves. They not only curl their Hair which makes it grow the streigheer, but also anoint it, not with fragrant Balsoms, or Oyles of Amber or Musk, but with Butter: not considering that they who are forc'd to turn their Noses from the stench of their Locks, have not the opportunity to admire the lustre of their Matted Tresses: yet lest an Ornament so slick and glittering should be rumpl'd or squeez'd in the Night, they by means of a most exquisite Invention preserve it, resting their Necks in a forked Stick, that so their Heads may hang at liberty, preferring their Pride before Pain and Torture.

Nor does their Poverty less appear in their Houses, for they that belong to the Camp, live all either in Tents, or in

Hutts made up of Reeds and Rubbish, daub'd over with Clay or Lome, and cover'd with Straw or Sedge, which they leave behind them when they remove their Camp with no dammage, or condoling for the loss of their Tenement, when they can as easily build another at the same rate. Not much better are their Villages, scarce secure against the Incursions of the Beasts of Prey. The *Cafers* like Wild Beasts lye without any other Curtains or Canopie than that of Heaven, in the open Field, where Night constrains them to rest. The Kings Houses are of two Fashions, the Longer which are call'd *Sakala*; and the Rounder, which if they be bigger then ordinary, are call'd *Beta Negus*, the Kings Houses.

They bewail their Dead after a most doleful manner; for no sooner do they hear of the Death of any great Personage, or any near Friend, but they prostrate themselves upon the Ground, where they lye knocking and bruising their Heads against it, with a cruelty very injurious to their Sculls. The Funeral of *Susneus* as being most Remarkable, I shall here set down, to shew their solemnities in burying their Kings. The Body, being wrapt up and covered with a most rich and costly Garment, was carryed from *Dancaza*, where the Camp then lay, to the Church call'd *Ganeta-Jesus*. Before the Hearse the Banners and Ensignes were born, not Revers'd, as among us, but upright and display'd, without any *Impresses* or *Motto's*, but only adorn'd with various Colours: the Drums beat slow and mournfully: after them followed Three of the best Horses which the King us'd to Ride, Magnificently caparison'd, as if it had been for some Triumphal Pomp: next to them follow'd several of the Noblemens Sons, carrying the Kings Royal Robes, and Ensigns of Regality, as his Diadem, his Sword, his Belt, his Spear, his Buckler, *&c.* taking their turns, and by their gestures and postures using all means to excite the People to Tears and Lamentation. To the same End the Queen her self, following at a good distance wore upon her Head her Husbands particular Diadem; accompanied with her Daughters and all the Ladies and Virgins of Noble Extraction, all riding upon *Mules*, and having their Tresses cut off: after them followed the Kings Son and Successor, with his Brothers and all the Nobility, some on Horseback, and some on Foot, in old tatter'd Habits, instead of Mourning: no Torches or *Flambeaus* lighted them along in their Procession: no Tapers burning in the Church, nor

was

was any thing to be heard from one end to the other of it, but Groans and Lamentations, till the Body was laid in the Tomb: only some few *Monks* standing before the Doors of the Church, read some few of the *Psalms* of *David*. Next day they return'd to *Dancaze*; and then so soon as they came in sight of the place, another sort of Pomp was order'd. For the Hearse being brought back again empty, was carry'd first, by which rode a certain Horseman, adorn'd with the Emperours Habit and Robes; and before him rode another upon a Horse richly caparison'd, and arm'd with Helmet and Spear: in which manner after they had proceeded a little way, some certain Bands of Armed Soldiers March'd forth of the Camp to meet them, testifying their Sorrow, by their bitter Lamentations and Howlings. Then the Princes of the Kingdome and chiefest Lords of the Court entring the new Kings Pavillion, renewed their Moans with all expressions of Sorrow, and concluded the Solemnity at length, with congratulations and well-wishes for his happy Government, and prosperous success in all his undertakings.

CHAP. V.

Of their Mechanic Arts and Trades.

Very few Handicrafts. The Jews *Weavers and Smiths. No Societies of Tradesmen. Certain Families of Trumpeters. Architecture formerly known, now forgotten; compar'd with the Antient* Germans. *Churches and Colledges built by the Fathers of the Societie. The Kings Palace Built after the* European *manner, admir'd. They are desirous of Learning and Sciences. What the King of* Ethiopia *chiefly wants.*

ALL this while, there is nothing of which they stand more in need then of Handicraft Trades: for thereby they are destitute of so many conveniencies of Human Life, as we abound in by the help of our Arts and Sciences. The *Jews* are almost the only persons that employ themselves among them in weaving of Cotton: they also make the Heads of their Spears and several other pieces of Workmanship in Iron, for they are excellent Smiths; a sort of Trade otherwise abhorr'd by the *Habessines*; which *Gregory* confirm'd with a smile, saying, That the silly vulgar people could not endure Smiths, *as being a sort of Mortals that spit fire, and were bred up in Hell.* As for other things, every one takes Care to supply his own wants either by his own or the pains of his Servants, which it is no hard matter to do, considering how little they have to use. And for the great Men, they have particular men for all their particular Employments: therefore there are no *Guilds*, or Fraternities of Trades-men among them, which are so frequent in all our Cities, who have their By-laws contriv'd by themselves, more for the good of themselves, than for the benefit of the Commonweale: for amongst us, the skilful and unskilfull, the just dealer and unjust, are all alike; as being all under the same By-laws; and they exercise a kind of Monopolie of their Trade, so that their fellow Citizens are as it were Forraigners among them, and compell'd to obey their Injunctions. But in *Habessinia*, what ever Art any one Professes, that he teaches his Children. The *Trumpeters* and *Horn-winders* are all of the same Families, and have their particular Country and Mansions by themselves. Formerly *Architecture*, as it was in request, so it was an Art well known among them, as is evident by the Ruines of the City of *Axuma*, and the Structures of Magnificent Temples cut out of the Live Stone Rocks: but the Imperial Seat being removed into *Ambara*, it grew out of date. For the Kings having deserted *Axuma*, by reason of their long and frequent Marches being accustomed to their Camps, rather chose to abide in Tents and Pavillions. Besides that, after the havocks of the *Adelan* Wars, and the Invasions of the *Gallans*, found that the *Caverns* and *Recesses* of their Inaccessible Mountains were far more safe and convenient and better shelter then sumptuous Palaces. Therefore what *Tacitus* hath written concerning our Ancient *Germans*, may be rightly apply'd to the *Habessines*. *It is sufficiently known, that Cities are not inhabited by any of the* Habessine *People, neither do they permit contiguous Buildings among them. They place their Villages not as we do, building our Houses close one to another; but every one encompasses to himself a space of ground peculiar to his Habitation, whether to prevent the accidents of Fire, or whether it be their ignorance in the Art of Building. They neither use Cement or Tiles, the whole composure of their Fabricks, being all of rude and Course Materials, without the least appearance of Elegancy or Ornament.*

But the Fathers of the Societies, having design'd their *European* Structures before, carry'd an *Architect* with them out of

 India,

India, and having found out Lime, unknown to the *Habessines* for so many Ages, built their Churches and their Colledges of Stone and Mortar, and encompass'd them with High-walls, to the amazement and dread of the *Habessines*, lest they should in time be made so many Impregnable Forts and Castles. But there was nothing which they so much admir'd as the Palace which they built for the King; of which the chief Architect was *Peter Pays*, both Labourer and Work-master, both Surveyer, Carpenter, and Mason himself, and Instructor of others. A Work which afterwards the People from all parts of *Ethiopia*, far and near flock't to see. However that the *Habessines* have a great desire to learn all those Arts and Sciences which are necessary both in Peace and War, is apparent by King *David's* Letter to *John* the Third King of *Portugal*, wherein he desires of the King to send him *Printers, Armorers, Cutlers, Physitians, Chirurgians, Architects, Carpenters, Goldsmiths, Miners, Bricklayers, and Jewellers*. *Ernestus* also, Duke of *Saxony*, demanding of *Gregory*, *What the King of Habessinia most desir'd out of Europe?* made answer, *Tebeb*, *Arts and Handicraft Trades*; well understanding, that neither Merchandize nor any other Calling could well be follow'd without the help of the Workmans Tool.

Alvar. Tom. 2. Hispan. Illustrat. p. 1297.

Chap. VI.

Of their Journies, and Travelling; as also an Account of the ways to Habessinia.

Pilgrimages now rare. They Travel upon Mules. No Inns or Waggons. Their Hospitality. The way into Ethiopia *dangerous. An account of the several ways to it.*

HOwever in the midst of all this penury of *Exotic* Arts and Conveniencies, the *Habessines* of their own accord never care to stir out of their Native Country, as being ignorant of Forraign Languages and Regions; nor can they distinguish between the *European* Nations, which they believe to be all *Franks*, and their Religion the *Latine Worship*; only they can tell the *English* from the *Dutch* Merchants. Neither do they understand the way of Exchange, or keeping Correspondence. Besides, they are deterr'd by their own Poverty from undertaking such dangerous Journeys through so many uncouth Deserts.

Formerly indeed they frequently made their holy Pilgrimages to *Jerusalem*, and so back again to *Rome*, when the *Mamalucks* were Lords of *Egypt*; their Government being more gentle, and the ways then far less dangerous then afterwards: but the Covetousness of the *Turks* has quite alter'd the Case, for the Basha's and Governours of the Islands of the *Red Sea*, and the upper *Egypt*, Men for the most part of base and sordid Condition, having bought their Employments at Court with Mony, without any sense of Law or Equity, so torment and vex all sorts of Travellers, and suck the Merchants Purses in such manner, though to the utter impoverishing the Subject and utter decay of Trade, have ruin'd all Commerce and Society with those Places: so that the *Habessines* now very rarely visit *Jerusalem*, and more rarely go to abide there, as they were wont. For though there, they are somewhat more free from the exactions of the Church, yet are they more oppress'd by want; in regard that the Revenues settled by the *Habessines* Kings upon Pilgrims in those Parts, are in the hands of the *Turks*; so that unless the Alms of the Place which are very sparing, God knows, support them, hunger presently destroys them.

In their Travelling, they only make use of Mules; neither can any other Creature perform that kindness to Man as they do, over so many craggie Rocks and Mountains, where it is impossible for Waggons, Carts, or Coaches to pass. Their Horses they preserve very charily for War, and Racing. *Gregory* wondred when he saw our cover'd Wains: He call'd that wherein He and I travell'd together *Bet*, a House, and wish'd he had such a one to carry him into *Ethiopia*. The Great Men and richer sort, carry all their Domestick Houshold-stuff along with them upon their Mules; and where Night over-takes 'em, there they pitch their Tents, and kindle Fires about them to skare the Wild Beasts. The poorer sort, when they have occasion to Travel beg upon the Rode; for there is not an Inn to be seen among them; and for Cooks Shops and Ordinaries, they know as little what belongs to them. Upon which happen'd a pleasant accident at *Rome*: Where the simple *Habessines* newly arriv'd out of the *East*, being walking in the *Suburbs*, were invited by a Cook into his Shop. They believing all Invitations to be made *gratis*, at first admir'd the Hospitality of the Man; but then considering that it might be done out of Curiosity, to see and discourse with strangers, went into the Shop, and very chearfully accepted of what was set before them: but at length, when they were going away, they consulted together for Phrase and Language to return their thanks to so kind an Host for his liberal Entertainment, which one among the rest, who best understood the Language was to deliver to the Cook in the behalf of his Companions. The Cook having listen'd a while to their Learned Speech, and not hearing a word of any Mony, without any respect to the smoothness of their Language, *Gentlemen*, said he, *who pays?* The *Habessines* like Men Astonish'd made answer, *That they came not into his Shop of their own accord, but by his Invitation, without any mention made of Expectancy of Payment; and that he, when he set his Wine and his Meat before them, never bargain'd for any Money, for that was the very thing they wanted.* But all this would not satisfie the Cook, who forc'd them to leave their Cloaks in Pawn, which were afterwards redeem'd at the *Popes* Charity, which made the Courtiers not a little Merry.

However the *Habessines* themselves are not ignorant of Hospitality, for that in their Villages they appoint the Chiefest of the Inhabitants for the Relief of the Poor: and indeed the Exercise of Hospitality is highly recommended by the *Apostolical Doctrine*, for the Relief of poor People driven from their abodes by the misfortunes of War, or other Calamities. Nor were our Ancestors defective in their Christian Charity, as having founded several Magnificent Pallaces, and endowed them with ample Revenues, were they but employ'd according to the Founders Design.

And here it may be very proper to set down the several ways that lead into *Ethiopia* by Land, and where they that go by Sea are to put in for a Landing Place.

The way from *Egypt* into *Habessinia* is most troublesome, difficult, and subject to many dangers, as well by reason of the Extortions of the *Turks*, the Robberies committed by several vagabond Nations, through which they are to pass, and the unwholesomness of the Climates; though formerly when those Kingdoms and Satrapies were under a stricter Government, the Passage was safe enough, and more frequented. Nevertheless there are at this day several Troops of Merchants,

Merchants, who setting out from *Gran Caire*, are carry'd up the *Nile* against the Stream as far as *Menfallut*, and thence Travelling in *Caravans*, first come to *Sijut*, and so in order to the following Towns.

Places.	Days Journeys.
Wach	3.
Meks	2.
Scheb	3.
Sellim	3.
Moschu	5.
Dungala	5.

Which is accounted the Metropolis of *Nubia*: Then they come into the Kingdom of *Sennar* under a Mahometan Prince, now neighbour to the *Habessines*, and sometimes also their Enemy, and therefore suspected by the Christians. From *Dungala* therefore they Travel to

Places	Days Journeys.
Kshabi	3.
Korti	3.
Tres	3.
Gerri	4.
Helfage	1.
Arbatg	3.
Sennar.	4.

In Travelling from *Wacha* to *Sennaar*, the Merchants staying in many places about the affairs of their Traffick, are wont to spend Three whole Months, though it might be done in a far shorter time, without stop or let. From *Sennaar* in Fourteen days time they arrive at the Confines of *Habessinia*. The Entrance is call'd *Tchelga*; but the safest and shortest Cut is through the *Red Sea*, so you can agree with the *Turks*; this Passage is Two-fold, for either the Merchants set out from *Caire* for *Suesso* a Port upon the *Red Sea*, from whence they set Sail for *Gidda* another Port upon the same Sea; from thence they set Sail again for *Suaquena* and *Mazua*; or if they cannot so long brook the Sea, they mount against the Stream from *Cairo* to *Girges*, then by Land they travel to *Gidda* in Two days, thence to *Alcossir* in Four days, where

where they take Shipping for *Gidda*, and so to *Suaquem*, &c. This way the Metropolitans use to take, as did *Abdelmesih* in the Year 1662. with whom it is the safest Travelling, if any of the *Europeans* are desirous to visit *Abassia*. *Michael*, the *Habessinian* Embassadour to the Emperour of the *Turks*, told *Thevenot*, That a Man may reach from *Gondar* to the Island of *Suaquem* in a Fortnight; and from thence, in forty or fifty days to *Grand Cairo* by Land. So that to Travel from the *Royal Camp* to *Grand Cairo*, will take up three Months. There is another way by Sea, round about *Africa*; but then you put in to some Port of *Africa*, that so you may take your opportunity to get into the *Persian Gulph*: Many would prefer this way as most facile, tho tedious and troublesom had the *Habessines* any Sea Port at their Command. They that have business at *Mocha* in *Arabia*, have the advantage of crossing over to *Mazua* that lyes over against it, and so from *Mocha* the Passage be easie: not so they amiss that make for *Baylur* a Sea Port belonging to the King of *Denkala*, in Amity with the *Habessines*; only the Journey by Land from thence is tedious and very much infested by the Robberies of the *Gallans*, though they that can Travel with a good Band of Musqueteers need little fear them.

Zeyla a Port belonging to the *Adelans* is more Remote, and altogether unsafe, because of the deadly hatred between them and the *Habessines*; as two of the Fathers of the Society found true. For mistaking this Port, for that of *Baylur*, they paid for their mistake with the loss of their Heads. The other more *Southern* Ports as *Melinda*, *Magadoxo*, &c. are too far distant from the *Habessines*; besides the whole Region is inhabited with none but wild and savage People, whose petty Princes are in continual Warr one with another, and exercise their Fury against all Strangers as Spies, nor are there any Guides to be found.

CHAP.

CHAP. VII.

Of the Merchandize, and Exchange of Merchandize in Habessinia.

The Arabians chiefly, next the Armenians the chief Merchants; all bargains by Exchange, of Gold, Iron, Salt. What Goods Exported, what Imported.

FRom what hath been said, it appears that the *Ethiopians* are no way addicted or expert in the Art and Intreagues of Merchandizing; for they that will not Travel into Forraign Parts must yield their gains to others; for gain is to be sought, not coming of it self. Therefore the *Arabians* who Inhabit the Ports of the *Red Sea*, especially, the *Mahumetans* scattered over the Kingdom, are the Chief Merchants in *Habessinia*, for being of the same Religion they have the free liberty of all the Ports of the *Red Sea*: next to these the *Armenians*, not much differing in their Form of Worship, from the *Abessines*, carry the greatest Trade, as being great Dealers in all parts of the World. They Import sundry sorts of Commodities, but carry out all the Gold; that 'tis no wonder the *Ethiopians* should be so poor; for neither Gold nor Silver is imported into their Country, but only an Exchange is made for *Indian* Wares. And then because there is no Money coin'd in *Ethiopia*, the more silly and ignorant sort of People, because they come easily by their Gold, as finding it among the Sand, or at the Roots of Trees, let it go again at low Rates. For if the Merchant deny it to be good, they exchange it for as much as they can get, never questioning the Merchants exception. But the Nobility and more cunning sort, carry a Touch-stone always about 'em, with which they try their Gold, then weigh it out, and pay it by the Ounce. The *Ethiopic Wakea*, or Ounce amounts, as *Gregory* told me, to the value of the *Spanish Pataccon*, or our Imperial *Dollar*: Therefore it is, that Exchange is far more frequent in *Habessinia*, then buying and selling; which Exchange is made with Iron sometimes, but chiefly for Salt hewn out of the Mountains; which in most Countrys supplies the Place of Mony, with which you may purchase all things. In the more remote Parts of *Ethiopia* you may buy a good

Mule

Mule with two or three Bricks of that Salt. Formerly Pepper had the same pre-eminence.

The Commodities Imported, are *Babylonian* Garments of all sorts, Velvet, Silken; but chiefly Woollen and Fustian, which the great Men wear instead of Purple, which at this day they have lost the skill of Dying. Spices, and especially Pepper they covet to season their insipid Dyet. Wares for Exportation they have few, besides Gold, Skins, Hides, Wax, Honey, and Ivory: scarce any thing else remarkable. Many more they certainly might have, did the *Habessinian* Kings encourage Traffick and Merchandizing, and if the Country were more commodious for Carriage. The best Merchandize in *Habessinia*, and most important for the Prince, were a more cultivated Ingenuity of the People; together with a perfect knowledge of the Latine Language, together with addition of our Arts, and Handicraft Trades, which would advance the Affairs of those poor Christians to a more flourishing Estate, and weaken the strength of the *Barbarians*.

The Almighty God stir up the Hearts of our Princes, to lend their Assistance to this Ancient Christian Nation, which might prove so useful to Propagate Christianity in those Remote Parts of the World; and so glorious to themselves and their Posterity.

THE END.

www.ingramcontent.com/pod-product-compliance
Lightning Source LLC
Chambersburg PA
CBHW030900270326
41929CB00008B/500
* 9 7 8 3 7 4 2 8 1 2 6 8 1 *